INDIAN ENGLISH AND THE FICTION OF NATIONAL LITERATURE

During the twentieth century, at the height of the independence movement and after, Indian literary writing in English was entrusted with the task of consolidating the image of a unified, seemingly caste-free, modernizing India for consumption both at home and abroad. This led to a critical insistence on the proximity of the national and the literary, which in turn led to the canonization of certain writers and themes and the dismissal of others. Examining English anthologies of "Indian Literature," as well as the establishment of the Sahitya Akademi (the National Academy of Letters), and the work of R. K. Narayan and Mulk Raj Anand among others, Rosemary George exposes the painstaking efforts that went into the elaboration of a "national literature" in English for independent India, even while deliberating the fundamental limitations of using a nation-centric critical framework for reading literary works.

ROSEMARY MARANGOLY GEORGE is Associate Professor in the Literature Department at the University of California, San Diego. She is the author of *The Politics of Home: Postcolonial Relocations and Twentieth Century Fiction* (Cambridge, 1996) and editor of *Burning Down the House: Recycling Domesticity* (1998).

INDIAN ENGLISH AND THE FICTION OF NATIONAL LITERATURE

ROSEMARY MARANGOLY GEORGE

CAMBRIDGE UNIVERSITY PRESS

CAMBRIDGE
UNIVERSITY PRESS

University Printing House, Cambridge CB2 8BS, United Kingdom

Cambridge University Press is part of the University of Cambridge.

It furthers the University's mission by disseminating knowledge in the pursuit of education, learning and research at the highest international levels of excellence.

www.cambridge.org
Information on this title: www.cambridge.org/9781316623077

© Rosemary Marangoly George 2013

This publication is in copyright. Subject to statutory exception and to the provisions of relevant collective licensing agreements, no reproduction of any part may take place without the written permission of Cambridge University Press.

First published 2013
First paperback edition 2016

A catalogue record for this publication is available from the British Library

Library of Congress Cataloguing in Publication data
George, Rosemary Marangoly.
Indian English and the fiction of national literature/Rosemary Marangoly George, University of California, San Diego.
pages cm
Includes bibliographical references and index.
ISBN 978-1-107-04000-7 (hardback)
1. Indic literature (English) – 20th century – History and criticism.   2. Nationalism and literature – India – History – 20th century.   3. National characteristics, East Indian, in literature.   4. Group identity in literature.   I. Title.
PR9485.5.N27G46   2013
820.9′954 – dc23   2013016360

ISBN 978-1-107-04000-7 Hardback
ISBN 978-1-316-62307-7 Paperback

Cambridge University Press has no responsibility for the persistence or accuracy of URLs for external or third-party internet websites referred to in this publication, and does not guarantee that any content on such websites is, or will remain, accurate or appropriate.

For my very own
Jayshree Marangoly Badrinath
and
Swaminathan Badrinath

Contents

Acknowledgements	*page* viii
Prologue	1
1 Many a slip between the literary and the national	13
2 R. K. Narayan and the fiction of the "ordinary Indian"	57
3 The in-between life of Mulk Raj Anand	91
4 The Sahitya Akademi's showcasing of national literature	136
5 Partition fiction and the "birth" of national literature	173
Epilogue	203
Notes	212
Bibliography	254
Index	267

Acknowledgements

This book has been written and rewritten in tandem with the many conversations on seemingly unrelated matters that I have had with friends and colleagues over the past few years. From start to finish, I have been lucky to have had many illuminating discussions with S. G. Badrinath, Lisa Lowe, David Ludden, Aparajita Sagar, and Khachig Tölölyan and so I thank them first.

San Diego, California, where I teach and live most of the year, often feels like it is at one end of the world, and when friends have come to visit I have often shamelessly thrust a chapter in their hands along with their morning coffee and then got to have the most splendid reward of their critique, questions, and suggestions. In August 2008, I received generous feedback on an early incarnation of this book from several of my colleagues at the University of California in San Diego, each of whom was working on her or his own complex transnational research project. I thank them here for their encouragement and genuine engagement with my work: Fatima El Tayeb, Yen Espiritu, Ross Frank, Takashi Fujitani, Lisa Lowe, Nayan Shah, and Lisa Yoneyama. My beautiful friendship with Jack Halberstam, Nicole King, Lisa Lowe, and Lisa Yoneyama has sustained me through the writing of this book and much else. A special thank you to Lisa Lowe, who, for the past twenty years, has been a most steady and loving friend and mentor. For generously providing friendship, reading materials, challenges, counter-arguments, clarifications, critique, encouragement, camaraderie, support, and sometimes all of the above in the past few years, I would like to thank Jody Blanco, Indrani Chatterjee, Vasudha Dalmia, Michael Davidson, Siddharth Dube, Ann duCille, Page duBois, Frances Smith Foster, Elaine Freedgood, Indira Ganesan, Huma Ahmed Ghosh, Sandra Gunning, Uday Khemka, Sukrita Paul Kumar, Malashri Lal, Neil Lazarus, Jin-Kyung Lee, John Lowney, Nandita Dhume Majumdar, John Marx, Yuko Matsukawa, Louis Montrose, Tejaswini Niranjana, Geeta

Acknowledgements

Patel, Ashish Rajyadyaksha, Chandan Reddy, Ellen Rooney, Paroma Roy, Mark Sanders, Kathyrn Shevelow, Dina Siddiqi, Minnie Sinha, Brett St. Louis, Muraleedharan Tharayil, Harish Trivedi, and Kamala Visweswaran. And my heartfelt thanks to Dr. Richard Schwab, Dr. Shridar Ganesan, Dr. Catheryn Yashar, and Dr. M. Varkey Thomas for their heroic efforts on my behalf from 2011 onward.

I would especially like to thank the following people who generously shared their time and expertise as I worked on specific chapters and whose enthusiastic response pushed me to continue working on this project. First, I must thank Aparajita Sagar who has read several sections of this book, often on short notice, and whose comments have compelled me to rethink and rewrite. Many thanks to Ann duCille who read the prologue and epilogue and added polish to both. I thank Kiki Skagen for giving me a box of priceless books from her stay in India in the 1950s and 1960s, including treasures like the 1943 Indian PEN anthology of Indo-Anglian Literature that I write about in Chapter 1. An early version of the chapter on the work of R. K. Narayan was presented at the Association of American Geographers Annual Meeting in Los Angeles in March 2002 and at the Rethinking South Asia II conference at UC Santa Cruz in May 2002. I would like to thank Kamala Visweswaran, Katherine Mitchell, and Cindy Katz for their very helpful suggestions early in my thinking on Narayan. My initial work on Narayan was published in *Antipode: A Journal of Radical Geography* and reprinted in *Life's Work* edited by Katz and Mitchell. I am grateful to David Ludden, Dilip Menon, and Ashis Nandy who read through different drafts of my work on Narayan and made some immensely insightful suggestions. I could not have written the section in this chapter on the TV serial *Malgudi Days* without the generosity and wisdom of Girish Karnad who shared many details about the production that would have otherwise remained unknown to me. I also thank Girish for introducing me to the dubbing director for this TV serial, the actress Padmavati (Pinty) Rao (screen name Akshata Rao), whom I would also like to thank here for thoughtfully answering my many questions on casting, language use, accents, and dubbing decisions.

I am indebted to scholars and associates of the late Mulk Raj Anand who gave generously of their time and shared materials or insights with me. At Lokayata, the Mulk Raj Anand Centre in New Delhi, I had enlightening conversations with the curator of the center, Kewal Anand. I also thank Siddharth Dube, Dilip Menon, Sukrita Paul Kumar, and Harish Trivedi for allowing me to discuss my ideas for this chapter with them. I am very grateful to the novelist and Anand expert Saros Cowasjee for many enlightening phone conversations and email exchanges and for sharing his unpublished interview with Anand with me.

I would like to acknowledge several debts that I have incurred in working on the chapter on the Sahitya Akademi and its shaping of a "National Literature" for India. Some of the research for this chapter was undertaken on two trips to the New Delhi head office of the Sahitya Akademi in November 2006 and July 2010. This second and very productive visit was funded by the UCSD Arts and Humanities Innovation Fund and I would like to thank the donors who consider it important to fund research in the humanities at UCSD. At the Sahitya Akademi, I need to thank several people who answered my many questions and helped me locate resources that were crucial to the writing of this chapter: Nirmal Kanti Bhattacharjee, Z. A. Burney, Richa Saxena, A. J. Thomas, and M. Vijaylakshmi. I am especially grateful to Mr. Padmanabhanam at the Sahitya Akademi library for his insights into the workings of the Akademi and for his invaluable help in locating documents from the early years.

An early version of the argument of the final chapter was presented at Brown University in 2001 and I thank Nancy Armstrong, Madhu Dubey, Sumit Guha, and Ellen Rooney for their most serious engagement with my presentation which gave me the courage to continue to question the usual assumptions about Partition and national literature. Vasudha Dalmia and Dina Siddiqi gave me encouragement and helpful suggestions on an excerpt from this chapter that was published in *SIGNS: Journal of Women in Culture and Society* in 2007. I need to especially acknowledge the extraordinary generosity of Muhammed Umer Memon (who had translated several of the texts I discuss in this chapter) in discussing big and small issues of transliteration and translation with me. I am grateful to the two anonymous manuscript readers appointed by Cambridge University Press whose queries and suggestions have helped identify and correct blind spots in my thinking. I thank Nandita Dhume Majumdar for our conversation that led to her wonderful cover photograph for this book. I am beholden to my editorial and production team at Cambridge University Press in the UK. I especially thank Linda Bree, my editor, as well as Anna Bond, assistant editor, Jessica Murphy, the production editor, Carol Fellingham Webb, my copy-editor, and Roberta Engleman, my indexer.

At the University of California, San Diego, where I belong to the best Literature Department in the world (despite the building in which it is housed), I have learned something new and important each day from my colleagues – faculty, staff, and students. I would especially like to

Acknowledgements xi

thank Christa Beran, Dawn Blessman, Heather Fowler, Nancy Ho-Wu, and Lucinda Rubio-Barrick, for all the special consideration they have shown me over the years. My graduate and undergraduate students at UCSD, too many to name individually, have provided me with an education in all kinds of cultural texts, patiently translating their world for me and expressing genuine interest in my work. I am very grateful for the work undertaken by Alexander Chang, Ashvin Kini, Kedar Kulkarni, and Lisa Vernoy, my research assistants at the department in recent years. I would also like to express my deep gratitude to Rob Melton, librarian extraordinaire at the Geisel Library at UCSD, who has gone out of his way to help with my periodic research queries of the most obscure and least documented kind. Over the years, I have learned so much from my English literature teachers – starting with Ms. Valarie Tellis and Mrs. Cynthia Dawson at Mater Dei School, New Delhi, and continuing with Dr. Harish Trivedi, Dr. Sharma, Madhu Dubey, and Dr. Rao at St. Stephens College, Delhi University. In the USA, I was fortunate to have studied with Guy Rotella, Michael Ryan, Roger Henkle, Robert Scholes, Neil Lazarus, Ellen Rooney, Nuruddin Farah, and Nancy Armstrong.

My friends/family on three continents have generously given me their love and support while I worked on this book. Most of them have not, and will not, read a word that I have written, but that is irrelevant to the major ways in which they have shaped my thinking over the years. In alphabetical order, many thanks and much love is due to Alka, Annie, Apu, Babu, Chandan, Christa, David, Dina, Huma, Jack, John, Lisa L., Lisa Y., Lucinda, Meena, Mutts, Nancy, Nandita, Nicole, Nirmala, Nusrat, Rana, Tarun, Uday, Vandana, and Yuko. A special acknowledgement is due to Prabuddha who would have quietly chuckled at the hubris of academic writing and put it all in perspective. My parents have my eternal gratitude and respect; their benevolence and their generosity to all around them has taught me more than anything I have learned in books. I thank in advance the next generation of my family – Nikhil, Smita, Nishant, Vasudha, Prashant, Uday, Uma, Chami, Jayshree, Rohan, and Ruben – who will no doubt read this book from cover to cover. But most of all I thank Badri and our daughter Jayshree whose unending love, profound wisdom, and joyous dispositions enrich my work and my life.

Prologue

The overarching concern of this study is to expose the processes by which an Indian "National Literature" was consolidated in the decades before and after independence from Britain in 1947 and the central role that the English language played in establishing the same for both domestic and international readerships. Indian national literature, as this book will demonstrate, was not a natural formation; it was, instead, a highly crafted and carefully deliberated entity that reflected an elite Indian understanding of the relationship between nation, identity, and literature. While English was understood to be a discomforting part of the legacy of the erstwhile colonizer, it was also the *lingua franca* of the Indian elite, the fashioners of this newly born nation and of its ambassadors to the world at large. And yet, English was patently not considered an Indian language as even those nationalists who were most dependent on it had readily or reluctantly acknowledged. This study tracks the construction of Indian national literature through several distinct locations, key authors, and significant texts. These include collaborative English language literary anthologies assembled from the 1940s onward, the establishment in 1954 of the Sahitya Akademi (the National Academy of Letters), and the work of the nationally acclaimed novelist R. K. Narayan, and of Mulk Raj Anand, whose work was assigned national status and significance by critical consensus.

Working through this diverse body of literary texts and institutions, *Indian English and the Fiction of National Literature* traces the many pressures and expectations that were placed on Indian creative and critical writing in the English language in the twentieth century. To speak or write in English, a language which migrated into the region fairly recently, is to address a national, and potentially, an international audience, and by doing so to take on the responsibility of presenting an ancient civilization in its modern phase. At various moments in the past century, literary anthologies with a selection of works written in or translated into English were presented as representative of national literature. The only questions asked of such anthologies were about adequate representation of India's linguistic diversity. It would have been counter to the modern sensibilities of the Indian English literary discourse to note the caste and gender specificities of what was being gathered together as national literature and what was being left out. And yet, at the same time, Indian literary production in the English language was also viewed as alienated from the rest of the nation and from its regional literatures. Nevertheless, Indian "national literature" was best presented in English.

Two critical questions have shaped this book. First, what specific practices have determined national literary canon formation in the Indian context and how is the English language central to this national endeavor? Second, how have changing normative practices in literary criticism (national and international) and the differing cultural capital assigned to specific languages, literary themes, and plotlines shaped our reading of the generation of Indian English writers from the mid-twentieth century? One of the primary concerns of this study is to question the very use of the "national" as a framework for the literary. Hence, each chapter in this book points to the limitations imposed by a strictly nation-based view of the literary, which undoubtedly provides a critical comfort zone but only at the cost of ignoring other, more delicate, more widely or deeply embedded affiliations in the literature.

Within the arena of literary studies in the middle decades of the twentieth century, elite Indian intellectuals were, understandably, highly invested in crafting a united culture and literature for the new nation. They were also firmly convinced of the pragmatic necessity of doing so in the English language. From a postcolonial critical worldview, the political highlight of the twentieth century was the burgeoning of independence movements throughout the colonized world. Literary texts produced in these locations were thus eagerly read as mirroring the heady national politics of the moment. Some of them did just that. But, as the chapters in this book will demonstrate, the nation was not the only concern, not even in literature written in the language in which this new nation was primarily imagined at this historical juncture. And yet, in the first flush of establishing and showcasing the newly independent nation and its unified culture and literature, most of these other themes and dynamics were rendered secondary.

By the late 1980s, when west-based postcolonial literary critics began attending to Indian literature (as part of their commentary on non-western literatures written in colonial languages like English), they unwittingly reproduced the elite Indian investment in a modern, nation-centric, secular discussion of Indian writing in English. In doing so, postcolonial criticism became and remains woefully unaware of how much it has taken its cue from the upper-class, upper-caste Indian literary discourses that have deliberately and firmly eschewed all literary texts that are not nation-centric in orientation as irresponsible and unworthy of serious consideration. And after all, thinking through the nation was the sign of modernity and was therefore to be applauded and encouraged everywhere. Hence, in focusing primarily on the national arena in its consideration of Indian (and other postcolonial) literature, postcolonial criticism has elevated this one theme over other subtler motivations to write and has also, perhaps unintentionally, adopted the mindset of the most elite of Indian colonial subjects for whom the ideas of national identity and subjecthood measured in terms of national sovereignty were central to their understanding of the function of literature. This is an ideological and thematic overlap that is augmented by the fact that both western postcolonial criticism and the elite postcolonial discourses in India (and elsewhere in the former British colonies) are primarily conducted in English. Hence, while the general view (especially in western academia) is that postcolonial literary criticism champions subversive writings from the margins, challenges conventional western literary canons, and gives voice to the unheard writers around the world, this book demonstrates that this is only a partial view of the trends and contestations that have shaped Indian literary production, even in the English language, before and since independence.

Today, postcolonial literary studies is increasingly at the risk of becoming a shallowly defined comparative field, because of publishing and pedagogical pressures as well as linguistic and research limitations rather than because the distinct literatures in the field are best studied in a comparative frame. The specific conditions and circumstances under which Indian national literature was consolidated from the 1930s onward that I examine in this book, make untenable the hitherto prevalent tendency to discuss the impact of colonialism on literary production in diverse parts of the globe without understanding the local conditions in which literature is produced and without taking into consideration the language(s) in which it is produced. The following chapters will show that even within a generation of authors writing in the same language and linked to the same national location there is considerable circumstantial variation in the literature produced. This is particularly evident in the chapters on Narayan and Anand that follow. Each chapter of this book reveals the different ways in which issues of caste, gender, and orientation to the national arena have had a significant impact on the valuation and canonization of literary texts in India. Reading literature in the Indian context should require analysis of caste-related issues which might be irrelevant to other postcolonial locations. This is not to argue that other postcolonial societies are not hierarchical, but to insist that Indian caste hierarchies are distinct in their presentation and impact and crucially relevant to cultural production.

Of course, in the first flush of anti-imperial Indian literary criticism in English, all discussion of caste was considered outdated and unmodern and consequently was expunged from the discourse. This was aided and abetted by the fact that even "Indianized" English is unable to convey all the nuances of caste and gender as blatantly as other Indian languages. In the late twentieth century, this seemingly caste-free stance was also adopted by postcolonial critics (either out of ignorance or in respectful imitation of Indian scholarship) when they discussed Indian literature alongside writing from other decolonizing venues under a generic postcolonial critical frame.

In insisting on the importance of paying due attention to the local dynamics such as caste in Indian literature, I am drawing attention to the limitations of the comparative survey mode that has become routine in postcolonial critical projects that discuss African, South Asian, Caribbean, and other British colonial or settler literatures in the same frame, each shorn of all local details. In many postcolonial literary scholarly projects, all of these heterogeneous literary/linguistic/political situations are arranged in sequence to produce a cross-continental literary analysis that is viable only because of its undue readiness to neglect, even deny, the crucial specificities of the literary terrain in each particular location. Viewed through the lens of nation and national literature, postcolonial criticism valorizes a few select themes, such as the creation of national identity, the disappointment after independence, the dynamics of gender and nation, the impulse toward colonial mimicry and national allegory, which in turn produce a reassuring sameness that apparently runs through all literature produced in all postcolonial locations.

In contrast to earlier stages in postcolonial scholarship that accommodated, if not required, such broad generalizations about literary production in all parts of the once-colonized world, *Indian English and the Fiction of National Literature* keeps local complexities firmly in sight. The focus on literary production in a particular cultural location, namely Indian writing in English in the mid-twentieth century, allows me to address the work of a generation of writers who have been too easily dismissed in postcolonial considerations of Indian literature. The massive negotiations that both writers and critics made in this era between languages, genres, audiences, and a host of related literary issues involved in writing in English have gone mostly unacknowledged. This study turns its attention away from the much-written-about late nineteenth- and early twentieth-century writers like Rabindranath Tagore and from the post-Rushdie era of the 1980s and beyond, in order to focus on the submerged yet clearly visible politics of Indian English literary discourse in the formative period, from roughly the 1930s to the 1970s.

Indian English and the Fiction of National Literature situates the very notion of "Indian national literature" in the context provided by the contradictory and changing status of English in India in the mid-twentieth century. Such a focus draws attention to the fact that most of the academic writing that is considered constitutive of modern "Indian" academic disciplines was and continues to be formulated in the English language and from an elite, upper-caste Indian standpoint. However, the issue of the language in which the authoritative Indian academic discourses are conducted is considered so fundamental, so taken for granted, so unchangeable, that it is rendered unworthy of sustained scholarly attention. The same is true for the class and caste parameters that accompany the use of English in academic discourse. This book, by contrast, is especially attentive to the implications of using English to articulate theories of Indian national literature as well as to the caste implications of linguistic choices. And, as the first chapter will demonstrate, the usual primacy afforded to mother tongues and national languages has to be reconsidered in this context. Through their focus on specific instances within the literary arena, the chapters that follow lead us to consider the unexplored impact of the fact that English is the indispensable (but discredited or underplayed) language of Indian academic discourse that aspires to speak *for* the national and *to* the international.

At its heart, then, *Indian English and the Fiction of National Literature* examines the literary consequences of placing nationhood and nationalism at the very center of the postcolonial literary critical framework that was collaboratively created from the 1980s onwards by scholars from/in different parts of the globe to serve as an analytical tool for "Third World Literatures" in the twentieth century. The readings of R. K. Narayan and Mulk Raj Anand that follow demonstrate that their radically different investment in, and critical placement in relation to, the nation and the realm of the national results in their very different stature in the Indian literary canon. The discussion of these writers will reveal how differently the works of each one might be re-evaluated once the assumptions about the close affinity of "nation and narration" are called into question.

Each chapter in this book explores in detail just how varied the interests and affiliations of individual writers working in English are: Narayan and Anand can both be considered pioneers who differently reworked the very genres they were writing within. Interestingly, their literary reputations may actually be enhanced when they are sprung out of the trap of literary nationalism fostered both by the patriotic fervor of scholarship in the independence period and by the nation-centric foci of the postcolonial critical apparatus in the late twentieth century. Hence, against the expectation that Indian literature and literary criticism would display a strong commitment to the nation, especially when produced in highly charged periods of the anti-imperialist struggle and its immediate aftermath, I present the varying degrees of affiliation to nation, a range and variety of commitments to forms of national identity and to events deemed national, as exhibited in Indian English writings of this era.

Prior to the postcolonial critical turn in the late twentieth century, in Indian critical circles as much as in the west, the assessment of Indian writers in English amounted to little more than an evaluation of the degree of their Indian "authenticity." Authenticity, simply put, meant that the writer managed to confirm the reader's view of what was accepted as representative of India and of Indianness. This book demonstrates why, despite the enormous critical attention paid to how "authentically Indian" the literature in English has been or can be, "authenticity" is ultimately a limited concern that erases the history of English in this region of the world and sidelines the amazing heterogeneity of the writing in this language. At mid-century there were many Indian fiction writers and poets besides Narayan and Anand who were writing in English, each with his or her own idiosyncratic interests, whose work has received scant attention outside the assessment of its degree of authenticity. Despite belonging to a small elite group of Indian writers by virtue of their choice of literary language, there is a vast heterogeneity in the work and worldview of these writers; they are not part of a collective, nor did they enter into any substantive correspondence or engagement with each other. In terms of literary reputation, the work of Raja Rao and that of R. K. Narayan vie for the top position as the representative Indian English author for this period whereas Anand is read as an earthier, less-refined writer. When the two prominent female writers of this era, Kamala Markandaya and Nayantara Seghal, are added to this picture, they are presented as lesser talents. Nation-centric literary criticism has also cataloged as "minor" a pool of writers whose work merits serious scholarly consideration now long overdue. This list would include G. V. Desani, Bhabani Bhattacharya, Kamala Das, Dom

Moraes, Sasthi Brata, Nissim Ezekiel, Eunice D'Souza, Pritish Nandy, and Saros Cowasjee, among others. All of these writers have been more or less systematically neglected because they cannot be easily accommodated within the currently dominant yet restrictive paradigm of what postcolonial literature is and what it needs as antecedents from the past century. For the most part, these writers did not put events in the national arena – the transfer from colony to independent nation – at the forefront of their literary projects. Hence their neglect. To be sure, on occasion the nation and nationalism are central to specific literary texts: Raja Rao's *Kanthapura* (1938) and Salman Rushdie's *Midnight's Children* (1980), to pick two critically acclaimed examples, are inspired nationalist novels. My interest is not in claiming major status for minor writers or in bringing down authors considered exemplary. I am, however, quite deliberately questioning the usual assessments of the "importance" of various writers when read within a national framework. In this book the imbrications of the national and the literary are examined through investigation of the production of critical and fictional anthologies of "Indian Literature" at three critical junctures: in the early 1940s as a prelude to national independence; from the mid-1950s under the aegis of the Sahitya Akademi; and in the 1990s as part of the celebrations of the fiftieth anniversary of Indian independence. What is worth noting is that in all three moments, anthologies of Indian national literature were assembled with both a national and a global audience in view; for possessing a national identity was and remains an essential prerequisite to claiming a place in the category of world literature. As my brief descriptions of the chapters that follow will show, the national and the literary are not always in lockstep with each other, even when voiced in English. However, in a world where, as Pascale Casanova notes, "our literary unconscious is largely national," those writers whose work is consciously synchronized with national projects or whose work critics can easily place in line with national preoccupations seem to capture and retain the attention of academic and mainstream readerships at home and in the world.[1] In the rest of this book and as briefly described below, I examine several distinct literary sites that produce surprising divergences and compliances between the national and the literary arenas.

The first chapter examines the contradictions posed by the deeply entrenched yet paradoxically precarious position of the English language in India in the decades just before and after independence from British rule in 1947. This chapter provides further amplification of a complicated linguistic scenario by arguing that English has had a special designation in the multilingual discourses around the struggle for independence from the British and in the establishment of an independent nation: the very use of this language implied that multiple audiences were being addressed and that identities were being consolidated and re-presented. Thus the public use of English in the context of "Indian Literature" or, by extension, "Indian culture," served a curatorial task that continues to be the purview of this language in the post-independence years. In a parallel move, literary discourse in English in the early years of the nation took on the editorial task of translating and compiling a national literature that was ancient as well as modern and made ready for the world.

This first chapter, then, establishes the literary landscape which I examine further in the chapters that follow. It examines the details of the official language policy instituted in the newly independent nation. It also articulates the importance and indeed the necessity of focusing on literary production as the cultural arena in which we can best trace the difficult position of Indian English in this era. A quick review of Indian cultural production in film, music, drama, fiction, and poetry would reveal that the English language has established itself as a viable medium for cultural production *only* in fiction and poetry. In every other cultural form, to this day, English is still not the language that will "touch the heart" (to use Gandhi's famous phrase) of an Indian audience. The linguistic situation is such that in most cultural production outside the literary, English is "rejected" as unusable except in brief citations, and yet it remains the prominent language in the vital transactions of the nation both domestically and internationally. This situation is changing in the twenty-first century as cultural production is born and circulates in a global remix that blurs origins, inspirations, and destinations. The first chapter explores the changing parameters by which Indian English literature has been evaluated both in India and outside. The chapter also attends to the equally relevant consideration of how the literary practitioners themselves interpreted their responsibilities as Indian writers in English or as critics of the same.

In the second chapter, I study the work of the acclaimed writer R. K. Narayan (1906–2001), paying special attention to his creation of Malgudi, the quintessential Indian small town in which all of his novels, from the 1930s to the 1980s, are set. Almost all discussion of Narayan's work has stressed the seeming lack of a political agenda in his novels; indeed, the resolute "apolitical" stance taken in them has been widely celebrated. In contrast, this chapter establishes the political significance of Narayan's creation of this fictional small town in the pre-independence days, by arguing that in his work written in the 1930s and 1940s, Narayan was creating a cityscape and community that was *Indian* (as opposed to British

Indian) and in essence unruffled by colonial rule, *prior* to the establishment of the independent nation. Narayan is not nostalgic for a pre-British India; rather, he insists that his protagonists already have access to a viable, locally understood everyday life as Indians. This confidant "Indianness," born of caste privilege, makes him paradoxically the most "nationalist" of the writers in this study. Narayan's Malgudi functions as a cultural reproduction of a Utopian present *and future* India sketched from the point of view of an upper-caste Hindu intellectual. Narayan's Malgudi is the utopia of a benevolent Hinduism – a model city whose order and set patterns cement a conservative nationalist anti-imperialism through its confidence that a caste-based Hindu India survives the assaults of outsiders. That Narayan writes his very first novel, *Swami and Friends*, in English rather than in his mother-tongue, Tamil, allows for a rendition of a nostalgic "Indian childhood" in a "typical Indian small town" that all readers can claim as their very own. Malgudi's success lies in the fact that it is imagined from the same linguistic, caste, and gender location as the Indian nation itself. The very complex but supremely successful process by which a specific caste and gender experience of childhood is rendered "typically Indian" and apolitical in Narayan's first novel is the central focus of this chapter.

In contrast, Mulk Raj Anand's first novel, *Untouchable*, published in 1935, the same year as *Swami and Friends*, has always been read, like all of his work, as fiercely political, socialist in its leanings, and committed to the independence struggle. In Chapter 3, I read this novel with its narration of a day in the life of Bakha, a Dalit youth, as a commentary on the crisis about caste discrimination that came to a head with the Dalit demand for electoral self-representation in the Round Table Conferences held between the British rulers and Indian representatives in the early 1930s that eventually led to the formulation of "The Government of India Act" of 1935. I consider how much of this climate of debate about the situation and destiny of the lowest castes is reflected in this first novel by Anand. As critics have duly noted, Anand's interactions with the Bloomsbury Group and the influence of European modernists and of international socialist writings is visible in this novel, but equally important is Anand's insistence that ending caste-based oppression is a struggle that is equal in importance and *yet not identical* to the struggle for Indian independence. Over the years, the brutality of caste discrimination that Anand brilliantly captures in *Untouchable* has been undervalued, his fundamental argument against caste practices such as untouchability has been sidelined, and his book has been cataloged as nationalist, even Gandhian. This chapter examines the literary and political confluences in Anand's writing and revising of his first novel, which make it a site where some of the complex affiliations of the writer in English, even at the height of Indian nationalist agitations, become visible. While attentive to the Dalit critique of this novel, my chapter on Anand exposes the gap between the predominantly nationalist readings of *Untouchable* and the many other inflections at play in this slim novel.

Perhaps no literary location in post-independence India has been more tightly or automatically linked with a nationalist agenda than that of the Sahitya Akademi. And yet, as I demonstrate in Chapter 4, there is many a slip between the literary and the national, even in this site where there are multiple convergences between the national agenda for literature and the literature itself. Established in 1954, the early history of the Sahitya Akademi provides a rich and previously underexplored institutional site from which to examine the mid-twentieth-century Indian literary and literary critical production in English in the shadow of a successful independence movement. The imbrications of literary discourses with governmental policy, as well as the simultaneous comfort and discomfort with the central role of the English language in formulating Indian culture in the early decades of the new nation, are ripe for analysis in the documents linked to this cultural institution. This chapter thus further investigates the literary politics of constituting a national literature and the necessity of English to curate this body of work.

The literary production of the first fifty years of the nation was evaluated and celebrated in the last decade of the twentieth century. While Chapter 4 discusses the Sahitya Akademi's particular shaping of the national literary trajectories of the post-independence period, the fifth and final chapter examines a similar moment at the end of the twentieth century, in which the forces which curate a national literature come not from a state/national institution directly but from the literary/academic marketplace. One of the many manifestations of the year-long celebrations in 1997 of the fiftieth anniversary of the creation of Pakistan and of Indian independence was the release by commercial presses of several English language anthologies of Pakistani and Indian national literatures. Most of these anthologies, which feature fiction translated from regional languages as well as written originally in English, are edited by academics. As with the earlier discussed anthologies edited from the mid-1940s and in the post-independence era under the auspices of the Sahitya Akademi, these end-of-the-century anthologies work hard to construct retroactively and to elaborate on retrospectively a distinct national tradition in English that pulls together the many distinct languages and literatures of the region.

Prologue

These anthologies, ostensibly showcasing the "best" national literature of the previous fifty years, are shaped by issues of translation, length, availability, editorial taste, and so on. However, almost every anthology begins with one or more of the now apparently requisite "Partition stories" which is presented as the traumatic tale of the birth of the nation(s) and of national literature. In these final pages of this book, I consider how the English language translations of "Partition stories" perform a distinct nationalization of what could more accurately be categorized as stories of people rendered into diaspora, who are heart-sick for the home left behind. This examination allows me to turn to some of the literary texts written in Indian languages other than English in the mid-twentieth century and to study what happens to these texts when they reappear in English translation at the turn of the century.

The epilogue that concludes this study allows for a summation of the larger questions that have hovered over all the preceding chapters, namely, what is a national literature and why, by the end of the twentieth century, in the Indian context, is it presented only in English? The epilogue also demonstrates that entry into the international category of world literature would seem to require rather than transcend national identification. What needs to be asserted upfront is that this book is not intended to serve as a literary survey of Indian writing in English in the mid-twentieth century and beyond. It does not provide comprehensive coverage of Indian fiction written in English; nor does it address English language poetry and dramatic writing in this location. Instead, my objective is to redirect the discussion on Indian English through the parameters of a specific argument about caste, language, and the invention of the national through literary discourse.

In this prologue, I have raised the many concerns about language, literature, literary criticism, nationhood, and the questionable links between these four terms that have provided the impetus for this study. This work is born of my evolution as a scholar in the fields of twentieth-century literary studies, transnational feminisms, cultural studies, and colonial and postcolonial discourse studies, all of which have been tested and challenged by my investment in and experience of cultural production in the Indian context. The standard scholarly work on the topic of Indian writing in English has tended toward a comprehensive survey of the entire field, with every "major" writer accounted for, a detailed discussion of all literary genres, and consideration of issues such as translation and the different destinies of English and vernacular literary productions. In contrast, this book focuses on specific authors, on literary anthologies, and on institutions, in order to illustrate that so-called "national literature" is a fiction maintained by nation-centric literary criticism. What themes and which writers are valorized, what and who are left out, what is remembered and what is forgotten in the many uses that English is put to in India in the mid-twentieth century, is the central focus of this book.

CHAPTER ONE

Many a slip between the literary and the national

> Is there a man who dreams that English can ever become the national language of India? Why this handicap on the nation?
> M. K. Gandhi, Banares Hindu University, 1916

> Willy-nilly, English assumed for a time the status of a common national language for India... It has long been, to us, as it seems likely to remain for some time to come, the sole key that we have to the many-chambered mansion of modern knowledge... It [English] will be shown its place, – but it will continue to have an important place in our scheme of studies.
> K. R. Srinivasa Iyengar, Introduction to the Proceedings of the first All-India Writer's conference, August 1947

Looking back at the imbrications of the English language in the Indian movement for independence from the British and then in the workings of the new nation, a distinct pattern can be traced from the turn of the nineteenth to the twentieth century and on to the end of the twentieth century. As I will argue in this chapter and in the rest of this book, literary writing in English took on an editorial and curatorial position as it showcased what was understood to be representative of culture and of cultural production in India in the mid-twentieth century. What needs to be noted right at the start is that it is the framing that the literary texts receive in the self-consciously nationalist literary critical discourse, *rather than the literature itself*, which insists on this close proximity of the literary and the national. So the "pattern" that this chapter traces in its attempt to show how vital writing in English was and remains in the construction of a "National Literature" demonstrates that the most painstaking effort in this endeavor was taken up by the critical apparatus surrounding the creative work. As with any pattern, of course, this one becomes visible only by fading out alternative designs that other researchers might discern in the same time and space. In this chapter, I argue that while the details of the pattern that I trace over the early to middle decades of the twentieth century change over time, the overall broad features of the role of English as curator to "Indian culture" remains fairly constant.

Both before and after independence is achieved, English is the indispensable medium through which a national identity is imagined and dispersed. Both before and after independence it is the language of a powerful minority of Indians – the urban caste/class elite who shape and voice the national agenda. In the early years of the struggle for independence, it is in this language that the very notion of a nation called India is formulated and presented to the world at large and to elite members of the diverse Indian linguistic communities. Literature and the arts are called upon to fortify this image of a single and singular nation that deserves to come into its own, to be free of imperial rule, and for this task English is a vital implement. Fueled by nationalist fervor, English language representations of modern India work hard to paint a picture of a forward-looking people who are ready for nationhood where detractors had dismissively noted only a plethora of often antagonistic religious, linguistic, caste, class, and regional groups each looking toward their own parochial interests. As the transfer of power took place, it became clear that the need to stress and safeguard the frail unity of the new nation, especially after the trials of Partition, was an even more urgent task. And as the debates around the selection of a national language for the newly formed nation revealed, the abundance of Indian regional vernaculars which competed against each other for a more significant role on the national stage meant that English had a continued role to play in the imagining/imaging of the new nation.

Furthermore, as this chapter will go on to argue, in the last quarter of the twentieth century with the advent of postcolonial literary studies, this imperative on Indian literary writing in English to translate India to itself and to the world received a further boost. Postcolonial literary analysis was a global discourse that, of necessity, had to be conducted in English and relied on "representative" national cultural texts from formerly colonized spaces that were written in English or had been translated into this language. In this chapter I elaborate on this narrative about English in India and the complex proximity of the literary and the national in the decades around 1947 and the resurgence of this proximity in the era of postcolonial prescriptions for literary writing from former colonies.

I

A detailed assessment of Indian literature in English cannot (or should not) begin without an account of the place of English in postcolonial

India. And yet, to investigate the history and spread of English usage in India is to be confounded with the paradox that while the language *seems* to be everywhere, in actuality it is used with ease only by a miniscule portion of the Indian population. Linguistic competence is a complicated feature of everyday life in India, where, until very recently, the comprehension of several languages, the ability to speak a couple, and, if literate, the ability to read and write in one or, sometimes, two languages was a commonplace skill. As Lisa Mitchell has brilliantly argued in her study of Telugu as mother-tongue in Andhra Pradesh, until the late nineteenth century, what we now see as distinct and different languages were routinely used by the same individual in different contexts on a daily basis. Other scholars such as A. K. Ramanujan and U. R. Ananthamurthy have commented on the use of different languages in the womanly spaces (kitchen, backyard) of the home and in the masculine domains (the formal living rooms).[1] But with *Language, Emotion and Politics in South India: The Making of a Mother-Tongue* Mitchell inaugurates a whole new understanding of the linguistic terrain in India in which, as she demonstrates, linguistic knowledge was never carved into different languages nor was there much investment in the "purity" of languages until the late nineteenth century. Mitchell demonstrates that by that time, colonial etymologists had introduced new notions of languages as possibly "foreign" and emphasized "purity" as a positive attribute of language use. Most significantly, Mitchell notes that the very concept of a mother-tongue or *Matr Bhasa* to which one is emotionally attached and which is granted the status of one's primary language came into circulation only in the late nineteenth century. However, well into the twenty-first century, there is great value placed on knowing one's *Matr Bhasa* since it is understood to be a repository of cultural wealth and the source of one's identity, even as proficiency in English is understood to be essential to material success in a rapidly globalizing world. In the 2001 census, out of a total population of over a billion, only 226,449 individuals – just 0.02 percent of the total population – claimed English as their mother-tongue.[2] And yet, this is not a straightforward statistic nor does it tell the whole story about English use in India. It is certain, of course, that many respondents might know another language better than their stated mother-tongue, and that other language may well be English, but this is not discernible from census data. Scholars estimate that, while a significant number of Indians, had they been asked, might have listed English as their third language, taking even the most minimal or informal knowledge of English into account would only expand this number of English users to between 5 and 10 percent of the total population.[3] And yet, despite the prominence of Hindi and the many vernacular languages in use, English was and continues to be the language in which India represents itself to the world and to its many disparate constituents.[4] Each subsequent generation of Indian English users moves the language away from its British colonial past and closer to a global use of the language. Hence "proficiency" in the language is a dynamic measure. The asymmetry between the small number of proficient English language users and the language's very significant role as the vehicle of Indian national discourses is such a staple feature of Indian political and linguistic reality that it has become a mostly unexamined part of the backdrop of national political, economic, academic, and cultural discourses.

From the very inception of the struggle to overthrow the British imperialists, English as the language of the Indian elites arrogated to itself the role of mouthpiece of the modern Indian national discourse, thereby rendering aspirations expressed in local/vernacular languages as parochial, regional, and excessively partial to the particular constituency from which they were speaking. English then became a critical vehicle for what Ranajit Guha has named the "elite's entitlement to hegemony."[5] More specifically, as D. L. Sheth elaborates in his essay on the language debate, in the postcolonial era, English users have accrued power on a national stage that is disproportionate to their actual numbers:

> In reality, power at the national level does not reside in the majority or even in the party elected to form a government. It resides in the apparatus of the state which in India is wielded by the neo-colonial Nehruvian elite to whom the power was transferred at independence. For its legitimacy, this elite only indirectly depends on numbers, which at the national level remain unaggregated on any issue. Since it is the members of this elite who usually supply terms of definition, the relationship between the merits of an issue and the weight of numbers behind it is generally kept unarticulated or obfuscated.[6]

This hegemony of English (despite the fact of its numerically unrepresentative nature) and of English users has been vigorously challenged and protested at various points in the struggle for independence and in the years thereafter. Yet, over the years it has become accepted (even when not explicitly acknowledged) as part and parcel of the circumstance in which power transferred from British to Indian hands in the mid-twentieth century. After independence these same Indian hands and minds ran the country. While English was still in use in the everyday business of running the modern state, the symbolic status of Hindi as the chosen official language grew, as did the usage of this language in numerical terms to 40 percent of the population. The fact that Hindi faced hostility and competition from several of the numerous other Indian languages for this favored status meant, ironically, that English continued to hold its place as the language of the state business. Moreover, after independence English continued to be used to affirm and reaffirm the coherence of this nation and did so as urgently as it had from the early days of the struggle for independence.

This laborious task of constituting a nation called India in the decades both preceding and following Indian independence in 1947 is clearly articulated in B. R. Ambedkar's *Pakistan or the Partition of India* (1940). Ambedkar, the foremost Dalit leader of the period and Congress Party member, presents the dilemma of Indian nationhood, as follows:[7]

> Whether India is a nation or not, has been the subject matter of controversy between the Anglo-Indians [British in India] and the Hindu politicians ever since the Indian National Congress was founded. The Anglo-Indians were never tired of proclaiming that India was not a nation, that 'Indians' was only another name for the people of India... The Hindu politicians and patriots have been, on the other hand, equally persistent in their assertion that India is a nation... The Hindu for these reasons never stopped to examine whether India was or was not a nation in fact. He never cared to reason whether nationality was merely a question of *calling* a people a nation or was a question of the people *being* a nation. He knew one thing, namely, that if he was to succeed in his demand for self-government for India, he must maintain, even if he could not prove it, that India was a nation.
>
> In this assertion, he was never contradicted by any Indian. The thesis was so agreeable that even serious Indian students of history came forward to write propagandist literature in support of it, no doubt out of patriotic motives. The Hindu social reformer, who knew that this was a dangerous delusion, could not openly contradict this thesis. For anyone who questioned it was at once called a tool of the British bureaucracy and enemy of the country.[8]

Here Ambedkar articulates an important yet under-acknowledged facet of the independence movement in the subcontinent in the first decades of the twentieth century: namely, the fact that "India" was a goal and vision rather than an established entity in whose name the battle for independence was being fought.[9] The high stakes involved in maintaining that India was already a nation are made very clear by Ambedkar. This is not to say that India was a mirage or ephemeral entity, but to point to the very active efforts, both material and ideological, that went into the construction of this nation in the years prior to and after independence. And writing in English had a very large role to play in this enterprise.

II

In the subcontinent, English had been the preeminent language since 1833, which is when it became the official imperial language. Like Persian before it, English had migrated into the subcontinent and was soon part of the linguistic mix that characterized this region. Consequently it has never stood alone or separate from regional/vernacular languages. As David Ludden writes in *India and South Asia: A Short History* (2004): "Cosmopolitan activities that built national identities always involved mediations between English and other languages."[10] Further, Ludden notes:

> Learning to read and write English fuelled social mobility everywhere in imperial society and English educated people concentrated in major cities. In 1911, Delhi and Calcutta together had more residents counted by the census as being literate in English than there were British citizens in South Asia. English schools boomed with funding from various sources...
>
> Literacy in general and English literacy in particular became the hallmark of social status and mobility. The seven million students reportedly in school in the 1911 census comprised about two per cent of the Indian population. Overall literacy then probably did not exceed the official figure of six per cent; and less than ten per cent of these literate people were officially counted as being literate in English, about one-half of one per cent of the total population...[11]

Ludden's analysis of the 1911 census presents a variegated presence of English among the different castes and regional sites. While English is known to only about 0.5 percent of the total population in the early twentieth century, it is already in place as the language of social mobility, of urban life, of the upper castes, and of male members of the population.[12] The noted Indian writer Nirad Chaudhari has pointed out that English was not forced on to Indians. As proof he cites the 1911 census which shows that more than 1,670,000 Indians were literate in English, even though at the time, the Indians employed by the British (and this included those in menial positions who didn't need English) numbered fewer than 300,000. Hence, Chaudhari notes, the ratio of those Indians who made the effort to learn English to those employed by the British was a striking 7 to 1. However, as the nationalist movement grew in fervor, there was great self-consciousness about the Indian use of English and discomfort at the "native" comfort in this language.

It was to such a linguistic scenario that Mohandas Karamchand Gandhi returned when he left South Africa in 1914 for India at the age of forty-five and after twenty-one years of living outside the country. Gandhi began his first political public speech after his return, which was delivered at the inauguration of the Banaras Hindu University, with an apology for arriving late and for speaking in English: "I wanted to say it is a matter of deep humiliation and shame for us that I am compelled this evening under the shadow of this great college, in this sacred city, to address my countrymen in a language that is foreign to me." Disturbed that the entire two-day inaugural proceedings were conducted in this "foreign language," Gandhi called for a new generation of educated Indians who would serve the country in multiple ways, especially through the spread of a "national language."[13] At Banaras Hindu University, in the presence of the British viceroy, prominent nationalist leaders like the theosophist Annie Besant, leading educationalists, and a handful of local Indian royalty, Gandhi lamented the limited worldview that was imposed by Indian education in English, as one that had greatly slowed down the struggle for self-rule:

> I have heard it said that after all it is English educated India which is leading and which is doing all the things for the nation. It would be monstrous if it were otherwise. The only education we receive is English education. Surely we must show something for it. But suppose that we had been receiving during the past fifty years education through our vernaculars, what should we have today? We should have today a free India, we should have our educated men, not as if they were foreigners in their own land but speaking to the heart of the nation; they would be working amongst the poorest of the poor, and whatever they would have gained during these fifty years would be a heritage for the nation. Today even our wives are not the sharers in our best thought. Look at Professor Bose and Professor Ray and their brilliant researches. Is it not a shame that their researches are not the common property of the masses?[14]

In his references to "our wives" and "the masses" as not being privy to the "best thought" of the intellectual leaders, Gandhi points to the thin constituency of those comfortable in English and the serious implications of such differential language knowledge between intimates and fellow countrymen. He suggests that, had English not intervened, the use of a *shared* language between educated men and women (the wives) and the masses would have more swiftly brought the whole nation into freedom. Here Gandhi overturns the usual assessment that it is precisely this English education that has led to the demand for freedom and self-rule. Later in this speech he states:

> I had the privilege of a close conversation with some Poona professors. They assured me that every Indian youth, because he reached his knowledge through the English language, lost at least six precious years of life. Multiply

that by the numbers of students turned out by our schools and colleges, and find out for yourselves how many thousand years have been lost to the nation.[15]

And yet, Gandhi acknowledges that, given the reality of English education, it becomes the unavoidable, albeit unsatisfactory, language of the struggle. Gandhi asked his audience: "Is there a man who dreams that English can ever become the national language of India? Why this handicap on the nation?" Commenting on this speech, David Lelyveld notes that Gandhi is "typically vague about what language other than English he might have preferred to use and why, as a matter of fact, he was not using it."[16] Gandhi himself was literate in Gujarati and had some knowledge of Hindustani, and in later years he was reported to have worked constantly on mastering a Hindi primer.[17] All through his political career Gandhi raised the issue of the need for a national language that would "touch" or "speak to" the "heart" of the nation in a way that English could not, and yet, English would continue to have its uses and its tacit advocates, however loudly its usage was protested and reviled.

Prior to independence, the use of English conferred a degree of control over information and official communication that was vital to the colonial state.[18] However, by the last decade of the nineteenth century, English provided nationalists with a linguistic location where the shape of a national community could be sketched, even as this shape was repeatedly negotiated against the British delineations of the "native" and with the competing images of self and society drawn by other language communities in the subcontinent. Hence when nationalist ideas and demands for self-rule/political representation first emerged, these demands and ideas, when directed *outside* the specific vernacular community where they originated, were made in English. Thus, from the late nineteenth century, when English was the language of any communication, what was indicated in *the very choice of language* was that the intended audience belonged to more than one specific linguistic community. Of course this does not imply that there was an automatic or necessary egalitarianism, or sensitivity to difference or to minority positions or other religious/linguistic/caste groups in the very choice of adopting English for speaking outside the immediate community. For example, when Hindu nationalists produced many of their plans for independence and for constitutional representation, in English, they were assuming that minority communities as well as the British in India would be among the audience, but there was no consequent adjustment to the subtle and not so subtle hierarchy of community interests that would be served in such formulations.[19] Muslim, Dalit, and/or other minority positions on issues of political representation and Indian identity, when articulated in English, were addressed primarily to the British and to the majority Hindu community, and in a secondary fashion to their own constituencies.[20]

As mentioned earlier, the fortunes of English in the pre- and post-independence period have been intimately tied to the political fate and implications of using other prominent languages of the region, especially Hindi, Urdu, and Hindustani. Scholars have carefully mapped the historical and linguistic overlaps in these languages, as well as the tensions that arose as the advocates of each jockeyed for recognition in the debates over the selection of a single national language in the independent nations that were under construction in South Asia.[21] Despite, or because of, debates over the national and official language to be used in independent India, English emerged from the fray as the language that survives, notwithstanding an almost uniform despair at the fact of its continued usage after the colonial era had passed.[22]

III

Prior to the successful achievement of independence in August 1947, an elected body of national leaders was assembled to formulate a constitution for the new country in the making. Beginning with their first meeting in December 1946, this Constituent Assembly of India held eleven sessions for close to three years in which each clause of the new constitution was first proposed then minutely debated and voted on. From August 1947 onward, this assembly served as the parliament for the newly established nation and by November 1949 the new constitution was approved by this body, being instated in January 1950. Participant commentary attests that no item on the agenda was as hotly debated as Article 115, the choice of a national language, which initiated a discussion that lasted for six weeks.[23] The initial vote to install Hindi as the national language was 78 for and 78 against. The final vote, put to the assembly after various arguments for and against Hindi were heard, was close: 78 for Hindi and 77 against.[24] As Asha Sarangi has commented, "The one vote margin has been seen as a sign of disapproval for Hindi more than any undisputed victory for it."[25] Several of the representatives from the non-Hindi belt put on record their objection to what they perceived as an automatic hierarchizing of north and south regions and languages as a result of this elevation of Hindi. Some non-Hindi speaking assembly members objected vigorously to those who pointedly chose to make their arguments in Hindi at these

Assembly sessions that were to determine the selection of what would be, after all, the national language. Speaking in English at the assembly even to argue *for* Hindi was seen as a gesture that indicated a willingness to accommodate non-Hindi speakers, whereas using Hindi was seen as a flexing of the power of the numerical majority. A very small minority even tried to propose that English itself should be the national language, but this was understood to be a lost cause despite the easy reliance on the language on the part of many national leaders. For example, assembly member Naziruddin Ahmad appealed against the adoption of Hindi as a national language because it would be an imposition on non-Hindi speakers and because of the "rudimentary condition" of Hindi to meet the requirements of a modern national language. Instead he proposed that:

> English should continue for such a period till when an All Indian language is evolved. You cannot make a language suitable for a modern world by a legislative vote. The suitability of a language requires a large number of things. It requires great writers, great thinkers, great men, scientists, politicians, philosophers, littérateurs, dramatists and others. I believe without giving any offence, that Hindi is a language that is in a very rudimentary condition in this respect.
>
>   After all, India is free. We have to contend with modern forces in the international field. I submit in this modern world we cannot avoid English. We must have English whatever other languages we may have. English is inevitable.[26]

Here, as in many of the arguments made to the Constituent Assembly members on behalf of or for English, the impetus comes from (or rather, is framed as coming from) the need to counter Hindi hegemony as much as from attachment to English and to literature in the language. Hence Ahmad's speech immediately followed one by Seth Govind Das who was a staunch Hindi advocate and whose speech implied rather broadly that Urdu had become a foreign language, in that Urdu had mostly drawn inspiration from outside the country: "You will never find your favourite *koyal* (cuckoo) in Urdu literature but, of course, *Bulbul* is there. In place of Bhima and Arjuna you will find Rustom who is completely alien to us. Therefore, I must say that the charge that we hold communal outlook [in advocating against Urdu and Hindustani] is absolutely unfounded..."[27] Das goes on to indict advocates of Urdu as holding communal views. Ahmad, in turn, concludes his comments with the suggestion that, if not English, then perhaps Bengali ("the most advanced Indian language in the whole Dominion," with fully developed and rich literature that had a long lineage that was second only to Sanskrit and "a galaxy of writers") was the worthiest claimant of the status of official language. In the course of arguing for English, Ahmad briefly suggests that perhaps Sanskrit should be the national language because it has all the literary requirements and, since no one at the present time used it, all Indians would be *equally* positioned in terms of having to painstakingly learn the national language.[28]

What is noteworthy is that every argument for or against any of these languages in the debates is made on the basis of claims for the worth and beauty of its literary corpus and only in a secondary fashion on its perceived ability to express modern ideas and scientific concepts and on the number of users.[29] This approach to evaluating the contesting languages in the assembly debates also carried over to other venues. For example, as early as 1943, Srinivasa Iyengar, the South Indian (Tamil) Brahmin scholar who was the foremost Indian English language literary critic of the time, concluded his assessment of "Indo-Anglian" literature (in English written by Indians) which had been commissioned by the Indian branch of PEN with the opinion that:

> it seems unlikely either that Hindi-Hindustani can ever become the national language in the dynamic sense of the term or that it can, for cultural purposes, take the place of English. After a taste of the munificence of the English language and literature for over four generations, it seems a short-sighted policy to think of giving it all up on sentimental issues only. It should surely be possible to study and love English literature without in any way prejudicing our love for or service to our own mother tongues.[30]

Every Indian intellectual no doubt had an opinion on the issue of the national language, but those who advocated for English or for literature in the language spoke quietly and obliquely, presenting themselves as fundamentally against Hindi domination rather than pro-English. Mid-century, English was already well established as the language of advancement, and especially in south India, the prospect of having to gain proficiency in Hindi in order to prosper in the post-independence era was not welcomed.

In November 1949 the Constituent Assembly passed the Indian constitution crafted under the guidance of B. R. Ambedkar, the Chairman of the Constitution Drafting Committee. The official version of this foundational document of the newly independent republic that came into effect on January 26, 1950 was written in English. Hindi, the language that was proclaimed *the* official Indian language in this constitution, was not the language used to record the national constitution. There were some leaders, like Rajendra Prasad, who wanted the constitution to be written in Hindi, but mainly because of Nehru's insistence that this would only cause delays over the choice of words, etc., the Hindi version was subsequently produced by professional translators. That this little detail was not viewed as exceptionally ironic or unusual speaks volumes about the ease with which English was accepted as a vehicle/curator/editorial frame for stating ideas, hopes, aspirations, and sentiments that were understood to be embodied more authentically by other more "Indian" languages but nevertheless were stated in English. The very language of the Indian constitution is symptomatic of the simultaneous use and disavowal of English that has marked the public use of this language in the post-independence nation. And the section from the constitution that has to do with language use echoes this equivocation between English and Hindi:

1. The official language of the Union shall be Hindi in Devanagari script. The form of numerals to be used for the official purposes of the Union shall be the international form of Indian numerals.
2. Notwithstanding anything in clause (1), for a period of fifteen years from the commencement of this Constitution, the English language shall continue to be used for all the official purposes of the Union for which it was being used immediately before such commencement: Provided that the President may, during the said period, by order authorise the use of the Hindi language in addition to the English language and of the Devanagari form of numerals in addition to the international form of Indian numerals for any of the official purposes of the Union.
3. Notwithstanding anything in this article, Parliament may by law provide for the use, after the said period of fifteen years, of the English language, or the Devanagari form of numerals, for such purposes as may be specified in the law.[31]

Hindi is declared the official language which will, it is hoped, come into its own in fifteen years, rather like an underage ruler on the throne who is represented by an able minister or counselor, the role essayed in this analogy by English. In the interim, English is very much the language in charge. Also to be noted is that in the passage in the constitution cited above, provision is made for the continued domination of English *if need be* even after the fifteen years has passed. As Srinivasa Iyengar had predicted in 1947, English will be "shown its place,"[32] but the language would occupy an important place. What usually remains unarticulated, but is obliquely acknowledged, is that English was understood to meet all the requirements that advocates had set up for the ideal national language (literary wealth, ability to express modern scientific ideas, internationality, etc.), except that it was now considered foreign and colonial. It is ironic that the very concept of a language being "foreign" to India was established through the work of British etymologists in the nineteenth century, as Lisa Mitchell's research demonstrates. And yet, in the independence era, the disparaging of English as a "foreign" language emerged as a deeply held patriotic and anti-colonial sentiment. A distinct ambivalence toward the continued use of this language has prevailed on or just below the surface of all discourse, including, as we will see, in the literary arena.

In 1950, after much debate, Hindi in the Devanagri script was instated as the *official* (*not national*) language of the nation with English as a secondary official language. The delicate distinction between Hindi as the official language and Hindi as the national language is generally lost, with "national" and "official" used interchangeably in everyday parlance, and yet the distinction was important enough to make in the final draft of the constitution. The constitution also included, in its provisions relating to languages, a list of languages that were recognized by the state. These eighteen languages listed in 1950 in the Eighth Schedule of the Constitution (Articles 344(1) and 351) did not include English. Over subsequent decades, several additional languages have won a place on this list, which now includes twenty-two officially recognized languages. English is still not one of them.[33]

The constitution as instated in 1950 included a provision to continue using English for all official purposes until 1965, at which point the issue would be revisited.[34] As Alok Rai has noted, though this period between Hindi's "unconsummated triumph of 1950 and the anticipated climax of 1965" appeared "deceptively quiet," advocates of this language were "assiduously at work, grooming Hindi for its exalted 'national' role" and developing Sanskritic reinventions of everyday words in Hindi that had originated in English or Persian.[35] During the 1950s and early 1960s, language-based disaffections became a consistent factor in the various regional resistances to control from the central government which was geographically located in the powerful Hindi belt of the north. At the same time, the Central Advisory Board of Education spent much time and effort in determining how many languages would be taught to Indians and how to balance local vernaculars, Hindi, the official language of the nation, and English. The "three-language formula" was proposed in 1956 whereby school students in non-Hindi regions were taught their local vernacular (or mother-tongue), as well as Hindi and English, and students in the Hindi belt were to learn another Indian language in addition to Hindi and English. The implementation of this three-language formula was uneven in different parts of the country, but the knowledge of a Sanskritized Hindi did gain foothold, especially since the third language offered by school authorities in the Hindi belt and in metropoles like Delhi was usually Sanskrit. However, because various language protests put pressure on the decision-makers, the Official Language Act of 1963 endorsed Hindi as the official language but stipulated that English would remain alongside it as an associate official language. In 1967, another constitutional amendment (the Official Language Amendment Act of 1967) guaranteed that English would continue as the associate official language alongside Hindi. Specific state governments could chose to use Hindi exclusively for their state business or for communicating with those other states that had also chosen to instate Hindi as their state language, but English would remain in use indefinitely.[36]

While Hindi (and its variant dialects) was the primary language of the largest proportion of the Indian population, its elevation to the official language status continued to be actively resisted in various parts of the country, especially south India, where this was interpreted as another hegemonic decision made for the entire country by north Indian politicians serving their own regional, linguistic, and caste interests. In the south, the anti-Brahmin movement in this period had a highly charged language politics which championed southern (Dravidian) languages, especially Tamil, and aligned them against Hindi (the language of the north) and Sanskrit (the language associated with the Brahmin caste).[37] And, as will be discussed in the next chapter, the educated upper-castes in the south were already well versed in the English language, and working to become proficient in Hindi in order to prosper in independent India was not an attractive prospect. In the late 1950s, the south Indian (Tamil Brahmin) writer R. K. Narayan wrote a brief essay on the fate of English in India in his weekly column for the Sunday edition of *The Hindu* which is illustrative of some of the tensions surrounding the continued use of this language after independence. In his short piece for this nationally circulating English language newspaper, Narayan notes that it is "almost a matter of national propriety and prestige now to declare one's aversion to this language, and to cry for its abolition."[38] Pointedly titled "Fifteen Years," this essay presents a courtroom scene in which "English" is the plaintiff who pleads her case in front of an unsympathetic judge who is determined to "deport" her after fifteen years. Despite complimenting him on his excellent English, despite asserting her rights under the Indian constitution, despite arguing that she has been in India for more than two hundred years, despite declaring that she is a devotee of the Hindu goddess of knowledge Saraswati, and not a "trident-bearing Rule Britannia," all her arguments are dismissed by the judge, who says:

"All that is besides the point. Even if you come in a sari with kumkum on your forehead we are going to see that you are deported. The utmost we shall allow you will be another fifteen years..."

"Fifteen years from what time?" asked the English language at which the judge felt so confused that he ordered, "I will not allow any more discussion on this subject," and rose for the day.[39]

In concluding his essay with this exchange, which clearly registers that the judgment to deport English is based on illogical blustering, Narayan was reflecting the widespread opinion among English users, especially in south India, that the plan to get rid of English fifteen years after independence was unfeasible and not well thought through. English survived in that it proved impossible to put this language aside in 1965 as had been planned in the Indian constitution because it was too deeply embedded in the workings of the nation and in the circles of the national elite. As Braj Kachru states in the opening paragraph of his influential *The Alchemy of English*, "knowing English is like possessing the fabled Aladdin's lamp."[40] The benefits of knowing this language were immense and not easily given up.

For the purposes of the discussion in this book, two significant inferences can be made from these early proceedings: first, English in India was established as a "neutral language" despite its colonial baggage and its clear upper-caste and upper-class affiliation. Second, at the very same time, it was a language which was expected to efface itself and was understood to have been "kept on in service," as Iyengar phrased it, only because of convenience and neutrality.[41] But convenience and neutrality are loaded terms. The neutrality of English, Braj Kachru suggests, stems partly from the fact that English does not make visible the caste and regional markers present in Indian regional languages. "Neutralization," he argues, "thus is a linguistic strategy used to 'unload' a linguistic term from its traditional, cultural and emotional connotations."[42] One of the examples that Kachru uses to demonstrate this "code-mixing" between languages is provided by the linguist E. Annamalai: "In Tamil, as shown by Annamalai (1978) *maccaan* and *attimbeer* reveal the caste identity of the speaker – not desirable in certain situations. Therefore one uses English *brother-in-law*, instead."[43] Thus the neutrality of English in the Indian context stemmed from the fact that not only was it not the mother-tongue of any region, but it rendered opaque all hints that other Indian languages provided about caste, rank, and region. The impact of this invisibility of caste dynamics in narratives rendered in English is amply demonstrated in Chapter 2 on R. K. Narayan.

As Braj Kachru argued in *The Alchemy of English*, a study of "non-native Englishes," there is a certain "alchemy" to the workings of English in the non-west. In this alchemy, English performs a "transmutation" of the subject since knowing the language promises entry into the realm of the modern, the powerful, and the elite. It offers entry into the category where caste is irrelevant simply because one is of the higher castes. And yet, as scholars such as E. Annamalai have noted, English is simultaneously representative of a native elite and, despite its class association, also a means for the dispossessed to enter, but not restructure, the realms of power.[44] Disadvantaged communities continue to argue vociferously for better access to English education as a means of improving their opportunities. For example, in the late 1990s, when the Bharatiya Janata Party (BJP, a right-wing Hindu political party that was in power at the time) declared 1999–2000 the year of Sanskrit and planned to extend Sanskrit education to Dalits who have traditionally been denied knowledge of this language of the high castes, Dalit groups rejected this and demanded better access to English instead.[45] In April 2010, Chandra Bhan Prasad, a Dalit intellectual and activist who has worked to promote English education in Dalit communities in north India, laid the foundation stone for a temple dedicated to "Goddess English" in a village in the Indian state of Uttar Pradesh.[46] A clear appreciation of the importance of English to non-elites is visible in Dalit activism, but its echoes are present even in Mulk Raj Anand's *Untouchable* (1935) as I demonstrate in Chapter 3 on this now too easily dismissed Indian English novel.

The claim made early in this chapter that English arrogated for itself the role of the linguistic medium that would/could represent all of India with seeming democratic impartiality and neutrality became touted as the *raison d'être* for its continued presence. The undeniable fact that it was the language in which the national urban elite was most comfortable, and in which caste and regional differences were veiled, was apparently of secondary importance, a mere coincidence perhaps. However, there remained the niggling sense that English could not express the "real India," that it did not meet the Gandhian ideal of a national language that could "touch the heart" of the nation. And literary work in English was subjected to especially harsh scrutiny; its ability to speak (from and to) "the heart of the nation" was especially suspect partly because the nuanced identity markers that were visible in the vernacular languages were "neutralized" in English. Thus, the ability of a literary work in English to convey "authentic Indianness," despite the limitations of this "foreign" language, became (and largely continues to be) the only yardstick by which the excellence of any literature in this language was measured.

Arguably, the cultural production that was quick to "touch the heart" and was readily embraced by large audiences from the 1940s onward has been cinema in Hindi and regional languages. Film production in several Indian languages found eager audiences both before and after independence. The reasons are many. Primarily, literacy was and remains low in any language, so visual arts had always found wide acceptance. Film was only the latest in a long line of pleasurable performance arts in different communities in South Asia. It drew on local dramatic, comic, and dance performance traditions like *nautanki*, *tamasha*, mythological/religious performances, and adapted these forms for circulation to a mass audience via the technology of modern cinema, imported, and often handled by technicians who were also imported, from the west. In the context of this present study, what is significant is that, despite the internationally collaborative technological endeavor that early cinema undoubtedly was in the Indian context, English was very rarely used in Indian cinema (even in representation of elite characters). To the present day only a handful of Indian films have used English in a substantial or even bilingual fashion and garnered commercial success.[47] Cinema has remained the domain of vernacular languages and unlike the official Hindi (heavily Sanskritized and shorn of Urdu and Persian inflections) used in government-controlled media like radio and national TV, Hindustani (with its linguistic medley of Hindi, Urdu and Persian words, expressions, and poetic forms) has flourished in "Hindi" cinema.[48] Unlike the imposition of the language itself, which was firmly resisted in the early decades of the new nation, Hindi cinema has been warmly embraced all over India, including in the southern states. So much so that one might wager that, in India, it is cinema rather than print commodities that create the kind of imagined community that Benedict Anderson theorized in his very influential work on nationalism in Asia.[49]

Like cinema, most other cultural texts with sizeable circulation in India have remained quite firmly impervious to the use of the English language even when the forms or technologies are adapted from the west. Hence Indian musicians certainly incorporate western popular and classical musical riffs into their compositions, but the language used for lyrics is rarely English. Western influences like rock, rap, and jazz go directly from the source to regional music composition. As is now well known, almost all feature films produced in India in Hindi or other languages include at least half a dozen songs; film music, a popular genre that uses classical and folk musical traditions of the subcontinent, also freely and frequently dips into jazz, big band, western classical, Latin American, African, and American sounds. But when lyrics have been added to the music, in only a handful of cases over the past sixty or so years have those songs used English in a sustained fashion. More recently reggae, rap, hip-hop, and other specific genres have been evoked in music compositions for films, but when it comes to the lyrics these musical numbers mostly bypass English (except for the odd refrain or two) to move directly to Hindi, Hinglish, or the appropriate Indian language. Needless to say, lounge singing, talent shows, and other musical performances do enthusiastically reproduce with startling precision the popular music of the west. Even before the advent of MTV and the internet, western popular musical stars and Hollywood cinema had their loyal fans among the English language elite in India. But when it comes to producing "original" cultural texts, *except in the literary arena*, English is kept at arm's length.[50]

In the realm of Indian cultural production, then, it becomes very significant that poetry, non-fiction prose, fiction, and, to a lesser degree, drama are the only genres in which English use is solidly entrenched. Consequently, the cultural site at which one can best read the impact of English in India is the small body of literary (creative and critical) activity once called Indo-Anglian (in the early to mid-twentieth century), then Indian writing in English (late twentieth century), and more recently, Indian English.[51] What needs to be said (perhaps only because this is often elided in English language literary discourse) is that Indian writing in English is a recent (from the mid-nineteenth century) and miniscule (in terms of volume of work) sliver of the multilingual and multifarious literary traditions in this region. This detail makes the elite underpinnings of literary production in the language clear especially in the early twentieth century when literacy in this language was, for the most part, the purview of men of the upper classes/castes.

IV

As the language debates summarized above indicate, in the very decades when a national culture was being proudly and painstakingly constructed around the Gandhian concept of *swadeshi* (indigenous, from one's own country), Indian writing in English was expected to earn its keep. It was entrusted with the task of constructing and consolidating the image of a unified, modernizing India for consumption both at home and abroad. Being Indian in one's theme, in content, and in the texture of English used became a crucial requirement and expectation from Indian literary writers; it was a manifestation of one's allegiance to and love for one's country and of the "authenticity" of the work. The very use of English, however, automatically imbricated the most parochial of Indian fiction with a cosmopolitan, transnational literary discourse. In its use of the language and some of the literary genres and aesthetics of the west, this fiction exposed the vulnerabilities of creative projects that tried to create "authentic" Indian literature in a language that was, in the context of those heady nationalist days, the colonizer's accursed legacy and newly considered "foreign." Often, the problem of using the colonizer's language was surpassed by the colonial subjects' ability to proudly and pointedly match the colonizers' ability to hold forth and/or create both national identities and fictional worlds in the language.

In retrospect what seems quite clear is the way in which this representation of India to the world and to the nation is understood to be the natural and rightful task of Indian writing in English; this was an assumption that ran through all kinds of literary and cultural initiatives that emerged in the 1930s and 1940s. Thus, English was a crucial and convenient linguistic tool when, in London in 1936, a group of Indian intellectuals (who worked primarily in Urdu, Bengali, Hindi, and English) led by Sajjad Zahir and Mulk Raj Anand launched the Progressive Writers' Association (PWA). As Talat Ahmed notes, "In London, linguistic or religious differences amongst the small Indian community would have seemed immaterial compared to their status as Indians and the cohesion this would have engendered."[52] Hence, their manifesto, which was drafted in Nanking Hotel in London primarily by Sajjad Zahir and Mulk Raj Anand, was composed in English. Once the manifesto was taken to India it was translated into the various other Indian languages, but it was initially printed in English in the February 1936 issue of London's *New Left Review*.[53] This manifesto was a boldly political declaration of the new literary themes and forms that were to be nurtured by this association:

> While claiming to be the inheritors of the best traditions of Indian civilization, we shall criticise, in all its aspects, the spirit of reaction in our country, and we shall foster – through interpretative and creative work (with both Indian and foreign resources) – everything that will lead our country to the new life for which it is striving.[54]

Hence, the deliberate aim of the PWA was to "produce and translate literature of a progressive nature and a high technical standard, to fight cultural reaction; and in this way, to further the cause of Indian freedom and social regeneration." Literature produced (and translated) under the banner of the PWA was to eschew "baseless spiritualism" and the "shelter of idealism" – it was to break away from old notions of literary value and boldly use both "Indian and foreign resources" to "bring the arts to the closest touch with the people." While the first draft of this manifesto advocated for the "acceptance of a common language (Hindustani) and a common script (Indi-Roman)," this recommendation was dropped from the printed versions of the manifesto.[55] The advocacy of Hindustani remained crucial to some branches of the PWA, but in the published versions of the manifesto there was no prescription as to the language(s) to be used. Rather, the reference to "foreign resources" and translation allows for more than a strictly circumscribed nationalist agenda and suggests that such progressive writing by Indian writers was to take its rightful place in a global body of left-leaning, communism-inspired literary writing produced in Europe, especially Eastern Europe, and the Soviet Union. Here the use of English signaled the entry into international literary conversations, but at the same time it was a gesture that was meant to include and represent more than one Indian linguistic or literary arena.

In fact, the foundation of this London-based manifesto for the Progressive Writers' Association was laid four years previously in Lucknow, with the furor created by the publication of a collection of short stories in Urdu titled *Angāre* [Burning Embers] by Sajjad Zahir and others.[56] Condemned for obscenity and for its lack of religiosity by conservative Urdu littérateurs and journalists and banned in March 1933 by the Government of the United Provinces under Section 295 of the Indian Penal Code, *Angāre*, Shabana Mahmud convincingly argues, caused a debate that led to the birth of this association a few years later in London. Mahmud cites a 1932 statement written by the authors of *Angāre*, titled "In defense of *Angāre*: shall we submit to gagging?" in which their "practical proposal is the formation immediately of a League of Progressive Authors, which should bring forth similar collections from time to time, both in English and the various vernaculars of our country."[57] Four years later, the PWA was formally launched in London and the first All India Progressive Writers' Conference was held in Lucknow in April 1936. The renowned Hindi and Urdu writer Munshi Premchand gave the presidential address (in Hindi) and a literary force that was to dominate the literary scene in the subcontinent across languages for the next few decades was born. The launching of the PWA in London in English thus must be understood as closely linked to the debates around literary and critical production in other Indian languages as much as to

European literary discourses — even though often the links were subterranean or forgotten or visible only in the editorial frames around the texts. Here too English was put to use as the language in which the project was announced on a global stage even though the majority of the literary work produced under this banner was in other Indian languages.[58]

English was even more instrumental to another literary initiative that was launched around the same time in India. In 1933, American-born Sophia Wadia founded the Indian branch of PEN (Poets, Essayists, and Novelists), twelve years after the international organization was founded in London.[59] The Indian branch of PEN was much more clearly and closely aligned with the nationalist leaders' priorities in the struggle for Indian independence than was the Progressive Writers' Association and it took very seriously the charge that literature had a role to play in proving Indians worthy of independence and as handmaiden to the independence movement.[60] In the editorial foreword that Wadia wrote for the series of books on Indian literature published by the Indian PEN Association in the late 1930s and early 1940s, she writes with absolute clarity of the political charge and importance of the multi-volume literary project she has undertaken. This foreword was included at the start of all the literary histories of vernacular literatures that were published in English in this series.[61] Wadia makes the argument that Indians have "undervalued the literary unfoldment of the last few years" which, "*if properly co-ordinated and helped*, would develop into a renaissance of the first order" (emphasis added).[62] She goes on to note the potential in literary texts to imagine and thus create a better future: "Visions of literary creators enshrined in books of today are likely to become the objective realities of tomorrow."[63] Wadia spells out the potential of literary writing (both creative and critical) to accomplish the work of the nation in this desired future:

> Moreover, the mystical intimations of the poet, the psychological analyses of the novelist, the philosophical expositions of the essayist, the tendency portrayals and the character delineations of the dramatist — these are related to the very problems which engage the whole consciousness of the politician, the economist and the sociologist. India cannot afford to be neglectful of her literary movement of today.[64]

Thus, in the editorial frame developed for this series, the urgency of this literary project is linked to and legitimized by the momentous national events that are in the offing. What Wadia sees as an urgent task is to change the perception that India's multiple languages are what holds it back: "India's many languages are not a curse, however much her enemies may call them so or her political and other reformers may wish for a *lingua franca*. Ideas unite people and rule the world; not words."[65] She firmly opposes the view that the multiple languages of the country lead to "chaos," and insists instead that "[o]ur many languages are channels of cultural enrichment."[66] And yet, she laments, the undeniable fact is that "[m]any educated Indians are not familiar with the literary wealth of any Indian language other than their own."[67] And, at the same time, "India suffers grievously in the Occident, which is ignorant of the present-day literary achievements in the different Indian languages."[68] It is to bridge this gap between the many Indian reading publics as well as that between India and the Occident that Wadia offers up PEN's "systematic attempt" to "popularize the story of the Indian literatures" and to "present gems from their masterpieces to the general public *in English translation*" (emphasis added).[69] Wadia concludes her editorial foreword with the declaration that this "labour of love" is "offered on the altar of the Motherland, . . . [which] will be greatly aided by the literary creations of her sons and daughters."[70] This slim book by Iyengar in the PEN series has been created with inaugurating the field of criticism on Indian writing in English.[71]

What is noteworthy and typical about Wadia's introduction is the absolute authority with which she assumes the responsibility of fulfilling this self-defined national obligation, on behalf of her associates who will write the individual books in the series. As the English language littérateur and general editor she occupies the linguistic vantage point from which all that is worthy of notice, once it has been translated into English of course, is visible. What is also noteworthy and also fairly typical of Wadia's project is that not much attention is paid to the fact that all of the proposed series of books (fifteen write-ups on different literary traditions) are written in English, and that without this language, the entire project would not have an inception of any kind. Time and time again, in this period we see English in India put to use as a *lingua franca* that does not have the coverage of a national language in a single language location, but which communicates across race, gender, class, caste, and location in a way with which no other Indian language could compete.

In 1940 when Japan withdrew its invitation to hold the next International PEN conference in Tokyo, Sophia Wadia offered that the meeting be held in the Indian state of Mysore, an offer that was accepted by the international body. This was a significant honor for Indian national and literary prestige in the pre-independence days. However, the war intervened and the Mysore conference, like all other conferences of the International PEN, was cancelled. Yet, in 1945 the first All-India Writers' Conference was organized by Indian PEN and was attended by global and local literary figures. The venue shifted from Mysore to Jaipur and it was funded primarily by the Jaipur royals and the Nizam of Hyderabad. The theme decided on was "The Development of the Indian Literatures as a Uniting Force." Fresh out of prison, Jawaharlal Nehru (who was one of the vice-presidents of the PEN India Center) agreed to attend the conference and to lead the discussion on the central theme. What is immediately striking about the attendees at this conference is how many were high-ranking national leaders even as they were leading literary figures. In addition to Nehru, who was to be the first Prime Minister of independence India and was himself a skilled English language writer as well as leader of the Congress Party, speakers included, Sarojini Naidu, the foremost English language poet of her time, activist for Indian independence, leading Congress Party member, and then President of Indian PEN; Sophia Wadia; S. Radhakrishnan (later to be the first President of independent India); E. M. Forster, who travelled from England to attend the conference; Mulk Raj Anand; Humayun Kabir; Srinivasa Iyengar; and other literary luminaries from India, England, the USA, France, Poland, and China.[72]

Despite the differences of opinions on the details, each and every one of the speakers at this conference was certain and vocal about the most important service literature could do for the nation – it would bring its various language groups into one strong union. Given the generous overlap among the conference attendees between the nation's foremost littérateurs and its national leaders gathered on the eve of national independence at this very first all-India literary conference, it is not surprising that a prescriptive agenda for literature and literary scholarship was drawn up at the conference. As K. R. Srinivasa Iyengar writes in his August 1947 introduction to the published conference proceedings, the Jaipur event "was an excellent opportunity for emphasizing the cardinal unity of Indian culture, not withstanding the many languages and literatures that flourished in our midst."[73]

Presentations were made in Jaipur by the leading political and cultural figures on the proximity of the tasks and responsibilities of the cultural producers to those of national and world leaders. In Iyengar's words: "Above all, if an integral national leadership is forthcoming, literature too, will hymn the notes of unity and harmony."[74] Furthermore, he goes on to insist that:

> If India sought unity within, she sought, no less earnestly and no less urgently, understanding with the outside world. Isolation was an unthinkable proposition in the era of the atomic bomb. And literature could promote international understanding, and such understanding would be a human understanding and therefore, a lasting understanding.[75]

A noteworthy proposition made at the conference with the aim of reaching out to the world was that "Indian classics should be made available to foreigners in reliable translations in English and perhaps in some other European languages as well."[76] A significant part of the last day of the conference was spent discussing a proposal for assembling an encyclopedia of India to compensate for the inaccuracies of sources such as the *Encyclopaedia Britannica*. This initiative was proposed by K. M. Pannikar, the Malayalam language writer and literary scholar, who argued that such new encyclopedic projects were necessary because the various Indian languages and literatures had grown to such an extent over the previous 150 years that the "unity of thought in India" had to be urgently "recreated" rather than assumed to preexist.[77] Pannikar argued that "the Sanskritic or the Persian traditions" had to be reconciled with the new ideas, new forms, new knowledge of the present.[78] The "modest proposal" that Pannikar presents is as follows:

> The most satisfactory method of providing this new basis for cultural unity is by the production of an Indian encyclopedia conceived as a scheme for providing authoritative instruction in every subject – a modern *Mahabharata* which would be a fifth and ever progressive *veda* for the future.[79]

In this proposed encyclopedia project, as elsewhere, there was a casual Hinduization which was not remarked upon because of the proposal's investment in national cultural unity. Several other anthologizing projects were proposed at the conference: a Bengali participant passionately offered to put together a bilingual volume of the "100 best poems" in Bengali which was to be published with an English translation alongside each Bengali original.[80] He then urged others to take up this task for their own mother-tongue – thus assembling a formidable source for Indians to get to know other literary traditions besides their own, and of course, to showcase the best of this Indian literary diversity for readers abroad.[81] Numerous such project ideas were floated at this conference; for example, an appeal was made by Bharati Sarabhai to the conference participants to write plays on the "authentic everyday life" of Indians (in English of course) which were to be performed by Indian actors but staged in the west.

The appeal of anthologies, encyclopedias, and translations showcasing the unity of India at this historical juncture is quickly apparent: first, it allows for a quick preview of the vast diversity and long literary traditions of a region which had a wealth of writing that could be classified as literature, and more importantly as "Indian Literature" *prior to the arrival of western literary genres*. Hence, the many literary genres in use in this region for centuries – narrative prose, epic drama in verse, epic poetry, essays and sermons, hymns, secular poetry, short narratives, folk songs, lullabies, biographies, lives of saints, and more recent forms such as autobiography, short stories, novellas, and novels – could be showcased, or, in the case of lengthy works, their rich textuality could, at the very least, be evoked even if not put on full display in such collections. Anthologies also served as evidence for the preexisting nation of India in the form of an unbroken literary heritage that had been painstakingly built century by century. The assembly of this literary lineage offered undeniable proof that such a nation had existed and now deserved to rule itself. Anthology editors could, both knowingly and unknowingly, also "claim" and "discard" regions, religious, ethnic, or caste groups whose literary texts were not considered worthy of inclusion.

Post-independence, as later chapters in this study will demonstrate, English continued as the seemingly invisible but indispensable language in such anthologizing of Indian literature. For example, the noted Bangla writer and literary critic Humayun Kabir edited an anthology titled *Contemporary Indian Short Stories* which had one story written in English and others translated into English from other Indian languages. Kabir's foreword to this collection, which was published in 1959 by the Sahitya Akademi, concludes with an account of already published volumes in the series and the plan for publication of many such anthologies. That this proposed series is published in English translation is only to be inferred from the sentence that states: "One of them, *Green and Gold*, a selection of stories from Bengal, has been well received in Britain, America, Germany and Italy."[82] Kabir continues: "Together, [these anthologies] will, it is hoped, give the reader in India and abroad some idea of the variety and vitality of the Indian literary tradition as well as the underlying unity of spirit which has characterized Indian civilization throughout the ages."[83] As discussed in later chapters of this book, the ubiquity of English in these literary projects that strive to systematically catalogue and bring together the "best" in Indian literature, continues in the anthologies that were published after independence by the Sahitya Akademi and later in the century to celebrate the fiftieth anniversary of Indian independence. The defensiveness about the need for English ebbs very slowly; its remnants can be traced in the anthologies from the 1950s, 1970s, and 1990s as in the 1940s.

While much of the discussion of English and of literary discourse in this language in the post-independence era will be conducted in greater detail in later chapters of this book, a brief preview is in order. The post-independence Nehruvian government was faced with the difficult task of reuniting the newly created country, which was shattered by the experience of the Partition of British India into Pakistan and independent India in the bloodied aftermath of independence. The 1948 conflict over Kashmir, as well as dealing with the fallout of Partition, led the leaders of the decolonizing nation to believe that establishing a coherent national identity was a mammoth daily (as well as a long-term) challenge. This task was enthusiastically tackled with a combination of force and persuasion. For example, post-independence India was forged with military force as the new nation state quite literally compelled the scattered princely states in their midst to join the union by force if enticement did not work.[84] Hence a rhetoric of national consolidation was considered, if anything, even more necessary in the post-independence era than before. Nehru, the first Prime Minister, in his *Discovery of India* (1946), written while a political prisoner in Ahmadnagar Fort prison from April to September 1944, coined the slogan "unity in diversity." Nehru was the chief architect of the construction of this modern state and this phrase "unity in diversity" soon became a byline for the Congress government in the first decades after independence.

In the early decades of the nation, the call for cultural displays of "unity in diversity" became a national slogan that presented itself as all-encompassing, as was only proper in a self-professed modern, secular, socialist state. But "unity in diversity" also served as a disciplinary dictum which actively discouraged and sought to control assertions of divergent views. To accept "unity in diversity" was to share in the patriotic vision of an independent India that was peopled by different religious, regional, cultural, class, caste, and language groups – all of which accepted their own as well as others' particular status in this extremely uneven "unity." That the slogan was expressed in English is significant, yet this choice of language was not what dominated the reception of this commonly used slogan: rather, unity in diversity was a sentiment that could be understood and accepted even by those with minimal access to elite circles. And yet, the other dominating slogan from this era that took hold in the public domain was expressed in Hindi: "*Garibi hatao!*" [Eliminate poverty!]. Coined apparently by Nehru's daughter, Indira Gandhi, then Prime

Minister of the nation, this slogan referred directly to the plight of those who would, in the linguistic logic of class in this location, be non-English speaking. It is important to note that in this era (roughly 1950 to the late 1970s), other slogans in Hindi that did not have English versions/translations were also being directed clearly at those outside the charmed circle of English. For example, pithy family planning slogans such as "*Hum dho, hamarey dho*" [We two, our two] or "*Ek kay baad abhi nahi; dho kay baad kabhi nahi*" [After one, pause a while; after two, never again] were also directed to the populace at large as was well indicated by the language choice.[85] What "unity in diversity" promised was *symbolic equity* rather than material or political equality among all Indians, a sentiment that functioned not unlike R. K. Narayan's fiction in providing the illusion of a shared Indian world that was available for all to partake in.[86]

With the death of Nehru in 1964, an era seemed to have come to an end. Nehru had served as Prime Minister since the dawn of independence and by the mid-1960s many of the national leaders and intellectuals of his generation had also expired. New faces and names appeared on the national stage as the spotlight moved away from the generation that bought the country to independence and had shaped it through the early decades. With Nehru's demise, the once significant correspondence between the political leaders of the nation and English language literary luminaries also became a thing of the past. However, the sense that there was an exclusive circle of national intellectuals, entry into which was marked by English language usage and membership in the higher castes and class, remained firmly in place. Correspondingly, in almost all the Indian academic disciplines, the dominant schools of thought were established in the English language. The shape that these disciplinary narratives took was no doubt influenced by the language they were narrated in, but over time this became an insignificant detail; English was the elephant in the room that was rendered invisible.

V

In the previous sections of this chapter, I have tried to set the stage for an examination of the place and focus of Indian literary criticism in English in the transition from British colony to independent nation. The rest of this chapter traces the dominant trends in the critical writing on Indian English literary texts in the years after independence, culminating with an assessment of the impact of postcolonial literary criticism's engagement with Indian fiction in English.

As early as 1943, Srinivasa Iyengar had lamented the paucity of authoritative Indian English literary criticism despite the growing body of literary texts in English. While Iyengar invariably found something good to say about each and every Indian creative writer he discusses in *Indo-Anglian Literature* (1943), his despair about the state of literary scholarship is relentless and unequivocal: "Literary criticism produced by the Indo-Anglians is almost inescapably derivative and imitative: and, naturally enough, criticism of metre and idiom is the most difficult of all."[87] In Iyengar's view, to participate in literary criticism was to enter a discourse that was not bound by the national affiliation of the writer(s) one studied. Iyengar's expectation was that the Indian critic would write on various literatures – British, American, and Indian – in English. Iyengar himself had published a well-received critical study of Lytton Strachey (1880–1932), the author of *Eminent Victorians* and other biographical works. Increasingly, Indian literary criticism in English in the mid-century focused on explicating contemporary Indian fiction and poetry and the work of British and US canonical writers – Shakespeare, nineteenth-century novelists, modernists like Eliot and Pound. However, the British literary canon provided the central texts in the instructional curricula that held sway over high school and university teaching of the English language and of literary study in the first four decades after independence. Hence well before Indian writing in English was established as worthy of study in the Indian classroom, critics were writing about this new genre of literary work.[88]

In the early post-independence years, the mainstream literary critical mode as best displayed by Iyengar's critical writing on Indian literature was geared toward consolidating, cataloging, praising, and encouraging literary production in all languages including English. The radical iconoclastic critique of the status quo that the Progressive Writers' Association had hoped to inject into assessments of Indian cultural production did not take hold in English language critical writing. By the early 1970s, however, this writing on Indian literature in English took on a more "critical" tone than exhibited in early critical accounts like those penned by Srinivasa Iyengar. Individual writers were held accountable for "non-authentic" writing and for pandering to the west, even while it was considered important to gain global attention for modern India through the country's cultural achievements. In the 1970s, 1980s and 1990s, small regional English language presses churned out many book-length studies and collections of critical essays on themes, images, metaphors, plot and character development, representation of women, and social issues in novels by a handful of prominent writers including primarily R. K. Narayan, Raja Rao, Mulk Raj

Anand, Anita Desai, Shashi Deshpande, Nayantara Sehgal, Kamala Das, and Kamala Markandaya. These volumes are written mostly by university professors in small town and urban centers, are often self-published, and are, for the most part, heavily invested in biographical details, narrow or "decent" interpretations of "Indianness," proper decorum for "respectable" female writers, "authentic" representation, and close readings of literary texts that relied heavily on detailed plot summaries.[89] Even though the focus of these scholarly works is on Indian writers, the comparison with canonical British and US writers continues, as does the use of a theoretical model that is more or less based on the new critical formalism of the early to mid-twentieth century in the west. This sense of participating in a global literary discourse was perhaps another reason why, typically, there was no discussion of the caste structures within which this literature was produced or consumed. Such use of western critical models attested to the modernity and professionalism of the literary scholarly work produced in post-independence India; caste considerations were viewed as a throwback to an earlier era. Oftentimes, new critical theory was matched with or supplanted by theoretical and interpretive aesthetic concepts from the ancient Sanskrit tradition like *dhvani* and *rasa* theory which remain vitally in use in other Indian high-cultural discourses and art forms such as classical dance. Proponents insisted that these classical theories of aesthetics and poetics could provide the most fitting critical coverage for Indian writing in English. These tools were then valiantly put to work to explicate all kinds of English literary texts from the subcontinent and beyond.[90]

The scholar and poet Arvind Mehrotra begins the "Further Reading" section at the end of his impressive edited book *A History of Indian Literature in English* with a head-note that reads:

> It is no secret that Indian literature in English, if not Indian literature as a whole, has been poorly served by its critics... That a modern literature could last almost two centuries despite this accumulation of neglect is a small miracle.
> Nevertheless, a large body of secondary material, like congress grass, has proliferated around this literature. Much of it is worthless and I have done my best to weed it...[91]

Mehrotra's book is a collaborative effort with leading scholars that systematically cleans up much of this "accumulation of neglect."[92] However, a critical work such as Meenakshi Mukherjee's *The Twice Born Fiction: Themes and Techniques of the Indian Novel in English* (1971) distinguishes itself from Mehrotra's choice phrase "congress grass," because it provides a historical map of the main themes and preoccupations of Indian literature in English up to the mid-1960s. Mukherjee's title suggests that this fiction in English was superior to the rest since the term "twice born" is conventionally used in reference to the higher castes (to mark their superiority over the lower castes and outcastes). However, on the very first page of her preface, Mukherjee clarifies that she has designated this fiction as twice born, not to elevate it to a superior caste, but to underscore the fact that it was "the product of two parent traditions," namely Indian and British.[93] Her book then goes on "to place such writing in its proper historical and cultural context and to evaluate it as literature."[94] In *The Twice Born Fiction*, Mukherjee, who was the most prominent of English language literary critics in Indian academia in recent decades, delivers a clearly articulated assessment of the literary texts of the past hundred years and her study remains a most influential resource.

Overall, Mukherjee argues, the period from the 1930s to the mid-1960s was the most productive period in Indian English writing and the themes she maps for each decade are presented as consistent across all Indian literatures.[95] She dismisses the earlier generation of writers from the late nineteenth century – Toru Dutt, Manmohan Ghose, and others – as not significant because they were "oddities," in that their texts were not "natural products of the general social and cultural conditions of their time."[96] Literature in every Indian language in the 1920s and 1930s is marked, according to Mukherjee, by a strong wave of protest and reform. The novels of the 1930s and 1940s are focused on the theme of national independence. After independence, Mukherjee notes that attending to social and economic problems was the dominant theme in all Indian language literatures. By the 1950s and 1960s, she finds that the most recurring theme is "the personal predicament" of the educated, sensitive protagonist torn between values of the east and the west.

Prior to the advent of what we now recognize as the postcolonial interpretive frame, scholars like Mukherjee were subjecting Indian writing in English to critical scrutiny and finding much to critique – both in the uneven quality of the primary texts and in the reception in India and abroad. A wide range of literary texts are discussed and it is understood that the urgency of supporting national projects through one's writing became less intense as other themes took center-stage, as in the writing of the generation of female writers (Anita Desai, Nayantara Sehgal, Shashi Deshpande, etc.) from the 1970s and early 1980s.[97] Mukherjee's assessments in *The Twice Born Fiction*, like Srinivasa Iyengar's before her, are written from the viewpoint that Indian English literature follows the same broad themes and motifs as Indian literature in other languages. This framing of the study of Indian English literature with works in and on other Indian literatures is best formulated in Sujit Mukherjee's approach to the writing of Indian literary history where he suggest that, rather than studying literature in each Indian language on its own, we need to look at literary form and content as it travels from one language to another.[98]

G. N. Devy's influential *After Amnesia: Tradition and Change in Indian Literary Criticism* (1992) also places the critical writing on Indian English literature within the larger context of literature in the modern Indian languages which he terms *bhāsā* literature, and which is consequently matched by *bhāsā* criticism. According to Devy, there is an "acute crisis" in *bhāsā* criticism marked by "a cultural amnesia which makes the average Indian intellectual incapable of tracing his tradition backwards beyond the mid-nineteenth century."[99] Instead, Devy argues, because of the "cultural demoralization" created by colonialism, Indian critics are "trapped between an indiscriminating revival of the past and an uncritical rejection of it, between Sanskrit poetics and Western critical theory," so much so that "*bhāsā* criticism today has ceased to be an intellectual 'discourse.'"[100] What Devy proposes is that Indian literary criticism recover from its amnesia by putting aside its "wild cravings for distant traditions" (both western criticism and Sanskrit poetics) and instead "remember" the *bhāsā* traditions that were established after the ancient period but before and during the ascendancy of the British in the subcontinent. Hence Devy begins his study with marking the emergence and survival of new languages from the third to the fifteenth century as the "greatest phenomenon in Indian cultural history."[101] While Devy's trenchant critique of the failure of Indian literary criticism is applicable to literary criticism concerning Indian writing in English (since it was also enamored of western and Sanskritic theories), his overarching argument about *bhāsā* traditions that could serve as a resource for every other Indian language does repeatedly draw attention to the different and distinctive historical trajectory of Indian English (and of the literature it begets) from that of other Indian languages.

Hence, while the urge to see a common or shared literary arena in which post-independence Indian literatures develop and evolve in tandem with each other was and remains an attractive vision, it was not necessarily accurate in the context of Indian English, whose emergence in the subcontinent was radically different from the birth of other *bhāsā* in this region. But by the early 1980s, this difference between English and other Indian languages was no longer intensely mortifying. There was a national literary arena and several regional ones of varying distinction. Hence, when the poet and novelist Kamala Das decided in the mid-1980s to move from writing in English and from the cities in the north in which she had spent most of her life, to writing in her mother-tongue, Malayalam, in her "home-state" of Kerala in south India, it was a shift from a national to a regional literary milieu.[102] Das had a very successful second career as a "regional" writer, but, read solely on the national literary register, her literary career, which reached its zenith with the publication of her English language autobiography *My Story* (1976), would seem to have had its moment in the headlines in the 1970s and 1980s when the work was discussed in nationally circulating English language newspapers, magazines, and journals. Not surprisingly, her reputation as an "Indian woman writer" corresponds to the period when she wrote primarily in English, thus asserting, once again, one of the central ironies tracked in this book, that writing in English, despite the fraught history of this language in the Indian subcontinent, is constitutive of the national literary arena and of "national literature" which thus comes into being in English or in translation from vernacular languages into English.

By the late twentieth century, Indian literature in English had legitimacy. Moreover, the increased authority that English carried because of its international usage in the era of globalization that intensified in the late twentieth century also played a role in carving out a separate destiny for literary works in this particular Indian language. And English language Indian literary critical texts worked overtime to secure the place of Indian creative writing in English. For example, in his evaluation of the late 1970s, Naik writes of Indian English as having weathered the storm of the national language debates and not just survived but thrived, despite the dangers of its banishment that had seemed so real in aftermath of independence:

> In spite of some early and hasty attempts to circumscribe the role of English in post-independence India, the importance of this world-language for a nation which had after centuries regained its legitimate place in international councils came to be increasingly recognized, and this provided further impetus to the study of English language and literature.[103]

And yet, in the concluding chapter titled "Retrospect and Prospect" Naik brings his "literary stocktaking" to a close by cataloging a long line of regional language writers and both Indian and international critics who, at worst, predict an imminent death for this literature, or at best, were doubtful about the "the very *raison d'être* of Indian English literature... even after this body of work has been more than a century and a half old and more."[104] The "Indianness" of such writing continued of course to be measured by its commitment to the Indian nation. Hence, in his "Introduction" to *Nationalism in Indo-Anglian Fiction* (1978), Professor G. P. Sharma notes that his purpose in writing the book was "that once I could show that Indo-Anglian fiction is nationalistic in spirit, all doubts about its not being Indian in spirit would be dispelled, and all prejudices against it will vanish. And once this happens in case of fiction – the biggest branch of Indo-Anglian literature – the readers should be able to study other branches of this literature with an open mind."[105] And any remaining doubts about the efficacy of English as an Indian literary language were swept away by the publication of Salman Rushdie's *Midnight's Children* in 1981.

VI

For Indian English literature, the 1980s were taken over, so to speak, by the publication of *Midnight's Children* by the London-based writer of Indian origin, Salman Rushdie. In retrospect, it is clear that Rushdie's writing of *Midnight's Children* and the rapturous reception it won in the early 1980s was symptomatic of a major shift in the very understanding of western colonialism, non-western nationalisms, and the politics of culture that had been gathering momentum in several locations in the late 1970s. Other developments elsewhere that were symptomatic of this shift would include the publication of Edward Said's *Orientalism* in 1978 and the related burgeoning of a new field of study called "postcolonial studies," which soon became a site for a formidable reassessment of the confluence of colonial and academic discourses. Another parallel development was the emergence of the "Subaltern Studies" collective of historians whose significant manifesto called for evaluating Indian history differently from the elite viewpoints established by colonial historians and inherited by early nationalist historians. If these academic endeavors of the early 1980s were declarations of independence from outdated colonial modes of studying the world, Rushdie's early work claimed self-rule and self-representation in the literary realm and was received in a manner that suggested such claims had not been made successfully enough by earlier writers. *Midnight's Children* did its share of brilliant theorizing on the impact of colonialism and of decolonization. In turn, this novel and *Shame* (Rushdie's next novel written in 1983) served as primary *literary* illustrations for almost every theoretical argument that was put forth by the early postcolonial literary and cultural theorists.[106]

When *Midnight's Children* was published in 1981, the cover carried a quote from the *New York Times* that said that in this novel "a country had found its voice." Despite irritation at the ignorance expressed in this vein of praise, *Midnight's Children* was received in the Indian subcontinent with overwhelming appreciation: the mix of irate affection, patriotism, and despair for the region that Rushdie displayed in the novel was instantly recognized by the elite as shared, even if seldom expressed in literary texts, and therefore deeply familiar.[107] This novel was embraced by the elite post-independence generation of English users in South Asia like no prior novel. This generation, born in the 1960s and 1970s, was no longer as reverential to the British literary canon as earlier generations of Indians nor as likely to be acquainted with a literary tradition in an Indian language other than English. Rushdie's novels spoke a language that was instantly familiar to this young, urban elite readership, many of whom, much like Rushdie himself, had a limited acquaintance with other Indian languages in the subcontinent.[108] In his extravagantly imagined novel, Rushdie adeptly showcased variations of local English (or Englishes) replete with jokes, multilingual puns, bilingual excess – all of which had hitherto been so carefully pruned out of South Asian literature in English but was around everywhere, every day – in the advertisements, films, speeches of national leaders, in the government offices, in the playgrounds and classrooms. And the plot of *Midnight's Children* was recognized in the subcontinent as delightfully Bollywood-inspired in its depiction of twists of fate, unrequited love, slow and secret courtships, babies switched at birth (so that the poor Hindu boy is bought up as son and heir by a rich Muslim family and the rich Muslim baby boy is brought up by a poor Hindu), class resentments ameliorated by faithful domestic servants, coincidences, repetitions, and the lavish use of mythological parallels. Rushdie's great achievement was that he had legitimized and licensed the use of this "mongrel" (to use his term) or "hybrid" (to use the more polished critical term) language *and reality* by elevating it into literature that had a global circulation. Unlike earlier international successes like Kamala Markandaya's *Nectar in a Sieve* (1954), which poignantly represented the suffering of a starving rural family in a proper "literary" English which had been bleached clean of local color and was supplemented by a glossary of the few non-English words that had been used, Rushdie's novel burst out with the wicked laughter of irreverence for standard English and other institutions that were conventionally held sacred. In *Midnight's Children*, Rushdie wittily contested the monolingual narration of a story, organized religions, "Indian" marriage and middle-class domesticity, the glorification of lineage, and family genealogy.

Shame, published in 1983, was Rushdie's chronicle of Pakistani history from its creation in 1947 to the fall of Prime Minister Zulfikar Bhutto and

Many a slip between the literary and the national 47

the military dictatorship of General Zia ul Haq in the 1980s. *Shame* needs to be read alongside Benedict Anderson's *Imagined Communities* published in the very same year and theorizing the very same ideas. Anderson's argument about the importance of print commodities like newspapers and novels in constructing the imagined community that is a nation could serve as a gloss for *Midnight's Children*, and even more acutely for *Shame* in which Pakistan (especially East Pakistan) is lamented as being destined to fail because it was "*insufficiently imagined*" (emphasis in original).[109] In the novel Rushdie writes: "My story, my fictional country exists, like myself, at a slight angle to reality. I have found this off centering to be necessary."[110] While *Shame* was a more somber novel than *Midnight's Children*, harsher in its criticism of the Pakistani state, it consolidated Rushdie's stature as an outsider who knew the inside story, who laughed at the national pieties, who thumbed his nose at humorless religious leaders, and who reveled in the power of the word, mocking authorities who would impotently try to control their world via censorship and intimidation. The Rushdie phenomenon opened up new possibilities for fiction writing in English and Rushdie's work itself drew both bouquets and brickbats. The issue of "inauthenticity" hounded his work, and Rushdie of course played up to (and even anticipated) this charge by inserting deliberate and glaring "mistakes" into his narrative (e.g. the date of Gandhi's assassination) and then drawing attention to such mistakes in the latter half of *Midnight's Children*.

Yet, for all his scintillating wit and irreverent bravado, Rushdie's early work was deeply nation-centric in that it was fueled by the national histories of the new nations in the subcontinent. His very plotline in *Midnight's Children* is propelled by historical events from the early twentieth century (the Jalianwala Bagh incident of 1919) to the 1970s (creation of Bangladesh, Indira Gandhi's imposition of the Emergency). The nations are the protagonists so much so that Saleem Sinai's very face and body are blatantly presented as following the contours of the Indian map. While most critics have focused on how Saleem Sinai's birth at the very stroke of midnight on August 15, 1947 when India was born makes him "handcuffed to history" as we are told on the very first page, much less has been said about how Rushdie very deliberately and self-consciously also handcuffs the novel's narrative to a textbook history of India, Pakistan, and Bangladesh. In Rushdie then, we have a novelist who is very consciously and carefully patterning his literary themes and plotline on twists and turns of national narratives.[111]

While Rushdie's writing is characterized as diasporic (especially signaled by his "mistakes" that are interpreted as proof of his diasporic distance), the issue at hand is much more complicated than what is usually represented as the alleged chasm between the India-based and the Indian diasporic writer. All through the twentieth century, novels written by writers of Indian origin from *either* location can and do partake of an "Indianness" that is deemed authentic and powerful *as long as* they are understood to be committed to the Indian nation and its people from within or from afar. This commitment can come in many literary guises: the celebration of ordinary yet "Indian" life (as in most novels by R. K. Narayan, and some of the novels by Amit Chaudhuri and Vikram Seth); in the form of critique colored with nostalgia (as in the early Rushdie novels and in Arundhati Roy's *The God of Small Things*); in the form of the denouncement of corrupt political and social practices and unequal economic status (as in the works of Mulk Raj Anand, Rohinton Mistry, Arundhati Roy, and most recently Aravind Adiga), and so on. As C. D. Narasimhaiah wrote in *The Swan and the Eagle: Essays on Indian English Literature*, "so long as the operative sensibility of the writer is essentially Indian it will be Indian literature."[112] While Narasimhaiah's specific and generally negative views on writers such as Rushdie, Roy, and Seth are not shared by all Indian literary critics, what is noteworthy is that the central evaluative vectors remain a commitment to "India/Indianness" and "authenticity," however loosely or strictly defined.[113] This question of "Indianness," of nation and national identity, which was, understandably, central in Indian literary criticism in the pre-/post-independence era, once again became valuable currency in the post-1980 period when postcolonial readings of literary texts proliferate. Under the aegis of postcolonial literary criticism, the non-western novel that garners global critical interest (as best epitomized by *Midnight's Children*) is once again that which foregrounds national history or histories through and after the transfer from colonial rule.[114]

In seminal essays like Fredric Jameson's "Third World Literature in the Era of Multinational Capitalism" (1986), a preoccupation with the national is presented as the unquestionable pivot on which non-western literature rests. As I have argued elsewhere, what Jameson's essay does is to domesticate this "alien" literature for the outsider (the western reader in his essay) by this declaration that "all third world texts are necessarily . . . allegorical, and in a very specific way: they are to be read as what I will call *national allegories.*"[115] In Jameson's cartography of western and non-western literatures, nationalism comes to be presented as the only authentic cultural attribute of the non-western parts of the world (p. 86). Despite some strenuous objection to the specific details of his essay, years after its initial publication, selective reworkings of the broad strokes etched by his argument substantiate the assessments of non-western literature, serve as a foundation for the teaching of non-western literatures in the west, for collections of essays, and as conference themes, and even undergird some of the most sophisticated writing on non-western literature.

The primacy of the coupling of "nation and narration" in postcolonial literary scholarship is perhaps best amplified in the influential collection of essays with that name which was edited by Homi K. Bhabha in 1990. All the essays in this collection postulate a close relationship between the literary and the national in the colonial world. They mostly harken back to Benedict Anderson's *Imagined Communities* and his argument about the importance of "print commodities" in creating national sentiment. In his essay for this collection, titled "DissemiNation: Time, Narrative, and the Margins of the Modern Nation," Bhabha argues that even that which is inscribed at the margins of the nation by marginalized groups (women, immigrants, the colonized) works to supplement the national narrative. The discourses produced by marginalized people, who are themselves the "shifting boundary" of a modern nation, write a doubleness, splitting, or ambivalence into the narratives produced at the margins. Hence Bhabha's claim that it is "through this process of splitting that the conceptual ambivalence of modern society becomes the site of *writing the nation*."[116] One could argue as I do here and elsewhere that "the nation" is precisely that which is not inscribed by the writing on the margins and often even in the literary texts produced at the center.[117] However, in Anderson's, Jameson's, and Bhabha's wake follow a long list of postcolonial critical works that cement this proximity of nation and narration especially through the fiction genre.

In the past three decades as postcolonial literary readings have achieved legitimacy in the institutional setup of both academia and publishing, scholars have formulated this nexus of nation and narration into a coherent critical framework for the literatures examined under this rubric. In retrospect, however, this *continued* centrality of nationhood and nationalism in the postcolonial literary critical reading is less a reflection of a dominant theme in the larger corpus of literary production in this period and more an imperative of the literary criticism that was brought to bear on the literature. The focus on the national in the literary criticism assumes that there is some common process that takes place in the literary arenas of disparate nations as they transition from the period of European rule to independence in the twentieth century. Of course this urgency to see the same dynamic emerging in every disparate decolonizing context meant that, to be equally applicable to every locale (with some allowance for local variation of course), it had to be a very slender or a very vague narrative.

The one commonality in the process of transferring from a colonial state to the institution of an independent nation is the emergence of some kind of nationalist sentiment. And more often than not, it is this emergence of nationalism that postcolonial literary critics find to be traceable in the literary texts produced from all such locations undergoing the processes of decolonization. Given the varying levels of linguistic nationalism in different decolonizing locations, it would be flawed logic to assume that English or other colonial languages function in identical fashion in all postcolonial literary contexts. While there are parallels and similar moments of tussle between the colonial and the local languages, any examination of literatures produced from such locations needs to be attentive to the specific local dynamics. Hence we cannot assume that the literary ramifications of writing in English are the same (give or take a few details) in, for instance, Kenya, the Philippines, and India.

In his introduction to *Narrating India: The Novel in Search of the Nation* (published by the Sahitya Akademi in 2005), E. V. Ramakrishnan begins by stating:

> The novels written both before and after independence in various Indian languages narrate the Indian nation in all its complexity, diversity and plurality. They constitute an unofficial history of the subcontinent depicting the people's version of what happened or what went wrong. They reveal to us the manner in which the nation was imagined and re-imagined from various locations in society. Yet moral dilemmas and failures of the national are nowhere documented with such clarity as in some of the best Indian novels produced in the last century.[118]

It needs to be said, of course, that none of the scholarly works listed above are using a formulaic or cookie-cutter notion of "nation + imagination = postcolonial literature," but despite all the contestations, cautionary qualifications, and multiple interpretations, the foundational status of the relationship between the nation and literature (especially the genre of fiction) is rarely questioned. At best the categories are expanded to fit the premise. Hence, the very nuanced introduction to the collection of essays titled *Nation in Imagination* concludes with:

> The discussions of nation presented in these papers show the disjuncture in current discourses of nation and stress the need for making the contours of nation and nationalism elastic, porous and resilient so that all historical and contemporary cultural formations, demographic transformations, political and economic affiliations, and ethnic as well as global aspirations are accounted for and accommodated.[119]

While these are laudable editorial aims, my quarrel is that in the push to find commonality, a very narrow definition of "the political" is instituted at center-stage: it is almost as if politics in third world literature is only recognizable when presented as national politics or when subsumed by the nation.

What is left out of literary analysis when we focus just on the national, on national allegory, and on nationalism? What is left out could be the many locally specific concerns (perhaps even with international implications) that surface as literary themes and are either delicately etched or deeply woven into the fabric of the literary text. These could be as varied as domestic concerns, caste struggles, themes of class, sexual/gender dynamics, linked to literacy, linked to modernity, and may not be legible even across all the regions of one nation or across literatures of former colonies over three continents. More often than not, such literary texts do not travel well unless their local themes are amenable to being elevated to and disciplined into the realm of the national. An excellent example of just such a novel from the era of national independence that has met with critical disregard despite its brilliance is G. V. Desani's *All about H. Hatterr* (1948). This novel is remarkable for its irresponsible relation to Indian nationalism and is therefore incomprehensible under the nation-centric framework. In the post-1980s period, accomplished writers such as Manju Kapoor, Jaishri Mishra, Anjana Appachana, and Nalinaksha Bhattacharya have published many nuanced and beautifully plotted novels in English that have not featured in the discussions of Indian postcolonial literature, possibly because the novels are centered on the minutia of the banal everyday life of mostly middle-class, mostly middle- and upper-caste, mostly female protagonists.

Some might argue that any substantial incursion into Indian literatures in languages other than English would radically change this assumption of a foundational link between non-western literature and the realm of the national. In fact in his rebuttal of Jameson's national allegory thesis, one of the most powerful counter-arguments that Aijaz Ahmed made was his insistence that the Urdu literary work of the pre-independence period had only passing interest in nationalism.[120] But here we come up against the mostly unspoken but very fundamental limitation of postcolonial literary criticism – its complete dependence on literatures written in or translated into English and other colonial languages. At a very distorted extreme was Rushdie's claim that the only good Indian fiction written in the fifty years after independence was in English.[121]

Emboldened by the emphasis on the nation in postcolonial literary criticism, and because the novel form first appeared in India in the third quarter of the nineteenth century, that is, around the same time as the idea of India as a single nation deserving of independence came into being, many literary commentators have argued for a causal relationship between the two. Even when not explicitly stated, the assumption seems to be that the novel form in India came into being in order to narrate the nation. In *Narrating India: The Novel in Search of the Nation* the editor Ramakrishnan writes: "The origin of the Indian novel in the second half of the nineteenth century coincided with the rise of nationalism as an ideology in the public sphere. The two discourses intermingled and, to some extent, even reinforced each other... Moreover the novel becomes the site where multiple discourses of nationhood become visible for examination."[122] Ramakrishnan's positing of the novel's "symbiotic relationship"[123] with the nation is *not* quite borne out by some of the essays in *Early Novels in India*, edited by Meenakshi Mukherjee and published by the Sahitya Akademi in 2002, which point to the heterogeneity of the impetus to write novels in the early history of this genre in India. For example, in his essay on Malayalam literature for this collection, Dilip Menon examines lower-caste Malayalam novels written in the nineteenth century to demonstrate that social reform movements especially around the status of lower castes and of women (rather than nationalism) are the more likely contemporaneous influences on the new genre of the novel.[124] In fact, he argues that this newness of the novel "combined with the protean form of the novel allowed its location in the exigent debates of an emerging public sphere, partly constituted through the engagement of native elites with the prospects of social modernity through the endorsement of colonial law."[125] Thus, rather than see the novel as an artifact of national sentiment, Menon argues that the novel expresses what might be termed a "colonial modernity" that "represented a compromise both with metropolitan modernity as well as indigenous traditions" and therefore centered on "the fashioning of the caste self and a new collectivity within a religious imagining."[126] In this particular context, Menon argues, "Christianity was the interface through which lower castes experienced modernity. And it was Christianity that allowed for their entry into a public sphere generated by inter-religious discussions."[127] Thus he refutes what he calls the "misapprehension of a connectedness between the nation and the novel... the axiomatic twinning of these ideas by Anderson" for, as Menon forcefully insists, "coevalness and causality are two distinct categories: imaginings of the nation and the writing of the novel happen at the same time, but the former is not responsible for the latter."[128] Menon goes on to demonstrate for example, how the pre-colonial world of oceanic travel and trade between networks that linked south India to Arabia, central Asia and southeast Asia are very much alive and celebrated in these fictions, so that the "imagination of subaltern groups has not shrunk as yet to the space of the nation, and still inhabits pre-modern geographies of freedom."[129] "Freedom" then, in these novels of caste, conversion, and rebirth, does not refer literally or allegorically to national independence; rather, for the low-caste protagonists, the freedom that is imagined and recorded is the movement out of slave-like existence to selfhood through travel, the protection of colonial law, or Christianity.

Compelling though Menon's arguments are, and backed by extensive archival research in the Malayalam literary realm, his is the only essay in this collection, *Early Novels in India*, that questions this fundamental assumption of the proximity of nation and novel. The leading essay in the collection by Namwar Singh, based on his keynote address at the conference where all these papers were first presented, categorically insists that "The idea of India as a country begins with 1857 [the Mutiny/First War of Independence], even though it did not become a sovereign state at the time, and we need to remember that novels in India came to be written only after that crucial year."[130] Singh continues: "Which are our novels that give us the sense of this birth of a country? I find most such novels have women at the centre... The oppressed woman frequently appears as a heroine in what appears to be a national allegory, to borrow Fredric Jameson's term. When the novel and the country were born together, in India, the focus became the woman's freedom."[131] Indeed, essay after essay in this collection points to the centrality of women in the early novel, not as author but as main protagonist and as imagined reader. In the critical reception of these novels, however, the discussion has already conflated woman and nation so thoroughly that one cannot access one without the other. To be of significance, anything and everything, anybody and everybody had to be elevated (or "shrunk" to borrow Menon's term) to the level of the national.

Ironically, in the early twenty-first century, even as the critical framework of "postcolonial literatures" gives way to the newly refurbished category of "world literature," this new discourse once again reinstates the nation through the category of the "national literatures," which is that which is worked on by "national scholars." As posed by Franco Moretti in "Conjunctures on World Literature" and in his collaborative anthologies on the novel genre around the world, within the "world literature" frame, both "national" scholarship and fiction are understood to be subsumed by the larger category of "world literature" which is then "coordinated" by the (west-based) comparativist scholar.[132] Under these critical circumstances, the non-western novelist (if she wants to be counted) had best present work that can be read in relation to the nation with which she is most closely associated.

VII

In conclusion then, if one places the dominant trends in post-1980s postcolonial literary theorizing within a larger narrative of the role and responsibility that critics had assigned to literature in English in the Indian context, we see a consistent pattern running through: the elevation of English above vernacular languages; the sense that the literature will respond to and reflect on the national situation; an elite and exclusive narrative which nevertheless assumes the burden of representing the "national"; a consolidation of this "national" that is in reality only a sliver of the whole – but because it is the sliver that is in power, it is the sliver that gets to define and to embody "national literature." Hence, for all its stated investment in margins, subalterns, and history from below, the literary arena in which postcolonial studies generally operates is of necessity mostly that of social and cultural elites. Given the critical impetus to track similar themes and preoccupations in literature produced from locations marked by the transfer from colony to independent nation, the "national" becomes a common critical currency. Hence, one could argue that postcolonial criticism's investment in the realm of the national becomes a larger version of the "unity in diversity" sloganeering with a global reach. And the category of world literature merely updates and refurbishes that ideological project. To understand the pitfalls of such literary critical projects we need to turn back to "unity in diversity" in the Indian context.

In the Indian context then, despite this national discourse of a shared worldview (exemplified by the "unity in diversity" slogan) that was symbolically available to all patriotic citizens alike, it only accurately fits the worldview of English-literates. Such scholars as D. L. Sheth have written eloquently about the distinct worldviews that different linguistic communities in India lived and continue to live within and engender.[133] Presenting the challenge that the "vernacular or regional elites" (those who represent large numbers and the increasing vocalization of aspirations that reach beyond regional boundaries) pose to the "national elites" (those who run the country and do so mostly in English) as an indication of healthy democratization, Sheth writes:

> The English-educated elites have so far enjoyed the privilege of determining the terms of discourse because they claim to represent a "national perspective" on every issue; in fact they define what is "national". But the regional elites have begun to operate with a newly acquired sense of confidence because of the numbers they represent. In the process, they are

seeking to change not only the terms of discourse on the language issue in their favour but are generally proceeding to challenge the role the English-educated elites have been playing since independence, both as norm-setters and pace-setters in India's public life.[134]

How does this translate in the cultural arena and specifically to Indian writing in English? Much of my impetus for this chapter came from a conviction that the whole project of defining and showcasing a "national literature" for India was a kind of critical sleight of hand deemed necessary for the consolidation of the nation and dexterously performed by English language cultural critics. Hence this chapter has narrated a very partial account of English in the early to late twentieth century which is not comprehensive but which hopefully provides a glimpse of the ambiguity and baggage that haunt all uses of English and which is especially complex and weighty as played out in the literary field. As discussed above, because English is so rarely used in other (non-literary) wide-ranging Indian cultural productions, literary work in this language is placed as standing outside or at best alongside, though removed from, the massive field of cultural production in many forms, languages, and hybrid traditions. However, as I hope to demonstrate in this study, the elite and their language of choice, English, too are a part of the cultural picture: their literature may have hogged the entire limelight, their choice of language may have given them an unfair advantage in the global literary arena, but historical circumstances gave them the task of consolidating and appropriating the mantle of national literature.

Most recently, the broad strokes of the understandable resentment against Indian English were exposed by the exchanges between Indian writers in English and writers in the vernaculars/regional languages in the aftermath of the first International Festival of Indian Literature that was held in New Delhi in February 2002. Literary practitioners working in other Indian languages have on occasion dismissed Indian writing in English as deracinated, shallow, rootless – an exoticized and unsubstantial performance staged for the western reader/tourist. At the 2002 literary festival, regional language writers of repute such as U. R. Ananthamurthy (Kannada), Sunil Gangopadhyay (Bengali), Balchandran Nimade (Marathi), Dilip Chitre (Marathi), Rajendra Yadav (Hindi), Gurdial Singh (Punjabi), and others were all quoted as having denounced Indian writing in English as "second-rate," "artificial western flowers," "a third-rate serpent-and-rope trip," "removed from their own ethos," "rootless," and other choice phrases.[135] This impulse to cast creative writing in English out of the category of "Indian literature" is deeply ironic because this very category is primarily a construct of English language literary criticism. Writers such as Shashi Deshpande (English) responded with astonishment and hurt at the degree of hostility expressed by vernacular writers: "We belong to the same world you did, all of us were part of the ocean called Indian Literature... This is our home, as it is yours; we did not drop out of the skies when we started writing in English."[136] I have tried in this chapter to trace the historical processes/circumstances that expose the logic and illogic of such assessments. The chapters that follow expose the pressures that this need to prove "authenticity" places on both English language writers and critics who were expected to justify the indulgence in English.[137] I will also demonstrate that this push to denounce literature in English as not authentically Indian is deeply ironic because this very category of "Indian literature" in the twentieth century is primarily a construct of English language literary criticism.

Since, as Sumit Sarkar has noted, written literature is "a guide to the ideas and values only of a minority," it necessarily marks out a reduced field of inquiry for literary critical work.[138] Furthermore, if the written literature in India that one examines is written in English, then the terrain is even more likely to be that staked out, at least initially, by elite-intellectual circles and therefore even tighter than more inclusive regional literary circles. However, as this chapter has tried to demonstrate, this sliver of the total literary production in this region, was seen as and saw itself as representative – as embodying the national, the modern, the secular. And in the years preceding and following independence, the elitist narrative of a unified India which could be represented in fiction through a representative "Indian" was embraced even by those who were not English literate, upper class, Brahmin, or even Hindu. For example, the enthusiastic nationwide acceptance (among English language readers) of R. K. Narayan's Malgudi as "their hometown," or of ten-year-old Swaminathan, the hero of his first novel (*Swami and Friends*, 1935) as embodying a commonly experienced "Indian childhood" and a shared past, suggests that this fiction could pass into reality. The efficacy of Narayan's fictional world of Malgudi, the focus of the next chapter, is what makes Ambedkar's ironic, even amused, reflections on the constructedness of the edifice called India to the point and, yet, conveniently put aside or even forgotten in the historical and literary accounting of these times and works.

CHAPTER TWO

R. K. Narayan and the fiction of the "ordinary Indian"

> First think of a good title (something like "Fires of Hate," "Death of love," "The Infatuated Raja," etc.), and add under it the sub-title that it is a "Novel of Indian Life". You must beg, borrow or steal a good atlas, and, if you have not forgotten how to handle it, you can easily find out where India is, and mark on it with a red pen the following important places: Bombay, Calcutta, Hyderabad, Himalayas, Ganges, Indus and North-West Frontier. This will give you the necessary topographical knowledge. After that you must cultivate the acquaintance of the following words (with their spellings): Hindu, Moslem, Brahmin, Crocodile, Bengal, Shikari, Dak Bungalow, Jungle, Great Mutiny, Sahib, English Men Out Here, Maharajas, GANDHI, Congress, Widows, Caste, My Servant, Chota Hazri, Tiffin. You can with a little practice, learn to use these words in combination with the names of places you have already memorized from the atlas. Here is an important point to remember. Never fail to use the words "Holy" and "Sacred" as often as possible. They can be used with almost every word in the list except Shikari, Dak Bungalow, English Men Out Here, Tiffin, Chota Hazri and My Servant, with which you can always use the words "Mystery" and "Intrigue," a pair of words without which it would be absurd to dream of writing an Indian novel.
> "How to Write an Indian Novel," *Punch*, 1933

In this chapter I examine the early work of R. K. Narayan (1906–2001), focusing on his creation of Malgudi, the small-town setting for all of his fiction written in the period roughly between the 1930s and 1980s. Despite the vast amount of criticism on his work, the political and literary significance of the processes by which this fictional small town was, seemingly effortlessly, naturalized into becoming the quintessential *Indian* small town remains to be fully explored. I argue in this chapter that what has been widely read as Narayan's apolitical vision could be viewed instead as the cultural reproduction of a utopian present and future India sketched from the point of view of a Hindu, upper-caste south Indian male writer.

I demonstrate that the presentation of this utopian Malgudi in English via a narrative style where "ordinary" events from everyday life are presented in a simple and seemingly transparent writing belies the craft with which the potentially disruptive aspects of caste, gender, and class are held under erasure so that a generic "Indianness" is shaped out of the specificities of the typical Malgudi narrative. Narayan's evocations of the contentment to be found in a simple familiar landscape, a simple plot, and simple resolutions were literary affects that were contrived with such a great degree of success that they were assumed to be "natural" attributes of his personality and writing style. Narayan's celebrated "artlessness" belies his careful and selective view of a world which was then deemed "ordinary," "typical," and authentically Indian. The easy sense of belonging that Narayan offered to readers created the illusion that this mode of Indianness was open to all despite the caste and gender specificities of the protagonists and of the disparate readers.

Expressed in English, Narayan's Malgudi becomes amenable to the vision of a new India that was shared by Indian nationalist leaders and intellectuals of the time: a Gandhian notion of the pastoral rural as the heart of India but upgraded to a small town in order to serve as a fitting setting for domestic plotlines. From the 1930s to the 1980s, Narayan's fiction served as a means by which urban Indian readers, who were more comfortable with the English language and its literature than with vernacular literatures and more comfortable with city life than with "village India," could recognize, experience, and participate in what was otherwise not available to them in such an immediate and aesthetically pleasing manner. Narayan's unadorned and straightforward presentation of narrative also served to welcome into the fold of English generation after generation of those upwardly mobile Indian readers who were taking their first steps into the literature in this language.

It is crucially important to keep in mind that Narayan begins writing his first novel *Swami and Friends* in a location where anti-Brahmin sentiments had coalesced into a well-established movement by the mid-1930s. Hence Narayan's Malgudi provides a bulwark against a rapidly changing world, even as it asserts that much satisfaction could still be had under this "timeless" social order where caste hierarchies and gender roles were not challenged in any radical fashion. These erasures, or authorial decisions, are so smoothly handled that we barely notice, for instance, that there are no girls in this novel about childhood. Tamil Brahmin girlhood in the 1930s was significantly different from boyhood in the same community. Swami and his friends encounter low-caste boys, but in these exchanges the inequality of power is completely camouflaged usually through reversals in that Swami is tormented by low castes. In this chapter I examine this careful construction of the narration of Swami's idyllic boyhood that, despite being carved out of erasures, was and continues to be claimed by Indians of all regions, religions, castes, and genders as their very own remembered past that Narayan had made available to all by his straightforward and simple rendition in English.

I

If, as can be surmised from a reading of the 1911 census results, a quarter of the Brahmin population of the Madras Presidency was literate in English, then it is not surprising that when the 29-year-old Tamil Brahmin fledgling writer R. K. Narayan published his first novel in 1935 (*Swami and Friends*) it was written in English.[1] Narayan's mother-tongue was Tamil and he had some proficiency in Kannada, two south Indian languages with prodigious literary traditions, but Narayan chose to write in English while living in a world where he was, no doubt, immersed in an English language literary milieu but was negotiating everyday life in other languages – a common enough situation in his caste and class circles.[2] In Tamil literary circles, from the early decades of the twentieth century, English served as an alternative to and an ally against what was experienced as linguistic domination from north India as the push to propagate Hindi in the south gathered force in the 1930s.[3] As Stuart Blackburn has demonstrated, the theme of Brahmin domestic life dominated Tamil magazine fiction and novels in the early twentieth century.[4] The thematic continuity between Tamil domestic fiction, with its use of romance and satire, and Narayan's writing is visible in all his early novels such as *The Dark Room* and *The English Teacher*.[5] By the 1930s, educated Tamil Brahmin men, like Narayan, had an ease with the English language that was unmatched by any other constituency. A combination of the collegial literary relationship between Tamil and English in this period, and his caste and gender location, produces the assured voice in which R. K. Narayan writes *Swami and Friends*, his very first novel, in English. Writing his novels in English in the early 1930s, then, makes Narayan a literary pioneer, but his work is also buttressed by literature in the vernacular which in turn makes his English a kind of Indian vernacular.[6] Despite the very few and brief published works that Narayan had to his credit before securing a publisher for *Swami and Friends*, he wrote his first novel in English with confidence and with a steady voice and style that did not falter or alter over the course of his lengthy career.[7]

In their impressive biography of Narayan's early years, Susan and N. Ram comment on the limitations of the literary scholarship on Narayan's work despite the vast amount of critical writing that his novels have engendered. While they view the lack of access to biographical information as the most "fundamental problem" for a full discussion of Narayan's work (a lack that their biography would fill), their evaluation of the other problems with literary scholarship on Narayan bears recounting. "For a start," they write

> to position Narayan within the Indo-Anglian writing stable seemed not very useful. There was no internal defining characteristic to this tradition other than the use of the English language by Indian writers in a milieu where English is rarely the principal spoken language but is nevertheless an important medium for communication in work, business, education . . . Nor was there any evidence of substantive interaction among unrelated writers who shared a tradition only in the most superficial sense. Even if Narayan could be placed here, he seemed to have no forebears or peers to relate to.[8]

All of the above is undoubtedly true and by his own account Narayan was more influenced by British fiction than by the, then, very young tradition of the Indian novel in English. In an interview with Susan and N. Ram conducted in 1985, Narayan states:

> I was not aware that I was writing in a foreign language. All these books, [indicating the bookcase], they've influenced me and they are in English. I could write more easily in English and I was fascinated with the London literary life of those days, the thirties, when Shaw and Belloc and Bennett and Chesterton and a whole lot of others had interesting encounters. News about them would always be there.[9]

Narayan's biographers do not directly comment on the influence of Tamil magazine literature and domestic novels that flourished in this time and place, but regardless, they are correct in claiming originality and genius for Narayan. At this early period in Indian novel writing, almost every novelist was a pioneer of some sort: detailed investigation will show that no writer was much like any other. Each new novelist was, to some degree, charting out a new course for themselves, some more successfully than others.

In the Indian subcontinent, the novel appears in the mid- to late nineteenth century. Bengali novels were already being written by Bankim Chandra Chatterjee and others by the mid-nineteenth century. *Rajmohan's Wife*, the first full-length novel in English, was written in 1864 but was overshadowed by the much more skillfully handled novels in the vernacular languages. Before and after this period there were, of course, several well-established literary genres in various languages that flourished in the subcontinent – epics, poems, drama, short stories, fables, long prose narratives, etc. But the novel form that newly emerged in the nineteenth and early twentieth century was the marker of a distinct literary renaissance in the subcontinent – especially in Bengal (modern-day Bangladesh and West Bengal state in India). These novels were romantic, mystical, and often historical; they were about upper and middle classes and castes – reflecting the readership for these novels (the educated upper and middle classes and castes). Popular themes included (unrequited) love, destiny, the pursuit of happiness against the claims of duty, (Indian) womanhood, masculinity, as well as topics central to social reform movements of the times – (child) marriage, widowhood, education of women, personal freedom, etc. As late as the 1930s, fiction in English was, to use K. R. Srinivasa Iyengar's term of assessment in a 1943 publication, "rather scanty."[10] S. Krishnan's account of the novel in English prior to the publication of *Swami and Friends* is equally uncomplimentary: "Hitherto, Indian fiction in English tended, by and large, to be philosophical, sentimental, political, or to ooze with an academic social consciousness. Naturally much of it was pretty unreadable, though chauvinist pride in the fact that we were using, moderately fluently, the language of the Englishman, gave Indian writing in English, a worth that was far from deserved."[11]

Hence, by all accounts Narayan did not have an established "Indian novel in English" tradition to look to for inspiration. The other predominant novelistic depiction of Indians was of course in the colonial novel. If one were to pause to consider how the "native" was portrayed in the popular colonial novel written in this era by European writers and set in the Indian subcontinent or Africa or in the Caribbean, we see a parade of colonial stereotypes which included both the requisite portrayal of extravagant, larger than life characters and settings, and the stock depiction of emaciated, unthinking crowds of unruly masses.

These, then, are the literary themes in circulation in writing in English by Indian and British writers as R. K. Narayan strove to be a full-time writer of novels in the language. In such a context, his insistence on presenting the ordinary, even banal, life of mainly middle-class citizens in their respectable homes restores the humanity that his subjects had been denied in English literary texts. Unmarked by the hyperbole of the colonial texts or the elevated heroism of overtly nationalist fiction, Narayan's characters epitomize an ordinary Indianness that is attractive to all. The radical difference of his fiction from prior Indian English fiction does bear out some truth in what the Rams claim – Narayan did seem to have "no forebears or peers to relate to." If he was influenced by earlier Indian novels *in English*, this influence is hard to track in the work. The influences that Narayan mentions are British writers whose work is in fact nothing like his (Shaw, Bennett, Chesterton, and others.) But influence works in mysterious ways and for each of the authors who are closely examined in this book, it is hard to name any clear literary forebears or peers with whom there was any meaningful interaction or of whom there are clear echoes. However, an early article written by Narayan well before he found a publisher for his first novel is very revealing of his absolute conviction about the kind of novel he would *not* write.

This rarely discussed initial publication by Narayan, titled "How to Write an Indian Novel," which was accepted for publication in the September 27, 1933 issue of *Punch*, reveals his astute sense of the literary world he was entering and further highlights the careful deliberation behind his choice of writing style.[12] An excerpt from this essay serves as the epigraph for this chapter. Published without a byline that would reveal the identity of the author, this essay serves as a humorous guide to writing a successful "Novel of Indian Life."[13] The tone Narayan adopts is that of an urbane and witty practitioner in the field whose "Englishness" is implicit, for example, in the use of English slang such as "bury your jemmy" and in the easy humor of the piece. Narayan, it would seem, could write like the witty English commentator in *Punch* as "authentically" as he could write as the authentic Indian writer! Hence, contrary to those who view him as simply writing "naturally" and without artifice, this essay reveals the careful construction of voice and worldview that was visible in his writing. The tone and content of this essay also gives pause to the image constructed by the critics of Narayan as the simple, south Indian, small-town writer who is unworldly and therefore authentic, and whose imagination/influences are barricaded from the outside world – the writer whose work is repeatedly compared to the clichéd image of Jane Austen myopically hard at work on her "small inch of ivory."

What this short essay in *Punch* reveals is that while Narayan was writing *Swami and Friends* and trying to get it published, he was well aware of the rules of the game, and, no doubt, painfully aware of the difference of his circulating first manuscript from the kind of novel that easily got published. His novel, which describes the antics of the nine-year-old middle-class Brahmin boy Swaminathan and his motley crew of young friends as they live their uneventful yet enchanted lives in a make-believe south Indian small town called Malgudi, was the antithesis of the novels he describes as certain successes in this essay. While his biographers, Susan and N. Ram, catalog this essay as a "satirical piece" in which Narayan "pokes sophisticated fun at foreign novelists writing on India,"[14] and while Narayan himself describes this essay in his autobiography as "lampooning Western writers who visited India to gather material,"[15] it also, perhaps unconsciously, voices his disenchantment with the kind of social reform/nationalist novel that *Indian writers* had been writing in English and getting published in previous decades. The essay's amused dismissal of the dominant modes of representing India in fiction is quite in keeping with Narayan's usual caution toward all forms of hyperbole. Narayan ends this essay on an ironic note by predicting that the "simple hints" he provides will lead the fledgling writer to "possibly in the course of time ... come to be looked upon as an expert on Indian affairs."[16]

The account of Narayan's difficulty in publishing his first novel and the heroic efforts of Kittu Purna, his friend who was studying at Oxford in the early 1930s, who managed to bring the book to Graham Greene's attention and thereby to a publisher, are well known. Briefly, Narayan had given the manuscript of his first attempt at a novel to his neighbor and friend Krishna Raghavendra ('Kittu') Purna who was en route to Oxford, with the instructions that if he could not place it with a publisher, he should tie a stone to it and drown it in the Thames. Purna did manage to get it to Graham Greene's desk and on a day with inclement English weather, Greene decided to read this manuscript by an unknown Indian, saw it as eminently publishable, and made sure that Hamish Hamilton did so.[17] Henceforth, Narayan embarked on a literary career in which he rarely deviated from the particularity of language, setting, and topic that were set in this first novel as the mould for all his later literary productions. As the author of fifteen novels (published at regular intervals from 1935 to 1993), five non-fiction books (including an autobiography and travel narratives), seven collections of short stories, and three books of mythology that he translated and adapted into English from other Indian languages, R. K. Narayan was undoubtedly the most prolific and the most widely read Indian author writing in the English language in the twentieth century.[18]

All assessments of Narayan's novels begin from the assumption that they are written in his "natural" voice. K. Srinivasa Iyengar's assessment of Narayan in his influential account of "Indo-Anglian" literature published in 1943 set the parameters for the literary critical approach to his work. In this survey of Indo-Anglian literature for PEN, Iyengar wrote: "Mr. Narayan is primarily an artist; he has no axe to grind, directly or indirectly; he is simply an engaging story teller."[19] This remains the dominant note in the literary criticism that Narayan's work has engendered. Almost sixty years later, Shashi Tharoor's assessment is not very different from Srinivasa Iyengar's:

> At his best, Narayan was a consummate teller of timeless tales, a meticulous recorder of the ironies of human life, an acute observer of the possibilities of the ordinary: India's answer to Jane Austen. The gentle wit, the simple sentences, the easy assumption of the inevitabilities of the tolerant Hindu social and philosophical system, the characteristically straightforward plotting, were all hallmarks of Narayan's charm and helped make many of his novels and stories interesting and often pleasurable.[20]

While Tharoor goes on to dismiss this writer for exhibiting the features described above, most literary critics have praised Narayan for precisely these attributes of the work. William Walsh writes: "If Anand is the novelist as reformer, Raja Rao the novelist as metaphysical poet, Narayan is simply the novelist as novelist."[21] The simplicity of Narayan's writing style belies the complex affiliations of his fiction and this is clearly visible when his work is read against the rather ornate English of Indian fiction writers in this period. In 1971 Meenakshi Mukherjee wrote: "Apart from a few exceptions, the bulk of Indo-Anglian writing even now is marked by two characteristics, which are conspicuous in Narayan by their absence: a meretricious, ornate and adjective-ridden style, and an excess of solemnity."[22] Thus, she argues, while the "unobtrusiveness of his style makes it appear an easy task... we realize how Narayan's artlessness really conceals art."[23]

Critics like William Walsh have noted in a broad sense the Hindu ethos in which Narayan operates. "Hindu myths and religious parables," Walsh writes, are not "theological scaffolding" to Narayan's fiction as much as a "part of a whole economy of feeling itself sunk deep into the constitution of the novelist."[24] In this first book-length study on Narayan published outside India, Walsh refers to Narayan in the very first sentence as "an Indian of the purest Brahmin stock."[25] Later in his book, Walsh concludes, "What one can say about Narayan without qualifications is that he embodies the pure spirit of Hinduism."[26] Walsh is correct of course in noting that Narayan's work is steeped in a Brahminical "economy of feeling" that is more than just a theological position or a caste category on a census table. While Walsh's obvious delight at the "purity" that Narayan embodies is disconcerting, Indian literary critics have gone to the other extreme and simply elided the whole issue of caste. Upon investigation one finds that none of the *Indian* literary critical accounts of Narayan's work in his lifetime mentions his caste background, which, while unobtrusive in the texts, is the very ground on which the edifice of these novels is created.

For example, in his chapter on Narayan in *The Swan and the Eagle: Essays on Indian English Literature* (1968), C. D. Narasimhaiah, an influential critic of Indian writing in English never once mentions Narayan's caste location or that of his characters; instead his assessment focuses entirely on Narayan's middle-class status and his ability to reproduce it in fiction: "Himself a product of the Hindu middle-class, sharing the beliefs, superstitions and perhaps the prejudices of his class in a small town and viewing its goings on with sympathy but also with a keen eye for the comic in the life around him, he had qualified himself to be a writer of his own class and provincial town."[27] Another landmark book of Indian literary criticism, M. K. Naik's *A History of Indian English Literature* (1982), introduces Narayan in the following manner: "A Tamil who has spent the major part of his life in the quiet city of Mysore, Narayan is the son of a school master."[28] In such critical placement of the author by class and region (with caste held under erasure), what is created is the ordinary, middle of the road, average, and representative figure.

As discussed in the previous chapter, the explanation for this silence on caste is that Indian English literary criticism (as much of the other Indian academic discourse) of this period prided itself on the modernity and secularism of its concerns, and in such a frame, overt or explicit considerations of caste-based formations of authors or literary protagonists are considered old-fashioned and are therefore rare unless, of course, the character under examination belongs to a low caste. Seeing oneself as unmarked by privilege is the privilege of elites everywhere. Nevertheless, references to "Indian traditions," "the Indian essence," "typically Indian values," "ideal Indian womanhood," "typical Indian village," or "typical small-town ethos" abound and are invariably coded according to the precepts of high-caste/hegemonic Hindu ideologies and practices. Hindu and Indian are interchangeable in such references, and the upper-caste location from which such formulations are proposed is naturalized into invisibility. Hence, to be producing that modern discourse known as literary criticism, from a high-caste position and heavily influenced by the western new critical investment in formalism, meant that explicit references to caste were much too old-fashioned, even retrograde, and extraneous to be included in any meaningful fashion in the discussion. This issue of the caste dimensions of what is considered "universal" or "typically Indian" and what is not is picked up in Chapter 3. That chapter examines Mulk Raj Anand's novel (also published in 1935) which follows Bakha, a young boy from the sweeper caste, as he goes about his day cleaning toilets in a military small town in north India. Despite being the more "typical" Indian childhood, in terms of sheer numbers, than that of Narayan's protagonist, Swami, the story of this Dalit youth has not been acclaimed for its universality precisely because his caste position makes him a "special interest" character.

In a recent essay on caste in the middle-class imaginary, the renowned sociologist M. S. S. Pandian begins his discussion of caste identity with a pointed critique of Narayan's autobiography, noting that in a text that runs to 186 pages, Narayan mentions his caste only in two instances when others (specifically, rabid Christians in one instance and exclusivist non-Brahmins in the other) incite a reference to his own caste.[29] Pandian goes on to argue that Narayan's "forgetfulness about caste" is typical of the upper-caste mode of transcoding caste into something else (division of labor, issues of hygiene), so that it becomes "an act of acknowledging and disowning caste at once."[30] Hence, in the public sphere, under the long shadow of modernity, Pandian finds two competing modes of representing caste either by transcoding, that is, "by other means" (the usual upper-caste mode manifest in Narayan's writing), or on "its own terms" (manifest in the work of non-Brahmin intellectuals like Ambedkar and E. V. Ramaswamy).[31] What Pandian finds is that in the dominant (upper-caste) discourses of modernity, caste as caste is rendered illegitimate and this delegitimization is achieved by pushing caste out of the domain of the political to, at best, the cultural domain where caste-talk is marked as pre-modern, uncivilized, and non-secular. This theorization then explains the reluctance of modern Indian literary critics to address caste in Narayan's work and the tendency noted above to transcode caste into class in discussions of Narayan's biographical and literary formation.[32]

In *Caste, Colonialism and Counter-Modernity* (2005), Debjani Ganguly astutely calls for academic work that does not treat caste as "merely an aberration that modern India needs to be educated out of."[33] Caste, she notes, is "not so much an essence that is responsible for South Asia's backwardness as a constellation of variegated social practices that are in a constant state of flux and that cannot be completely encapsulated within a narrative of nation building and its progress."[34] On the other hand, one could argue, as I have, that the narrative of nation building in India rests very firmly on an upper-caste understanding of national sovereignty as their birthright. As M. S. S. Pandian has succinctly stated, "what looks like the unmarked modern is stealthily upper caste in orientation."[35] Ganguly argues that it is "imperative to make a theoretical shift from the ideological (caste is oppressive) to the phenomenological (caste generates ways of living of which, no doubt, pain and oppression are a part) in conceptualizing caste."[36] Further, Ganguly notes that caste and caste practices are "a struggle to keep alive a life-form in ways where the questions of modernity, while not irrelevant, are not central to the ways in which people make sense of their lives."[37] Hence, it is perfectly conceivable to read the lives of Narayan's Brahmin characters through Ganguly's theoretical frame, as Chitra Sankaran does in her reading of his *The Painter of Signs*, where she demonstrates that "caste is rendered visible through daily acts that are endorsed by it."[38] Sankaran notes that despite Narayan's "elusive concept of caste," ultimately, both "Hinduism and its ingrained caste system emerge in more affirmative than negative terms" in *The Painter of Signs*.[39] In her conclusion to this essay that draws heavily on Ganguly's work, Sankaran writes: "caste as it is conceived of here becomes a future possibility rather than an ancient hurdle."[40] The effort to rightfully insist on a consideration of caste sometimes skates close to a reinstation of caste.

The deliberate absence, or at best, oblique ambivalence, of caste-talk in Narayan's literary world allows the illusion that Narayan focused on the mostly unremarkable lives of "ordinary folk" and it thereby becomes a means of laying claim to the identity of the typical Indian and of the Indian novel. Correspondingly, in Narayan and his depiction of "ordinary India," a varied Indian English readership found and embraced this attractive self-image whose caste and cultural particulars were unmentioned and yet visible and eminently desirable, a process akin to the phenomenon described in other contexts as "Sanskritization." This term was coined in the 1950s by the anthropologist M. N. Srinivas who argued that lower and middle castes might seek to improve their social status by adopting and adapting the customs and practices of higher and/or dominant caste communities.[41] As discussed later in this chapter, Srinivas and Narayan were close friends and this detail adds to the affinity between Srinivas's sociological theorizing and Narayan's literary writing. While Sanskritization theory is not without its own upper-caste bias, it offers one means of accounting for the reason why readers felt such a tight identification with Narayan's Malgudi characters, and it does provide a context in which to understand Narayan's success in the dominant discourses of Indian literary culture.[42] In an essay in *The Blindness of Insight* that argues that communalism in India is actually about caste, Menon elaborates his critique of Sanskritization theory as one that emphasizes "harmonious change through ritual adaptations over social antagonism" so that the "actual material violence involved in the maintenance of caste" is buried and instead the desire for "gradual social transformation on the part of the post-colonial elite" is once again upheld.[43] Consuming Narayan's fiction, as so many Indians do with complete enjoyment regardless of their caste or gender, is the perfect secular example of a ritual/reading practice that buries the material violence of caste maintenance and in its place promotes a glacial pace of social transformation which is further delayed by nostalgic longing for the way things were. Most importantly, Narayan's depiction of this ordinary India was so in keeping with the hegemonic discourses on Indianness which were (as described in Chapter 1) the purview of the caste and class elite, that its naturalness, authenticity, and representativeness is taken for granted by both lay readers and literary critics.

II

From his first novel, *Swami and Friends* (1935), to his writings in the late 1990s, all of Narayan's novels and most of his short stories are set in the imaginary small south Indian town, Malgudi.[44] Malgudi society is one that does not change under outside pressure: over the sixty-odd years that Narayan wrote about Malgudi, the town and its inhabitants remained essentially the same. From the very first novel, then, the contours of Malgudi are lovingly prescribed. Most of Narayan's protagonists are, like himself, Tamil Brahmins. All middle- and upper-class children, the class categories to which all central protagonists of all Narayan's novels belong, go either to the Albert Mission School or to the Board High School. All teachers, such as the protagonist of *The English Teacher*, teach in one or the other of these two educational institutions. All prosperous families live in Lawley Extension. All films are seen at Palace Talkies. All road travel in and out of Malgudi is conducted via the trunk road. The map of Malgudi provided in *Malgudi Days*, a collection of short stories assembled by Narayan and published in 1982, neatly marks the spots where characters from various novels live or go through momentous events in their lives, as well as quasi-historical sites such as the place where Gandhi made a speech in 1937 or where the Buddha preached in earlier times. In the "Author's Introduction" to this collection, dated September 1981, Narayan provides this discussion of Malgudi:

> I have named this volume *Malgudi Days* in order to give it a plausible geographical status. I am often asked, "Where is Malgudi?" All I can say is that it is imaginary and not to be found on any map (although the University of Chicago has published a literary atlas with a map of India indicating the location of Malgudi). If I explain that Malgudi is a small town in South India I shall only be expressing a half-truth, for the characteristics of Malgudi seem to me universal.[45]

Narayan and the fiction of the "ordinary Indian" 69

In the hegemonic Indian nationalist context, Malgudi does indeed have universal appeal. Narayan's Malgudi functions as a utopia of an essentially upper-caste view of benevolent Hinduism – a model city whose order and set patterns cement a conservative nationalism through its confidence that Hindu India survives the assaults of outsiders. Every Malgudi novel ends with the "outsiders" evicted and some semblance of order and tranquility restored. "Outsiders" in a typical Narayan novel are those who disrupt the established social order – Shanta Bai, the single working woman in *The Darkroom* who disrupts the domestic life of her boss, the main protagonist Ramani, and of his wife, the long-suffering Savitri; Daisy, the caste-less independent heroine of *The Painter of Signs*. In *Swami and Friends* too, Rajam, the westernized schoolboy from the big city of Madras who triggers rivalries amongst the simple small-town boys of Malgudi, leaves town at the very end of the novel.

In retrospect, it is quite logical that Narayan chose to construct Malgudi as the setting for his fiction. Narayan's domestic tales are in keeping with general literary trends in the late nineteenth- to early twentieth-century fiction in his mother-tongue Tamil, and yet the difference is that in Narayan's work, this world of Brahmin domesticity is represented in English and this immediately widens its purchase. Like other upper-caste thinkers from his time and place, when Narayan conceived of Malgudi, as a small-town merging into the villages that surround it, he was tapping into the widespread intellectual fascination with village India and adapting this trope for Indian fiction in English. Malgudi the small town, with its villages, forests, and hills on hand, becomes the flexible space between urban and rural. For urban Indians, Malgudi bridged the gap between their own experience and what was everywhere (or at least in upper-caste narratives) promoted as the spiritual core, the rural heart of India.[46] This romance of the unspoilt small town or village which supports a private, communal life that is visible despite the changes brought by British rule is ever present in the films, fiction, and even the early anthropological studies produced in India from the 1940s to the 1970s. If we consider M. N. Srinivas's many anthropological works (*India's Villages*, *The Remembered Village*) or the classic anthropological study, *Behind Mud Walls 1930–1960* by William and Charlotte Wiser, or the early films of both art cinema (Satyajit Ray's *Apu Trilogy*) and commercial cinema (*Mother India* in 1957), or Rajarao's novel *Kanthapura* (1938) – we see the very same recording of the mythologized, representative "Indian" small town or village captured as it crosses the threshold of modernity. In the 1930s, well ahead of the other cultural manifestations mentioned above, what Narayan produced via Malgudi was a way for upper-caste (or caste-observant) urban Indian bourgeois readers, who were comfortable in the English language and its literature and with city life, to experience and participate in what was otherwise not available to them in such a pleasurable manner unless they were readers of academic work such as that by Srinivas or bilingual readers of literature. Malgudi captured the imagined "innocence" of the unspoilt village and the comforts of the small town. Narayan's very selective presentation of life in Malgudi, as this chapter demonstrates, glossed over some of the more difficult realities of such locations that were indeed marked for upper-caste Indians by the pressures of colonial rule and/or by low-caste or middle-caste uplift movements. As for the lowest castes, the village and small town were primarily locations of intense caste oppression.

In contrast to Narayan's fiction, many Dalit autobiographies and novels begin with a recollected narration of a miserable childhood spent in the village where caste oppression and discrimination are presented as most severe and brutal. This is usually mapped through an exposé of the exploitative and hierarchal relationship between villagers of different castes and especially through first-hand accounts of caste cruelty to Dalit children in village schools.[47] The protagonist in all these Dalit narratives makes every effort to escape from the village into the relative caste anonymity afforded by urban spaces.[48] Not surprisingly Dalit leaders like Ambedkar, for example, had, in contradistinction to upper caste national leaders like Gandhi, repeatedly denounced Indian villages as the site of intense caste oppression and misery. But for the upper-castes there was an entirely different narrative around the village.

M. N. Srinivas's *The Remembered Village* records a fascinating account of the attraction that village India held for patriotic, England-educated, urban, upper-caste Indian young men of the 1940s and the simultaneous sense of the difficulty of actually dedicating one's life to such places. Srinivas recounts his own romanticized expectations of village life even as he presents the trials of doing fieldwork in a village in south India in the late 1940s. As an Oxford-trained anthropologist and Tamil/Mysorean Brahmin (like Narayan) from a wealthy urban family, Srinivas sets out to look for a village untouched by modernity. Very quickly, his resolve to pick a village that is not on the bus route or train line to the big city of Madras falters, because he finds that he really needs to maintain his contact with urban life. Having chosen his village, he escapes to the city as often as he can. He realizes that he needs much more of the accoutrements of modernity to survive in the village, thus arriving with more baggage for one man for a few months than many village households have acquired over a lifetime.

He repeatedly dodges villagers' offers to visit him in the city, even as he goes to great lengths to establish his own rules of privacy during his sojourn in the village.[49] Narayan's Malgudi retained enough of the village to provide an immensely readable literary alternative and solution to the difficulties of anthropological sojourns in the village that M. N. Srinivas captured so beautifully in his work.

Interestingly, Narayan's autobiography, *My Days*, as well as the very authoritative biography written by Susan Ram and N. Ram, makes clear that Narayan was himself less than tranquil in the small towns in which he, briefly, held several jobs as schoolmaster and budding journalist/writer. His autobiography and biography record his repeated escapes from placid small towns and quiet respectable jobs back to the big city of Madras. In his other writing, such as essays that display his love of New York, Narayan displays an immense capacity to make any place home-like simply by recognizing the Malgudi-like permanence and the hints of a village community at the heart of the city.[50]

The larger implication of this commonly held interest in the city–village dynamic among Indian intellectuals in the mid-century is best explored by Ashis Nandy in *An Ambiguous Journey to the City: The Village and Other Odd Ruins of the Self in the Indian Imagination*.[51] Here, Nandy eloquently tells the "the story of India's ambivalent affair with the modern city through the myth of the journey between the village and the city and the changes that myth has undergone."[52] Nandy expands his thesis in many nuanced passages of which I quote some that illuminate my discussion of Narayan's Malgudi. Nandy begins by establishing that:

> the village of the imagination has become a serene, pastoral paradise. It has become the depository of traditional wisdom and spirituality, and of the harmony of nature, intact community life and environmental sagacity – perhaps even a statement of Gandhian austerity, limits to want, and anti-consumerism. The village, too, is no longer a village in itself: it is a counterpoint to the city. India lives in its villages – social reformers and political activists love to say, usually as a glib, ideological ploy. That statement has acquired a deeper meaning today. The village symbolizes control over self: the city reeks of self-indulgence and the absence of self-restraint. Beyond the temptations and glitter of the city lies the utopia of an idyllic, integrated, defragmented self, not tyrannized by the demands of atomized individualism. It is the utopia of the village as self, controlling the self-that-is-the-city.[53]

Nandy rightly begins his exploration of this modern understanding of the Indian village with an analysis of Gandhi's well-known association with "village India." He points to the less discussed fact that it was only in his late forties that Gandhi, under the guidance of Gopalkrishna Gokhale, began to actually experience life in rural India. Nandy ruminates:

> After a while, it began to look as if he came from a village, as though he had lived in and fought for villages all his life. How did a finished product of the city begin to speak and even look like a villager? Was there latent in Gandhi a retrievable imagination of the village which he could revive when he physically encountered the village? The answer might well be that the village was never dead within him. Its survival within him was ensured through the rituals, folklore, epics, legends and myths to which he was exposed through the traditions of his family, peer-group, caste, sect and language. That imagination was waiting to be reclaimed. When Gandhi reclaimed the village within him, he could easily slip into the role of the larger-than-life Indian village headman. He had been only apparently an outsider.[54]

Understood in Nandy's terms, then, Gandhi's endeavor was to awaken the village consciousness that lay dormant within the urban Indian. Note that even Nandy seems to suggest that the village lives (and dies and can be revived) within all urban folk. Hence, he goes on to name Gandhi's village as "Indian public life's first village" and the film director Satyajit Ray's village in his debut film *Pather Panchali* as "cinema's first village." Nandy notes that Ray too, like Gandhi, was a latecomer to the village — indeed, it was not until he started shooting the film that this urban Bengali advertising executive from a distinguished cosmopolitan family had any personal experience of village life. Nandy then goes on to hail M. N. Srinivas's village in *The Remembered Village* as "the first Indian village of the social sciences."[55] Narayan's Malgudi, though more small town than village, is fitted into this paradigm by Nandy in the following fashion:

> The village of the mind shapes the city of the mind, too... By now, all English-speaking Indians and large parts of the Anglophone world know the town and its human-scale adventures and rhythms of life. By now, Malgudi is English literature's first Indian small town. It is such a living reality that one is sometimes surprised that maps do not show it; it is more real than many real-life Indian towns... The Malgudi stories supply clues to the imagery of the village that empowers the creativity of Gandhi and Ray.[56]

In Nandy's analysis, of course, as is typical of most intellectual work by academics on India, the caste parameters of this worldview are not delineated, and yet, the glowing account of village life reveals its upper-caste underpinnings. This empowering "imagery of the village" is simply understood to be the arena of the "Indian" imagination/psyche/creative realm. Within this realm, and upgraded from village to small town, Malgudi allowed for a fictional discourse of the arrival of modernity and the domestic and social frictions it produced. Whereas other elite nationalist public discourses lauded the processes of modernization reaching the Indian village and transforming agricultural production, Narayan was able to offer his urban Indian readers something they could identify with more easily: the arrival of an intellectual and cultural modernity – in sum, a comfortable sort of fiction for the newly awakened Indian national bourgeoisie. Hence his 1938 novel *The Dark Room* narrates the disruption that ensues when Ramani, the middle-aged, married, Brahmin manager of the Englandia Insurance Company hires the company's first female insurance agent, the westernized outsider Miss Shanta Bai, and then promptly becomes infatuated with her.[57] Clearly this is not a plot that could be convincingly set in an Indian village in the 1930s. However, later in the novel, when the plot requires that Savitri, Ramani's hitherto obedient and submissive wife, walk out of her comfortable home (in protest over the extramarital affair that her husband refuses to end) with a determination to live outside of masculine protection and without her children, the small-town milieu of this imagined city ensures that she comes to no harm as she roams the streets and riverbanks at night. She does find shelter and even a job of sorts in a local temple, but decides to return home after all.

In Malgudi, Narayan had worked out a quasi-urban location that was necessary to support the domestic plots of his early novels, such as the joys and trials of childhood, the travails of education, young love, the everyday triumphs and failures of the middle-class householder, upper-caste domesticity, the educated housewife's daily troubles, the young schoolteacher's frustrations, etc. And all these themes evoked a rich response from the English-reading Indian audience. Narayan's seemingly minimal interest in tracing the national struggles for independence, even though most of his novels were written during the freedom struggle period, is read either admiringly or disapprovingly by literary critics as a measure of his apolitical, even simplistic, worldview. But while Narayan's early fiction did not loudly proclaim its support for Indian independence or for social change like some of his contemporaries' work, his novels performed the subtler task of imagining a viable, albeit casteist, "Indian" small-town community where the otherwise overwhelming fact of being under foreign, imperial rule was a minor detail.[58] The domestic tale that each novel narrated strengthened this image of ordinary Indian life that was firmly rooted in places like Malgudi and therefore indestructible.

Meenakshi Mukherjee notes in *The Twice Born Fiction* that it is "often in the rural context that the regional reality and the *Indian* reality more or less merge" (emphasis in original).[59] What she means to suggest is that Indian readers "recognize" Raja Rao's Kanthapura as an Indian village despite the regional (Karnataka) details because it is accepted as a truthful narration. Even small towns like Narayan's Malgudi, Mukherjee suggests, "have something universal about them so that no Indian has any serious difficulty in identifying them in his experience."[60] By "universal," then, Mukherjee means to imply "Indian despite the regional details," and by "Indian" she means those who will not have "serious difficulty in identifying them in [their] experience" – as in, not shaped by a different caste experience of village life.[61] C. D. Narasimhaiah, in his *The Swan and the Eagle* (1968), presents Malgudi as "the microcosm of traditional Indian society."[62] Charles Larson, like many other critics, compares Narayan's Malgudi to Faulkner's Yoknapatawpha County.[63] So, at some level, Malgudi is a fictional setting like other fictional settings and at the same time it is rendered universal precisely because it sits comfortably within the hegemonic understanding of the "typical" Indian village/small town.

Narayan's reward (or punishment) for his investment in Malgudi was that his Malgudi became solidified in the national imagination as more truthfully Indian than any actual Indian city. Thus, in his introduction to *Malgudi Landscapes: The Best of R. K. Narayan*, the editor S. Krishnan writes: "*What is a fact* is that Malgudi takes its contours from the sleepy little South Indian towns of those days, . . . a placid little backwater full of gentle and gently eccentric persons" (emphasis added).[64] By the late twentieth century Malgudi presented an ideal Indian past that is a fiction and yet is so entrenched in the national and diasporic imaginary as to appear real. Narayan's early delineation of Malgudi was concerned with providing roots in the "real India," or rather the preferred mythic version of India, for Indian and western readers, and each subsequent work set in this city added nourishment to these roots. As younger writers in India and in the diaspora crafted their own representative "Indian worlds," each new fictional locale further consolidated Narayan's Malgudi as the Ur text – effortless, even artless, and firmly grounded in reality. Hence, in relation to later fictional cities like Madhupur in Indira Ganesan's novels written from the diaspora and set on the island of Pi, Malgudi becomes the original, the authentic, Indian city.[65]

A good illustration of the post-independence investment in Malgudi (on the part of both the author and his audience) is provided in an essay titled "Misguided 'Guide'" written in the 1970s in which Narayan berates the Bollywood and Hollywood collaboration that led to the production of a film based on his novel, *The Guide* (1958).[66] Much to the writer's chagrin, *Guide* was shot on location in Rajasthan, north India, which the American film director and Indian producers considered more picturesque and exotic than the Malgudi-like places in south India that the writer had proposed.[67] In this essay, Narayan recounts, with his usual comic undertones, the tussle between himself and the film director on this issue of location:

> Our next meeting was in Bombay, and I wasted no time in speaking of this problem. "My story takes place in South India, in Malgudi, an imaginary town known to thousands of my readers all over the world," I explained... "You have to stick to my geography and sociology. Although it is a world of fiction there are certain inner veracities."
>
> One of them replied: "We feel it a privilege to be doing your story." This sounded irrelevant as an answer to my statement.
>
> We were sitting under a gaudy umbrella beside a blue swimming pool on Juhu beach, where the American party was housed in princely suites in a modern hotel. It was hard to believe that we were in India. Most of our conversations took place somewhat amphibiously, on the edge of the swimming pool, in which the director spent a great deal of time...
>
> "Please remember," one of them tried to explain, "that we are shooting, for the first time in India, in wide screen and Eastman colour, and we must shoot where there is spectacle. Hence Jaipur."
>
> "In that case," I had to ask, "why all that strenuous motoring near my home? Why my story at all when all you need is a picturesque spectacle?"
>
> I was taken aback when the reply came! "How do you know that Malgudi is where you think it is?"
>
> Somewhat bewildered, I said, with what I hoped was proper humility, "I suppose I know because I have imagined it, created it and have been writing novel after novel set in the area for the last thirty years."
>
> "We are out to expand the notion of Malgudi," one of them explained. "Malgudi will be where we place it, in Kashmir, Rajasthan, Bombay, Delhi, even Ceylon."[68]

While the Hindi version of the film *Guide* (1965) won national awards and critical acclaim, and was moderately successful in a commercial sense, in his essay "Misguided 'Guide'" Narayan triumphantly quotes both then Prime Minister of India, Indira Gandhi, and the most prominent Indian filmmaker, Satyajit Ray, as having told him of the foolishness of trying to move a Malgudi story out of its (imagined) location in south India to elsewhere in India.

Post-independence, the Malgudi milieu was one that the author could not or would not update: its simple pleasures, conflicts, and triumphs became ossified by popular demand. From being a projection into an idealized version of the present and future, it became the map of a lovingly remembered and equally idealized past. Sometimes Narayan was frustrated by the liberties that others took with Malgudi, and yet, in other essays, he expressed resignation at his own imprisonment within the confines of this small town. When invited to join the American Academy and Institute of Arts and Letters in 1982, Narayan wrote in his acceptance speech:

> It had just occurred to me when I started on my first novel, *Swami and Friends*, about fifty years ago, to be exact in September 1930, that it would be safer to have a fictitious name for the background of the novel, which would leave one free to meddle with its geography and details as I pleased, without incurring the wrath of any city-father of any actual town or city. I wanted to be able to put in whatever I liked, and where ever I liked – a little street or school or a temple or a bungalow or even a slum, a railway line, at any spot, a minor despot in a little world. I began to be fascinated by its possibilities; its river, market place, and the far-off mountain roads and forests acquired a concrete quality, and have imprisoned me within their boundaries, with the result that I am unable to escape from Malgudi, even if I wished to... [69]

In the years after independence, Malgudi had become the unviolated/inviolable India of the Indian bourgeois nationalist fantasy and was replicated as such in the diasporic imagination. But, one might argue, India is also not equal to the nationalist fantasy that is produced from within the Indian context nor equal to the quite similar diasporic fantasy of the homeland. Against such impossibilities, Malgudi continues to serve as the best example of this serenely consumed fantasy. Not that places *like* Malgudi or childhoods *like* Swami's did not exist, but that Narayan offered his readership the chance to partake of a very particular experience as the heritage and legacy of *every* Indian, regardless of region, religion, caste, class, or gender. Hence, to be socially reproduced as an urban, modern Indian was to accept this rendition of one's roots and to find complete satisfaction in Narayan's picture of a benevolent, caste-ordered, Hindu world. Thus, from being a projection into an idealized version of the present and future in the 1930s when Narayan began writing fiction, post-independence, his Malgudi became the map of a lovingly remembered and equally idealized past that was formative of "Indianness" the world over. Especially for the far-flung south Indian, who was away from his "oor" or "naad" because of employment elsewhere in India or abroad, Narayan provided a nostalgic escape back home. And his very first novel, *Swami and Friends*, being as it was a story of a blissful childhood recollected by an indulgent, amused adult narrator, was instantly recognized as every Indian's childhood with the usual allowances made for fictionalization.

III

In *Swami and Friends*, the story revolves around the daily antics of nine-year-old Swami and his classmates in the Albert Mission School. Narayan's plot weaves the days Swami spends memorizing maps of Europe and Africa, dodging the blows of teachers, resisting Christian scripture lessons by the devout convert Ebenezar, setting up the Malgudi Cricket Club, evading his father's surveillance, pretending to study, faking illness with the hope to thereby avoid a potentially difficult day at school, being spoilt by a doting grandmother with an unending fund of Hindu mythological tales, impressing his friends, running through the streets of Malgudi, relaxing at the banks of the River Sarayu, and generally enjoying a carefree childhood. We are very quickly made to understand that young Swami lives in perfect satisfaction with his world. Chapter 2 ends with:

> The river's mild rumble, the rustling of the *peepul* leaves, the half-light of the late evening, and the three friends eating, and glowing with new friendship – Swaminathan felt at perfect peace with the world.[70]

Unlike in more recent fictional depictions of childhood, where such an early staging of childhood "happiness" is almost a guarantee that things will fall apart in unimaginably cruel ways, forever banishing protagonist and reader out of the idylls of childhood, here Narayan is only warming up to the story about the joys of boyhood.[71]

Swami and his friends are local boys; Malgudi is their universe, their playground where not much harm can come to them. The safe, happy, uncomplicated childhood does, of course, come with trials and terrors, but there is nothing that will permanently scar or harm these boys. They are at home in a way that is unshakable. They may long to speak better English or to have more of the British toys that Rajam the wealthiest boy in the group owns, but none of this detracts from their sense of belonging. There are, of course, in this novel, as in some of the later novels, the constant references to English literature, international cricket stars (the Australian Donald

Bradman and England's Maurice Tate are Swami's idols), British items of everyday use (pens, paper, perfumes, books, clothes, ties, cars, films), etc. In fact Narayan's initial title for the manuscript was *Swami, the Tate* but this was changed to *Swami and Friends* by the British publisher Hamish Hamilton who hoped thereby to draw attention to the novel's similarity to Rudyard Kipling's *Stalky and Co.*[72] And yet, for all this swirl of British colonial culture through Malgudi, there is a very strict demarcation of those who belong and those who don't. Consider this passage that begins chapter 11 titled "In Father's Presence":

> During summer Malgudi was one of the most detested towns in South India. Sometimes the heat went above a hundred and ten in the shade... The same sun that beat down on the head of Mr. Hentel, the mill manager, and drove him to Kodaikanal, or on the turban of Mr. Krishnan, the Executive Engineer, and made him complain that his profession was one of the hardest, compelling him to wander in sun and storm, beat down on Swaminathan's curly head, Mani's tough matted hair, and Rajam's short wiry crop, and left them unmoved. The same sun that baked the earth so much that even Mr. Retty, the most Indianised of the "Europeans,"... screamed one day when he forgetfully took a step or two barefoot, the same sun made the three friends loath to remain under a roof.[73]

The ability to bear the heat is one of the many not so subtle (to literary audiences) ways in which Narayan attests to Swaminathan and his friends' secure sense of belonging in Malgudi as fully enfranchised young boys. The heat – which is, not coincidentally, a constant theme in the European novel set in the colonies – is no big deal for Swami and his friends. In their hesitant use of English, their confusion when faced with complex math problems, the fearful encounters with tough low-caste boys, the pain of being caned by headmasters, the excitement of participating in a rampage through the school under the pretext of a nationalist strike, and the thrill of breaking the headmaster's window pane, Swami and his friends are local boys.

The brilliance of Narayan's writing is such that we do not notice how selective a presentation of everyday life, even of upper-caste domestic life, this novel showcases. If, for instance, we were to pause to consider why there is such a paucity of girls in all the households we are given access to (namely, those of Swami and his friends), we would immediately see the potential complications that "realistically" depicting girlhood in this caste/class community in the 1930s would entail. If Swami were to have a sister who was around his age, the difference in her mobility, education, and relation to the outside world and to the domestic sphere would serve as too vivid a contrast to the freedom that Swami is presented as enjoying. Such a presence in the novel would also underline the fact that his childhood joys are those that are the exclusive purview of boys. A nine- or ten-year-old Brahmin girl from a respectable family would be at the threshold of marriage and would have a much more closely monitored mobility through Malgudi. There is no occasion to refer to the Brahmin practice of isolating menstruating girls and women even from family members to avoid having their "unclean" presence pollute others. Without such a "sister subplot," when Swami chafes at the increased surveillance he suffers from his lawyer father when the courts are closed for the summer (and consequently his father is at home and ready to assign math problems or other tasks that require Swami to be industrious), it is simply another occasion to chuckle at his boyish outrage at being isolated from friends and oppressed by the elders until he can sneak out of the house. In the "girl-free" narrative that Narayan presents, we do not see that being boys rather than girls in an orthodox patriarchal community has so much to do with the quality of childhood that Swami and his friends enjoy. Two recent scholarly works by Mytheli Sreenivas and Mythily Sivaraman shed light on the condition of girlhood in the early part of the twentieth century and both studies focus centrally on the Tamil Brahmin society that Narayan's work is set within.[74] These studies analyze the impact of the Child Marriage Act which came into force in 1830 and fixed the legal minimum age of marriage for girls at fourteen and for grooms at eighteen. Sivaraman documents how this act was vigorously opposed by orthodox Brahmins well into the twentieth century and notes that underage girls were routinely married off despite this law. She cites female activists like Chinnamalu Amma and Muthulakshmi Reddy (1886–1968) who publicly protested child marriage as no less than a "death sentence" for girls. Sivaraman quotes from Subhalakshmi Ammal's (1886–1969) testimony to the Age of Consent Committee (1928–1929) in which she stated: "99% of child marriages were consummated much before the girl attained puberty or before she completed thirteen years . . . There is no girlhood at all among Brahmins . . . many girls of fourteen or fifteen, had to have a minimum of three or four abortions every year and many gave birth to still born babies at the age of eleven and twelve."[75]

Given this radically different experience of childhood for Brahmin girls, it becomes clear why neither Swami nor any of his friends are scripted as having female siblings. The complications of presenting Brahmin girlhood would be too numerous to fold into the narrative even with Narayan's trademark deft use of humor and understatement. While Narayan does not draw attention to how gender shapes childhood by risking a female sibling for any of the boys in the novel, he does present Swami's interactions with boys and men from lower-class and -caste backgrounds whose lives are also very different from his.[76] Here the comic skills of the writer come into play as Swami's negotiations with low-caste boys are narrated without directly drawing attention to the caste hierarchy that marks every such interaction. In the course of the narrative, Swami attempts to get back a small sum of money from a cart driver (referred to as "the coachman") who had tricked him into believing that he could "grow" big sums of money from the small amount. When the coachman refuses to give back his initial investment, Swami arrives with his friends at the coachman's segregated slum neighborhood, hoping to intimidate him and his son into returning the money. Swami, meanwhile, both resents and fears the coachman's son: "He had in his heart a great dread of the boy. And sometimes in the night would float before him a face dark, dirty and cruel, and make him shiver. It was the face of the coachman's son."[77] The use of "dark, dirty and cruel" might seem merely descriptive, but it serves as a mode of transcoding caste into other registers, in this case of skin color and hygiene, which has been noted, as discussed earlier, in writing that avoids direct reference to caste. Swami's friend Mani, who is the tallest, oldest, strongest, and bravest of all the boys, tries to bribe the coachman's son with a shiny red spinning top which the boy grabs and runs away with. Mani tries to retrieve the top but the coachman's neighbors set the neighborhood's dogs on them and pelt them with small stones until the boys flee into the safety of their own streets, having lost both money and top. In the very next chapter, we are told of how Swami, Mani, and Rajam restore their bruised egos by harassing a little village boy who drives a bullock cart into Malgudi, by demanding to see his "pass" to enter the town and insisting on issuing one with much display of their version of governmental officialese. The following chapter describes a visit that Swami makes to "the club" when he accompanies his father to a tennis match. While idly watching the tennis match, Swami notices that the very same coachman's son who had hounded Mani and him out of his neighborhood is the ball boy at the club. Swami is in turn recognized by the ball boy, who "grinned maliciously and hastily took out of his pocket a penknife and held it up."[78] The humorous tone of this passage depends on the reader's complete identification with the child protagonist Swami and the easy assumption that the "dark, dirty and cruel" ball boy is naturally prone to violence.

Narayan's focus never shifts from Swami's terror at this encounter with his "enemy." We are told with great comic effect of Swami's elaborate arrangements to protect himself from being killed at any minute. That

Swami's class and caste privilege will protect him should be visible to the reader, but Swami's "cold fear" is indulgently narrated:

> After the set when his father walked toward the building, Swaminathan took care to walk a little in front of him and not behind, as he feared that he might get a stab any minute in his back.
>
> ... He [Swami] stooped and picked up a stone, a sharp stone and held it ready for use if any emergency should arise. The distance from the tennis court to the building was about a dozen yards, but to Swaminathan it seemed to be a mile and a half.
>
> He felt safe when he sat in a chair beside his father in the card room... This was the safest place on earth...
>
> An hour later father rose from the table. Swaminathan was in a highly nervous state when he got down the last steps of the building. There were unknown dangers lurking in the darkness around. He was no doubt secure between father and his friend. That thought was encouraging. But Swaminathan felt at the same time that it would have been better if all the persons in the card-room had escorted him to the car. He needed all the guarding he could get. Probably by this time the boy had gone out and brought a huge gang of assassins and was waiting for him...
>
> ... When they came to the car, Swaminathan got in first and occupied the centre of the back seat. He was still in suspense. Father's friend was taking time to start the car. Swaminathan was sitting all alone in the back seat, very far behind father and his friend. Even now the coachman's son and his gang could easily pull him out and finish him.
>
> The car started. When the engine started, it sounded to Swaminathan's ear like the voice of a saviour. The car was outside the gate now and picked up speed. Swaminathan lifted a corner of his *dhoti* and mopped his brow.[79]

So intent is Narayan on presenting Swami's terror as comically disproportional to the actual threat that many of the other ramifications of this club episode are completely sidelined. For example, the coachman's son who works as a ball boy at Swami's father's club is only presented through the lens of Swami's childish terror and so we do not know (or care) if he goes to school in the day or if, like the village boy driving the cart whom Swami and his gang accost, he is a young worker with a very different "childhood" from that of our primary protagonists. Swami is a part of the Indian elite who were allowed, albeit reluctantly, to enter European colonial clubs as patrons or who established their own clubs modeled on the European ones. His family may not be as wealthy as Rajam's, but Swami is part of the local elite and clearly not in any danger from the coachman's son. Yet Narayan does not let up on this line of vision in this episode and hence, neither the exclusivity of such clubs nor the details of caste privilege or of child labor interrupt the humor of this scene. Caste is never mentioned but appears everywhere. In Narayan's text, ultimately Swami is safe but the potential threat of violence in the self-assertions of low-castes is registered with great comic skill.[80] Swami's great fear at falling victim to the ball boy's penknife establishes the potential for violence in any assertion of selfhood on the part of low castes, but the hyperbole involved also dissolves some of this fear as childlike panic. Comedy becomes, as K. Ravi Srinivas and Sunder Kaali have demonstrated in their study of Tamil cinema, a very effective means of temporarily rendering unstable the power dynamics in a caste-based society.[81]

It is to be noted that in the 1930s, and in fact to date, there have not been many substantial accounts of childhood in the non-west, and those that exist are mostly anthropological works that examine specific child-rearing practices in different parts of the non-west. As Allison James and Alan Prout have argued, childhood is a social construct in that while the immaturity of children is a biological fact of life, the ways in which this immaturity is understood and made meaningful is a fact of culture.[82] There is of course some scholarly work on local understandings of the stage of life called childhood, but much of our understanding of childhood in different locations comes from literary texts. It is very hard to recreate what childhood means or meant in a time and place – because of the unreliability of source materials and because children are usually represented, rather than representing themselves. The experience of childhood is mediated not just by geography and century, but even within the same time/space parameters by gender and class. Even within the same family, children can have very different childhoods depending on their gender and birth rank and on the family circumstances in their early years. None of this is of course relevant to Narayan's novel, because no childhood but that of Swami and his friends matters. What childhood entails is constantly being redefined, and this in itself makes a stable rendition of a past, but seemingly timeless, happy childhood, like that Narayan creates in his first novel, extremely attractive. A cultural text like *Swami and Friends*, in its spatio-temporal manipulations, demonstrates that desire, memory, fantasy are all at play in the processes of creating the representative Indian childhood. And nowhere is this clearer than in the huge success of the TV serial *Malgudi Days* (based on *Swami and Friends* and on short stories by Narayan) which completely enthralled Indian audiences in its first run in the late 1980s.

In the mid-1980s, the Kannada actor and director Shankar Nag was commissioned by the national (state-owned) TV channel, Doordarshan, to make a TV serial based on some of Narayan's short stories and on two of his novels, *Swami and Friends* and *The Vendor of Sweets*.[83] This TV serial, titled *Malgudi Days*, began airing in 1987, ran for thirty-nine episodes, and was an instant success.[84] Episodes 19 to 26 of *Malgudi Days* covered the plot of *Swami and Friends* and, unlike the novel they were based on, were narrated in Hindi. This TV serial was generously financed by Doordarshan, and so it was shot in 35 mm film negative and not on video, and on location in Agumbe village in Shimoga district in Karnataka rather than in an urban studio set like most other TV serials.[85] *Malgudi Days* had a cast comprising mostly actors from Kannada cinema and theatre who spent several months in Agumbe living together like a film unit on location. Every detail of this production carefully recreated Malgudi as it might have existed in south India in the early 1930s.[86] In every episode, the camera lingers over many household devices of the time, now mostly out-dated, or distinctly old-fashioned but still in use, such as nib pens, spinning wheels, brass water containers, and other accoutrements of domestic life that no doubt appeared quaint to urban TV viewers in the 1980s but were still recognized for what they were.

This was a production that did not try to present a generic Indian village, but made the regional and caste specificities very explicit: in fact the carefully orchestrated visual cues in the first episode based on *Swami and Friends* (Episode #19) straight away establish that Swami belongs to an Iyer Tamil Brahmin family.[87] Since this was a national TV production, the language used was Hindi, rather than Kannada, the local language of the actors and director, and known to the writer, which would perhaps have been more appropriate. Tamil, the mother-tongue of the novelist and of the characters, and a language in which there had been a translation of the novel under the title *Swamiyum Snegithargalum* by V. Krishnaswamy as early as 1939, was also not chosen as the primary language of the serial.[88] In the scenes set in public spaces, voices in the background speak Kannada or Tamil, the architectural styles, styling of clothes, markers of widowhood, and a thousand other details mark this as a small town/big village in Tamil Nadu or Karnataka state, but the language used is Hindi. So why this choice of language when everything else is so painstakingly recreated as "authentic"? As discussed in the previous chapter, because Hindi was chosen as the official language of post-independence India, it was the favored language of national television in the era before the arrival of multiple, privately owned alternative TV channels. Up until the late 1980s, TV viewing was restricted to two government-run channels that broadcast a mix of news, educational, and entertainment programs in Hindi, English, and regional languages in specific regions. A few episodes of the *Malgudi Days* series (though none of the episodes of *Swami and Friends*) were reshot with English dialogue (financed by the producer, S. Narasimhaiah) for the purpose of international sales. Those episodes that were reshot in English immediately after the Hindi language take used a local, south Indian accented English. However, these English episodes were not broadcast in India and were apparently very successfully marketed abroad. The Hindi screenplay for the *Swami and Friends* episodes was written by the well-known poet and film scriptwriter Sharad Joshi, and in this version, English is used in those situations where that language would be used – such as when Swami's father writes to his school principal to register his protest at the ear-pulling Swami receives from the Christian scripture teacher Ebenezar.

According to Padmavati Rao, the dubbing director of this TV serial, all decisions about language were deliberated and carefully thought through. The choice of Hindi for the serial was not imposed by the government but rather chosen by the producer and director, since it was, after all, the national language:

> We were very sure that Malgudi was a place that could have been anywhere in India and not just the south. That being the case we found Hindi to be the best choice for nation wide viewing and understanding. While the costumes are south specific in India there is always a cultural overlap and it was the cultural ethos that broke the north-south barrier of acceptance, if ever there was one.[89]

For Indian viewers, the logic of the medium took over: if it was a serial by Doordarshan set anywhere in India, the language would quite likely be Hindi; there was no strenuous protest of the use of this language for the TV serial. And despite the passionate anti-Hindi politics of the past decades, the Hindi version was apparently as successful in the south as in the Hindi belt.[90] Shankar Nag's presentation of Hindi (rather than Kannada or Tamil) as the home language with English used in official correspondence actually mimicked well the everyday bilinguality of the majority of TV viewers in the country. And in fact, some scenes, like the schoolboys' discussion (in Hindi) about the new student Rajam's superior command of English, coming as he does from an elite private school in Madras, is all the more effective for being conducted in their "home" language – here, Hindi. In the novel, when Narayan's young characters speak in very serviceable English (which we are led to understand is "really" being said in Tamil) to express their admiration, envy, and disdain for the big-city boy and his command of English, the difference in the use of English is harder to discern.

This decision to broadcast the serial in Hindi and to use English as needed cemented the already established reputation of Narayan's world as representative of everyman's India. And it also reinforced the fact that Hindi was the national/official language for the nation. As Padmavati Rao recalls from her perspective as dubbing director for the TV serial:

> Having decided to use local actors as far as possible the southern accent was both inevitable and deliberate, as we did want the rest of India to get a feel of the way the language is spoken here. As dubbing director of the series, I made sure that when an actor had too thick an accent, which made the dialogue difficult to understand, we used dubbing artists to maintain the accent to a certain degree without losing the rhythm of the language. As for the English, we thought it was time for an Indian English accent to be given its place. After all people all over the world speak English in their own accent and people do make the effort and understand British, American and Australian accents to name a few. As an actress (I played the wife of Jagan, the vendor of sweets) I remember using typically southern forms of interjection which I got other actors to include in the dubbing for their own roles to find for myself the balance between the comfort of speaking Hindi as it is spoken in the north and avoidance of a put-on southern accent.[91]

By the late 1980s, this south Indian production in Hindi no longer felt the need to replicate a generic north Indian accent and instead retained a very pronounced south Indian accented Hindi. By that time, English too had been gathered into the fold of Indian languages and was confidently presented in its very own accent to an international audience. Finally, in contrast to his many concerns about the film adaption of *Guide*, according to those who created the serial, R. K. Narayan was apparently very satisfied with the television serial based on his works.

In the decade that followed the weekly broadcasting of Nag's *Malgudi Days*, there was a blossoming of several multilingual, 24-7 TV channels as government control over this medium was relaxed as a matter of state policy. In this rapidly changed landscape, this particular TV serial from the late 1980s took on an enchanted, prelapsarian status as is apparent in the many nostalgic internet comments around the uploaded episodes on You Tube and other net venues and in discussion in the blogosphere. While *Swami and Friends*, the novel, enabled an earlier generation of Indians to indulge in a nostalgic revisiting of a "shared" innocence of childhood in the pre-independence era, current internet discussion of *Malgudi Days* is unequivocally nostalgic and appreciative of this series. The television series serves as an opportunity for now globally located, young, net-savvy Indian techies to recall this recently passed time of "innocent" TV viewing in their individual and collective memories of growing up in India in the 1980s era of Doordarshan. The "reruns" of this TV serial on the internet allow for a stepping back into the chatter-free, less frenetic era of state television where programming was restricted to the evening hours and made up of a daily dose of news in Hindi (and/or the regional vernacular) and in English, instructional programs, a once-a-week half-hour program of film songs (*Chitrahaar*), a Sunday night Hindi movie, and a daily program for farmers (*Krishi Darshan*) that was beamed into urban households regardless of their distance from any kind of farmwork. In comparison to such state-designed programs aimed at maintaining a link between the rural heart of India and the urban centers, *Malgudi Days* was a delightful demonstration of the hold that the small-town/big-village ethos continued to have on the heart of the nation. As with the novel, this TV serial was acclaimed for depicting every Indian's childhood in truthful detail.

IV

When R. K. Narayan died of heart failure in 2001 at the age of ninety-four, his passing was mourned by his readers in India and by diasporic Indians all over the globe. While the literary critical world may have written him off as a faded star, he was honored by his readers (and by a few critics) as the quintessential "Indian" writer whose work spanned a whole era in Indian history: from the pre-independence days of his early novels to the final essays written at the close of the 20th century. In an assessment of Narayan's work published in 2003, the essayist and novelist Pankaj Mishra points to the fact that Narayan's realism never sheds light on the larger social and historical setting of his fiction, and provides only "a few, easily missed domestic details [that] hint at the fact that Swami and Chandran, along with many other Narayan protagonists, are Brahmins marginalized by a fast-changing world."[92] "Nevertheless," Mishra continues:

> the lack of direct political comment doesn't prevent one from seeing in Narayan's novels all the anxieties and bewilderments and disappointments of a generation of Indians expelled from the past into a new world. This tortuous initiation into modernity, which Narayan himself underwent, is what gives his work, particularly the early novels – and despite the inevitable comedy of small-town ambition and drift – an unexpected depth of suffering, which is all the greater for not being perceived or acknowledged by the characters in his novels.[93]

Here Mishra homes in on the precise quality of Narayan's realism. However, contrary to Mishra, I have argued in this chapter that it is *not despite* the lack of direct political statement or of a plethora of signposts signaling the caste and regional setting of his novels that his works are so compelling to his Indian readers, *but precisely because* of this lack of explicit commentary and specific detail that his work allows for such easy identification. The astounding success of *Swami and Friends*, and of the Malgudi novels and TV serial that followed which are centered in the very particular slice of life represented in Narayan's novels (foibles of the middle-class Brahmin community in the fictitious small town of Malgudi), comes from the fact that it is scripted out of the upper-caste Hindu ideologies that were hegemonic in the period and which invited participation and identification from his fellow country men and women, even from those who would not otherwise belong to a typical Malgudi narrative. In the imaginary town created by Narayan, the subject is cocooned in a hometown that seamlessly supports and is perfectly adequate to the narrative that unfolds within the text. In this lovingly imaged hometown, nostalgia is managed, mixed with memory and desire, and offered up for the pleasures of consumption by those who are "hailed" by the text. Hence, for example, the much-quoted statement by Graham Greene, that Narayan "wakes in me a spring of gratitude, for he has offered me a second home. Without him I could never have known what it is like to be an Indian."[94] S. Krishnan, editor of *Malgudi Landscapes*, ends his introduction to the collection with this quote by Greene, followed by this final sentence: "To which it can be added that even to Indians born and bred, he [Narayan] performs a similar service by revealing truths about ourselves we have not been aware of."[95]

After Narayan's death, of the many obituaries and assessments that were written and published in newspapers around the world, a couple tentatively questioned the exalted position of the writer, even going to the extent of speculating as to whether he was "seriously over-promoted."[96] In a widely circulated article written after Narayan's death, prominent writer and critic Shashi Tharoor, apparently reluctantly but none-the-less bluntly, pointed to "the banality of Narayan's concerns, the narrowness of his vision, the predictability of his prose, and the shallowness of the pool of experience and vocabulary from which he drew."[97] This was echoed by Tunku Varadarajan, a critic whose article about a visit to the aged and ailing Narayan pays stinting homage to the body of work even as the elderly author's unseemly interest in sweets is reported with quiet derision. Such negative assessments of Narayan's literary work by Tharoor and Varadarajan, at the time New York-based members of the Indian intelligentsia who are also widely published in English language newspapers and magazines in India, were met with a barrage of irate letters from readers from all over the globe who self-identified as "ordinary Indians" despite the globally dispersed locations from which their letters were sent. Consider, for instance, these excerpts from a letter to the editor written by a diasporic Indian in New Jersey to the *Wall Street Journal* after Narayan's death in 2001:

> R. K. Narayan is revered by Indians like me who come from the lower-middle-class, run of the mill milieu that Tunku Varadarajan treats with disdain. Swamy, the little boy of Malgudi, continues to epitomize average Indian boyhood despite the intervening decades between Narayan's fictional creation and twenty-first century India.
>
> Swamy holds the same charm for most ordinary Indians, that Tom Sawyer and Huck Finn might hold for the average American (or Anglicized Indians like Mr. Varadarajan) . . . The "spare prose, simple tales, unvarying vocabulary and no obvious philosophy" that Mr. Varadarajan derides, is precisely what is so appealing about Mr. Narayan's writing because it does capture the essence of the life and attitudes of ordinary Indians who live next door, around the corner and across the street in small-town India.
>
> Painting the landscape of the daily lives of a few hundred million people might not be enough to get the applause of a pundit of the *Wall Street Journal*, but that is not the kind of writing that should be treated so dismissively either . . . R. K. Narayan needs neither the Nobel Prize, nor the "literary affirmative action" of American academia. He is respected where he truly belongs: in India. (Anil Sivakumaran, Lawrenceville, NJ)[98]

Written in response to a less than complimentary essay on Narayan by Varadarajan, this letter to the editor is testament to Narayan's success. These ordinary admirers of Narayan absolutely refuse a reading of Narayan as inferior because he is "artless" and instead testify that what makes Narayan a great Indian writer is precisely because the "artlessness" of his work speaks directly to them and confirms what they believe is the essential India. For Sivakumaran, who writes in indignation at the disrespect shown Narayan by Varadarajan, there is clearly no dissonance or explanation necessary to explain the authority with which, given his location in Lawrenceville, NJ, he can assert that R. K. Narayan "is respected where he truly belongs: in India." There is an interesting marshalling of national geography and national identity in this letter to the editor: on the one hand, there is the conventionally understood geographic India that is held in contrast to geographic America. On the other hand, there is the "India" where Swami, the nine-year-old protagonist of Narayan's first novel, and his childhood in Malgudi "epitomize average Indian boyhood." While this letter is fascinating in its reference to "literary affirmative action" and its dismissal of the Nobel Prize, the point to be noted is that Narayan's astute grasp of the political and literary power of the narrative about "the simple life" is what escapes sophisticated critics who have written him off.

If, as the saying goes, the past is a foreign country, then all memory is diasporic.[99] An understanding of diasporic aesthetics that can encompass the travel from Graham Greene to S. Krishnan to Anil Sivakumaran is one that blurs the perceived distance between national and diasporic imaginings. Malgudi as discussed in this chapter reproduces a serviceable imaginary hometown that both pays homage to and rebels from a full exposure to what has always passed for the real. Social reproduction, Cindi Katz has argued in an essay on the topic, is "precisely not 'revolutionary,'" because it "is focused on reproducing the very social relations and material forms that are so problematic."[100] Hence, as is true for social reproduction in most contexts, Narayan's fictional world does not radically alter the hegemonic social and economic relations that are in place. Narayan's early work is radical because of the pioneering context in which it was imagined and created in English. And yet, in the years after independence, as Narayan's fame grew, his fictional city solidified into an inflexible model for a mythologized, sentimentalized, unchanging India as apprehended through a small town/big village that was grappling with the arrival of modernity. It was a model city that neither author nor readers were willing to rebuild or alter.

In the next chapter we will examine Mulk Raj Anand's first novel, *Untouchable*, also published in 1935 and also focused on the lives of an Indian boy/youth Bakha, aged eighteen, and his fifteen-year-old sister Sohini. They belong to a Dalit caste, and live in the outcaste slum neighborhood on the outskirts of a small military town in north India. Bakha, who is unlettered, cleans the latrines in the town and in the British cantonment, and in his free time hangs out with his posse of low-caste youth. His sister labors at whatever task she is assigned by the upper castes and also constantly works to safeguard her budding sexuality from her caste superiors. Numerically, of course, these children's lives would be much more representative of the "ordinary Indian life" than that of Swami and his friends. But ordinary is a tricky word. On the one hand, we have R. K. Narayan's much-celebrated "ordinary" characters who populate his fictional town of Malgudi. Here "ordinary" is of course epitomized by a very specific class, caste, and gender, but regardless, Narayan's ordinary man is accepted as the Indian Everyman. With Anand's *Untouchable* we have yet another rendition of ordinary. Numerically the majority of Indians belong to the lower castes, and yet Bakha is not representative of India; instead he is representative only of his specific class and caste. It seems almost blasphemous to even suggest that Bakha is more representative than Swami for this is not how they are presented, or how their stories are received. As we have seen in Chapter 1, the logic of numbers has always been irrelevant to Indian writing in English and to the India it imagines.

CHAPTER THREE

The in-between life of Mulk Raj Anand

Someone christened him Muck Rake Anand. And that remains the best epitaph on him.
 ... He was an incurable unregenerate leftist who, we believe, consistently wrote, spoke and worked for the despicable creed of socialism which has now been defeated on all fronts on this earth... his novels... bring our great, ancient, and noble people into contempt among people in Britain, America, France, Germany, Poland, Finland, Czechoslovakia, Hungary, Rumania, Bulgaria, Russia and China, where his obscene writings had been eagerly translated and lapped up by certain dirty minded, low, materialists who despise our great spiritual heritage.
 ... Knowing that he would be found out to be the empty windbag he was if he wrote in one of our own great languages, he began to bluff all innocent people abroad by writing in English and managed to pass off as a representative Indian writer.
 No fraud can outmatch that perpetuated by this charlatan. For he took advantage of our temporary differences with the British at the time to write certain books, like *Untouchable, Coolie, The Village,* showing in exaggerated, animalistic language, things about which the less said the better... The wretch always denied the charge made by one of our esteemed critics that he had sold Indian local colour to the western world to great advantage to himself...
 Unfortunately, during the difficulties of a transition period he seemed to us too unimportant a person to bother about and was, therefore, allowed to disseminate his vicious liberation ideas, thus doing untold harm to our nation during the early years of our Ram Raj.
 The political sympathies of Anand were clear enough, but the clever plausible rogue that he was, he tried to disguise all his most sinister impulses and ideas behind the vague terms of what he called humanism.   From Mulk Raj Anand's "Self-Obituary," 2005[1]

Mulk Raj Anand has been acknowledged, along with R. K. Narayan and Raja Rao, as one of the three most important Indian writers in English of his generation. These three male writers, we have been told, display between them the full range of Indian literary responses in English to the momentous changes in the subcontinent in the 1930s and 1940s. Anand's attention to India's most underprivileged sectors of society, his narration of his close association with Gandhi, and the allegation that all of his early novels were banned by the British Indian government have together earned him a place in a national(ist) literary canon from the very first catalogs of such works. In this chapter, I will examine the literary and political confluences at work in Mulk Raj Anand's writing of his first novel, *Untouchable* (1935), and trace how the critical understanding of the significance of this work has shifted in the years since. Anand's *Untouchable* provides an exemplary site in which it is visible that, even at the height of Indian anti-colonial agitations, the affiliations of an Indian writer in English are much more complex than can be categorized under the term "nationalist." This chapter will focus on how the wide-flung affiliations that surpass nationalist sentiment are shaped by Anand's self-presentation and also harnessed and interpreted in literary critical discourses. I will also demonstrate that while Anand was much more attuned to Dalit aspirations than has been critically acknowledged, once Dalit literature was established as a substantial literary field in its own right, this well-meant novel was pushed further into the larger category of national literature in English and its insistence that freedom from caste oppression was more urgent than the national independence struggle also faded from critical memory.

I

A narrative that glosses over certain problematic details, erasures, exaggerations, and gaps could present Mulk Raj Anand as a man of many worlds – a contributor to an international socialist literary movement in the 1930s, a participant in European modernism, an anti-fascist participant in the Spanish Civil War, a founding member of the Indian Progressive Writers' Association (PWA), an anti-imperialist intellectual committed to Indian independence from the British, an advocate for the most downtrodden and disempowered sectors of Indian society, a prominent writer of Indian fiction in English, a humanist (with a clearly articulated definition of what that meant to him), a champion and preserver of art and culture in post-independence India, a secular and vocal public intellectual in an increasingly communal South Asia, a facilitator between African and Indian writers and artists, and a Gandhian.

The difficulty with such a description of Anand as a man of many worlds is that while each aspect is somewhat accurate, Mulk Raj Anand was distinctly marginal in most of these literary/political endeavors. And this marginality is almost always a direct consequence of his being who he was in this particular time and place: brown-skinned, middle-caste Hindu, middle-class, colonial subject, literate in Punjabi and Urdu but educated in English in colonial institutions, and writing in that language with very clear leftist affiliations. He is marginal to the central actions/events to which he contributed, especially as recollected by other participants in most of these endeavors. In more recent decades the margin has been retheorized as a place of great potential within critical theory. But Anand was "marginal" in his early and most productive years without enjoying the benefits of the current critical valorizations of the margin as a vantage point that gives access to both the inside and the outside of any specific charmed circle. In the second half of his (very long) life, many of the projects to which he had devoted his early years were either being written up without acknowledgement of his contributions or were themselves (PWA, socialism, socialist realism) long forgotten and abandoned. In later years Anand himself tried valiantly to reposition his early life in a series of semi-autobiographical books that insisted on his participation in several literary and political ventures, but with limited success. It is this sense of marginality that colors his witty self-obituary with anger, irony, and sorrow as is palpable in the excerpt that serves as an epigraph to this chapter.

Anand's reputation has ebbed and flowed with the changing emphases in critical trends; but in every literary and political framework within which his work has been placed, he is tacitly or often overtly found wanting in some fashion. He is the wrong man at the right place: making astoundingly acute contributions from the periphery no doubt, but inevitably overtaken by more authentic subjects who better embody the project under way. Hence, he is the Indian among Euro-American modernists, the colonial subject among British colonists, and one of the very few English language writers among Progressive Writers' Association founders. Anand was upper-caste among Dalit writers who focused on Dalit everyday life, and similarly not a devout enough Gandhian nationalist amidst those whose work embodies this creed. He was allegedly communist or, again, not communist enough; not Dalit but on the other hand not part of the Brahmin elite with its fluency in language and power. He was not considered a good writer but was prolific; not an artist but a self-trained art critic and curator. Believed to be prone to exaggerating his contacts, arena of influence, friendships, encounters, he was also done the disservice of being left out of his associates' memoirs and other writers' accounts of the very years in which he claims association with them.

The in-between life of Mulk Raj Anand needs to be examined as such because it provides an excellent example of the actual messiness of authorial affiliations even in texts written at the height of specific nationalist struggles. *Untouchable*, Anand's first novel (written and revised during the 1920s and early 1930s and published in 1935), bears the traces of several different literary and political movements and of his own personal experiences, and yet, this novel is usually read through the singular lens of nationalist literature. *Untouchable*, as this chapter demonstrates, takes from Euro-American modernism for its style, from Indian nationalist, Dalit, and Irish struggles for its content, and from the PWA manifesto for its literary politics, even as it showcases international socialist ideals, considers Gandhian reform, and remembers Anand's own interactions with low-castes in his youth in Punjab. At present, scholarship on Anand reads his body of work within one or at best two of these critical frameworks which are then invariably overwritten by the nationalist reading. However, to do the novel justice, to appreciate just how many disparate "influences" Anand was welding together in *Untouchable*, we need to see all these inflections at play in the text. The intention is not to reach a definite reading of Anand's motivations and affiliations, but rather to illuminate the power and continuing resonance of this slim novel that was produced in the intersecting margins of so many literary/political movements. And yet, as we will see, this novel has been pushed out of the catalog of progressive writing on caste, a situation that needs to be fully understood if not reassessed.

II

Mulk Raj Anand was born in 1905 and received his early education in Peshawar in Punjab, in British India.[2] His was a lower middle-class family that belonged to the Kshatriya caste which is ranked second in the four major caste categories in the Hindu caste hierarchy.[3] His father worked in the British Indian army as a result of which Anand was eligible for and awarded a scholarship to study in England under the Silver Wedding Fund Scholarship scheme. He left for England in 1925 and lived there till 1945, earning a Ph.D. in philosophy (1929), writing arguably his strongest works of prose and fiction (from the early 1930s to 1945), meeting members of the Bloomsbury Group (late 1920s to early 1930s), helping draft the Progressive Writers' Association manifesto as a founding member (1934), volunteering to fight fascism in the Spanish Civil War (1937), working as a lecturer in philosophy and literature with the London County Council Adult Education Schools and the Workers Educational Association (1939–1942), and working alongside George Orwell at the BBC's Eastern Service propaganda radio program from 1941 to 1945. By 1945 he had published seventeen books including seven of his best-received fictional works. In 1945, Anand returned to Bombay and almost immediately set up an Indian magazine dedicated to the arts. Titled *Marg* this beautifully produced art magazine was funded by a leading Indian industrialist. Anand published another eighty-six books after his return to India – several novels, four volumes of a seven-volume fictionalized autobiography, short story collections, edited collections of essays, and single authored books on art, beauty, architecture, poetry, selected personalities, etc. Anand died in 2005, a few months short of his hundredth birthday, and was given a state funeral of the kind reserved for notable cultural figures.

For the most part, the critical reception of Anand's work, in both Europe and India, casts him as an Indian nationalist whose best work was done in the early novels that championed the outcastes of Indian society and brought their difficult lives to the attention of those in power.[4] As mentioned above, Anand quickly earned a place as one of the three most important writers of his generation: while his place in this trilogy is secure, his talents are understood to be considerably less magnificent than those of R. K. Narayan and Raja Rao.[5] Anand is always presented as the least polished or refined of the three patriarchs of Indian writing in English, with the rough topics that he wrote about presented in a correspondingly rough style. The early novels, namely *Untouchable* (1935), *Coolie* (1936), *Two Leaves and a Bud* (1937), *The Village* (1939), *Across the Black Waters* (1940), and *The Sword and the Sickle* (1942) were rumored to have been banned by the British government and this in itself earned him the badge of nationalist writer.[6] *Untouchable*, Anand's first novel, has been read as a "Mahatma novel" alongside Narayan's *Waiting for the Mahatma* (1955) and Raja Rao's *Kanthapura* (1938), novels that are categorized as such because they have M. K. Gandhi present as a guiding light through the narrative or as an actual character in the text. *Untouchable* features Gandhi as himself, the acknowledged leader of the national struggle for independence, and so, without too much discussion of the nuances of the political and literary allegiances on display in his work, critics quickly classified Anand as a staunch nationalist and Gandhian.[7]

As early as 1943, Srinivasa Iyengar, in his assessment of Indo-Anglian literature sponsored by the All Indian PEN, had given Anand his due in his compact seventy-page introduction to Indian literature in English:

> In the past few years, Mulk Raj Anand and R. K. Narayan have published a few novels and short stories that have won recognition in India and abroad... [Iyengar goes on to list several of Anand's fictional and other prose works]... Anand's sympathies are with the masses, with the underdogs in Indian social life; hence "the coolie" and "the untouchable" are to him symbolic of man's cruelty to man in unredeemed India.[8]

By the time Iyengar wrote his expanded *Indian Writing in English* in the 1960s it was more than eight hundred pages in length and Anand was one of the dozen or so public intellectuals or creative writers who had a chapter to himself.[9]

Anand offers an interesting counterpoint to the elite positions inhabited by other Indian writers in English of this time period. Mulk Raj Anand's work has usually been classified (and often dismissed) as socialist realism of the sort internationally favored in the 1930s. His writing is in stark contrast to the Narayan kind of writing – his heroes/protagonists were not young, middle-class, upper-caste men idly dreaming of romance.[10] Instead Anand focuses in his first novel on Bakha – lowest caste, illiterate, flawed, sensitive yet rough, a part of humanity as manifest in his desires and aspirations for dignity. A variety of scenes and sentiments are considered uncharacteristic of Bakha and so, the critical assessment has mostly dismissed such moments as striking "a false note." This includes scenes in which Bakha's explosive anger is expressed to the reader (though not to other characters in the novel) or when, at the end of the novel, Anand's hope for a socialist future takes over the narrative and is coupled with a very clear authorial distancing from the Gandhian position on caste. Prominent literary critic Meenakshi Mukherjee in her path-breaking *The Twice Born Fiction: Themes and Techniques of the Indian Novel in English* (1971) concluded her discussion of Anand's work as follows:

> However, when he imposes his convictions directly upon his heroes, who are usually country-bred or unsophisticated people without the advantage of his wide background, the characterization fails because instead of becoming fully rounded individuals they become mouthpieces of the author's ideas. Anand's characters are lonely misfits – not lonely in the tradition of the modern European protagonist of fiction, whose loneliness is a form of intellectual alienation, but lonely because they do not arise out of the soil they inhabit, because Anand has stuffed them with his own beliefs.[11]

Such an evaluation is based on the belief that a character like Bakha could not himself hold the convictions he is portrayed with. Mukherjee refers to Bakha as "the sufferer–in–chief" amongst all of Anand's protagonists in all of his novels about social institutions that need reform. Mukerjee's argument is based on the belief that while Anand's characters do suffer immensely, they cannot, at least not without upper-caste leadership, articulate their experience into thoughts and ideas of self-empowerment, of resistance. Hence, the protests voiced by these protagonists in the novels are understood to be "stuffed" into them by Anand. Most of the early scholarship on Anand operated from the assumption that Dalit activism and political identity were in a very nascent stage in the 1930s and 1940s and that Dalit consciousness was publicly voiced only in the late twentieth century; this misinformation informs most early literary criticism on Anand's *Untouchable*. In recent years scholars like Ramnarayan Rawat and others have demonstrated that the core foci of post-independence Dalit politics were formulated from the early decades of the twentieth century. In Anand's home state of Punjab by 1925 the Adi Dharam movement had begun to gather force around the figure of Ravidass, the Chamar caste Bhakti saint from the fourteenth to fifteenth century. Dalit consciousness emerged in the Ravidass Deras (spiritual and social service centers) that emerged in the early twentieth century in Punjab, in other parts of north India, and in migrant communities abroad. As Ronki Ram has documented, Ravidass advocated neither assimilation to upper castes nor conversion to other religions; instead his message was one of "self-respect and dignity of labor."[12] At the other end of the critical spectrum from Mukherjee's dismissal of Anand's characters as his "mouthpieces," Dalit intellectuals have argued that novels such as *Untouchable* are at best a manifestation of the middle-class novel writer's benevolent and patronizing depiction of the lower echelons of society.

If literary scholars take into consideration Anand's role in the formation of the Progressive Writers' Association in London in 1934 and the impact on his work of literary trends developed under the association's aegis, then his work could be viewed in a different light. As discussed briefly in Chapter 1 of this study, the PWA was formally set up in London in November 1934 and its manifesto was drafted by Mulk Raj Anand and Sajjad Zahir. *Untouchable* closely adheres to the prescription for progressive literature set out in this manifesto.[13] Among the statements made in the PWA manifesto as published in London in *New Left Review* (February 1936) was:

> We believe that the new literature of India must deal with the basic problems of our existence today – the problems of hunger and poverty, social backwardness and political subjugation, so that it may help us to understand these problems and through such understanding help us to act.[14]

Untouchable, then, was the first of Anand's novelistic attempts to write fiction that adhered to this; it also strove to "bring the arts into the closest touch with the people." Further, it was art that was calculated to help one face the "actualities of life" rather than serve as a "refuge from reality in spiritualism and idealism." So while the PWA's mission was to "give expression to the changes taking place in Indian life and to assist in the spirit of progress in the country," it was not simply championing the idealization of India and Indian culture in a spirit of conventional nationalism. Rather, it was a call to sweep out the old stagnant formalities of literature and usher in the new progressive era. Nuanced political scruples about speaking of/for/to "the people" were not under investigation in this impassioned bid to revolutionize literature. Hence Mukherjee's dismissal of Anand's protagonists as his "mouthpieces" has to be read against the excitement generated by the notions and literary practices advocated by this radical literary movement.

Interestingly, a clause in this manifesto that Anand helped to draft pledged that members would "strive for acceptance of a common language (Hindustani) and a common script (Indo-Roman) for India." While this clause, especially the part about the Indo-Roman script, was dropped fairly quickly after the manifesto made its way to India and when it was translated into other Indian languages, what its presence in the original PWA manifesto signals is that here too (as elsewhere) Anand was participating in a literary endeavor that would necessarily place his own writing in the periphery. Over the years, works in Indian languages other than English were more easily viewed as authentic claimants to the legacy of the progressive ideology.[15] However, in the early years, Anand's fiction certainly lived up to the pledge made by PWA members in their manifesto. What writing in English did facilitate to some degree was the harnessing of "both native and foreign resources" as authors were encouraged to do in the manifesto.

The "foreign resource" most utilized by Anand in writing *Untouchable* was of course the techniques developed by European modernist writers like James Joyce and Virginia Woolf. *Untouchable*, which according to the author was begun in Dublin in the early 1920s, was completed in the early 1930s. However, Anand writes of this intertwined set of influences, separating out Joyce from a wider net of Irish nationalist cultural productions:

> As I saw some of the plays about peasants, fishermen and slum-dwellers... I felt that my own sweeper-boy hero was rather like the new people whom these Irish writers wrote about, than the sophisticated literary gentleman,

Stephen Daedalus. And just then I came across a poignant story about a sweeper-boy, Uka, by Mahatma Gandhi in *Young India*, written with utmost simplicity.[16]

Despite his distancing of his protagonist from Joyce's Stephen Daedalus, Anand's novel is modeled on Joyce's *Ulysses* in that it covers a day in the life of Bakha, an eighteen-year-old untouchable youth whose job of removing night soil takes him to the British cantonment and to the neighborhoods of local residents of Bhulandsher, a small military town in northern India, possibly in Punjab, much along the lines of Leopold Bloom's wanderings around Dublin in *Ulysses*.

In recent years, some critical energy has been directed toward placing Anand in the context of European modernism. In her essay on Joyce and Anand in *Modernism/Modernity*, Jessica Berman argues that "Anand's position as a constitutive part of modernism thus helps to realign modernism along global lines."[17] Berman goes on to argue that "placing Anand in this way forces us to reconsider Joyce's writing within the context of Anand's direct political engagement." Berman continues: "When we read Joyce and Anand together, what emerges is a complex intertextual exchange that highlights the specificity of their colonial critiques; the challenges their work poses to conceptions of a representative, ethical subject; and the very real political engagement, extended and made more overt in Anand's oeuvre, of their modernist narrative modes."[18] Berman argues that what Anand drew from Joyce is "engagement with the self within the context of a colonial reality rather than the metaphysical world" and then argues that their work jointly revises the European *Bildungsroman* narrative by challenging, in their presentation of their protagonists' progress through the world, "the absolute universality of the representative man" of the standard *Bildung* tradition. Thus, she writes, in reference to Anand's *Coolie*, "reading Anand into the body of modernism rather than as its appendage, mirror or mime, means that the heroism of a coolie who suffers every conceivable setback on his road to maturity, even while becoming a spokesman for a grassroots movement of rebellion before his death at an early age, ought to be seen as a model of modernist engagement with the consequences of Enlightenment historicism and the *Bildungsroman*."[19] Berman uses Anand and Joyce to infuse political "engagement" into European modernism, which is nevertheless visible only from this transnational vantage point. Or, as Berman puts it, "Perhaps then *Coolie* is teaching us a lesson about how to read *Portrait* [*of an Artist as a Young Man*]."[20] Despite the use of terms like "complex intertextual exchange," we are not told what Joyce draws from

Anand, but according to Berman's model, reading Anand's work helps us to read Joyce's politics more effectively. What Berman seems to be invested in is using Anand, and to some extent even Joyce, to infuse a progressive political agenda into European modernism, a difficult task by any measure, and a task in the course of which she does not or cannot name a single other modernist other than these two.

Berman aims to "bring Anand to the center of the conversation about modernist experimentation and its connection to politics and [she] makes a case for his work as a constitutive element of international modernism."[21] In retrospect, his work can be seen in this fashion, but from Anand's many accounts of his time in England it is clear that his actual position within the modernists' circles was nowhere near the center. And once we move out of this enchanted circle of modernists, and the outer ring of intermodernists (discussed below), these essentially European categories are too limited to fully explicate the multiple worlds in which Anand was situated. In his *Conversations in Bloomsbury* and in other accounts like the third volume of his fictionalized biography, *The Bubble,* Anand meticulously describes the hierarchy-ridden literary and social circles that he is constantly trying to break into or present himself as a part of. Again and again, what we can glean, against the grain of these later Anand narratives, is a group portrait of the coterie around the important male personage, who is usually a well-respected poet or Oxbridge professor. Around him hovers an intelligent but deferential white woman, attached to him, who is his intellectual equal but also the cook and cleaner, as well as the acolytes who attach themselves and wait for the much longed-for invitation to Cambridge, to lunch, to tea, for the weekend, or to accompany the professor/poet/essayist to visit some other Big Man (Bertrand Russell, Bernard Shaw, T. S. Eliot). Among the acolytes there is often a colonial subject who is on occasion Indian – sometimes Krishna Menon, sometimes Mulk Raj Anand. In these accounts, the "Indian" is extremely polite, charming to the ladies, sometimes vegetarian, capable of offering a spot of eastern wisdom or a quote from Ghalib, the Upanishads, or Shakespeare, as the need arises. Anand is especially acute in noting the gendered and racial aspects of this intellectual hierarchy, which is manifest in a network of letters, invitations, reviews, and parties, introductions given or withheld. Colonial subjects like himself occupy the marginal spaces – at best that of the "budding writer" who remains in the apprentice mode. Anand bluntly notes in *An Apology for Heroism* (1946) that "There could be no dignity in the personal relations of British and Indian intellectuals."[22] Many years later, in his *Conversations in Bloomsbury* (1981) he smooths much of the roughness of some of these interactions, but the distance between the British elite and colonials like himself remains visible. Consider the account he gives in a 2005 essay of having his first published and anthologized story, "The Lost Child," read out in Virginia Woolf's salon in the 1920s:

> Also, I dared to show my story "Lost Child" to Virginia Woolf. She asked me to read it out at her next home party. Desmond McCarthy, Victoria Sackville West, Edward Garnet, clapped after I read my story.[23]

Eighty years after the event, writing about a moment of attention received from the Bloomsbury circle, Anand is able to see the distance of his world from the Bloomsbury Group. He recalls that with the publication of Virginia Woolf's essay "Mr. Bennett and Mrs. Brown" a few months after reading aloud in her salon, he realized that his kind of literary subject – "Low class sons of sweepers, washermen and bandsmen" – would not meet with her approval.[24] He writes that his sense of the negative reception he might receive was confirmed when the young poet Edward Sackville West advised him to "leave your Cockneys in their sordid world."[25] As Anand remembers it, he left the Bloomsbury circle because of such exchanges. Somewhere along the way the "budding writer" sadly becomes viewed and remembered, if at all, as a minor writer within European circles.

Another mode of accounting for Anand is to categorize him as an "intermodern" figure. In *George Orwell and the Radical Eccentrics* (2004), Kristen Bluemel coins the term "intermodern" to account for the "spaces between modernisms" and for writers who are best understood as occupying such spaces. Intermodernism becomes for Bluemel a way of accommodating the "diversity of radical personages" in the 1930s and 1940s for whom, she claims, George Orwell served as a figurehead and central focus.[26] Writers and intellectuals that she groups around Orwell include, in addition to Mulk Raj Anand, Stevie Smith and Inez Holden. Bluemel suggests that intermodernists were those young people who did not fit into the Oxbridge networks because they were not endowed with the "right" gender, class, and/or colonial background and so were on the margins of celebrated literary groups. Anand no doubt fits right into this category that Bluemel describes as comprising mostly working-class aspiring writers (all holding down day jobs to supplement their income), whose writing style is essentially realist but experimental, whose work is political and features working people rather than the leisured Mrs. Dalloway stepping out to buy flowers for her evening party.

Not quite modernist or postmodernist, Bluemel's intermoderns wrote in the period between the wars. Her meticulous research on this period sheds light on Anand's time in Europe especially in the early 1940s, thus freeing us from overly relying on the older Anand's "recreations" of these years. On the basis of her thorough research through the memoirs and letters of the intermoderns, Bluemel points out that, on occasion, in his later writing, Anand patently misrepresented events and relationships that he may or may not have had with famous people.[27] She notes that it is hard to tell whether his relations with the prominent literary and intellectual personages he mentions in his later works were personal (i.e. he actually knew them) or primarily intellectual (i.e. in that he was acquainted with their work). This uncertainty about his "contacts" is severely complicated by the account that both Saros Cowasjee and Bluemel give of Anand's serious falling out in the 1940s with many of his friends and acquaintances among London intellectuals because of his insistence on condemning British imperialism and because of his refusal to denounce Stalin after the signing of the non-aggression pact with Hitler. In *Letters on India* (1942) and *An Apology for Heroism* (1946) Anand was unequivocal in his denouncement of both western imperialism and capitalism.[28] Consequently perhaps, as Bluemel notes, "Anand's name is rarely mentioned in memoirs that evoke London's literary culture in the 1930s." Anand's social and literary alienation from his peers, his "diminishing reputation," Bluemel argues, had "less to do with any failure of his literary imagination and more to do with many English leftists' allegiance to England's imperial identity and specifically its right to rule India."[29]

There is yet another feasible explanation besides the possibility that Anand embellished and exaggerated his interactions with European intellectuals or that his anti-British writings caused them to deliberately cast him out of their memoirs. This third explanation is offered by Sushila Nasta in her compelling analysis of the ways in which white British intellectuals routinely minimize or develop amnesia about non-white participants in cultural activities in Britain in the 1930s and 1940s. As prime evidence of a trend that continues into the present, Nasta discusses a group photograph from the BBC's Eastern Radio Service in 1942 that was used as an illustration for a review of a book on modernism in the *Times Literary Supplement* in October 2000. Despite the fact that the photograph clearly shows eight regular contributors to this radio program, namely Venu Chitale, J. M. Tambimuttum, T. S. Eliot, Una Marson, Mulk Raj Anand, C. Pemberton, Narayanan Menon, George Orwell, Nancy Barratt, and William Empson, who were named in the caption that accompanied the photograph in the BBC archive, when this photograph was reproduced in the 2000 *TLS* article, the caption for the photo read: "Among others – T. S. Eliot, George Orwell and William Empson." Nasta comments:

> the occlusion of these major colonial writers not only pinpoints an ongoing critical failure to acknowledge the role writers such as Anand played in the reinvention of Britain as a transnational site for the growth of a global modernity, but comfortably relegates these supposed "others" to yet another containable location on the margins of mainstream literary studies; namely that of the "colonial" or the "postcolonial", placed *outside* and conveniently separated *from* the key tenets of the body of European modernity.[30]

Another international literary grouping, a distinct alternative to modernism, that Anand could conceivably be placed *inside* would be the genre loosely called socialist realist writing of the 1930s and 1940s. Talat Ahmed has recently narrated Anand's life as a journey that ended with his achievement of the stature of the most important Indian writer in English and a socialist writer of international significance.[31] In such a narration, Anand's political and literary awakening begins with his early awareness of the oppression of British imperialism in India which crystallized, as it did for many Indians of that era, with the massacre at Jalianwala Bagh, Punjab in 1919. A year after Anand came to England, he witnessed the 1926 General Strike in London and the harsh measures taken to end it. Anand writes that he had been struck by the "particular dignity and self-respect with which the porters, sweepers and other workers bore themselves here as against the coolies in India who were always being kicked about and intimidated."[32] Soon after his arrival in London, Anand had imagined that the working-class man in England was "a free citizen of a democratic society."[33] "But," he continues, "this illusion of mine had been shattered with a bang" by the force with which this General Strike was put down: "all these liberties seemed to evaporate in a crisis."[34] And he concludes: "The general strike showed me that the people of Britain, no less than the people of India had yet to win their liberty. And freedom became for me again the most compelling ideal."[35] Elsewhere, Anand calls these workers "the better off untouchables of Europe" and for sure, he was marking the connections between all kinds of struggles in Europe and in India.[36] Talat Ahmed and other scholars interpret Anand's representation of India at the "World Congress of Writers against Fascism" in Madrid in 1935 and his travel to Spain in 1937 to fight with the Republicans in the Spanish Civil War as testament to his strong commitment and central role in the dynamic international socialist movement of the 1930s.[37]

But Anand's attention was also turned toward India, where, in the 1930s, the struggle for national independence from the British had intensified dramatically. In the early 1930s, while Gandhi and the Congress had emerged as the major players, it was absolutely clear that there were many other vocal leaders of communities that did not believe themselves to be adequately represented by Gandhi or the Congress. The demand for independence from the British was clearly articulated, but there were deep and distinct divisions about how political, electoral, and territorial power was to be handed over and to whom. The Round Table Conferences (RTC) held in the early 1930s between the British rulers and Indian representatives that led to the controversial formulation of "The Government of India Act" of 1935 were the crucial political events in this period. This act was to set the terms for the post-independence Indian constitution and for political representation of its diverse population. In negotiations prior to the formal constitution of this act, Muslims, Dalits, and other minorities had wanted to enshrine a constitutional basis for their rights via separate electorates for minorities. Hence, in November 1931, the representatives of many minority communities attending the Round Table Conference worked out a "Minorities Pact" which was presented to the British authorities by the Aga Khan and agreed to by Sikhs, Muslims, Anglo-Indians, Depressed Classes (Dalits), Christians, and British/European Indians who together claimed to be 46 percent of the total Indian population. However, the Congress, led by Gandhi's vision of a united India, of Hindu–Muslim brotherhood, of Dalits as Harijans (Gandhi's term for the lowest castes that translates into "God's people") whose uplift was imminent, strongly opposed communal representation as another "divide and rule" ploy of the British. Gandhi was insistent on being the sole representative for *all* Indians; he viewed all other arrangements as a clear capitulation to another British ploy to splinter Indian interests. While Gandhi eventually conceded that Muslims and Sikhs could get separate electorates, he was adamant in denying the same to untouchables. In his speech to the RTC denouncing the "Minorities Pact," Gandhi stated: "I claim myself in my own person to represent the vast mass of untouchables."[38] He renewed his pledge to remove untouchability and thus the need for separate electorates, because, as he argued, while Muslims, Sikhs, and Europeans "might remain as such in perpetuity," the crucial question was "will untouchables remain untouchables in perpetuity?"[39]

While the details of the kinds of political safeguards to be put in place were being worked out, Gandhi declared his decision to go on a hunger strike to death if separate electorates were given to untouchables. The decisions were announced in August 1932. A communal award was made whereby untouchables were given what amounted to a double vote (special constituency and votes in the general constitutions), but not separate electorates. Nevertheless, Gandhi went on a fast unto death, primarily to force Ambedkar (the primary representative of Dalit interests) to drop the demand for separate electoral representation. Ambedkar was compelled to revise his position on self-representation and settled instead for a small number of reserved seats for the Depressed Classes. The Muslim League, under the leadership of Jinnah, did not surrender its demand for separate political representation which it saw as a necessary safeguard for minority interests in "a majority Hindu electorate led by a predominantly Hindu Congress."[40] Ambedkar, on the other hand, even though he firmly believed in the legitimacy of Dalit demands, reluctantly acquiesced to the position of the Congress Party (which he was himself a member of) and ultimately worked some of his concerns into the national constitution for independent India that he drafted after independence. In September of 1932, immediately after the fraught negotiations and bitter compromise (on the part of Ambedkar) led to the signing of the Poona Pact, Gandhi ended his fast and set up an organization for the uplift of untouchables which, after a number of name changes, was settled as "Harijan Sevak Sangh" (Harijan Service Society). In its founding statement, it was clearly stated that the HSS would "work [to end untouchability] by persuasion among the caste Hindus."

It is in this climate of debate about the situation and destiny of the lowest castes and below – the "achhuts" or literally "untouchables" – in the larger community of Indians that Mulk Raj Anand published his first novel, *Untouchable*. The novel has been read primarily as Gandhian text (a Mahatma novel) and/or as modernist literary endeavor (Joycean in style), and the critical commentary has focused on the ways in which Anand accommodates both projects. In 1996, Theresa Hubel included a thoughtful chapter on *Untouchable* titled "Gandhi, Ambedkar and *Untouchable*" in her book *Whose India? The Independence Struggle in British and Indian Fiction and History*. Hubel's nuanced chapter reads Anand's novel in the context of the nationalist debate about untouchability. Hubel writes:

> On the pages of *Untouchable*, Gandhi's ideas are enacted and found wanting. Later, another more practical solution is offered in its stead. But this other solution has its own problems, of which the novel is not aware. Ultimately Anand is conditioned by the same historical shortsightedness that made Gandhi incapable of seeing the limits of his own stance in regards to the

untouchables. Neither is about to imagine a world without themselves, the elite, to lead the despised and downtrodden out of their subjugation.[41]

After a lengthy discussion of realism, Hubel criticizes Anand for presenting "Bakha's powerlessness" as "a condition of untouchability in general," and insists that the novel confirms this "overall image of communal emasculation." Ultimately, for Hubel, Anand's and Gandhi's positions on caste are equally compromised. Hubel asserts that: "Anand's text pulls back at the same time it pushes forward. The place of its revolutionary consciousness is also the place of its conservatism."[42] Similarly, Arun Mukherjee has argued on the basis of a detailed reading of *Untouchable* that there is "a gap between its [*Untouchable*'s] intentions and execution, its overt radical surface and its covert bourgeois nationalist unconscious."[43] Mukherjee insists that "texts written by ostensibly radical writers with radical cognitive intentionalities need not necessarily be radical or subversive and ought to be subjected to a 'hermeneutics of suspicion' . . . like any other text."[44] She goes on to note that "It is in the refusal of the text to consider the possibility of strategic action on Bakha's part that one must look for the repressions and omissions of the text."[45] Mukherjee notes that the "possibility of revolutionary violence" is "totally absent" in this novel, as are the "dissenting and angry voices of the contemporary untouchable leadership."[46] She insists that "[t]he 'heteroglossia' of the novel, is ultimately, constituted of middle class voices alone."[47]

By the late twentieth century, Anand's *Untouchable* is squarely placed within the category of narrative born of upper-caste sentimentality toward Dalits. In an interview conducted by S. Anand and Ravi Kumar with Raj Narendra Jadhav, a Marathi Dalit writer, a dismissal of Anand's book is taken for granted: "Mulk Raj Anand's *Untouchable* is completely outdated now. The situation is totally different. And frankly that book is very patronizing."[48] In the same book, Arundhati Roy is addressed by the interviewer in no uncertain terms: "I hope you agree that non-Dalits cannot claim to produce 'Dalit literature.' Mulk Raj Anand or Ananthamurthy or you can have a Dalit character or protagonist in your work and write as empathetically or as fantastically as each wishes to, but this is also an issue of a long-suppressed community finding its own voice."[49] Over time, Anand's *Untouchable* was eclipsed by Dalit literary texts that presented a radically different understanding of the individual protagonist at the center of the autobiographical or fictional narrative and his/her relationship to the Dalit community represented in the text. All of this criticism holds water, but its logic depends on a singular understanding of Anand as no more and no less than an educated, elite, upper-caste Indian writer with "covert bourgeois nationalist" sympathies covered over with a veneer of Marxist ideology.

In the section that follows I will suggest that we need to rethink such a total dismissal of Anand's motivations and of his literary project. Anand's first novel could be read as a fictional text that is much more attuned to Dalit aspirations than has been appreciated. The fact remains that Anand belongs to the category of the elite by his education and by caste. However, this "elite" status needs to be filtered through and against the many locales described above that shaped Anand the writer and his first novel. Doing so will reveal that Anand's own experience of multiple marginality pressed on his understanding of untouchability. In the next section, *Untouchable* is read for its very keen understanding of the key tenets of the Dalit fight for freedom from caste-based oppression.

III

> Mahatmas have come and Mahatmas have gone. But the Untouchables have remained as untouchables. (From the statement by B. R. Ambedkar on Gandhi's fast, September 19, 1932.)[50]

In Anand's first novel, which records a day in the life of Bakha, a young untouchable who cleans toilets by collecting and disposing of excrement, *the* Mahatma (great soul), as Gandhi was respectfully and lovingly hailed, comes and goes, but untouchables remain as untouchables. In this section I will explore some of the ways in which Anand, despite his distance from Dalit struggles for equality and respect, produces a novel in 1935 which is, despite the class and caste location of the author, in tune with Dalit activism and demands of the time and of the years to come. I will argue that because of Anand's location on so many margins, in *Untouchable* he produced a novel that warrants a second look as a worthy evocation of Dalit aspirations. Contrary to the readings of *Untouchable* as a Gandhian novel, I see this as a text that deeply questions Gandhi's plan for "Harijans" and insists on the vast gap between a nationalist, Gandhian approach and a Dalit-centric approach to several key issues: untouchability and its eradication, the meaning of selfhood for Dalits, the meaning(s) of independence/freedom, and the future course to be taken on all these endeavors. Nothing is so telling of Anand's distance from a faithful Gandhian position as the final equation that the novel makes between Gandhi and the flush toilet: we leave Bakha debating the efficacy of "the machine" against that of "the mahatma." From a reverent Gandhian position this is as close to blasphemy as a writer has come.

As discussed above, Anand was not himself of the lower castes; consequently this novel is read, if not as faithfully Gandhian, then as primarily invested in caste and class privilege and no more than a benevolent outsider's view on caste-based discrimination. As Anand himself mockingly writes in his 2005 self-obituary: "His family, though of low caste, was never really poor, so how could he have had any real sympathy or knowledge of outcastes and coolies and *babus* and *banias* about whom he wrote?"[51] Here Anand is voicing a common complaint about his being an outsider's representation of the outcastes of Indian society; no one has really complained about his lack of first-hand knowledge of the professional and merchant class (*babus* and *banias*), but by drawing attention to this, Anand makes the rest of the complaint seem equally questionable.

Literary scholars, both Dalit and upper-caste, have overlooked the formative influence of Anand's experiences as a colonial subject on the margins of British social, political, and cultural/literary circles for twenty years in the early twentieth century. I will insist that this experience gave him sharp insight into the condition of being treated as a pollutant who is literally untouchable. Racism as practiced against people of color in the west can teach harsh lessons even to upper-caste Indians as has been repeatedly evinced in the life and works of prominent Indians of the twentieth century. A succinct commentary on this dynamic is presented in the work of a leading Dalit intellectual and poet, Daya Pawar (1935–1996). In 1974, Pawar published a collection of poems in Marathi titled *Kondwada* (Cattle-pen), which included a poem titled, in its English translation, "You Wrote from Los Angeles," in which the narrator responds to his upper-caste friend's letter in which he evidently complained about being subject to racism in LA. The poem in its entirety is as follows:

> "In the stores here, in hotels, about the streets,
> Indians and curs are measured with the same yard-stick;
> 'Niggers' 'Blacks'! This is the abuse they fling me.
> And deep in my heart a thousand scorpions sting me."
> Reading all this, I felt *so damn good!*
> Now you've had a taste of what we've suffered
> In this country from generation to generation . . . [52]

The racism that Anand must have routinely encountered as an Indian in England in this time period (1925–1945) is rarely mentioned in his works.[53] And yet, as the narratives on M. K. Gandhi's life have also shown, hardship related to racism and racial segregation outside India often serves as an eye-opener for upper-caste Indians. Various accounts of Gandhi's life mark his being thrown off a train in South Africa in June 1893 (for presuming to occupy a first-class compartment despite being "a coolie") as a political turning point. This is perhaps best detailed by Gandhi himself in his 1927 text, *An Autobiography or My Experiments with Truth*.[54] However, as discussed below, by the time Anand wrote about his early experiences in the west in the late 1970s and 1980s, what he produced was calculated to enhance the significance of his encounters and associations in his time in Europe, and thus he downplayed not just the racism that he no doubt encountered, but even the slights and dismissals he faced from friends and acquaintances. All of this has to be inferred from oblique references. And yet, in a 1967 essay, Anand acknowledges the racism that he faced aboard a ship journey from England to India and its impact on his writing. He recalls the contempt for Indian and for Australian passengers exhibited by British passengers on board, and Anand writes "I began retouching my novel *Untouchable* from the new anger I felt about being an outcast of the society on the ship."[55] Anand is able to recognize and acknowledge the parallel structures of humiliation that underlie race- and caste-based insult and discrimination. More recently, in an edited collection of essays titled *Humiliation: Claims and Context* (2009), the scholar Gopal Guru has proposed that we interrogate and theorize these very structures of humiliation that underlie social life. In his introduction to this collection, he suggests that "in the West it is the attitude of race that is at the base of humiliation. In the East, it is the notion of untouchability that foregrounds the form and content of humiliation."[56] Guru goes on to note that the nationalist response which "remains silent over caste-/gender-based humiliation and shows hyper-sensitivity over racial humiliation necessarily acquires Janus face."[57] Citing the writing of Bankim as an example, Guru argues that Indian nationalist thinkers "ignore the question of self-respect for women and the lower castes. In fact, they tend to produce the same mechanism of humiliation of which they were the victims at the first instance."[58] Once again, Anand's writing marks his difference from this club of nationalist thinkers; *Untouchable* stands witness to how Anand reacted to his own marginality within so many of the projects that he participated in. And this was what lent acuity to his novel on untouchability as practiced in India at the time.

"Untouchable," the term Anand uses in his novel, was the English word used by Dalit leaders like Ambedkar (who were Anand's contemporaries) in their English language discourse to refer to "those castes lowest in the

Hindu scale of pollution."[59] The Hindi language word also in use, and of which "untouchable" was a direct translation, was "achhut." Hence in the 1920s and 1930s, depending on the language in use, either untouchable or achhut was used by Dalits to make a claim to a more inclusive identity that would unite disparate untouchable castes. The Marathi term Dalit (downtrodden, oppressed, crushed), coined by the nineteenth-century Marathi social reformer Jyotirao Phule (1826–1890) and popularized by Ambedkar in his later years, came to replace previously used terms like untouchable/achhut by the 1960s and 1970s. Though individual caste and subcaste names also continued in use, Dalit was meant to signal a political identity and was not a caste name. By the 1980s, Dalit was understood to be the single term that indicated a united political formation that would, as Ramnarayan Rawat states, "contest earlier dominant ascriptions of these communities" and both question and reject "the notions of impurity and pollution attached to their community, identity and history."[60]

It is noteworthy that Anand does not title his novel or refer to his characters by the name that Gandhi was fervently trying to get all Indians to adopt, namely the term "Harijan" which loosely translated as "people of god." From the early 1930s, it was the term for untouchables that Gandhi tried to popularize and was understood to display upper-caste benevolence to untouchables. In September 1932, immediately after the negotiations between all parties and Ambedkar's bitter compromise that led to the Poona Pact as recounted above, Gandhi set up the Harijan Sevak Sangh for the uplift of untouchables. This organization, comprising upper-caste managers and workers, was to carry Gandhi's message on ending untouchability to caste Hindus. As the founding statement of the HSS noted, the plan was to proceed "by persuasion of the caste Hindus" to give up the practice of untouchability. There was no discussion of rethinking or abolishing the caste system. Through the end of the twentieth century, Gandhians and mainstream nationalists used this term Harijan to refer to India's Dalit population. In fact, Harijan has been replaced by the term Dalit in general usage only very recently and only selectively. In contrast, the vast majority of Dalits have, from the very first, rejected the term because it patronizingly offers inclusion without equality.

Alternately, Anand did not choose to use either the term "Depressed Classes" (the official government term in use until 1935), or the new official term "Schedule Castes" which replaced the former term in official government references (subsequent to these castes being granted certain special rights in 1935). Of course, it can be argued that such official titles (Depressed Classes, Scheduled Castes) are singularly unappealing in terms of their aesthetic value or as a means of drawing readers to a literary text. But Harijan was certainly a term associated with Gandhi, who was the best-known Indian on the Indian and global stage at the time, and Anand's decision not to use this term in/as his title, even as he struggled to get the novel published, is a telling detail. It was the addition of E. M. Forster's preface which ultimately "purified" (Forster's term) the novel's contents and allowed it to be deemed worthy of publication.[61] The use of the Gandhian term Harijan would perhaps have helped to further "purify" the novel, for purification was at the heart of Gandhi's strategy for ending untouchability. But, as discussed later in this chapter, Anand's decision to hitch his star to Gandhi, as it were, came much later in his life.

If Anand were indeed as centrally influenced by Gandhi as he himself and others make him out to be, there would have been no alternative but to have called the novel "Harijan" and/or at the very least to have referred to the characters as Harijans. Instead we have the one instance toward the end of the novel when the term is introduced by a Congress volunteer who explains to the gathering crowd that Gandhi will speak about untouchability: "'Mahatma ji is not speaking about *swadeshi*, or on civil disobedience,' put in a Congress volunteer authoritatively. 'The government has allowed him out of gaol only if he will keep strictly within the limits of his propaganda for *harijans* (men of God as Gandhi chooses to call the Untouchables), for the removal of untouchability.'"[62] Bakha's reaction is as follows:

> "*Harijan!*" Bakha wondered what that meant. He had heard the word before in connection with Gandhi. "But it had something to do with us, the *bhangis* and *chamars*," he said to himself. "We are *harijans*." He recalled how some Congress men had come to the outcastes' street a month ago and lectured about *harijans*, saying they were no different from the Hindus and their touch did not mean pollution. The phrase, as it dropped from the mouth of the volunteer had gone through Bakha's soul and body. He knew it applied to him. "It is good that I came!" he thought.[63]

While Bakha is depicted as deeply affected by this "phrase," Anand leaves unclear what exact phrase is being referred to: the use of the *term* Harijans or the *phrase* "removal of untouchability."

That *Untouchable* is written in English is also used to castigate Anand for his elitism and to point to the impossibility of this novel's ability to speak to the generic or particular Dalit condition. However, as argued in the first chapter of this book, English has a very particular function in the Indian context in this period as a medium of communication across linguistic, class, caste, religious, and national communities. Hence, the very fact that Anand writes his novel in English (as opposed to in Punjabi or Urdu, the two other languages of which he had some significant knowledge) indicates that he hoped his novel would be read across different constituencies. It is not as simple or straightforward as Ben Conisbee Baer states in a recent essay: "We have seen that *Untouchable* is neither addressed to the subaltern nor to a popular Indian readership, but is rather written in English so that it will speak to the metropolis."[64] Baer is not, of course, the only critic to see Anand (or, for that matter, all Indian writers who use English) as writing to and for the west. And in Anand's case, he did perceive himself as a participant in European modernist experimentation, so a significant part of his audience was indeed located in the west.[65] More importantly, as discussed in Chapter 1, what consistently runs through Dalit discourses in the past century is the deep and consistent engagement with English as a desirable language *especially for Dalits* to acquire. Ambedkar's conscious decision to write in English (rather than in Marathi) gave a wider circulation to his work than, for example, that of his predecessor, the Dalit leader Jyotirao Phule who wrote in Marathi.[66] And this importance of English to Dalits is something Anand seems to have understood very well indeed as manifest in his depiction of Bakha's aspiration to learn the "tish mish" (Anand's onomatopoeic rendition of how Bakha hears spoken English) of the British soldiers. Bakha earnestly attempts to teach himself the English alphabet from a primer he buys with his scarce resources and also attempts to bribe upper-caste children to teach him English from their school textbooks. Dalits, as much as other Indians, have understood the power of this language to transform one's social and economic options.

In the novel, Bakha is depicted as being enamored of the English language and equally entranced by British men's clothing as worn by the British army soldiers in the military barracks where he cleans toilets. His daily outfit is, thus, a carefully put together set of cast-offs from British soldiers, either given to him by the Tommies or bought from second-hand stores. This decrepit, soiled, and ill-fitting set of clothes is a great source of pride for Bakha and something that endows him with a vestige of manhood and dignity in his own eyes. Interestingly, the Penguin cover of the 1989 edition of *Untouchable* uses as a cover visual an undated photograph of "An Untouchable" from the India Office Library and Records. This young man, staring directly into the camera, is dressed in somewhat generic Indian clothes (a long kurta over a dhoti), and is bare-footed with a turban on his head. Except for his basket and broom placed at an angle that ensures that the viewer can recognize him as a cleaner, there is nothing that marks

Right from the start of *Untouchable*, the novel's English is ironized as a kind of self-defeating, transvestite medium, for the moment precisely unsuited to the task of accessing and giving voice to subaltern consciousness and idiom. Indeed, Anand underlines this connection by dramatizing Bakha's own desire to speak English: "He had he felt a burning desire, while he was in the British barracks to speak the tish-mish, tish-mish which the Tommies spoke" (U 39). The novel represents a displacement of the sound of English (the language in which it is written) as meaningless onomatopoeia, and thus as a lingual space as yet inaccessible to the very subaltern whose consciousness is being depicted in that language.[74]

Rather than "self-defeating" or "meaningless," I would argue that Anand is carefully working through the gaping divides between language, his plot, the aspirations of the nationalist elite and those of his young Dalit protagonist. This can be read as "transvestite" only if transvestite acts are understood to be profound and active attempts to bridge gaps between desires and access to the means of fulfilling these desires. However, in Baer's reading, as in other critical responses, Anand's depiction of these elements (the desire for English and for western clothing) as dominant in the interiority or sense of self that he endows Bakha is interpreted as an indication of the protagonist's hollow sense of self and his political naivety. It has also been wrongly read as indicative of Anand's patronizing disdain toward his low-caste protagonist or as an indication of Anand's upper-caste ignorance about what the Bakhas of the world desire for themselves.

For Bakha, learning English and getting together a "gentreman's" outfit are part of the dream of bettering his lot in life through education and self-improvement. It is only in the final scenes of the novel, when Bakha is caught up in the fervor around Gandhi's appearance, that his usual interest in British clothing is surmounted by a mainstream nationalist sentiment. We are told that Bakha observes every detail of the uniform of the English District Superintendent, and yet: "Somehow, however, at this moment Bakha was not interested in sahibs, probably because in the midst of this enormous crowd of Indians fired with an enthusiasm for their leader, the foreigner seemed out of place, insignificant, the representative of an order which seemed to have nothing to do with the natives."[75] Instead it is now Gandhi who Bakha identifies with. "'He is black like me,' Bakha said to himself. 'But, of course, he must be very educated.'"[76]

Unlike his befuddlement at the conclusion of the novel over sections of Gandhi's speech which do not connect to his own experience of being an untouchable, Bakha's dream of getting an education and his realization that this dream has been deferred is articulated with utmost clarity all through the novel. Early in the novel, the eighteen-year-old Bakha recollects the moment when he fully understood why getting a formal education was not an option for him:

> And he had wept and cried to be allowed to go to school. But then his father had told him that schools were meant for the babus, not for the lowly sweepers... Later at the British barracks he realized that there was no school which would admit him because the parents of the other children would not allow their sons to be contaminated by the touch of the low-caste man's sons... But the masters wouldn't teach the outcastes lest their fingers which guided the students across the text should touch the leaves of the outcastes' books and they be polluted. These old Hindus were cruel. He was a sweeper, he knew, but he could not consciously accept that fact. He had begun to work at the latrines at the age of six and resigned himself to the hereditary life of the craft, but he dreamed of becoming a sahib... [77]

To put this narrative in some perspective, we need to read it against a statement by Mrs. Annie Besant, who, in 1917 as President of the Indian National Congress, passed a resolution urging the people of India of "the necessity, justice and righteousness of removing all disabilities imposed by custom upon the Depressed Classes..."[78] Yet, her views on education for this sector of the Indian population as stated in a 1909 article titled "The Uplift of the Depressed Classes" are revealing:

> In every nation we find as the basis of the social Pyramid, a class of people, ignorant, degraded, unclean in language and habits, people who perform many tasks which are necessary for Society, but who are despised and neglected by the very Society whose needs they minister... In India, this class forms one-sixth of the total population, and goes by the generic name of the "Depressed Classes"...
>
> What can be done for them by those who feel the barbarity of the treatment meted out to them... Here, as elsewhere, education is the lever by which we may hope to raise them, but a difficulty arises at the outset, for one class of the community, moved by a noble feeling of compassion and benevolence, but not adding thereto a careful and detailed consideration of the conditions, demands, for the children of the pariah community admission to the schools frequented by the sons of the higher classes, and charges with the lack of brotherhood those who are not in favour of this policy... The children of the depressed classes need, first of all, to be taught cleanliness, outside decency of behaviour and the earliest rudiments of education, religion and morality. Their bodies, at present are ill-odorous and foul with the liquor and strong-smelling foods out of which for generations they have been built up; *it will need some generations* of purer food and living to make their bodies fit to sit in the close neighbourhood of a school-room

with children who have received bodies from an ancestry trained in habits of exquisite personal cleanliness, and fed on pure food-stuffs. We have to raise the Depressed Classes to a similar level of physical purity, not to drag down the clean to the level of the dirty, and unless this is done, close association is undesirable.[79]

Here, concerns about caste-based pollution are recast as modern concerns about hygiene and breeding but the essentials remain the same. In her account of caste, Besant manages to recast it as a natural process: according to her logic, the base of the pyramid in every society is sordid and unredeemed. Thus as early as 1909, Besant articulates the Congress and later Gandhian emphasis on benevolence, purification, and the rejection of what she calls "artificial equality" – all of which together keep eager pupils like Bakha shut out of an education. As discussed in Chapter 2, almost every Dalit autobiography from the twentieth century begins with an account of the Dalit child's battle against all odds to get an education in which the writer recounts experiencing exactly what Bakha's father warns him about – teachers and fellow students who fear pollution and are affronted by a low-caste child's desire to study.[80] Significantly, writing in 1933 in a statement on the agitation for temple entry by Dalit organizations, Ambedkar argued that Dalit resources and efforts should be focused instead more centrally on the more important issues of education and employment.[81] He stated:

> The depressed classes think that the surest way for their elevation lies in higher education, higher employment and better ways of earning a living. Once they become well placed in the scale of social life, they would become respectable and once they become respectable the religious outlook of the orthodox towards them is sure to undergo change, and even if this did not happen, it can do no injury to their material interest.[82]

Bakha's interest in getting an education and thereby a chance at "better ways of earning a living" is thus entirely in keeping with Dalit aspirations of his time and place. To read Bakha as politically naive because of his lack of interest in the nationalist movement or because of his investment in the English language or in the British masculine dress code is to be caught in a discourse of generic postcolonial nationalism that is not able to read the caste dynamics attendant to nationalism in the Indian location. Once again, the blind spot of the high-caste reading overlaps neatly with that of the academic mainstream of postcolonial discourse.

The events in this one day in the life of Bakha that serves as the structure and plot of the novel, while marked by defeat, humiliation, failure, and irony, are neither arbitrarily chosen nor without resonance in the "real world" inhabited by untouchables in the 1930s. Anand is to be commended for his focus on just those nodes that are central to Dalit activism and self-representation in this period and beyond: namely, the notion of selfhood, the daily public humiliation of being considered a pollutant in a shared public space, the agitation for education, temple entry, and use of public wells, the sexual vulnerability of Dalit women and girls, and the seeming impossibility of escaping from caste oppression. The novel begins with a description of the scavenging work that Bakha does, that his father Lakha has done his entire life, and that his younger brother Rakha and his future offspring will also do – the inherited job of manually cleaning toilets and disposing of the excrement. All oppression, the novel suggests, stems from these dirty tasks assigned to the untouchable. As Bakha declares in a moment of outrage, "they think we are mere dirt because we clean their dirt."[83] Ambedkar's vision for untouchables was that they could walk away from these inherited jobs if they were educated to be able to pursue alternative means of livelihood. Gandhi's vision for untouchables was that a change of heart among caste Hindus about the practice of untouchability would change the situation and he attempted to work toward this by compelling caste Hindus to join him in cleaning toilets even as he exhorted Dalits to purify their lives.

The incidents in the one day of Bakha's life that Anand narrates are, each and every one of them, central issues around which Dalit agitation was focused in the early 1930s and beyond. As best articulated by Ambedkar in his various speeches, petitions, and documents, equality for Dalits was understood to follow from political safeguards such as separate electorates and improved educational opportunities that would open up improved and alternative employment opportunities for scavengers. Along the way, Dalit activists protested the prohibitions that governed their daily life: they conducted Satyagrahas and other agitations to compel the admission of untouchables to Hindu temples; they agitated against the compulsion to eat leftover foods; against needing to wait for a caste Hindu to draw water for them from public wells; against the barriers to getting their children educated; against the very concepts and practices of untouchability and pollution. Each of these Dalit preoccupations forms the kernel of an event that Bakha or his sister Sohni experiences on this particular day as recorded in the novel.

In an event which serves as the climax of the plot, Bakha walks through this small town attending to his scavenging tasks as well as taking time out for small pleasures, when he accidently bumps against a high-caste Hindu on the street. Bakha is slapped across the face for his impudence in thus polluting his caste superior and heckled by a crowd of caste Hindus. This is the lowest point of Bakha's day and his every little physical and cognitive response to this humiliating sequence of events is minutely detailed in the narrative. Anand is expansive in his presentation of the conflicting emotions of rage, remorse, vengeful thoughts that crowd through Bakha's mind as he alternates between fear, anger, humiliation, and humility. But even as the modernist stream of consciousness technique is skillfully employed to narrate this encounter, Anand is carefully mapping out the deep schisms in Indian society as well as pointing to possible coalitions between different minoritized groups. Hence, it is not incidental or accidental that it is a Muslim man who drives his *tonga* (horse cart) into the ruckus right before Bakha is slapped and thus breaks up the hostile Hindu crowd, a virtual lynch mob, that had gathered around him. Caste Hindus bond together over Bakha's "crime," but those who are outcastes for different reasons (untouchables and Muslims in this instance) can come together over their mistreatment by members of the dominant community. Anand underlines this formation of a coalition across minorities by writing the scene in such a fashion that the slap is reported to the reader from the point of view of the Muslim *tonga-wallah* (cart-driver):

> "You've touched me," he [the tonga-wallah] heard the Lalla [Hindu merchant] say to Bakha. "I will have to bath [sic] now and purify myself anyhow. Well, take this for your damned irresponsibility, you son of a swine!" And the tonga-wallah heard a sharp, clear slap through the air.
> Bakha's turban fell off and the jalebis [cheap Indian sweets] in the paper bag in his hand were scattered in the dust. He stood aghast. Then his whole countenance lit with fire and his hands were no more joined. Tears welled up in his eyes and rolled down his cheeks. The strength, the power of his giant body glistened with the desire for revenge in his eyes, while horror, rage, indignation swept over his frame. In a moment he had lost all his humility, and he would have lost his temper too, but the man who had struck him the blow had slipped beyond reach into the street.
> "Leave him, never mind, let him go, come along, tie your turban," consoled the tonga–wallah, who being a Muhammadan and thus also an Untouchable from the orthodox Hindu point of view, shared the outcaste's resentment to a certain degree.[84]

The implications of this scene would not be lost on Indian readers; the turban is understood to be a sign of a man's dignity and honor regardless of caste or religion. That it is knocked off in this humiliating fashion by caste Hindus and then restored by the kind intervention of a passing Muslim registers as significant. Here Anand skillfully works over the most dominant fear that had guided Gandhi's every move in the negotiations over separate electorates in the Round Table Talks and in his many attempts to get the delegates who represented Muslim and Sikh communities to separate their demands from those of untouchables. Ruled by the fear that minorities would bond together, Gandhi offered all kinds of guarantees to Muslim delegates to try to keep them from supporting Dalit demands for self-representation in elections as a political safeguard. When all these attempts failed to compel minority delegates to agree to see untouchables as part of the Hindu community, Gandhi undertook a fast unto death which was what ultimately compelled Ambedkar to sign the Poona Pact under duress.

At the conclusion of the novel, Anand offers several possible solutions that have the potential to ameliorate, if not change, Bakha's position as a lowly untouchable. The first of these solutions is presented by Colonel Hutchinson, chief of the local Salvation Army, who offers salvation through Christianity. Hutchinson's ineffective efforts to convert Bakha do mostly miss the mark, especially when he tells Bakha to "confess his sins" which is an alien concept to Bakha. Nevertheless Hutchinson does bring Bakha to the entrance of the church, within view of his Christian god, "*Yesuh Messih* [Jesus Messiah]" who, as Bakha acknowledges, "makes no difference between the Brahmin and myself."[85] But Hutchinson's efforts are ruined by the racist outburst of his working-class wife, the former barmaid, whose shrill angry tone reveals her disgust at his association with "blackies, *bhangis* and *chamars*."[86] From the few words of her diatribe that Bakha understands ("Bhangi" and "Chamar" are names of the low-castes who clean toilets, dispose of animal carcasses and work with leather) he knows he must flee the scene, and so he does. Anand here presents conversion to Christianity as overshadowed by the very racialized status afforded to "native" Christians, a staple feature of western missionary work in the empire. Also in operation is Anand's characteristic inability to present white women as anything but devouring, screechy, over-sexed caricatures of working-class British women. Bakha is momentarily intrigued by the possibility of belonging to a religion where Brahmin and Bhangi are treated alike, but the memsahib ruins this possibility. Literary critic Arun Mukherjee rightly points to the fact that there were, in this period, several instances of mass conversions of untouchables to Christianity and Islam. She is also correct when she notes that those Dalits who did not convert did use this possibility as a bargaining tool for better treatment from caste Hindus. Hence she argues: "The documents of the time are full of such instances, testifying to the will and political astuteness of the untouchables. Anand's novel, however, makes no space for such oppositional activity."[87] It is true that from the early 1920s Dalit agitations for temple entry had been directly linked to the threat of leaving Hinduism. In 1921, for instance, in Travancore, Yerawas (a local Dalit community) had threatened to convert to Christianity (a well-established religion in this region with its own powerful elites) en masse if the rulers did not grant to untouchables entry to the Vaikom temple and the use of the road that ran in front of it. The Vaikom Satyagraha of 1924–1925, organized by untouchables themselves, was successful only in 1936 and only after a Yerawa conference which seriously debated mass-scale conversion out of Hinduism. In 1936, a year after *Untouchable* was published, Ambedkar announced decisively that while he was born into Hinduism, he would "not die a Hindu, for this is in my power."[88] But when he did convert in 1956 along with 300,000 other Mahars, it was to Buddhism – a religion that he had been interested in since the 1930s and which he had claimed as part of the past history of untouchables.[89] "In Buddhism," Zelliot writes, "Ambedkar had found an Indian, not a foreign, religion which could legitimize the claims of the Mahar."[90] So while Christianity is understood to be a foreign religion, it did win many converts from all castes but especially from the lowest of Hindu castes. However, the dynamics of the conversion scene in *Untouchable* primarily stage Anand's repeated insistence in this novel and elsewhere that caste discrimination is not the only oppressive burden that an underclass struggles against: here and elsewhere in this novel, class and race domination is in full display even by those like the Hutchinsons who do not practice untouchability. Anand's twenty years in the west had no doubt impressed this upon him in an indelible fashion. Once again, Anand demonstrates that he is not willing to hold racial and caste inequality apart in his understanding of social hierarchies; thus in his writing he does not adopt what Gopal Guru has identified as the Janus face of conventional nationalist thinkers.

After his escape from the colonel, his wife, and his *Yesuh Messih*, Bakha happens to come across a crowd of Indians of every class, caste, and color, eagerly awaiting the arrival of another messiah – the Mahatma. The speech that Anand ascribes to the Mahatma is taken almost verbatim from a speech that Gandhi made at the Fourth Conference on "Suppressed Classes" in Ahmedabad on April 13, 1921 and published in *Young India*, on April 27 and on May 4 of the same year. In Anand's novel, Gandhi does mention his fast to death in 1932 that was aimed at keeping untouchables from demanding separate electorates and his Gandhi does refer directly to this demand as something to be resisted at all costs. But for the most part Anand relies on the 1921 speech for the substance of Gandhi's message in the novel. This is the speech in which Gandhi mentioned the great impact on his life of Uka (the young scavenger in his childhood home) and famously declared untouchability to be "the greatest blot on Hinduism." For the most part, every utterance of Anand's Gandhi is taken from this 1921 speech which contains the kernel of his views on the practice of untouchability and on ending it. Some of his analysis and solutions are clearly rejected by Bakha. He reacts with approval and dismay at different propositions that Gandhi puts forward. For instance, Bakha feels "thrilled" when Gandhi says that he would like to be reborn as an outcaste. And yet, a moment later when Gandhi urges untouchables to "purify their lives... to rid themselves of evil habits" Bakha is outraged at the unfairness of the message: "But now, now the Mahatma is blaming us," Bakha felt.[91]

As important as what Anand includes from Gandhi's 1921 speech is what he omits. In this speech, Gandhi had passionately declared: "Yudhishthira would not enter heaven without his dog. How can, then, the descendants of that Yudhishthira expect to obtain swaraj without the untouchables?" That Anand leaves out this specific sentence while retaining almost all of the rest of Gandhi's speech is indicative of his attempt to edit that speech of truly offensive materials. This detail in itself is a critique of the Gandhian approach to untouchability. Dalit leaders had on many occasions protested the animalistic depiction of untouchables in caste Hindu representations. For example, in 1936 when Gandhi asked a Christian missionary to pray for Harijans rather than attempt to convert them, because they did not have "the mind and intelligence to understand... would you preach the gospel to a cow?" (*Harijan*, December 19, 1936), Jagjivan Ram, then a young Dalit Congress member, had protested this equation of the Dalit with the cow. Gandhi's response was that for him the cow was a symbol of gentleness and patient suffering, which were clearly qualities he saw (or wished to see) embodied in Dalits.[92]

After Gandhi leaves the podium, Bakha overhears a debate about the value of his ideas that breaks out among educated members of the audience. While the majority of the crowd is inspired by Gandhi to set to flame their foreign items of clothing as was the nationalist ritual following such speeches, a light-skinned Indian dressed in western clothes dismisses Gandhi as a fool and hypocrite who "is in the fourth century with his swadeshi and his spinning wheel."[93] This monocled Muslim gentleman has recently returned from England and shows off his knowledge of democracy, Rousseau, Hobbes, Bentham, and John Stuart Mill. Yet, confident in his class privilege, he shouts an order to Bakha, who is a stranger to him, because of his supreme confidence that he can do so: "Eh, eh, boy, come here. Go and get a bottle of soda-water for the sahib."[94] The Penguin edition of *Untouchable* gives this line as: "Eh, eh, Black man, come here. Go and get a bottle of soda-water for the sahib."[95] Here race as marked by skin color is evoked in the monocled gentleman's assumption of superiority over Bakha. Anand is always insistent on drawing parallels between race- and caste-based structures of discrimination. The irony here is that while this England-returned modernized Muslim Indian is not concerned about Bakha's caste or that his touch might be polluting, he nevertheless flaunts his class authority over Bakha with aplomb. Fortunately for Bakha, a young Indian poet engages this gentleman in conversation and so the order for soda water is forgotten, and instead Bakha can stand close by and overhear the poet's assessment of Gandhi. In a lengthy meandering philosophical speech, the poet pontificates on many topics, including the nobility of the Indian peasant and the need to modernize India, before finally mentioning the machine that will end untouchability – the flush toilet system. This "machine," then, is proposed by Anand as the third and final mode of eradicating untouchability and it proves to be very attractive to Bakha.[96] Ultimately Bakha resolves to tell his father all that Gandhi and the poet had spoken about. He walks home thinking alternately about the Mahatma and the machine. The image we are left with – the hero slowly, painstakingly, figuring out the elements of possible new worlds as he walks homeward – is familiar to us from several modernist fictions.

Jessica Berman sees the political rewriting of the *Bildungsroman* in Anand's work, especially as manifest in the hero who is not in a position to simply perform his growth into adult selfhood and his integration into society, as stemming from Anand's contact with writers like James Joyce. Bakha has been read by Meenakshi Mukherjee, Berman, and other critics cited above as the modernist hero – unheroic, lonely, and alienated from his world. And in retrospect, the Bakha that Anand creates owes much to the usual portrait of the hero in the modernist novel – the flawed, inadequate young man on the road to self-discovery. But *Untouchable* and its representation of Bakha is also deeply colored by Anand's acknowledgement of the struggles for liberty by Dalits and by disenfranchised people elsewhere in the world. As Anand has written in *Apology for Heroism*:

> Thus the urges of the people, to rule themselves, cannot be halted. Strange, that when all seems lost, how the deeply-seated urges for liberty, in the smallest of the small, express themselves, and answer back the oppressors and win through to the right of the many freedoms, here and there and everywhere.[97]

For Anand, untouchables were participants in a struggle for selfhood and liberty that was being globally manifest "here and there and everywhere" by different peoples who shared the same deep-seated urge for liberty. The "many freedoms" that Anand championed encompassed scales that were both larger and smaller than the struggle for national liberty.

In 1992, Anand, along with the prominent Ambedkar scholar Eleanor Zelliot, edited and published the first English language anthology of Dalit poetry.[98] This anthology featured translations from Marathi, starting with an acknowledgement of the work of the fourteenth-century Bhakti poet-saint Chokhamela, to selections from the best-known Marathi Dalit poets of the mid- to late twentieth century. Later that year, *Poisoned Bread: Translations from Modern Marathi Dalit Literature*, edited by Arjun Dangle, was published by Orient Longman, a mainstream English language press with better production values and wider distribution. The Dangle anthology became the publication that forced mainstream English language literary criticism to pay attention to this literary development in their midst.[99] As S. Anand has rightly noted, the publication of *Poisoned Bread* by Dangle, who was one of the founders of the Dalit Panthers, showed up the Anand and Zelliot anthology as "carelessly produced," albeit the first of its kind.[100] Of course most Indian editions of Anand's novels and other publications have been plagued by shockingly shoddy editing and proofreading, but the dedication and passion with which the Dangle anthology showcased Dalit literature made the lack of attention to publication details in the Anand and Zelliot anthology seem indicative of editorial inattention or, worse, a casual approach to the Dalit works anthologized in this collection.[101]

As many scholars have noted, the primary genres in Dalit literature are poetry and the autobiography form.[102] Prominent works within this prose genre include Hazari's *Untouchable: The Autobiography of an Indian Outcaste* (1951), Daya Pawar's *Balute* (1978), Laxman Mane's *Upara* [The Outsider] (1980), Sharan Kumar Limbale's *Akarmashi* [Outsider] (1984), Laxman Gaikwad's *Uchalya* [The Petty Thief] (1987), Bama's *Karukku* [Double-edged Palm Leaf] (1992), Baby Kamble's *Jivan Hamara* [My/Our Life] (1995), Mohandas Naimi Sharay's *Apne Apne Pinjare* [Each One's Cages] (1995), Om Prakash Valmiki's *Joothan* [Leftovers] (1997), and Surajpal Chauhan's *Tiraskrit* (2002). Sarah Beth, a scholar of Dalit literature, points to the common assumption that "members of a marginalized group will both *want* and *need* to write autobiographical literature in order to express their experiences of oppression" (emphasis in original).[103] In an interview with Beth, Rajendra Yadav, literary critic and editor of a progressive Hindi journal, *Hans*, states: "Early Dalit writing has been in the form of autobiography because this is the only authentic experience they [Dalits] have since they have been separated from the experiences of the world."[104]

Almost all scholars writing on this literature agree that Dalit autobiographies or testimonios or "life-writing" are collective documents. Pramod Nayar insists that such texts have no "problematic hero"; rather what is showcased through the story of an individual is "a problematic collective situation."[105] Even the individual bodily suffering, scholars insist, is presented as communal in Dalit texts. Writing on the publication of the English translation of the Tamil autobiography *Karukku* (1992) by Bama, Nayar writes: "Bama suggests that one suffers as a Dalit, even though the pain is singular to the suffering *individual* body" (emphasis in original).[106] Writing about the same testimonio, M. S. S. Pandian notes that Bama's text is "a case of willfully violating genre boundaries" because: "Bama's narrative, even as it verbalizes her own life story, depletes rather effortlessly the autobiographical 'I', an outcome of bourgeois individualism, and displaces it with the collectivity of the Dalit community. Her story, to put it differently, refuses to be her own but that of others too."[107] As Pandian continues, "It is as though the autobiographical 'I' does not have an autonomous life outside the collective 'we.'"[108] What is privileged in Dalit narratives like Bama's is not "her own voice, [instead it] functions as a site for the criss-crossing of multiple voices from within her community."[109] In her essay on Dalit autobiography, Ganguly perceptively reconsiders the neat opposition posited in this scholarship between "individualist and collectivist genres" whereby the individualist genres are seen as "proxies for privilege and power" and as "expressive modes of the dominant majority," and the collectivist genres are "seen as products of marginalization and oppression" and as "expressive modes that draw the readers in as witnesses to suffering and that aspire to circulate in a communal context of healing, amelioration and resistance."[110] But for the most part, Dalit literature is viewed as committed to the presentation of individual subjecthood that is always deeply rooted in and validated by the communal.

This reading of the communal in the individual story is echoed by most commentators on Dalit literature as the primary distinguishing factor between Dalit writers' and non-Dalit writers' presentation of Dalit protagonists. Sarah Beth notes that with the autobiographical mode, Dalit writers have "constructed a powerful counter-discourse emphasizing the authority of *svanubhuti* (self-perception) and discrediting literature based on *sahanubhuti* (sympathy) as elitist and oppressive, concluding that only Dalits can write Dalit literature."[111] This absolute rejection of upper-caste representations of Dalits in fiction is the dominant stance in all Dalit scholarship on literature.

While the events in *Untouchable* echo Dalit political concerns, Anand's Bakha is not like the protagonists of texts written from within Dalit communities by Dalit writers. Bakha's desires and aspirations for a better life are presented as individualistic; he is alienated from his brother and father, he is not conscious of his community interests except fleetingly. Ultimately his character is cut from the same cloth as the middle-class hero of the modernist novel. Bakha is the low-caste version of the bourgeois subject at the center of the modernist novel. Like Leopold Bloom he wanders through the city and ultimately returns home musing over the day's events. Every aspect of his day, each encounter, each event is shaped by his caste identity, but he is not a spokesperson for his community.

Anand's *Untouchable* is not a part of Dalit literature; nor is Anand the first nor the last upper-caste writer with socialist/leftist sympathies who wrote empathetically on Dalit everyday life. Anand himself names *Untouchable* as being "in the tradition of" non-Dalit writers like Munshi Premchand (1880–1936), who wrote in Hindi and Urdu, and Kota Shivaram Karanth (1902–1997), who wrote in Kannada.[112] In 1947, the Malayali writer Thakazi Sivasankara Pillai wrote a novel titled *Thottiyude Makan* which was translated from Malayalam into English as *Scavenger's Son*. Like Anand, Thakazi (as he is popularly called) was also a member of the PWA, also upper-caste, also a leftist in his political leanings, and deeply influenced by Marx and other European thinkers. *Thottiyude Makan* tracks a scavenger community's unsuccessful attempts to consolidate via unionizing what power they, as latrine cleaners, have over the everyday functioning of elite caste lives. By the mid-twentieth century, Dalit writers had themselves written and published fiction and autobiographies that have reprioritized the core political issues at stake and have better illuminated the very struggles raised in the earlier novels by upper-caste writers. Especially after the renaissance in Dalit literature from the 1960s through the 1990s, Anand's novel was, inevitably, cast aside for more gripping accounts by more authentic subjects who better embody the many fronts on which Dalits have had to fight for recognition and respect.

IV

What has been foundational to much of the discussion of *Untouchable* is Anand's account of how it came to be written, revised, and published. Several critics have written in detail about the process of publication, the rejection of the manuscript by nineteen publishers, and its eventual success when it was championed by E. M. Forster, so I will not rehearse their arguments here.[113] Instead, I would like to grapple with a very difficult and delicate issue – namely the claim that Anand first made in the mid-1960s that M. K. Gandhi himself helped him revise and rewrite the novel. I turn our attention to this issue in order to understand how (if not why) Anand himself greatly contributed to the nationalist, even Gandhian, reading of his first novel.

When *Untouchable* was first published in 1935 by Lawrence and Wishart the book carried a preface by E. M. Forster and was dedicated to a certain Edith Young. Subsequent editions, such as the one published in 1947 by Hutchinson International Authors, also included these features. However, in 1967 in an essay titled "My Experiment with a White Lie," a title that interestingly alters and echoes that of Gandhi's autobiography (*My Experiments with Truth*), Anand claimed that the Mahatma had himself read and helped him revise the manuscript of *Untouchable*.[114] Initially published in the Sahitya Akademi's literary journal *Indian Literature* and then reprinted in the seminal *Critical Essays on Indian Writing in English* edited by M. K. Naik, S. K. Desai and G. S. Amur, Anand's claim has been accepted at face value. Henceforth, the 1970 Indian edition of *Untouchable* published in New Delhi by Arnold Publishers included an "Author's Afterword" titled "On the Genesis of *Untouchable*" in which Anand claimed that Gandhi oversaw the revisions that he made to the manuscript for this novel in 1927 while the author was in residence at Gandhi's Sabarmati Ashram, near Ahmedabad in Gujarat. In this afterword, Anand claims to have deleted a hundred or more pages of the original manuscript on Gandhi's urging: "he [Gandhi] suggested I should cut . . . especially those passages in which Bakha seemed to be thinking and dreaming and brooding like a Bloomsbury intellectual."[115] And to the original dedication to Edith Young were added the names of K. S. Shelvankar and M. K. Gandhi. Subsequent editions, such as the popular paperback edition in the Penguin Twentieth-Century Classics series, carry the Forster preface and the revised dedication but not the authorial afterword.[116]

The degree, if any, of Gandhi's involvement in the crafting of this novel on untouchability in the very period when he was formulating his program of caste reform remains uncorroborated. Even so basic a fact as the date or year of Anand's visit to Sabarmati Ashram is variously represented by Anand himself and scholars. In the 1967 "white lie" essay, Anand mentions receiving a postcard from Gandhi inviting him to visit the ashram on a Sunday in April – no year is given. In the "Author's Afterward" to the novel, Anand claims the visit took place over a hot weekend in April 1927. Elsewhere, as in Marlene Fisher's book, the year given is 1929 or, as in the preface to the 2005 reader edited by Atma Ram, Anand says he made the visit in January 1927 and stayed in the ashram for two months.[117] In *The Bubble* (1984) and in *The Little Plays of Mahatma Gandhi* (1991) Anand does not give specific dates for this visit and consultation with Gandhi. Naik's 1973 book-length study on Anand starts with a chronology of Anand's life that notes under the year 1932: "Returned to India; studied ancient monuments; lived in Sabarmati Ashram with Mahatma Gandhi and wrote first draft of *Untouchable.*"[118] Saros Cowasjee, a leading scholar on Anand who had a close relationship with the author and has published his extensive correspondence with him, in addition to writing several books and articles on his work, also gives the year of the visit as 1932. In an unpublished interview, Cowasjee asked the author quite directly: "There is still a lot of confusion about when you first wrote *Untouchable* and when you showed it to Gandhi." Anand's response was reportedly as follows:

> I first met Gandhi in Sabarmati Ashram in 1927 when I showed him the immature draft in Joycean English. I did not write the book in 1930, but began it 1925, as part of the Confession. I went to see Irene in Dublin in summer/autumn of 1926, and met A. E. and Yeats. I can't vouch for the day and month in each case, but what I have put down there [in *The Bubble*] three or four times are factual references.[119]

My efforts to authenticate this claim that the revisions of this novel were closely or loosely supervised by Gandhi have been unsuccessful. A close perusal of Gandhi's correspondence and appointment records shows no mention of Mulk Raj Anand or of this novel or of any visit by Anand to the ashram. In fact Gandhi was travelling and away from the ashram in January and April 1927 and April 1929, and he, along with many of his associates, spent all of 1932 in prison.[120] To the best of my knowledge, none of Anand's written work or interviews prior to the 1960s mentions this visit to Sabarmati Ashram or Gandhi's direct involvement. It would be useful to speculate as to why Anand waited till 1967 to make public this story of Gandhi's involvement in the writing of his first novel.

And so to speculate. In his masterful *So Many Freedoms: A Study of the Major Fictions of Mulk Raj Anand*, published in 1977, Saros Cowasjee ends his account of Anand's life to that date with the assessment that Anand is "an angry old man."[121] Of course, Anand went on to live for another thirty years, and some of that anger is very visible in his self-obituary published in the year after his death in 2005. In this final document, Anand is defiantly and coherently anti-nationalist and very critical of the Hindu right-wing ideology that was cast over Indian national politics in the last years of his life. Notably this self-obituary does not mention the visit to Sabarmati Ashram even though it traces the important events in his life.

As mentioned above, Anand returned to India in 1945 at the age of forty and settled in Bombay.[122] His prose work from the 1940s, especially *Letters on India*, which was vocal in its anti-imperial stance, had alienated him from most of his British intellectual friends and acquaintances. However, in India his relations with the Bombay branch of the PWA were also less than cordial. According to Cowasjee, the Bombay PWA openly disapproved of Anand's "bohemian" lifestyle. Cowasjee reports that the rejection by the leftist PWA was a "serious blow" to Anand, but one that pushed him toward a deeper involvement with the then Indian Prime Minister and Congress Party leader Jawaharlal Nehru, who roped Anand into representing India and Indian culture, as a member of official Indian delegations to international conferences and other cultural venues. In 1966 Anand broke ties with the Bombay PWA when he refused to serve on the Organizing Committee for the Sixth All-India Progressive Writers' Conference. Anand, who had always maintained his distance from mainstream nationalism, was now a part of that state machinery. And, as Cowasjee notes, this meant that it was no longer admissible for Anand "to criticize a government which had become his patron."[123]

Very soon Anand was heavily involved with the cultural institutions for the arts established, in the mid-1950s, by the new national leadership: the Sahitya Akademi, the Lalit Kala Akademi, and the Sangeet Natak Akademi. Anand participated in or judged competitions organized by these institutions of literature, visual arts, music, and drama even as he was associated with the National Book Trust, the Indian Council of Cultural Relations, and other government-funded cultural organizations. His primary work was with the art journal *Marg* which was funded by the philanthropist and industrialist J. D. R. Tata, thus forcing Anand, who had stood by the worker and the laborer in his fiction writing, to now make his livelihood through the largesse of the most prominent business house in India. His commitment to international organizations also continued apace: he was closely involved with the World Peace Council, the Afro-Asian Writers' Association, and UNESCO's Dialogues of East and West. He also made several trips within and outside India to write for *Marg* about historic monuments and artworks around the world.

Once he was based in India, Anand found himself repeatedly having to work his contacts with the Nehru family to expedite the everyday bureaucratic business of being a widely travelling cultural figure. Anand's association with Jawaharlal Nehru has been well documented. The third edition of *Apology for Heroism* (the 1975 Arnold-Heinemann reprint) carries the following dedication: "for J.L.N. with whom I share many ideas." After Nehru's death in 1964, no doubt Anand's affiliation with the central government became more tenuous.[124] There was a need to bolster his importance for the new generation of leadership, and perhaps this accounts for his announcement in 1967 of Gandhi's role in the writing of *Untouchable*. Perhaps.

On his return to India in 1945, Anand began narrating his life story on several fronts, but primarily through a seven-volume fictionalized autobiographical project which was left incomplete at the time of his death. The title of each of these texts, four of which were published prior to his death, was taken from the well-known speech in Shakespeare's *As You Like It* (Act II, sc. vi) where life is divided into seven ages and which begins "All the world's a stage / And the men and women merely players..."[125] Anand was not alone in writing his memoirs, for several others who had been active in the London intellectual scene were writing memoirs of the 1930s and 1940s. Anand was left out of several of these memoirs for reasons discussed above. In the post-independence critical reception of Anand's work, the general assessment seemed to be that *Untouchable* and *Coolie* were his best work and that later novels and autobiographical fiction did not measure up to the promise of the early writing.[126] The story about Gandhi's contribution to the writing of *Untouchable* at the exact period in his political career when he was working on eradicating untouchability no doubt enhanced the general interest in this early novel and helped to anchor its reputation. More than mere fiction, it became a work that was "corrected" and edited by none other than the father of the nation, and thus the interpretive frame bought to bear on it was primarily that of the national struggle for independence.

Anand had claimed close association with a wide range of well-known figures besides Gandhi including Picasso, Freud, and others. In 1981, at the age of seventy-six, Anand published his account of his association with literary figures in England in the 1920s and 1930s titled *Conversations in Bloomsbury*.[127] This book has chapters dedicated to Anand's recollection of individual figures he was acquainted with to varying degrees, such as Virginia Woolf, T. S. Eliot, D. H. Lawrence, Leonard Woolf, Nancy Cunard, Clive Bell, Aldous Huxley, E. M. Forster, and others. In the preface to this book, Anand tells us: "In *Conversations in Bloomsbury*, I emerge as an electric, miscellaneous and unconventional romantic, in my concentration on the human predicament, the Hamletian 'to be or not to be.'"[128] Clearly Anand had close friendships with influential figures like Bonamy Dobrée and professional associations with others like Leonard Woolf, and thin acquaintance with some of the others in this write-up. Regardless, the conversations that Anand presents in this collection of essays are wonderfully created in that one can imagine T. S. Eliot or D. H. Lawrence or Virginia Woolf saying or doing exactly what Anand claims they did. For example, Anand's report of his first meeting with Eliot at a party at Harold Munro's bookshop, where Eliot is described as shy but arrogant, disdainful, blushing, unable to look directly at Anand and his friend Nikhil Sen, but nevertheless confident of his view that Gandhi is an "anarchist" and that "Indians should pursue their culture and leave government to the British empiricists," is very credible given the poet's general reputation.[129]

But no association was as impressive as the claim Anand made in the "white lie" essay in 1967 that Gandhi helped him revise *Untouchable*. It is of course perfectly feasible that such a collaboration took place. Gandhi's correspondence mentions several instances in which fictional texts were presented to him or where he comments about not having had time to read or having read and enjoyed certain books. He did have strong opinions on texts he read and his judgment was highly regarded and could make or break the success of a publication.[130] And Gandhi certainly may have sent out postcards that were not recorded in the correspondence and received visitors at the ashram whose visits were not mentioned in the logs. Part of the uncertainty comes from the fact that Anand's papers are presently uncataloged and inaccessible to scholars.[131] There is no record of the existence of a manuscript either with or without the hundred or so pages that Gandhi allegedly advised Anand to discard.

Most Anand scholarship does not question the verity of this account of the stay at Sabarmati Ashram.[132] The only exceptions are Jessica Berman who refers to this visit to Sabarmati Ashram as "an apocryphal story," Sushila Nasta who cites Berman and seems to agree, and Leela Gandhi who uses the term "allegedly" to refer to this story.[133] And ultimately, more interesting than establishing whether or not Anand had direct interactions with Gandhi is the impact of this claim on the critical and mainstream reception of this novel. As Nasta notes: "this tale . . . has continued to feed . . . Anand's credentials as an authentic 'social realist' and literary icon of Indian nationalism." Interestingly, this reported stay at Sabarmati and consultation with Gandhi on Anand's first novel has also come to be read as an indication of how Gandhi felt about fiction writing in English. Consequently, in his introduction to the outstanding study *A History of Indian Literature in English*, the poet and editor of this collection, Arvind Mehrotra, persuasively uses this account of Gandhi giving the young writer Anand advice at Sabarmati Ashram as symptomatic of Gandhi's "characteristic forthrightness" and of his lack of serious opposition to English, despite the claims of others who cite chapter and verse in Gandhi's writing to point to his general disapproval of the Indian reliance on English.[134] Mehrotra writes of his great satisfaction with Anand's report of Gandhi's attitude to the use of English: "'the purpose of writing is to communicate, isn't it?' he [Gandhi] said. 'If so, say your say in any language that comes to hand.'" Based on Anand's account of Gandhi's openness to Indian writing in English, Mehrotra confidently asserts: "Between Gandhi's many-sided opposition to English and his encouragement of Anand there is no contradiction."[135] Anand's story thus manufactures the much sought legitimacy and approval for writing in English from the father of the nation.

Ultimately, it is not crucial to figure out the exact degree of Anand's actual association with Gandhi.[136] Gandhi was and remains an overwhelming presence on the Indian landscape: as has been well documented, his impact on cultural production in India and beyond in the twentieth century was undeniably massive. That Anand narrated this Gandhian prehistory to *Untouchable* in the 1960s could be viewed most generously as no more than a conciliation with an ideological giant whose influence could be belatedly acknowledged especially when the other shaping forces faded or, rather, when other shaping forces faded out Anand's contribution.

V

Anand's literary reputation may have waned after his return to India, but his interventions in the art world were crucial to the development of avant garde cultural production in India, especially in the first two decades after independence. The radicalism he had exhibited in the early literary works evolved into a curatorship of modern Indian art and architecture that he promoted with much dedication and energy.[137] At *Marg* Anand shepherded, judged, and recorded Indian cultural production in different venues – architectural projects like the building of the city of Chandigarh, the cultivation of Indian abstract art and sculpture, the legitimizing of photography as art – even as he sought to ensure governmental preservation of historical monuments and other ancient sites. In keeping with the self-assigned task of writers in English discussed in Chapter 1 of this book, Anand's greatest success was perhaps in this role of curator of modern

Indian culture to the world and to the nation. As Annapurna Garimella has noted, Anand shaped "Indian modernity" through the positions he took in early issues of *Marg* on "matters such as urban planning, contemporary art, architecture, arts education and training, heritage, tourism, popular and folk cultures, and museology."[138] Anand's creed of humanism was also no doubt nurtured and nourished by his work for/at *Marg*. In the 1950s Anand also initiated and nurtured cultural exchanges between Indian, Asian, and African writers and artists. His efforts to sustain a South–South dialogue in the arts in an era of global decolonization remains to be fully acknowledged or appreciated.

Mulk Raj Anand's life demonstrates the opportunities and limitations that someone of his linguistic, class, regional, caste, national, and educational background grappled with in the course of a century in which so much of the world changed and so rapidly. In an age of transition, Anand lived (for almost a hundred years) and wrote in the interstices of colony and independent nation, of nation and empire, and of communism, socialism, and capitalism. In his own words he was "floating between Asia and Europe, through the mental struggles of our tragic century."[139] Ultimately, the political stance that Anand settled on was a personalized version of humanism that he had begun formulating early in his life. In *Letters for India* (1942) and *Apology for Heroism* (1946) Anand had spelled out what a non-nationalist humanism signified for an Indian of his time(s) and place(s). In the final pages of *Apology for Heroism*, this "autobiography of ideas" as the work is subtitled, Anand writes:

> I suggest that a new society will only be born through the coming together of all the multifarious peoples of the world, inspired by this tenderness for each other, to build new democratic communities of the various free nationalities and peoples, local collectives which while retaining their own languages and cultures, might emerge into the bigger collectives and federations in which there is room for adjustment of the economic and social needs of people through free exchange and barter.[140]

In the mid-twentieth century, with national independence and an end of empire in view, there was an opening up of European intellectual circles to countless former colonial subjects like Anand from India and other educated elites from the non-west. These intellectuals of color thought themselves to be participants in a new global discourse which would be based on the belief in the common humanity of all and would usher in a new multiracial, multinational, and multicultural society. Anand continues in this passage in *Apology for Heroism* (1946) to envision the new humanism appropriate to this new world that would not be consumed by colonialist or nationalist fervor:

> I believe that from this very attempt at tenderness will spring the dynamic of the new life, a new humanism. For it will bring a realization of the dignity of manhood, of the urge for men to rise to the full heights of their individual and collective genius from the mutilations and frustrations they have suffered so long.[141]

"Floating between Asia and Europe," Anand was ushering in a new humanism that would "tenderly" draw in the oppressed of the world and give intellectuals from all corners of the globe a shared platform to speak from. There was a whole slew of English language writers from this mid-twentieth-century period whose placement between India and the west somewhat parallels Anand. These writers, such as Kamala Markandaya, Dom Moraes, Raja Rao, Aubrey Menon, Sasthi Bhrata, Shanta Rama Rau, and Saros Cowasjee, were all writing (mostly fiction but also travel guides, autobiographical texts), in English and all straddled at least two different worlds. These writers' degrees of investment in nationalism and internationalism, their particular aesthetics, their attempts to rethink humanism, and their mostly tenuous place (except for Raja Rao) in the Indian literary canon are all worthy of scholarly investigation.[142] All of these writers were negotiating their world(s) on their own; there was not much dialogue between them, at least very little that has come to light in the intervening years. There are, of course, tantalizingly brief or tangential references to conferences, cultural exchanges, and correspondence between these decolonizing constituencies, which await scholarly detective work. For, by mid-century, there were signs that the very real possibility of independence for India signaled the end of colonialism everywhere and the dawn of a new era of global interactions on a more equal footing.

As Anand wrote in the preface to a later edition of *Apology for Heroism*: "The world becomes our task."[143] On his return to India, Anand found that in a post-independence India, he had a whole country and its cultural production to represent to the world. From his vantage point at *Marg*, with his involvement in the workings of the cultural institutions set up in the new nation, and with his easy access to Prime Minister Nehru, Anand had the credentials to lead cultural delegations to his former haunts in Europe and, even more excitingly, to Africa and other parts of the world that were casting off the shackles of European imperialism. And as the next chapter on the establishment of Sahitya Akademi in 1954 will demonstrate, in the mid-twentieth century, with decolonization in sight around the world, it was believed that literary/cultural institutions and individual cultural producers would finally be able to lay claim to India's rightful place in a global discourse on humanity, art, and culture. What was well understood, as the founding documents of the Sahitya Akademi made clear, was that India would occupy the place appropriate to its immense cultural wealth in this global conversation, only when it presented a well-defined, united, and specifically "Indian" voice. That this "authentic Indianness" had to be voiced in English was understood to be a prerequisite of participation in an international cultural world.

CHAPTER FOUR

The Sahitya Akademi's showcasing of national literature

> You will find that while all the languages named in the Indian Constitution are represented in the Academy, English does not find a place there. You will agree that the Academy would remain incomplete if some distinguished writers of English had not been included. We have to admit that for the last 100 or 150 years, English has served not only as the vehicle of knowledge and learning but also as the medium of expression of many of our finest writers. This was inevitable, for English had achieved such a pre-eminence that the status of an author was not assured till he had expressed himself through its medium.
> From the speech by Maulana Abul Kalam Azad, Minister of Education, at the inaugural meeting of the Sahitya Akademi, Central Hall of Parliament, New Delhi, March 12, 1954[1]

> Another thing I feel is that we need not be unduly narrow in the choice of the languages with which the Akademi should concern itself. Besides Hindi to which I have already referred and the other great languages of India which are listed in our Constitution, there are several other languages in India of which we should take note. We should also remember that even in the present, English is a language in which Indians are writing and have written with distinction. This is a fact we should not ignore.
> From the speech by Jawaharlal Nehru, Prime Minister of India and Chairman, General Council of the Sahitya Akademi, at its first meeting, on the afternoon of March 12, 1954 at the Prime Minister's residence in New Delhi[2]

The establishment of three national cultural institutions in the early 1950s was a key component of the central government's efforts to consolidate and define the newly independent Indian nation as a singular entity. The Sahitya Akademi (National Academy of Letters), which will be the focus of this chapter, was set up in 1954 along with the Lalit Kala Akademi (for the visual arts) and the Sangeet Natak Akademi (for music, dance, and drama). Together these three government-funded yet autonomous institutions were to serve as the machinery that would continuously reproduce and propagate the concept of a singular and strong Indian culture that was manifest in many traditions, languages, and art forms. In this chapter I argue that even though no literary location in post-independence India has been so deliberately established with a nationalist agenda to fulfill than the Sahitya Akademi, there has always been a gap between the governmental imperatives and the critical and creative works produced under the aegis of the Sahitya Akademi. The official critical framework (usually articulated in English) that the Akademi has cast across a diverse body of literary works insists on locating a commonality of origins, themes, and foci to all literature in all the languages – a commonality or unity that is marked as "Indianness." But it was well understood that cultivating unity from diverse sources needed careful nurturing and had to be coaxed into full bloom. And yet, as I will demonstrate in this chapter, despite the imposition of this organizational structure and philosophy on the Akademi's projects, the literary works and their critical assessments produced therein did not always perform "unity in diversity" or "Indianness" as expected. From the outset it was acknowledged by all concerned with the Akademi, that a national literature could not be commanded into existence by governmental decree; even so, much effort was put into achieving this very goal.

This chapter will examine the early history of the Sahitya Akademi to demonstrate that despite it close association with the departed colonial power, the English language was essential to the project of creating a unified national literary consciousness. Even though English was not one of the Indian languages listed on the Eighth Schedule of the Indian constitution, it had a pivotal role to play in the Sahitya Akademi's articulation of a unified Indian literary arena. From the start it was well understood that a national literature had two distinct audiences: Indian and foreign. Creating a national literature was in itself a goal which required literary interactions and engagements on an international stage and this meant that the "National Academy of Letters" had to be cosmopolitan, international, and simultaneously attentive to specific Indian languages. Again English was indispensable to the attainment of international prestige for Indian literature, for such recognition was understood to be a measure of the worth of a national literature. A variety of instances discussed below demonstrate that the necessary reliance on English in this showcasing of Indian identity was not an easily accepted feature of making a national literature. Consequently, there was a very deliberate emphasis on the part of the Akademi on propelling Hindi (and the Devanagari script in which it was to be written as per the Indian constitution) to the national forefront, on supporting literary ventures in "Indian languages," and on consciously creating an ethos of linguistic equal opportunity for the more vulnerable among the many Indian languages. This chapter will primarily examine the explicit agenda of the Sahitya Akademi to create a singular united national literature out of diverse linguistic and literary traditions and the practical difficulties that unraveled some of the efforts to reach this goal. Along the way it will demonstrate that a national literature is a carefully orchestrated assemblage of cultural texts, more held together by the critical framework cast around it than evolving from the literary contents of the body of work. A secondary focus in this chapter is the consideration of what has been gained and what lost in this single-minded pursuit of diversity interpreted solely as linguistic diversity. How have caste, religious, and gender diversities been sidelined in this determined attempt to secure linguistic diversity? The early history of the Sahitya Akademi provides a mostly unexplored site from which to examine one of the central concerns of this book, namely the contours and reverberations of the mid-twentieth-century Indian literary discourse in English in the shadow of a successful national independence movement.

I

As discussed in earlier chapters of this study, a multi-pronged effort to knit together a singular Indian cultural identity from the diverse cultural traditions in the region had been launched by national leaders prior to independence. These efforts continued apace in the early 1950s. In his *Discovery of India* (1946), Jawaharlal Nehru had coined the slogan "unity in diversity" as a rallying call for all Indians.[3] In the immediate aftermath of the bloody Partition that had followed national liberation, Nehru, now serving as the first Prime Minister, found that forging this unity from diversity was a difficult but crucial task. In the early years after 1947, the former princely states were slowly falling into line and joining the Indian union through either persuasion or force. The regions that were now West and East Pakistan were erased from the map of independent India and were regretfully and bitterly acknowledged as a separate country. Hence, the consolidation of a national identity was considered, if anything, an even more necessary task in the post-independence era than before. It was with the aim of harnessing literature to this task that the Government of India decided to establish a National Academy of Letters by its resolution of December 15, 1952.[4] This institution, named the "Sahitya Akademi," was formally inaugurated on March 12, 1954.[5] Nehru, who simultaneously served as first President of the Sahitya Akademi and first Prime Minister of the new nation, was the chief architect and guiding force of this Akademi. Krishna Kripalani, literary critic, ardent nationalist, and close associate of Nehru, was its first general secretary and, as such, the man at the helm in the formative years of this institution.

As set forth in the opening passage of its constitution, the Akademi was to serve as "a national organization to work actively for the development of Indian letters, to set high literary standards, to foster and co-ordinate literary activities in all the Indian languages and to promote through them all the cultural unity of the country."[6] Specifically, these goals were to be met in multiple ways: mainly, by promoting "co-operation among men of letters for the development of Literature in Indian languages"; by arranging for translations of literary works between different Indian languages as well as of texts from and to non-Indian languages; by assisting in the compilation and publication of bibliographies, dictionaries, encyclopedias, and vocabulary guides in the various Indian languages; by sponsoring conferences, seminars, and exhibitions; by awarding prizes; by promoting teaching, especially of regional literatures; by encouraging "the propagation and study of literature among the masses," etc. Especially noteworthy in the constitution's listing of goals are numbers (ix) and (x) which bear quoting in their entirety because they will be discussed in this chapter:

(ix) to improve and develop the various scripts in which the languages of the country are written, to promote the use of the Devanagari script and to encourage publication of select books in regional languages in the Devanagari script;

(x) to promote cultural exchanges with other countries and to establish relations with international organisations in the field of letters.

In essence, the overarching task of the Sahitya Akademi was to co-ordinate and produce a national literature out of the many disparate literary traditions in the newly formed nation. A secondary yet related goal was to push Hindi to the national forefront even while other Indian languages were to be promoted regionally. The bifurcation of Hindi and Urdu into two languages with two separate scripts which resulted from the constitutional decision to exclusively use the Devanagari script for Hindi was supported by the Sahitya Akademi's many ventures that were to popularize this script. In such a scenario, the diversity between languages was valued and hybridity within any one language was not. A "pure" language reaching back to Sanskrit roots was the desired history for all Indian languages. What is also cemented into this project of showcasing a national literature is that diversity is understood to be linguistic diversity. With the many languages and dialects that proliferated in the nation, ensuring linguistic diversity as described above was enough of a challenge; so much so that other manifestations of diversity such as those created by gender, caste, and religion were rendered less urgent.

The primary contradiction that is visible in the narratives around the inception of this institution was that this unity *despite* diversity was treated as an established fact even while the difficulties in the path of establishing such a singular national literature or national identity were being articulated in several avenues. A citation from the introductory section of the first *Sahitya Akademi Progress Report (1956–57)* will illuminate this conundrum, whereby the official narrative of the Akademi presented the urgently desired "unity in diversity" as something that was already achieved even as it laid out the difficulty of reaching this goal. The report states:

> But the main activity in the Sahitya Akademi's programme is directed to meet the challenges of the peculiar circumstances in India which result in the anomaly that while Indian literature is one, though written in many languages, writers in one language hardly know anything of what is being written in a neighbouring language of the same country. It is therefore very necessary that Indian writers should come to know each other, across the barriers of language and script, and should appreciate the immense variety and complexity of their country's literary heritage.[7]

In the passage above, which was written a couple of years after the inception of the Akademi, the phrase "Indian literature is one, though written in many languages" is presented as a truism even as the practical difficulties that need to be overcome in order for the statement to hold true are being discussed. A few decades down the road, this "anomaly" does become a truism. For example, the prominent Indian poet and intellectual A. K. Ramanujan, in his influential essay "Is There an Indian Way of Thinking?" (1989), offers the Akademi's line as one among the catalog of answers to his title question. Ramanujan writes: "So, under the apparent diversity, there is really a unity of viewpoint, a single supersystem. Vedists see a Vedic model in all Indian thought. Nehru made the phrase 'unity in diversity' an Indian slogan. The Sahitya Akademi's line has been, 'Indian literature is one, though written in many languages.'"[8] While Ramanujan is not in full agreement with this statement, he does quote accurately from the Akademi's literature and gives this phrase the status of a foundational truth even as he sets it aside without any further consideration of the logic it espouses.

The Sahitya Akademi and national literature

By the late twentieth century the ideological positions adopted by the Sahitya Akademi may have hardened into clichés about "Indianness," but the early documents of the Sahitya Akademi contain powerful instances of the intellectual care and self-consciousness with which this institution was envisioned and these ideological positions were reached. Consider the choice of "Sahitya Akademi" as the name for this institution. The name is usually translated or interpreted as the "National Academy of Letters" in the official documentation on this institution. However, the title "Sahitya Akademi" was clearly chosen after some deliberation. The variant spelling and pronunciation of "Akademi" (pronounced phonetically as spelt) came from the Greek: specifically from Plato's Akademi established in the garden of the Greek hero Akademos whose name supplies the root of the English word "academy." Calling this cultural institution an "Akademi," as opposed to the more standardized "Academy," brilliantly allowed for an Indianized pronunciation of the term and also strategically bypassed the colonial baggage associated with English by directly accessing the Greek root of the English term. At the inaugural ceremony of the Sahitya Akademi which was held in the central hall of the Indian Parliament on March 12, 1954, S. Radhakrishnan, then Vice-President of the nation and Vice-Chair of the Sahitya Akademi's General Council, noted in his inaugural address:

> The phrase, Sahitya Akademi, combines two words: "Sahitya" is Sanskrit and "Academy" is Greek. This name suggests our universal outlook and aspiration. Sahitya is a literary composition; Academy is an assembly of men who are interested in the subject. So Sahitya Akademi will be an assembly of all those who are interested in creative and critical literature.[9]

Radhakrishnan went on to speak about the freedom of the spirit and mind that is "the first essential of any kind of creative literature."[10] In his comments, the worlds of ancient Greek and ancient Sanskrit are aligned and literature sustains this lofty realm of global interactions. Radhakrishnan continues:

> We have a saying that all *kavya* [literary composition; poetry] is for *visva sreyas*, for the good of the world. The literary artist has not merely to reflect the world, he has to redeem the world. He has not merely to portray the experience which he has, but he has to recreate that experience. He has to enter into solitude, glimpse the vision of truth, bring it down to earth, clothe it with emotions, carve it into words. That is the purpose of literature.[11]

Hence its literature will elevate India into this world discourse that is not bogged down by petty, worldly strife. Radhakrishnan ends his speech with a call to look beyond the "sickness and violence," the "confusion and conflict", the "economic greeds" of the times, for, as he says in conclusion:

> If we are to make any contributions to the literature of the world, if this Akademi is to serve any useful purpose, it has to recapture the dignity, the mission, the destiny of the spirit of this ancient race, try to reorient it and produce a new climate of ideas which will make for a universal republic of letters and a world society.[12]

Maulana Azad, in his comments on the same occasion, also speaks of the word "Akademi" in terms that stress the international consciousness behind this endeavor: "There is no other word in any Eastern or Western language which can convey the full flavor of the Academy. That is why we have resisted the temptation of a vain search for a new term and have kept the original word in its adapted form as 'akademi', in conformity with the requirements of Hindi pronunciation."[13] Azad's inaugural speech touches on several European national academies, and lingers on the French academy, established in 1635 by Louis XIV, which serves for him as the model that the Sahitya Akademi should follow especially in insuring that the highest literary standards are maintained. Once again, the British are passed over in this citation of ancient Greeks and the French in more recent times.

In comments made later in the same day, Nehru also called for a "broader" interpretation of "sahitya," matching that of "similar academies in other parts of the world."[14] In Azad's, Nehru's, and Radhakrishnan's narratives on the genesis and inspiration for the Sahitya Akademi, there is a deliberate evocation of the international arena of literature to which a claim is being made, but significantly there is no mention of similar British institutions in all of these speeches. India, these Akademi officials make clear, was not aping its erstwhile colonial master, but it was intent on establishing a literary institution that would be on a par with the best-known European institutions of art and literature. Interestingly, none of these speeches mentioned the proposal to establish a National Academy of Letters in India that the British Indian government had agreed to consider in 1944, which had served as a blueprint for the initial post-independence discussions that resulted in the establishment of these three main Akademies.[15]

The British may well be bypassed in this discussion of the Greek roots of the Sahitya Akademi, but the English language, the medium in which these speeches were made, was crucial to this lofty literary endeavor. In their respective speeches, both Nehru and Azad speak of the necessity of including Indian-authored literature in English in the Sahitya Akademi's projects as indicated in the passages that serve as epigraphs to this chapter. In his inaugural speech Azad elaborates on this very point:

> Tagore, who is the greatest poet of modern India, had been writing in Bengali ever since his childhood but his fame was not fully recognized even in his own province till the English version of the Gitanjali declared him as one of the greatest poets in the world. Mahatma Gandhi's contribution to national awakening and the achievement of independence is acknowledged universally. His writings in Gujarati are, however, only known to the people in Gujarat. It was his writing in English that enabled him to evoke a new political consciousness and give a revolutionary turn to Indian life. Similarly, Aurobindo Ghosh's claim to distinction rests upon the quality of his writing in English.[16]

English here is fully divorced from the erstwhile colonists and is instead the language in which Indians speak to each other and to the world at large. English was understood to be the facilitator of this assumption of India's rightful place in a global literary arena that the establishment of the Sahitya Akademi would accomplish.

In this scheme of gaining international legitimacy for Indian literature, English was to serve as a curatorial or editorial language, the gateway to and from the legitimate languages and literatures of India. This would be achieved in multiple ways. Primarily, the Akademi planned to publish several series of comparative critical studies of Indian literature and anthologies of Indian literatures, which would be written in English and translated into other languages. Some of these volumes are discussed below. Another plan was to embark on a massive translation program which would bring the diversity of the world's literature to the readers of Indian regional languages and to simultaneously translate the best of Indian regional literary texts into other Indian and foreign languages. Between 1955 and 1957 a great majority of the thirty-seven books published by the Akademi in the fourteen constitutionally recognized Indian languages (and two in English) were translations, and of these the majority were of Hindi literature into other Indian languages.[17] Foreign classics selected for translation into Indian languages in these early years included: from the Arabic – Al Biruni's *Kitab-ul-hind* and *One Thousand and One* Nights; from Chinese – the works of Confucius and Lao Tze; from English – selected Shakespearean plays (*Hamlet, Macbeth, Othello, King Lear*), Milton's *Areopagitica*, Whitman's *Leaves of Grass*, and Thoreau's *Walden*; from the French – works by Molière, Voltaire, and Victor Hugo; from the German – Goethe's *Faust*; from Italian – *The Prince*; from Japanese – Murasaki Shikubu's *Genji Monogatari* and a selection of No plays; from Latin – selections from Commentaries by Julius Caesar; from Norwegian – the plays of Ibsen; from Persian – selections from poets and the work of Jalaluddin Rumi; from Russian – the works of Tolstoy and Dostoevsky; and from Spanish, Cervantes's *Don Quixote*.[18] In parallel, a detailed list of Indian classics in fifteen Indian languages (excluding English) were recommended to UNESCO for translation into foreign languages.[19] Translations were a quick way of demonstrating the wealth of Indian literature to Indians themselves and to the world at large. Simultaneously this program of translating world classics into regional Indian languages ensured that it was not just the English-literate who would be adept at navigating foreign literatures.[20]

A busy schedule of national and international conferences has also kept up this interaction with foreign littérateurs and literary/cultural institutions around the globe.[21] Over the years, the Akademi has nominated (unsuccessfully) various Indian writers for the Nobel Prize in literature as another means of adding value to Indian literature.[22] The Akademi had gifted its publications to various visiting dignitaries, held book exhibitions, and participated in countless book fairs around the world.[23] In 1961, the Akademi became a member of the Union Academique International – an international association located in Brussels that creates avenues for interaction and joint projects between national academies in different nations around the globe.[24] Furthermore, the Akademi's constitution had provisions for inducting five "Honorary Fellows" from among "Literary persons of outstanding merit who are not nationals of India." Poet, President of Senegal, and theorist of "Négritude" Leopold Sangor was elected the first Honorary Fellow of the Sahitya Akademi in 1974.[25] This group was to complement the category of "Fellows of the Akademi" whose number was at no time to exceed twenty-one in total and who were to be living Indian writers of undisputed excellence – "the immortals of literature." S. Radhakrishnan was the first "Fellow of the Akademi" to be given this title in 1968 after he left the service of both the government and the Akademi. K. R. Srinivas Iyengar was the first scholar of Indian literature in English to be inducted into this select group of Fellows in 1985; Mulk Raj Anand was the first Indian English writer to be inducted in 1989 and R. K. Narayan the second Indian writer working in English to be inducted in 1994.[26]

A vital part of the rationale behind the setting up of the Sahitya Akademi was to establish an institutional base from which independent India could make its mark on a world literary community. This ability to imagine entry for Indians and their literature into a "universal republic of letters and a world society," as Radhakrishnan had phrased it, was the corollary to imagining and establishing an independent nation. As I have argued elsewhere, this cosmopolitan aspiration for entry into "world society" on equal terms is the flip-side of the elite colonial subject's self-confident demand for national liberation.[27] In fact such a stance, whereby anti-imperialism was expressed via an investment in Eurocentric universalisms, was a commonplace feature among the western-educated local elite all over the colonial world. And indeed in the mid-twentieth century, with India attaining its independence, for a fleeting moment it seemed that the world had changed so dramatically that a newly decolonized nation and its rich national literature would be given a place in a "universal republic of letters and a world society."

In her influential *La république mondiale des lettres* (1999) Pascal Casanova argues that there exists a literary world space which is relatively independent of the political divisions of the everyday world, and whose customs and rules are not influenced by, or at least are not reducible to, those of ordinary political space. In the preface to the English language translation of her book, *The World Republic of Letters* (2004), Casanova indicates that her purpose is to restore to literary studies "a point of view that has been obscured for the most part by the 'nationalization' of literatures and literary histories, to rediscover a lost transnational dimension of literature that for two hundred years has been reduced to the political and linguistic boundaries of nations."[28] It was their belief in and their ambition to stake their claim to just such a world community that the founders of the Sahitya Akademi put on display in their inaugural speeches. Thus, I will insist that aspirations for a national literature are also international aspirations at the very same time. In the selections from the inaugural speeches excerpted above, Casanova's arguments are validated but also complicated. On the one hand, these founders' vision for the Akademi makes clear that efforts to showcase a national literature were made with a view to gaining due respect in a world republic of letters as much as to establishing the contours of the hegemonic understanding of national identity within the newly created nation. But it was also well understood by these Indian leaders that this literary world space was not as independent of the political world as Casanova would make it out to be fifty years down the road. While Casanova acknowledges that there are "relations of force" and violence in this "international literary space," she insists that one must take "care not to confuse this domination with the forms of political domination, even though it may in many respects be dependent upon them."[29]

The founders of the Sahitya Akademi well understood that a non-European country that had just recently thrown off the yoke of imperial domination would have to marshal an illustrious and ancient tradition of literary activity, as well as display a contemporary ease with the literatures of its own region and of the world, in order to participate in these exalted international literary circles. Hence the Akademi's deliberate moves to translate in both directions, and to encourage literary interactions nationally and internationally. In the very name chosen for the Indian Academy of Letters, the Greek of the European past was shown to be highly compatible with Sanskrit, the Indian language with equal cultural capital and an even longer literary reach into the past.[30] Such claims about the wealth of "Indian culture" that equaled or surpassed that of the west had been routinely made since the mid-nineteenth century. For example, in his epilogue to his English translations of the *Ramayana* and *Mahabharata* published in the early twentieth century, R. C. Dutt had stressed the parallels between these two epics and Homer's *Odyssey* and *Iliad*: Ram and Odysseus are both wandering princes and the *Mahabharata* and *Iliad* are both epics of war.[31] The Sahitya Akademi was not simply evoking a glorious past, it was also insisting on its right to participation in a contemporary and global literary space.

Such a project would use English yoked with an ancient Indian language, Sanskrit, in order to, as Radhakrishnan puts it, "recapture the dignity, the mission, the destiny of the spirit of this ancient race."[32] It is in this context that we need to understand the tendency within their English language speeches of almost all of these leaders, from S. Radhakrishnan onwards, to occasionally pointedly use a Sanskrit word or phrase, especially when expressing a philosophical thought or a universalism. It is almost as if only a Sanskrit term would do justice to the universal concepts being evoked in these speeches – *vishwa sreyas, kavya, tejomayi vāk* – as shown in the excerpts cited in this chapter. Clearly there is an explicit Hinduization of this singular Indian past being called forth in these citations from Sanskrit, but they also serve to allude to the cachet of having an ancient linguistic and cultural past to lay claim to in an international arena – one that matches and was, according to some scholars, in collaboration with ancient Greek.[33] The use of Sanskritic terms in English utterances also rendered English into an Indian language. Alok Rai and others have noted that many Indian languages went though a Sanskritizing stage in which the languages were pruned of words that originated in English, Urdu, and Persian that were newly deemed "foreign" and Sanskrit equivalents were added wherever possible. In Hindi, for example, the frequently used word for language, "Zabaan" (a Persian/Urdu word that literarily meant "tongue" but which also connoted "language"), was replaced with the Sanskrit word "bhasa."[34] Sanskrit was the "Deva Bhasa," or the language of the gods, and the Devanagari, the script that was chosen for Hindi, was the script of the scriptures. Alok Rai notes that in this period, Hindi scholars worked hard to establish that "Hindi had a direct filial relationship with Sanskrit – eldest daughter to be precise, *jyeshtha putri*. This eldest daughter then takes precedence over other daughters – Bangla, Marathi, Gujarati."[35] The Sahitya Akademi absorbed and disseminated this Sanskrit-centric account of languages in India; Hindi was indeed the eldest daughter, and even English occasionally needed a Sanskrit word or two to express the more profound cultural notions. But despite the historical reach of Sanskrit and the parallels to be made with ancient Greek, English is nevertheless the language that is pressed into service to present an Indian familiarity and ease with the circuits of international literature, and more pragmatically to present the more "authentic" Indian literature in other languages to the world.

Perhaps the most significant fallout of this hyper-attentiveness to language (managing the discomfort with English despite the compulsion to use it; the advocacy of Hindi despite the resistance from other regional languages; the clamoring for recognition of minor languages) is that diversity is narrowed down to mean *only* linguistic diversity. Hence the slogan "unity in diversity" is interpreted by the Sahitya Akademi only in terms of bringing together the literary production in diverse languages. In its preoccupation with balancing the necessary reliance on English with a championing of Hindi and other "Indian" languages, a wider understanding of diversity has not been formulated except in very minimal gestures. From its very inception, the Akademi's carefully calibrated showcasing of "one Indian literature in many languages" has sidelined other important forms of diversity. For example, the bias toward male littérateurs is deeply engrained in the language of the constitution which refers to "men of letters" in its key passages. Curiously, in the more pedestrian situations, such as when listing the administrators required for various administrative posts in the Akademi, the constitution uses the gender-neutral word "persons." The various documents of the Akademi are strewn with categories such as "Men of Promise" and "Men of Achievements."[36] Looking at the various lists of Akademi honorees over the years, such as induction to the exclusive twenty-one-member circle of Akademi Fellows, it is immediately evident that there are very few writers who belong to minority religions or women who have been awarded this highest literary honor given by the Government of India. Vaikom M. Basheer (inducted in 1970) and Kaifi Azmi (in 2002) are the only two Muslim male writers who have been considered worthy of this honor. For the most part, the Fellows are upper-caste Hindu male authors, except a few female writers (Mahadevi Verma, Krishna Sobti, Nalapat Balamani Amma, Qurrantulain Hyder, and Ashapurna Devi). Needless to say, many women have won the Akademi awards for their writing and translation work, and so the expectation is perhaps that they will see themselves included in the category of "men of letters" and, as in other situations, everyone concerned was adept at reading women into the category of "men." It was only in 1996 that the Sahitya Akademi launched a forum called *Asmita* "for women writers, Dalits, and others seeking an identity of their own." Of course some of these writers had been included in the previous activities of the Akademi, but this conscious plan to create a forum for writers of promise and achievement who were not upper- and middle-caste and male was launched only in the mid-1990s.

This issue of a narrow understanding of diversity needs to be routed through the argument made earlier in this study that the slogan "unity in diversity" reverberated only within a small elite stratum of Indian society.[37] It might be useful to once again rehearse this argument in the context of the Sahitya Akademi's heavy investment in working toward a linguistic unity in diversity. As discussed earlier, "unity in diversity" was envisioned as the proper (modern, secular, patriotic) vision for an independent India that was populated by persons of different linguistic, regional, and religious groups. To share in this vision was to accept one's place in this undoubtedly uneven unity. The slogan was understood, even in the Akademi's reliance on it, as providing a primarily symbolic equity between all diverse groups. Of course it was patently clear that some languages (Hindi, for example) would be more important than others. Literatures which extended back into the ancient period (Tamil, Sanskrit) or had enjoyed a recent literary renaissance (Bengali in the nineteenth century) were clearly more valued than newer languages, those that were not backed up with territorial representation, or that represented territorial spaces that were politically marginal in independent India. But on the whole, the Sahitya Akademi's national anthologies and translations bestowed literary value even on marginal literatures. English was the medium in which this message of "unity in diversity" was most often expressed; this detail revealed the elite origins of this vision, but here too English was marshaled forth as a convenient, self-effacing medium that would voice Indian sentiments, imperfectly but with a wide national and international reach. As the literary scholar Srinivasa Iyengar had presciently noted in 1947, English, after independence, would be "shown its place... but it would be an important place."[38]

The Sahitya Akademi worked hard to fulfill the language mandate enshrined in the nation's constitution. And the men at the helm of the Akademi were drawn from the very same elite (upper-caste, male) class of intellectual leaders who led the nation in the independence movement. It is because this caste and gender nexus at the core of this institution is so pervasive that it has gone mostly unnoticed. Instead the more standard criticism leveled against the Akademi concerns the perception that there is extensive governmental interference in its operations. Interestingly, at the inaugural ceremonies, almost every speaker expressed both regret at and resignation to the fact that there was no ready alternative to governmental sponsorship of these institutions of Indian culture and art. Anxiety about the autonomy of the Sahitya Akademi, which was present since inception, continues to shadow its operations. Nehru's witty comment made in the course of inaugurating a film seminar organized by the Sangeet Natak Akademi in 1955 while he was both President of the Sahitya Akademi and Prime Minister of the nation bears repeating here: "As President of the Akademi I may tell you quite frankly I would not like the Prime Minister to interfere with my work."[39] This widely quoted comment succinctly acknowledges and assuages the anxiety about the autonomy of such government-sponsored cultural institutions. Furthermore, in all the early documentation of the Sahitya Akademi there are explicit statements of justification for the rationale behind choosing such high-ranking political figures as Nehru and Radhakrishnan for the highest offices in the Sahitya Akademi. Time and time again, it is stated that it is their great skill and experience *as writers* rather than their high rank in government office that earned these individuals this honor of shaping the agenda of the Akademi. But the general criticism was not about the multiple tasks assigned to these "lettered" national leaders, rather it was about the potential for governmental control of the arts via censorship or propaganda.[40]

The Sahitya Akademi has conscientiously fulfilled its mandate of working actively "for the development of Indian letters," but it has not shaken off the mistrust that its close association with governmental policy has generated for skeptics. The proximity of "poetry and power" and the general ambivalence about this proximity has been kept in the spotlight all through the history of this organization. Concern about its autonomy serves as the driving question behind the self-assessment of the Sahitya Akademi as written by D. S. Rao in *Five Decades: A Short History of Sahitya Akademi*

(1954–2004). Commissioned in 2003 and released in 2004 to commemorate fifty years of the organization, Rao's study offers an impressive and mostly impartial account of the establishment of and challenges faced by this "Indian Academy of Letters" and has served as a primary source for the issues discussed in this chapter. Rao, a retired Akademi official when he compiled this book, writes with a clear and critical eye. His comprehensive account is in no way a panegyric to the institution and focuses primarily on examining the relationship between "poetry and power." Rao's assessment, after a careful consideration of five decades of this institution's operations, is that in all its workings the Sahitya Akademi has self-consciously and successfully kept the Indian government out of its operations.[41] Regardless, the harshest criticism the Akademi has faced is that it is not autonomous in its decision-making and it has been repeatedly characterized as no more than yet another department in a lumbering, nepotistic, and corrupt government machine.[42]

In his comments at the inauguration of the Sahitya Akademi, the Minister for Education, Maulana Azad, presented the government's involvement as no more than "a curtain-raiser" even as he distanced himself from Nehru's and other leaders' regret that a governmental initiative rather than a literary body or individuals in the field was instrumental in setting up this academy. Azad declared:

> Today there is hardly any country in the Western world that does not have one or more National Academies. All these academies were established by Governments under letter patent of the Sovereign or by legislation. There was, therefore, no reason why Government of India should not take the initiative for the establishment of the academies. In fact, if we had waited for the Academy to grow from below we might have had to wait till the Greek Kalends.[43]

In his comments at the Akademi's General Council meeting later that day, Nehru elaborated: "speaking to Maulana Saheb I did say that in a field of this kind affecting literature, language and all that, I was a little afraid of the very heavy hand of the government in all these things. To impose things by an order of government is not right."[44] Interestingly, Nehru went on to mention the process by which Hindi became the national language as his example of such heavy-handedness and ended this train of thought with the insistence that English, despite not being included in the Indian constitution, be included in the Sahitya Akademi's program of activities.

As the heated debates in the Indian Constituent Assembly over the selection of the national language had made clear, the whole business of language was a deeply fraught issue in the early years of the nation.[45] The tensions clearly seeped into the Sahitya Akademi and into the setting of its agenda. Note, for instance, the subtle distinction that Nehru draws between the "languages *of* India" and the "languages *in* India" (of which English is his prime example) in the passage from his speech that serves as the second epigraph to this chapter. When the Sahitya Akademi was established in 1954, it was to work with literature written in fifteen Indian languages that were at the time recognized in the Eighth Schedule of the Indian constitution as formulated in 1950. English was not (and still is not) one of the now eighteen Indian languages recognized by the Indian constitution. However, at the second meeting of the Akademi's General Council, which was held on March 13, 1954, a day after the Akademi was inaugurated, the council revised its language policy to include English.[46] Hence, from *almost* the very start, in the Sahitya Akademi, English was legitimized and recognized in a manner in which it has never been acknowledged in the Indian constitution.

Much of the antagonism and anxiety about the place of English in the Sahitya Akademi's workings remained subterranean over the years. Yet it is visible in many of the ordinary memos, in the award decisions, in controversies that have arisen periodically about specific publications or actions of the Akademi. For example, the hesitation over giving Indian writing in English its due can be glimpsed, in retrospect, in the record of annual awards that the Akademi granted for the best literary writing in each language. While awards were given for the best book in twelve languages in 1955, and to twelve books in twelve languages again in 1957, and so on each year, the first book written in English to win an award was *The Guide* by R. K. Narayan in 1960. Interestingly, in the period between 1955 and 2007, English has been second only to Kashmiri as the language which has gone for the maximum number of years with no award given for outstanding writing. In comparison with the sixteen years without an award for writing in English, awards in Hindi have been given every year since 1955 except one, in Bengali every year except three, and so on. No awards were given for Sanskrit in thirteen years, and awards for this language in the first five years were given to texts on Sanskrit literature and culture but written in Hindi or English.[47] It is worth mentioning here that India's most prestigious private literary award, the Jnanpith Award, which has been presented annually since 1965 and is administered by a private organization, the Bharatiya Jnanpith Trust (established in 1943), is only given for work written in the languages that are listed in the Eighth Schedule of the Indian constitution. Consequently, there has never been an award for an Indian English literary work. Ironically, the selection of the award-winning work is made by a jury who usually read the nominated works in English translation if they are not written in or translated into the jury members' mother-tongues or a language they are familiar with. Hence, in her consideration of translation from and into Gujarati, Rita Kothari notes that when the 2001 Jnanpith award was not given to the well-known Gujarati writer Rajendra Shah, Gujarati literati complained it was because few of his works had been translated into English.[48]

Award selection in *all* the languages in the Sahitya Akademi was and continues to be a fraught and hotly contested process, but choosing worthy recipients seemed especially hard in the English language category. It could not have helped that an English language writer of the stature of Bhabani Bhattacharya recommended his own work for the award in both 1955 and 1956 or that, in later years, prominent critics like Khushwant Singh often found no English book worthy of the award.[49] It would be useful to consider one set of justifications proffered for the refusal to recommend Indian English writers for this award. Hiren Mukerjee, a barrister with a law degree from London, famous orator (in English and Bengali), life-long communist, and member of Parliament from 1952, wrote to Krishna Kripalani in 1963: "Please do not think me rude, but I cannot honestly think of suggesting, for the Rs. 5000/- Sahitya Akademi award, any book in English by an Indian author, which is, to quote the conditions governing the award 'an outstanding contribution in the Language and Literature to which it belongs.'"[50] He goes on to amplify, that while R. K. Narayan had received the award in the recent past,

> even he, however, cannot in my view (which some may think perverse) be said to have made an "outstanding contribution" to English Literature. Perhaps you will not agree, but if I were in authority I would scrap the Akademi award for English. I would do so not with any animus against the English language, but because I have such a great respect for it that I can hardly conceive of anything that we write in English to be outstanding in English standards.[51]

While Hiren Mukerjee's hesitation was based on his exquisite standards that no Indian writer could meet, this demand to end the annual awards for writing in English was made at regular intervals with less lofty justifications. Most recently, in 2002, while the BJP (Bharatiya Janata Party, a Hindu nationalist party) was in power and Atal Bihari Vajpayee, a Hindi poet of some repute, was Prime Minister, the "Hindi Consultative Committee" of the Government of India advised the Akademi to stop issuing the annual award for best writing in English because this language was not on the language list of the Eighth Schedule of the constitution. In response the Akademi noted that since such awards were also given in other languages such as Dogri, Maithili, and Rajasthani which were also not on the Eighth Schedule, the Hindi committee's advice could not be heeded.[52] Hence, the questioning of the legitimacy of English in the workings of the Akademi extended into the twenty-first century and continued to be linked to anxiety about the fate of Hindi and other languages.

II

This section focuses on some of the Sahitya Akademi's early published work to examine the means by which the problematic reliance on English was subsumed by the massive task assigned to works in this language. Projects in this language were to curate the government's agenda for Indian literature. The Sahitya Akademi's primary literary journal, *Indian Literature*, was launched in 1957 and is published in English. The Akademi's Sanskrit journal, *Samskrita Pratibha*, was launched in 1959. A Hindi language literary journal, *Samakaleen Bharateeya Sahitya*, was launched by the Akademi in 1980. The Sahitya Akademi indeed funded projects that called for the strengthening of national unity through literary activities in other Indian languages, besides English, but when such activities had to be coordinated through *all* Indian languages, the project was usually routed through English. Depending on approval of the English edition, the end product was translated into Hindi and other Indian languages.[53] However, as an examination of selected English language works will show, these literary endeavors did not always follow state dictates. There are many slips between the literary and the national even in so regulated a site as the Sahitya Akademi. This is evident in the Akademi's very first publication in English which was titled *Contemporary Indian Literature* (1957), a collection of fifteen short essays that provided histories of the literatures in all fourteen constitutionally recognized languages and in English.[54]

Contemporary Indian Literature begins with a single-page foreword by S. Radhakrishnan, who was at the time Vice-President of the nation, a senior Akademi officer, and a littérateur of high standing. His two-paragraph foreword reiterates the main tenets of the Akademi's position on Indian literature. Radhakrishnan writes:

There is a unity of outlook as the writers in different languages derive their inspiration from a common source and face more or less the same kind of experience, emotional and intellectual. Our country has never been insensitive to ideas which come from abroad but gives to all of them its own peculiar turn and imprint.

Literature is a sacred instrument and through the proper use of it we can combat the forces of ignorance and prejudice and foster national unity and world community. Literature must voice the past, reflect the present and mould the future. Inspired language, *tejomayi vāk*, will help readers to develop a humane and liberal outlook on life, to understand the world in which they live, to understand themselves and plan sensibly for their future.

I hope this small book will give to its readers an account of our travail of mind and heart, our hopes and aspirations.[55]

Radhakrishnan's foreword is a lyrical restatement of the governmental policy as manifest in the establishment of the Akademi. His main stress is on the "unity of outlook" that will be on display in the essays and the "national unity and world communion" that literature will produce through its "proper use." He does not spell out what the "common source" that all Indian literatures draw their inspiration from might be, but his comments seem to indicate that the referent is well known at least to the first of the two readerships for the book. This first readership is the Indian readership that could use the book to get to know themselves and "plan sensibly" for their future by developing a "humane and liberal outlook," and the second is an international readership who could learn of "our" travails, hopes, and aspirations from this collection.

Contrary to what one might expect after such an introduction that presents literature as a sacred instrument, what follows is not a selection of literary texts but brief critical essays that outline the histories of fifteen literary traditions. It seems that a national literature that shares a "unity of outlook" could not be put on display via a literary selection; instead, a set of critical essays was deemed the better vehicle for presenting this common theme that would cover disparate texts in multiple languages. The literature itself, as I have argued in all the chapters of this book, usually had multiple concerns that may have very little in common with official nationalism or even with each other, and so the task of yoking literature to a singular national tradition falls to literary criticism.

The essays in *Contemporary Indian Literature* instruct the putative reader of the major developments within a specific literature and provide a selective, annotated list of authors to read. These essays were commissioned

The Sahitya Akademi and national literature

from established experts in each of the literary fields represented. It is not clear as to what exact instructions were given to these scholars as they embarked on their assigned task. Nevertheless, it would be useful to refer to the comprehensive set of rules compiled by the Akademi's first secretary, Krishna Kripalani, for the *book-length* literary histories that were also commissioned by the Akademi in the 1950s. *Contemporary Indian Literature* serves as a handy preview of this ambitious multi-volume literary histories project that Kripalani's instructions were written for. In fact some of the essay-length histories in this book were authored by the same scholars who went on to write the book-length histories of the literature in their particular language of expertise.[56] The very first paragraph in Kripalani's "Note on the Proposed Histories of Literature" concedes that this series of "standard histories of Indian Literatures" is needed to enable "readers in one language to know something of the creative elements in literature in other Indian languages. The differences in language and script have tended to cloud the basic unity of Indian literature as a whole which needs to be emphasized in as many ways as possible."[57] The general tenor of the instructions is that the tone, organization, analyses, and selections should all aim to "illustrate the cultural unity of India" and toward achieving this end, it was firmly stated, there should be no belittling of other languages, religions, or regions.[58] Then come the specific instructions as to length, use of jargon, and writing for a lay audience, etc. The "Note" suggests that whether the history is written in the language concerned or in English, it should be easily translatable into other Indian languages.[59] Kripalani urges a uniform pattern in organizing the materials: each history should begin with an introduction that dates and describes the origin of the language, and then explicitly link this origin to Sanskrit and Prakrit.[60] This requirement would of course make Indian writing in English and Urdu less "Indian" – but their "foreignness" was in any case never to be overcome. Kripalani also stressed that the literature is to be presented through the categories of the ancient, medieval, and modern periods with the understanding that the length of discussion in each of these three periods would differ from language to language.[61] In the ancient and medieval periods, "undue stress on religious and sectarian controversies might be avoided," according to Kripalani's note, and the modern period may be "assumed to begin with the rise of British rule in India and the introduction of the Printing press" and "should be treated with particular sympathy and understanding."[62] Kripalani also calls for "impartial evaluation" of the contemporary scene, though he acknowledges that would be difficult. He further specifies that

"No school or branch of modern literature should be ignored because of the ideological content of its writings or because of the experimental nature of the forms employed."[63]

Each essay in *Contemporary Indian Literature* reveals itself to be differently focused and organized. Each literary tradition has its own rhythm and high points that are mirrored in the different organization for each of the essays. Kripalani's well-meaning instructions for a smooth and orderly narration of multiple literatures developing from the same source and covering the same intellectual and emotional terrain simply could not be followed. Thus this alphabetically arranged collection begins with an essay on Assamese literature that is organized in the following sections: Introduction, Modern, Early Romantics, Post-War Verse, Drama, the Novel, Short Story, and Essay. The essay on Bengali literature is simply organized under Introduction, Nineteenth Century, and Twenteeth Century. The essay on Indian literary writing in English is organized by a very specific time-frame: an introduction that is followed by sections marked by the following dates: 1820–1870, 1870–1900, 1900–1920, 1920–1947, and after independence.

Judging by the contents of the different essays it would seem that the "the basic unity of Indian literature as a whole," if indeed it existed, was still "clouded over", to use Kripalani's metaphor. For instance, some essays give deep consideration to folk and oral traditions, others do not. Some essays extend their consideration of literature in the modern period to writing for radio and film, others do not. Some essays discuss writing by women in a sustained fashion in a separate section of the article (Sindhi, Marathi), others include no more than a minimal discussion of female writers (Gujarati). Still others do not distinguish between writers by gender, with both male and female writers being discussed at any given historical moment (Urdu). Children's literature receives serious attention in the account of writing in Sindhi, but is missing from most other essays. Humor writing, journalism, etc. are differently weighted in different essays. While the national movement and achievement of independence gets some mention in most of the essays, this event seemed to have had varying resonance in the specific literary worlds described in these essays. The trauma of Partition is directly linked to literary production only in the specific languages (Urdu, Sindhi, Punjabi) most effected by the creation of West and East Pakistan. That the essay on Hindi literature does not consider the impact of Partition in any fashion speaks eloquently to the language politics of the post-independence years. After decades of agitation toward this goal, Hindi in India was consolidated into the national language precisely as a result of the trauma of Partition. It ousted from the competition for national language Hindustani, which was an amalgam of Hindi and Urdu, precisely because of the distrust of such hybrid formations especially after Partition. Partition created seemingly unbridgeable rifts between the religious communities and solidified the alignment of specific languages with specific religious communities and nations: Urdu/Muslim/Pakistan and Hindi/Hindu/India. In India, Hindi had attained national prominence after independence and thus the essay on Hindi literature did not have losses to catalog after Partition.[64]

Interestingly, the essay on Urdu literature in *Contemporary Indian Literature* does not distinguish Pakistani from Indian writers in the post-independence period and this in itself disrupts the concept of contemporary "Indian" literature. Clearly no historically accurate scholarly essay on Urdu literature could conjure up an exclusively "Indian" (as opposed to a subcontinental) trajectory for literary production in this language; hence being true to the literature's history required stepping out of the national narrative. Furthermore, Kripalani's instructions had suggested that in their introductory section, such scholarly accounts could buttress the fundamental "Indianness" of the literature under investigation by tracing the language's origins to Sanskrit and Prakrit. Urdu, unlike the other languages in the book (besides English), is not presented as having roots in Sanskrit or Prakrit, a feature that again marks it as outside this Akademi umbrella of "Indianness."

There was no place for pessimism or discontent in *Contemporary Indian Literature*, a book project that was to showcase the many vibrant literatures of India, all of which were to be braided into one impressive cultural tradition. For instance, the essay on Sanskrit ends with a section titled "Future of Sanskrit," which gives several suggestions for ensuring that this language has a literary future. This plan for the future in itself obliquely gestures toward the overwhelming difficulty of sustaining the use of this language into the future. V. Raghavan, author of this essay, calls for "purifying" the language, so that it "should smell less of English and be more in conformity with the genius of the language," and thereby "re-emerge into a creative language, adding to its long record, fresh achievements."[65]

All through the various essays one can see signs of the reshaping of literary history and compromises being advocated in order to ensure that a language and literature would be considered a worthy claimant to space within the national literary arena. Some languages had thriving literatures that were not necessarily "united" even within their own literary trajectory, and while such divergences had proved to be no obstacle to literary reputation or production in the past, after independence a streamlined profile was called for. For example, as Khushwant Singh notes in his essay,

Punjabi was born in the works of Muslim sufis and Sikh gurus, had served three different religions (Sikhism, Islam, Hinduism), and was written in three different scripts (Arabic, Devanagari, and Gurmukhi). And yet, after independence, Singh argues, given "the recognition of Urdu in Pakistan and the patronage of Hindi in India," the survival of post-independence literary production in Punjabi would "depend on Sikh writers using only Gurmukhi."[66] Singh acknowledges that much will be lost in the streamlining of Punjabi that he proposes, but he insists that the regeneration of Punjabi literature in the post-independence period would depend on imposing these "restrictive measures" and in convincing Sikh writers like Rajinder Singh Bedi to shift from writing his "absolutely first-rate stories" in Urdu to writing in Punjabi.[67] As Khushwant Singh sees it, in the postcolonial period, Urdu would be tended to by Muslim writers and Hindi by Hindus, and so the task of writing Punjabi and in the Gurmukhi script would fall to Sikh writers. Gone were the days of Munshi Premchand, who barely twenty years earlier had presented his daily writing rhythm as one in which he wrote in Urdu in the morning and in Hindi in the afternoon. As Singh's essay on Punjabi literature amply demonstrated, by mid-century, choosing which language one wrote in was no longer just an aesthetic decision but one with deep political implications.

In several instances, fashioning a literary history also required realignment in the link between language, literature, and territory. Some languages, like Sindhi in independent India which had been separated from the region of Sind which was now in Pakistan, were thus rendered instantly vulnerable. But under the linguistic division of India, other literatures were instated more securely within the new nation. Thus, for example, when Kannada speaking districts were gathered into the state of Karnataka, literature in Kannada had a newly gathered geographical space to speak from. V. K. Gotak, the author of the essay on Kannada literature, begins his discussion with this geographical realignment that consolidated the strengths of literature in this language: "The newly formed Karnataka State includes parts that were formerly in the Bombay, Madras and Hyderabad states and the states of Madras and Coorg. The new State has an area of about 85,000 sq-miles and a population of about twenty-five million."[68] In the case of the essay on Hindi literature, S. H. Vatsyayan, the essayist, ends the discussion of whether Hindi and its various dialects had been historically the dominant literary language in north India with: "It is not necessary to go further into this intricate and controversial matter: today at any rate Hindi is incontrovertibly the language of about 150,000,000 people and its region comprises roughly half the territory of India."[69] Thus the details of the division of independent India into states on the basis of linguistic conformity meant that different literatures could lay claim to space within the national literary arena with differing levels of confidence that was directly proportional to their share of the actual geographical space.

Also notable is the differing degree of attention paid to religion in each of the essays. In some cases, as in the essay on Punjabi literature, the connections between literature, language, and religion are presented as central to writing the literary history. But for the most part the assumed religion from which secular and devotional literatures arise is Hinduism. What remains unspoken in these essays is a discussion in any form of caste background or affiliations of the writers or even of the "Indian cultural traditions" under review. Hence there is no opportunity to understand the caste underpinnings of this singular national Indian literature that is manifest in multiple languages. As discussed earlier in this book, references to caste are few and far between in the modern literary discourses of the post-independence era because any discussion of caste is viewed as a throwback to an archaic world that is now pushed firmly into the past by upper-caste writers who control the national public discourse.

Despite the seriousness with which the charge of writing an impartial history of one's literature is taken up by scholars who contributed to *Contemporary Indian Literature*, each of the essays is passionate and opinionated; the scholars are ruthlessly dismissive of trends and literary figures of whom they are not enamored and lyrically praiseful of those who meet their approval. Despite Kripalani's suggestion that "derogatory criticism and rapturous eulogy should both be avoided," both were equally apparent in the essays. Khushwant Singh writes on the Punjabi poet Amrita Pritam in his characteristically patronizing fashion: "Popularity has come Amrita's way somewhat easily and she frequently seeks the applause at the cost of quality."[70] An instance of biased writing that led to serious action entailed the essay on Hindi literature which had been written by the well-known writer S. H. Vatsyayan (pen name "Ajneya"). When the first edition of *Contemporary Indian Literature* was published, this essay met with immediate criticism from Hindi littérateurs in Delhi for two reasons: first, the excessive self-praise and second, because of Vatsyayan's highly selective narration of the modern period in which he belittled the contributions of the Progressive writers and of those who did not belong to the major groups (Chhāyāvāda, Pragativāda). The self-praise was seen as egregious because Vatsyayan wrote the essay under his given name and referenced himself in the essay only by his pen name "Ajneya." In the essay, "Ajneya" was presented as leading the writers with the most potential for excellent work into the future. As was noted by Ramdhari Sinha (pen name Dinkar), a member of the Akademi's Hindi advisory board and himself a leading Hindi writer, the problem with the essay was the difficulty of distinguishing between scholarly freedom and the responsibility of writing a commissioned essay for "official or semi-official bodies."[71] Dinkar, in his letter of complaint to the Akademi, suggested that "Agyeya" (variant English spelling) be pasted at the end of the writer's name in all the available copies of the first edition of the book so that rather than censor his work, his self-praise would be made explicit. Dinkar was of the opinion that no deletions should be accepted and that rather a "post-script" written by the Hindi advisory board should be added to the essay. This campaign of criticism which was aired in the national daily newspapers compelled Ajneya to cut parts of his essay before the book appeared in Hindi translation and in its second English edition. Significantly, the essay's virulent anti-Urdu and anti-Islamic statements were not considered problematic and remained unaltered in subsequent editions.[72] Clearly when it came to discussions of Urdu and Islam, there was some leeway in the application of the general caution against, as Kripalani had put it in his instructions, causing "hurt [to] the religious sensibilities of any sect or community."[73]

Most of the essays in *Contemporary Indian Literature* end on a note of anticipation of the coming of a new dawn of literary production. For example, in his conclusion to the essay on literature in Kannada, after describing eight groups of writers with dramatically different orientations in the contemporary period, Gotak writes:

> But a close scrutiny is sure to reveal the fact that the contribution of all these schools meets and mingles and is unified in a rich and new life, a new and complex individual and social awareness... But there is a unity in this multiplicity and that is the unity of the new and complex symphony that Indian life is going to attain.
>
> It cannot be claimed that modern Kannada literature has sounded all the depths of this complexity or that it has carried sensation [*sic*] into the heart of all knowledge. It is towards a new synthesis that our literature is evolving today, as everywhere else in India...[74]

The sentiment seems to be that a new synthesis was surely evolving and that literature in Kannada would make its contribution to the Indian symphony which was being composed. All literatures, we are to believe, were moving toward this unity.

Ultimately, one might argue the similarities or differences in the trajectory of each literary tradition mapped in this book do not decisively prove or disprove the "unity of outlook" or the "common source" of inspiration that Radhakrishnan claimed for Indian literature in his foreword to the book. What is significant is that such unity in diversity was being actively claimed as the official policy of the Sahitya Akademi and echoed at varying pitches and with some distortion by each of the essay writers in the collection. Despite the disagreements over specific essays, the collection was considered very successful in that it enjoyed record sales of five thousand copies in the first two years, which was unusually high for a non-fiction book in English. Consequently an English language second edition was published in 1959 and the book was translated into several Indian languages. When it was published in translation in other languages (Hindi, Dogri, Kannada, Malayalam, Marathi, Punjabi, Tamil, and Telugu) the Akademi added a publisher's foreword that stated that while the authors were "originally selected by the SA and each one is a distinguished writer in his field," there had been criticisms and challenges to the opinions expressed. The statement noted that the opinions expressed in each article belonged to the authors and did not have the Akademi's "endorsement."[75] Thus the claim of autonomy prevailed and at the same time authors were tacitly expected to undertake revisions and rewriting if their views were deemed objectionable.

III

To celebrate the twenty-fifth anniversary of Indian independence, in 1973 the Sahitya Akademi published a companion volume to *Contemporary Indian Literature* discussed above. Titled *Indian Literature since Independence* (1973) this English language book brought together twenty essays on twenty literatures in as many languages. K. R. Srinivasa Iyengar, who was the leading scholar of Indian English literary criticism from the 1940s onward and Vice-President of the Sahitya Akademi from 1969 to 1977, both edited and wrote the introduction to this collection of essays. As with *Contemporary Indian Literature*, many of the writers of individual essays were also the authors of the Akademi's Literary History book series.

Among Srinivasa Iyengar's many prior accomplishments was his work for the Indian branch of PEN established in 1933 by the theosophist Sophia Wadia. As discussed at great length in Chapter 1, in the pre-independence years, Indian PEN took the position that their literary curatorial work would prove Indians to be a united force and worthy of being granted national independence, and toward this end, they began the publication of a series of English language books that showcased each of the literatures in Indian languages.[76] Srinivasa Iyengar wrote *Indo-Anglian Literature* (1943) as part of this PEN series and this book was later considered by many scholars to inaugurate the consideration of Indian literary writing in English as a legitimate field of study. Like Iyengar, several of the other literary scholars who were associated with Indian PEN in the pre-independence days gravitated to, or were recruited by, the Sahitya Akademi to take charge of the literary projects such as those discussed in this chapter. In fact there was some correspondence between Sophia Wadia and Krishna Kripalani in the early years of the Akademi concerning coordinating the activities of the two institutions.[77] As discussed in Chapter 1, Iyengar had also been one of the chief architects of the first All-India Writers' Conference organized by Indian PEN in 1945 which had as its theme "The Development of Indian Literature as a Uniting Force." This conference was attended by leading Indian public figures of the period, and many of the ideals and actions that became foundational to governmental policy in the realm of literature and culture, and to the Sahitya Akademi, were set in place at this conference. When the conference proceedings for this monumental event were published in 1947, the document was edited and the introduction was written by none other than Srinivasa Iyengar.[78]

What the career of a scholar like Srinivasa Iyengar demonstrates is that in the period of transition from colony to new nation, there was not much distance between the new governmental policy on literature and culture and the critical writing of elite public intellectuals; all shared a common vision of facilitating the unity of "Indian culture" and showcasing its fitness for inclusion in a global literary arena. Given his established expertise in the field, Srinivasa Iyengar was assigned the chapter on Indian writing in English in the previously discussed Sahitya Akademi publication, *Contemporary Indian Literature*. Iyengar thus came to the task of editing and introducing the 1973 publication of the Sahitya Akademi, *Indian Literature since Independence*, after many years of working closely with national leaders and with other leading literati, and after being central in the official and non-governmental efforts to, as he had written in 1947, "emphasiz(e) the cardinal unity of Indian culture, not withstanding the many languages and literatures that flourished in our midst."[79] And the task of writing the chapter on Indian literature in English in this 1973 collection was assigned to the Aurobindo Ghosh scholar, Prema Nandakumar, who was Iyengar's daughter.

The Sahitya Akademi and national literature 163

In his introduction to the 1973 collection, Iyengar is less unequivocal than he was in 1947 about this "cardinal unity" of Indian culture or, rather, more willing to question this truism. Unlike Radhakrishnan's lyrical two-paragraph foreword to *Contemporary Indian Literature*, Iyengar's introduction is a lengthy text that deliberates on the past and the present, on literature and film, and on the culturally and linguistically hybrid everyday life of Indians. Iyengar begins with an account of the languages heard on his daily morning walks on the marina in Madras (now Chennai):

> As I take a walk on the marina in Madras, I hear snatches of Tamil, Telugu, English, Hindi, Malayalam, Kannada, Marathi, Gujarati, Bengali... It is said of the Tamil mystic poet, Tirumoolar, that when he traversed the country fifteen hundred years ago from Himalaya to Kanyakumari, he found that while the people spoke several languages the same heart spoke through them all.[80]

Iyengar's introduction casually sets the scene with his morning walk (possibly in Mylapore, the Tamil Brahmin neighborhood) in Madras, with south Indian languages (and a few others) heard on the marina, and a Tamil poet from antiquity. And from this location, too, the essential unity of Indian literature ("the same heart" speaking through all the languages) is evident. Yet Iyengar's introduction goes on to significantly deconstruct this tried and tested cover story by refusing to smoothly knit together the twenty literatures that his edited book surveys. He asks: "Is 'Indian literature' no more than the sum of these twenty literatures or is it rather a single literature with divers [sic] manifestations?"[81] His meandering essay toys with this question with almost Zen-like detachment. Later in the introduction, in his discussion of poetry in post-independence India, he writes: "There is always the risk of oversimplification to the point of near-falsification in all attempts at making sweeping reviews of poetic activity in twenty different languages over a period of 25 years of stress and change."[82]

After some evocative writing on the difficulty of making "exact evaluation" of the "impact of historical events – like the coming of independence, the death of a great national leader, or the eruption of war – on a literature," Iyengar goes on to carefully make inexact evaluations of the same.[83] National independence and Partition, Iyengar suggests, are the crucial formative influences on postcolonial Indian cultural texts. However, his introduction repeatedly balances the impact of Indian events with that of world events on the contours of the many literary works produced after independence. For example, he muses that:

> Perhaps, the second world war, the Jap [*sic*] invasion, the Bengal hungers, the fall of Hitler, the unleashing of the atomic bomb and the logistics of the cold war had as much to do with the moulding of our consciousness as the coming of independence and the trauma of partition.[84]

A couple of pages further into the introduction, Iyengar circles back to elaborate on these national and international issues that impinge on the Indian writer's consciousness:

> While independence, partition, the influx of refugees, the pangs of rehabilitation, Gandhiji's martyrdom, the decline of standards in public life, the simmering crisis in the national character, all offer ready material to the writers in free India, they were also exposed to certain influences from abroad. Marx, Lenin and Freud on the one hand, Eliot, Joyce and Gorki on the other, were not unknown in the thirties or even earlier, but after 1947 their influence was more marked and widespread.[85]

The discussion covers the same parameters of early Akademi publications discussed above, for Iyengar goes on to write about an "Indian sensibility" that is visible in the "best Indian critical writing" and which is attuned to Indian as well as to world events.[86] Like earlier Akademi intellectuals, he argues that reaching a "universal aesthetic" should be the goal of literary and literary critical endeavors. Hence this "newly awakened Indian sensibility" manifest in the critical discourses is perfectly compatible with the "first stirrings of a global human sensibility, partly including and partly exceeding Western, Oriental and African sensibilities."[87]

On the whole, and especially in comparison with earlier Akademi-sponsored editorial commentary, Iyengar's introduction offers only a gently prescriptive framework within which to read the essays that follow. Perhaps the fact that the nation and the Akademi had flourished in the years since both were established lent some measure of equanimity to his pronouncements. And as a result, perhaps, some of the earlier urgency to depict the various literatures as walking in lock-step toward this vision of one national culture was eased in this volume marking the twenty-fifth anniversary of Indian independence. Also, perhaps the heterogeneity of the reports on individual literatures in the volume made it almost impossible for a meticulous scholar like Iyengar to insist more vigorously on a singular narrative frame that would encompass all that followed his introduction. But Iyengar does suggest that winning national independence is the watershed event of the past twenty-five years and as such has left an indelible mark on postcolonial Indian cultural texts.

The very first essay, on Assamese literature, however, contradicts Iyengar by beginning with the assertion that national independence was "a political event and not a cultural turning point."[88] Navakanta Barua writes that when Sylhet, which constituted the largest Bengali speaking area of British Assam, was rendered into East Pakistan, many linguistic patriots in Assam celebrated the end of what they had seen as Bengali domination in the literary field. These patriots believed that "a purely Assamese Assam, language and literature would flourish" as a result of the departure of a million Bengali speakers, but this did not happen. Barua explains that except for this "strangely exclusive and negative" linguistic patriotism, the Assamese literary world was oriented away from nationalism. Patriotism, Barua writes, was "not the immediate reaction of the creative artists. It was not the keynote of the post-independence world of letters . . . it was hardly a note at all."[89] Instead, Assamese literature was still in the grip of a movement that had grown in the wake of World War II, one that was concerned with "the socio-political emancipation" of its people. Barua clarifies again that the Assamese literati's "political views were of course not national, but based on class struggle"[90] Barua concludes his essay with this assessment:

> The variety and the colour of the writing of this period would not have been possible had the creative artists been busy trying to forge a "national will" to fight the British Raj or continued in the old decadent romantic tradition. National liberty gave the artists a sense of respite to think of other values of life. There had been a romance in the national struggle and in the search for Indianness – but when independence became a reality it made us feel that we are men and not merely Indian.[91]

In Barua's declarations, literary nationalism is rendered into an idea whose moment had come and gone; past its expiry date, such insistence on the national would be a creative straightjacket. His claim to be part of humanity and not "merely Indian" is perhaps the resistance that literary discourse from a geographically marginal state in the northeast corner of the country might offer to totalizing schemes. After all, to belong within such schemes, marginal language groups have to erase much of their identity. But Barua's essay also shows how the insistent declaration of the early years of the Akademi (and of the nation) of being both human and Indian was now confidently altered, twenty-five years after independence, into a claim to be "men and not merely Indian."

The essay that follows in this alphabetically organized collection is on Bengali literature, which is commonly viewed as the most culturally hegemonic of all the regional literatures and languages in India. However, even within this report on Bengali literature since independence, there is a critical distancing from the doctrine of a uniform national literature spurred into production by the struggle for independence. The essay on Bengali literature in this collection, written by Alokeranjan Dasgupta, begins by categorically refusing the impact of national independence on Bengali literature: "A student of Sociology may legitimately ask whether Indian Independence had no instructive bearing on our writers. If one had to answer this in one word, it might be a plain 'no.' But that would be a case of complacent generalization. For one thing, Bengali creative writers of the day do not subscribe to any *a priori* critical criteria."[92] Dasgupta goes on to say, "The independence of India has not brought any element of bellicose patriotism in our writings. On the other hand, a world-vision in literature has been cultivated by the leading writers of the day. There have been bold attempts to reconstruct Tagore's concepts of world literature."[93] He continues: "Bengali writers when asked, would not particularly focus on the significance of Independence for their thematic or spiritual development."[94] Dasgupta insists that for some Bengali writers, World War II was the bigger influence, for others it was Tagore's writing. He adds that one has to take into account the literature published in Bangladesh as well as in India to really understand Bengali literary trends and changes since independence. And yet, his essay is peppered with references to themes or motifs being "typically Indian" or "quintessentially Indian" but more in a timeless, essential fashion (which would no doubt envelope Bangladeshi writing as well). Dasgupta ends his essay with a provocation: "The pertinent query then, is: Whether the *independence* of a country has anything to do with the *freedom* of its artists?" (emphasis in original).[95]

Other essays in this collection are somewhat more compliant with evaluating the contribution the literature under investigation has made to a singular national literary discourse in the twenty-five years after independence. But the assessments reached do not add up to a smooth narrative about a nation sharing the same hopes and aspirations or writing the same story in different languages. The essay on Dogri literature by Shivanath begins with the acknowledgement that this body of work is "more or less, a post-independence phenomenon."[96] However, the concluding section of the essay asks and responds to the question of the contribution made by Dogri literature to the Indian literary scene with: "Not much perhaps... a bit of literature that is thoroughly indigenous, steeped in local colour, preoccupied with local problems, and self-absorbed in discovering itself."[97] Thus, almost every essay in this collection in its own fashion contributes to the unraveling of the Sahitya Akademi's long-term goal of emphasizing "one Indian literature in many languages."

As with *Contemporary Indian Literature*, many of the views expressed in *Indian Literature since Independence* were considered highly controversial. The essays on literature in Kannada and Hindi were considered especially biased in their evaluation of individual authors and trends. Complaints were made to the advisory boards in both languages and the authors of both essays were requested by the Sahitya Akademi to "restore balance" to their assessments. Namwar Singh's survey of Hindi literature was viewed by the Hindi advisory board of the Akademi as so objectionable in its omission of worthy materials that the board recommended that the book be withdrawn from circulation. D. S. Rao reports that for the first time in its history, the Sahitya Akademi actually withdrew one of its own books from circulation for a few months because of the protests, this despite the fact that Srinivasa Iyengar, the editor of the collection, was the then Vice-President of the Sahitya Akademi.[98] Rao notes that a few months after the withdrawal of this book, when the protests died down, it was back in stores and sold out fairly rapidly. It is indeed noteworthy that the advisory boards did not have access to this and other Akademi publications in manuscript form and all complaints (or praise) had to wait until the work was published. However, this critical anthology with its assessment of Indian literature after independence in twenty languages was not reprinted in English nor was it translated from the original English into other Indian languages. The quick sale of the first edition once it was put back in stores did not result in any reevaluation of the decision not to publish a second edition or to translate the book.

One can speculate whether it was these protests about specific essays, or the vast heterogeneity of the assessments in the individual essays that the introduction refrained from papering over as was the usual practice, that led to the Akademi's decision to deviate from its usual publication procedures of multiple translations and editions. Regardless, the "damage" that the book was perceived to have done was thus contained within the single English edition of 1973. What this confirms is that despite the deep imbrications of Sahitya Akademi's literary discourse with governmental policy on building a unified national culture, the contours of the literature and literary criticism produced in English under the aegis of the Akademi did not always conform to state dictates or even to the Sahitya Akademi's vision for national literature as curated in such collections of essays.

IV

Examining the "failed projects" of the Sahitya Akademi and its language politics can also be very instructive. Time and time again the Sahitya Akademi envisioned various projects that would work toward the larger goal of consolidating Indian literature under one banner and in widening the purchase of the nation's official language, Hindi. One such project was the *Bharatiya Kavita* (Indian Poetry) series which was originally planned as an annual poetry anthology that would have select poems from each of the Indian languages that were translated into Hindi as well as transliterated into the Devanagari script used for writing in Hindi. Rao writes about the massive bureaucratic machinery that was put to work in producing the editions of this "laudable project to present in one volume the best of Indian poetry."[99] The project required the initial selection of the poems, clearance of copyright, contracting scholars for transliteration and translation, from twenty languages. The advisory boards for each language were expected to make the initial selection of poetry; some boards appointed committees to do this job. Translators and transliterators had to be identified, the poets' permission had to be sought, and approvals had to be obtained from the Akademi officials at every stage. Given this elaborate procedure for assembling each volume, it is not surprising that the volume for 1953 appeared in print only in 1957. The next three volumes were biennial and the publication was delayed by several years, so that the 1954–1955 volume appeared in 1961, the 1956–1957 in 1967 and the 1958–1959 in 1972. The fifth volume, which was initially to cover five years, and then, because of delays, ten years (to 1970), was ultimately abandoned.

However, the failure of this project was not just due to the logistical difficulties of coordinating original texts in twenty languages. While promotion of the use of the Devanagari script and of Hindi was mandated by the Akademi's constitution, this task was hard to accomplish for various political and linguistic reasons. As discussed in Chapter 1, there was serious opposition to Hindi being selected as the official language of the new nation and the *Bharatiya Kavita* project was an undisguised means of proposing that Hindi would be *the* language and Devanagari *the* script in which to showcase *Bharatiya* or "Indian" poetry. However, there were practical difficulties in such an ambitious project. As early as 1957, C. Rajagopalachari (Rajaji), a leading nationalist from south India and close associate of both Gandhi and Nehru as well as a respected writer and translator of ancient texts from Sanskrit to Tamil and into English, had questioned the wisdom of such transliterations into the Devanagari script.

Rajaji wrote to Kripalani in 1957 listing some of the limitations of using the Devanagari script to convey sounds that did not exist in Hindi but were central to several southern languages: "some other diacritical devices too would be necessary but what is it all for? The transliterations are of no use to any mortal."[100] Despite such complaints and listing of practical obstacles, in 1958, the General Council of the Akademi resolved that within a period of six months each of the other languages' advisory boards would submit a list of additional letter-symbols and diacritical marks that would facilitate the Devanagari script to adequately express sounds that were not commonly used in Hindi but routinely used in other Indian languages. When the suggestions came in, they were so numerous that had they been adopted, they would have swamped the existing Hindi/Devanagari alphabet. Such complications led to delays until finally the entire project was shelved.

Despite such failed projects, in its early years, Akademi officials had been highly optimistic about such schemes that would link Indian languages to each other via translation and transliteration. The Annual Reports of the Sahitya Akademi for the early years of operation abound in plans such as the proposed translation of the top hundred of a list of three hundred foreign books into all Indian languages, and plans to translate widely from one Indian language to another. One such Annual Report stated:

> With the help of members of Advisory Boards and other scholars, lists are being compiled of writers who have adequate command over more than one Indian language. There are several such bilingual writers. There is no dearth of talent and scholarship in our country. The difficulty is that the country being large and the languages many, adequate information about existing resources is not readily available.[101]

D. S. Rao notes, however, that such optimism was premature, for "Experience in later years showed that there were many languages in the country, which were not directly linked even by basic tools of reference like dictionaries, not to mention the absence of competent translators."[102] In fact, it was only when the implementation of a lofty plan began in earnest that the difficulties (linguistic and ideological) emerged and derailed project after project.

While translation between Indian languages remained a major though difficult goal, projects that were to consolidate Indian literature in the English language continued apace in the last quarter of the century. However ambitious or successful these large-scale projects were, the lament about the inability of English to capture the nuances of Indian languages continued to be voiced. For example, in 1992, the first volume of an ambitious ten-volume anthology of Indian literature in English translation was published with much fanfare. This first volume was edited by K. M. George and was one of the three planned on the "modern period," which were to be complemented by three volumes for the ancient period and four volumes on the medieval period. In his speech at the book release of this first volume, titled *Modern Indian Literature*, Prime Minister P. V. Narasimha Rao, himself a translator (from and to Marathi, Telegu, and Hindi) and a writer of some renown, called for many more anthologizing projects that would "develop into a massive movement, a massive movement of understanding Indian literature..."[103] And yet, the Prime Minister, who, it is said, knew seventeen different Indian languages, was unsatisfied with the use of English in such a project:

> It is unthinkable how the English language can bring out the spirit of a poem written in Malayalam or Tamil. Maybe Malayalam can bring out the spirit of a poem written in Tamil. Maybe Marathi can bring out the spirit of a poem written in Gujarati. But English, unless we take what comes out as being better than nothing, only in that respect English could bring out... Translations, yes. But the spirit, and particularly if it happens to be poetry, for heaven's sake, no. It is extremely difficult... When you say "Lotus feet," it looks so odd, so incomprehensible... Immediately you are reminded of *charnakamal*, which is known all over India. So lotus feet although it does not make any sense in English, it makes a lot of sense to any Indian translator... [to] any Indian who is interested in literature.[104]

The papers and publications of the Sahitya Akademi show many such instances in which despite being only "better than nothing," English is relied upon as the language without which the Akademi cannot fulfill its mandate.

V

What are the implications for postcolonial literary studies, with its deep investment in "national literature," of this lengthy examination of the workings of the Sahitya Akademi? As in the academic discourse called postcolonial criticism, in the Akademi too, this imperative to read nation and literature off each other is voiced more stridently in the critical rather than the creative literary discourses. The details of the establishment of the Sahitya Akademi reveal that nurturing a coherent national literature was a top priority of the independent Indian state as it emerged from centuries of colonial domination. But as this chapter demonstrates, this blossoming of national literature was not a natural or a spontaneous phenomenon. If anything, the discussion of the various Akademi projects shows that the very concept of a national literature was a highly crafted, manipulated, albeit discordant, entity. This is of course completely belied by the "Table of Contents" page of any of these edited collections of critical essays or of literary selections from various languages, which show an orderly and alphabetical progression through twenty or so "equal but different" literatures. While each contribution to such a collection may tell a different story, bound together between the covers of a book, they are *de facto* a singular national literature. Despite the impossibility of the task, the Akademi worked relentlessly to fabricate a single national literature, in a highly politicized and fractious linguistic arena, mostly with inspired editorial oversight. These literary endeavors were often successful, often seemingly successful, but sometimes they faltered, unraveled, and were abandoned. The "failures," such as the *Bharatiya Kavita* series, are as instructive as the successes. Ultimately, the Akademi's accomplishments will be judged by the many book series, translations, awards, conferences, seminars, and literary events that it has overseen. At a glance, what has been produced under the aegis of the Akademi is a formidable, historically deep, linguistically wide, body of work. And, minus the pesky details, it all seems to add up.

In more recent years, especially under the visionary guidance of K. Satchidanandan, Malayali literary luminary and head of the Akademi from 1996 to 2006, new questions about literature and the nation have been raised. In his Inaugural Address at a conference on diaspora writing held in New Delhi in September 2000, Satchidanandan noted:

> We are living at a time when the idea of "Indianness" is being interrogated from different perspectives – those of Dalits, tribals, women, gays, lesbians and minorities for example. The essentialist, often Orientalist, conception of India derived from colonial-Indological and nationalist discourses is beginning to give way to a more federal democratic perspective of a polyphonic India, a mosaic of cultures, languages, literatures and world-views.[105]

Interestingly, Satchidanandan suggests that it is the critical and creative discourse from the diaspora that is yet unwilling to interrogate "the exotic eternal India," whereas "several Indian writers writing in the languages today are engaged in projecting different imagined communities, alternative nationhoods."[106] The use of the phrase "in the languages" signals the deliberate exclusion of English, but it also gestures toward an acknowledgement of literary developments as yet outside and independent of the purview of the Akademi. More significantly, there is in this speech a recognition of the exclusions inherent in the very concepts of "Indian culture" and "unity in diversity" that are foundational to the Akademi.

In the 1950s when the Sahitya Akademi was established, the expectation was that it would shape and then shepherd this national literature into the international arena that was opening up culturally and politically in ways that were unimaginable just a few years prior. As discussed at the conclusion of the previous chapter, there was a sense among the intelligentsia from the colonies that the world was undergoing rapid and radical change in the post-war period. For instance, on his release from prison in 1945, Sardar Patel, one of the leaders of the movement for Indian independence, had exuberantly declared: "Today it is Quit India; Tomorrow it will be Quit Asia and then Quit Africa."[107] In the 1950s, under the cosmopolitan leadership of Nehru, a newly independent India was poised to play a prominent role in this new, decolonizing, non-aligned world. And the three national Akademis were entrusted with the task of curating Indian arts and culture for the nation and the world beyond it. Chapter 5 on English language anthologies that were published around the fiftieth anniversary of Indian independence will demonstrate how the literature produced from very specific local and regional contexts is drawn into a national narrative via translation into English. Such edited projects have positioned themselves as representative of all Indian fiction. Inclusion in such anthologies ensures a national and international readership, a chance to be put on curricula, and an opportunity for the work to be in conversation with other literary texts. Looking at the anthologies of Indian literature published around 1997, and the seeming necessity of a "Partition story" to get the anthology going, we shall see how renditions of that "extraordinary" period in Indian and Pakistani history also comes to mark the "birth" of national literature.

CHAPTER FIVE

Partition fiction and the "birth" of national literature

> Why have you married and sent me so far away
> To an alien land, dear father?
> I am like a bird in your garden
> Here only for the night
> The next morning I fly away, dear father,
> I am like a mute cow tied to a post
> Whichever way you drive me I go, dear father,
> You have given my brother your palatial home
> But you have given me an alien land, dear father.
> "Kahe Ko Byahi Bidesh," traditional wedding song[1]

In the sixty-odd years since the 1947 Partition of British India into independent India and the new state of Pakistan, a vast body of fictional texts about this traumatic event has been translated into English and gathered into a genre that is now read as inaugurating the national literatures of both nations. In this final chapter, through close analyses of short stories by Saadat Hasan Manto, Syed Mohammad Ashraf, and Jamila Hashmi that have been translated from Urdu into English, I demonstrate how, in this process of English translation as a prelude to inclusion in a national literature, much of the nuanced literary and cultural world in which this fiction was once embedded is obscured even as the rhetoric of the nation takes over the literary commentary. The interdisciplinary "new Partition studies" of the late twentieth century has revised much of the earlier analysis of Partition produced in disciplines like political science and history, but the nation remains the central focus of this new scholarship. As this new scholarship's corollary, the newly assembled literary genre called "Partition fiction," circulating in English translation, is roped into these new interdisciplinary projects to illustrate this difficult birth of new nations. When read within a national framework, there is a distinct gender discourse through which Partition violence in cultural texts is viewed: it is understood that violence against women is metonymic of the violence done to the land. Ultimately, in such a reading what is forcefully reinscribed is this very equation of woman and nation. This chapter once again troubles the category of "national literature" and questions the automatic linking of the national and the literary, even in texts that are undoubtedly produced in response to the violent creation of the nations in the subcontinent in the mid-twentieth century. Importantly, as this chapter demonstrates, when these literary texts reappear at the end of the century in English translation and in anthologies in which they are shorn of the details of their original publication milieu in the original language, they provide the scaffolding on which the national literary canons of India and Pakistan have been raised. And yet, the aesthetics of these stories are more "diasporic" than nationalist and, more importantly, what is visible even in the English translations is that these stories brilliantly put to use a deeply etched and gendered cultural vocabulary which allows for a nuanced presentation of the gendered impact of dislocation without resorting to rhetoric of the nation. What I argue in this final chapter is that in the richest "Partition fiction," the usual rhetoric of the exceptional and gendered violence requisite to the grand narrative of birthing new nations is put aside in favor of less dramatic expositions of the parallels between ordinary and extraordinary times within patriarchal societies. Hence I demonstrate that these works convey the trauma of Partition through an intricate weaving of narrative and aesthetic which echoes familiar cultural texts such as folk and religious stories of love, loss, exile, and dislocation that are also replayed in film songs, legendary love stories, and everyday metaphors of marriage and leaving home.

I

The vast body of South Asian Partition-themed fiction has been read, quite understandably, within the framework of nation building as the quintessential national literature documenting the birth pains of the nation(s). The literary details of individual works in this category of "Partition fiction" make it a transnational genre which undercuts the fiercely policed political boundaries between India and Pakistan. While Partition fiction is easily read as inaugurating the national literatures of these two countries, these stories resolutely refuse to produce patriotism toward the new nations. In this chapter, I will argue that much of the fiction written about Partition can be more accurately be read as local narratives, more concerned with the trauma of relocation and with homesickness for the place left behind than with celebrations of independence and the formation of new nations.[2] This "local" is replicated in story after story in a fashion that follows the

Partition and the "birth" of national literature

precepts of diasporic longing rather than of nation building. The idiom of diaspora is appropriate not just because of the movement of populations that ensued after Partition, but because of diaspora's deep resonance as metaphor. In these fictional texts, themes that are habitually identified with diasporic aesthetics – the articulation of loss, homesickness, trauma, travel, the longing for return – are not just the large-scale expressions of the angst of a people who have indeed left their home country en masse in tragic circumstances; rather, such tropes also operate on a metaphoric level to articulate the gendered trauma of Partition in individual lives.

In this chapter, I consider the means by which some of this fiction, written originally in Urdu and since translated into English, makes sense of and provides alternatives to the usual nationalist narrative about Partition's violation of women and of undivided India.[3] Furthermore, I suggest that when we look more closely at the fictional articulations of diasporic longing in these texts, we find that such desires are articulated in very specific and gendered cultural codes expressed through an existing gendered vocabulary. Against the general consensus that Partition violence was part of an exceptional moment of insanity in which "men went mad," and women were reduced to symbols of the nation or community they belonged to, we have stories that theorize differently: the violence that Partition brought to women is understood to be exactly the same in essence but of a different magnitude than the usual fare doled out to them in a patriarchal society. As for the male protagonists in this fiction, the sense of violation and homelessness that ensued after Partition challenged the very foundations of their manhood and subjectivity since most of the existing modes of expressing and protesting the sorrow of leaving home were gendered feminine because they were linked, as in the epigraph to this chapter, with marriage and travel away from the natal home.[4]

Some Partition fiction, I argue, adopts the vocabulary, tropes, and aesthetics that we now readily recognize as endemic to the fictionalization of diasporic situations. Yet gender prescriptions in this fiction do not automatically change when the cartographic certainties of nationhood give way to the flexible and mobile spaces of diaspora. Of course, during and immediately after Partition there were very few cartographic certainties associated with nationhood, since villages and even cities that seemed destined for Pakistan stayed in India and vice versa. Clearly, the birth of the two nations in this case cannot be separated from the birth of the two diasporas, who are wrenched from one home to a more "fitting" home. As currently practiced, however, critical discourses on the national and on the diasporic proceed as if the two were diametrically opposite objects of study when in actuality the two are intimately intertwined. It would be productive to bring the diasporic privileging of mobility, travel, memory, split affiliations, and so on, to bear on the hallowed ground of national discourses because it reveals the scaffolding on which the national is raised.[5]

During the Partition months, violence against women (in the form of sexual assault, mutilation, murder, and abduction) rose to unprecedented levels, and this gendered violence has mostly been read as metonymic of the violation of the land.[6] It is generally understood that Partition was an aberration – a period of temporary insanity, the memory of which was best repressed in the aftermath since every aspect of it was horrific and since the violence was evenly replicated on both sides of the border. "Madness," Ravikant and Saint have astutely noted, "itself has a privileged status in the discourse on Partition."[7] These authors suggest that Gandhi (who appealed to the populace not to meet "madness with madness") and other national leaders as well as social commentators repeatedly used the metaphor of madness in a manner that both communicated a "sense of incomprehension" toward this violence as well as a "refusal to understand."[8] Such an emphasis on madness, Ravikant and Saint add, "achieved a double purpose. The Partition could be dismissed as an aberration and the responsibility of owning up to its ugly reality, denied."[9]

National histories written in the first decades after independence tended to focus on the realm of high politics and therefore on issues of triangular (British, Pakistani, Indian) national political interests that were served by Partition. As many scholars have subsequently noted, these early historical and political accounts were for the most part silent about the high level of gendered violence; the official narrative seemed to be that it was a time of extraordinary violence and shame for men, for women, and for the two new nations, and so was best forgotten or buried deep. Silence allowed for a saving of face, on both a national and a familial level; silence became, as Ashis Nandy phrased it, an anti-memory and a psychological defense, a way to move forward.[10] And yet, the fiftieth anniversary of independence from British colonial rule arrived in 1997 with no one willing or able to say that the wounds of this Partition have healed or been forgotten, despite the official policy of silence.

Since the last decade of the twentieth century, for a variety of reasons, academic and mainstream discussion of the 1947 Partition has been greatly vitalized and intensified. This is especially the case in the Indian context in comparison with Bangladesh and Pakistan.[11] Primarily, the resurgence of communal violence in the 1980s and 1990s forced a reconsideration of the silence regarding Partition violence.[12] In recent years, a whole new body of social histories has been added to the numerous political histories of Partition written from 1947 onward. Left-leaning and/or feminist scholars have variously revised the official national readings of this event and process called Partition – in what amounts to a distinct body of work that can be called "new Partition studies." Gendered analysis is central to this multidisciplinary scholarship, primarily because of the pivotal and early contributions of feminists to this discussion. In this new scholarship, however, in an attempt to break the decades of silence on the gendered implications of Partition, there is now a resolute determination to read gender dynamics into, and often only through, the fabric of the nation state.

This late twentieth-/early twenty-first-century scholarly rethinking of Partition has opened up space for more diverse readings that focus more on the social and psychological effects of the trauma of Partition than allowed for in earlier scholarship. New Partition studies goes beyond the official nationalist rhetoric and offers instead "richer definitions of the nation" (to use Gyanendra Pandey's term) through an examination of fragmentary evidence such as government documents, memoirs, newspaper articles, interviews with Partition survivors, ethnography, and so on.[13] Feminist scholarship by Urvashi Butalia and by Ritu Menon and Kamla Bhasin and others has especially forcefully argued for a gendered understanding of communal violence and of state restorations of order.[14] And yet, the focus of much of the new scholarship on Partition remains solidly grounded in the national. The question of "how were we to link the stories of women's lives with the story of the nation, the history that we had been told?" is especially central in motivating Menon and Bhasin's moving and impassioned feminist accounts of the particularly gendered victimization of women during Partition.[15]

While this focus on the nation state that intervenes in everyday life is justified in Partition analysis, it effectively restricts women to being evaluated only in terms of a framework in which they are, of necessity, positioned as symbols, communal sufferers, familial victims, and second-class citizens. In Menon and Bhasin's words: "Women's sexuality, as it had been violated by abduction, transgressed by enforced conversion and marriage and exploited by impermissible cohabitation and reproduction was at the centre of debates around national duty, honour, identity and citizenship in a secular and democratic India. The figure of the abducted woman became symbolic of crossing borders, of violating social, cultural and political boundaries..."[16] Menon and Bhasin go on to define their project as:

> Country. Community. Religion. Freedom itself: a closer examination of what meaning they have for women has led feminists to ask searching questions about women's asymmetrical relationship to nationality and citizenship; and to appreciate the role assigned to them in any renegotiation of identities, whether ethnic, communal or national. Such an analysis of the experience of abducted women, for instance, sheds light not only on the Indian state and its articulation of its role and responsibilities vis-à-vis its female citizens, but also on its perception of its role vis-à-vis Pakistan, Hindu and Muslim communities, and displaced Hindu families.[17]

This text and the other equally prominent feminist study by Butalia advocate paying attention to the fragments – fragments that may, as Menon and Bhasin write, "at their most subversive... counter the rhetoric of nationalism itself."[18] But neither of these studies nor other work on Partition is quite able to (or considers it necessary to) theorize Partition outside the "story of the nation," as Menon and Bhasin phrase it.[19] In her edited collection *No Woman's Land: Women from Pakistan, India and Bangladesh Write on the Partition of India*, Menon's inclusion of texts by Pakistani, Bangladeshi, and Indian women demonstrates her feminist deconstruction of reading within a singular (usually Indian) national framework.[20] What is ironic is that national identity in all three states is established primarily through differentiation of each from the other, so that nation and nationalism are the currency even within this cross-border feminist coalition.[21]

II

Not surprisingly, given the tight links that have been forged in literary criticism between third world literatures and nationalism, the essays on "Partition fiction" that are written by literary critics mostly assume that the national is the predominant framework within which such literary texts must be read.[22] The very coherence of the term "Partition fiction" to describe fiction written in several languages in two countries (three countries by 1971) and over a long stretch of time – from 1947 to the 1970s, if not later – is debatable. This coherence comes largely from the new attention that Partition received in both mainstream and scholarly venues from the late 1990s onward. One of the many manifestations of the year-long celebration in 1997 of the fiftieth anniversary of the creation of Pakistan and of Indian independence was the release of several English language anthologies of Pakistani and Indian national literatures. These anthologies, ostensibly showcasing the best literature of the past fifty years, were shaped by issues such as translation, length, availability, and editorial taste.

However, despite these constraints, the first few entries in most of these collections are what could be classified as Partition literature – fiction that in some shape or form addresses the trauma of the 1947 Partition.[23] Additionally, around the late 1990s, several publishing houses commissioned scholars to assemble anthologies on Partition fiction in English translation even as several literary critical evaluations of this literary genre were published.[24] And finally, in the late twentieth century, several previously published and out-of-print novels and memoirs dealing with Partition were translated into English, printed and/or reprinted, and reviewed.[25]

Today, more than a decade after 1997, Partition fiction/film studies has congealed into an established field of inquiry (a subfield of Partition studies), and the disparate works gathered under this term do come together as a complex genre. While this new scholarship on Partition radically altered the terms and practices of knowledge production in several disciplines, literary texts continued to be utilized in unaltered fashion. Historians and other social scientists have used Partition literature as a means of supplementing their historical analysis: literature is a treasure trove of realistic, even confessional, chronicles of horrors from which examples of "emotional trauma" can be extracted.[26] Looking through these literary anthologies, it seems almost as if the particularities of each story *need* to be held at bay, so that a more cohesive statement about partition and its place in Indian literature is presentable. Hence it is significant that in most anthologies published around the fiftieth anniversary of Partition in 1997, information about the original publication of each entry is typically not included; rather, the anthologies provide the new, and often the only, context for these disparate works. The notes on the contributing authors are minimal and there is next to no discussion of translation issues since almost all anthologies have individual stories translated by different persons. In the introduction to these anthologies there is barely any reference to the literary milieu in which these stories first circulated; instead there are varying degrees of pedantic instruction on how these stories need to be read, what they can teach us about the past in ways that are useful to deal with the present.

The most commercially successful of the literary anthologies on Partition is undoubtedly *Stories about the Partition of India* edited by Alok Bhalla, first published as a three-volume set and in 1999 as one book. In his very brief "Editorial Note," Bhalla states that the stories in the three volumes "have neither been arranged chronologically nor according to the original languages in which they were written. I have chosen, instead, to let a variety of different voices and the complexity of experiences which they narrate, resonate in each volume."[27] Utterly uninterested in the literary setting from which these stories are plucked, Bhalla's project is instead framed by a naive Gandhianism that very soon becomes a disabling feature of the collection. In his introduction Bhalla identifies "utter bewilderment" as the common note struck in all Partition stories and organizes the stories by four themes that he considers most useful: those that are "communally charged," those that are predominantly about "anger and negation," those that concern "lamentation and consolation," and finally, those absorbed by the "retrieval of memory."[28] While such categorization can be debated on many points, the actual fictional texts and literary analysis presented become secondary to Bhalla's project of insisting on an idiosyncratically Gandhian discussion of the fiction. Hence Bhalla begins and ends with posing questions about conduct during the Partition months, such as "Why did we not follow Gandhi, as we had done before?" and "Why did we, as Gandhi wondered, 'meet madness with madness'?"[29] Gandhi becomes an arbiter of literary value as in Bhalla's assessment of the story titled "Where is my Mother?" by Krishna Sobti. Dismissing this story as communal for using common stereotypes about Muslims, Bhalla writes: "Her narrative structure, however, doesn't permit us to remember the fact that one of the gentlest of Gandhi's disciples was Khan Abdul Ghaffar Khan, a Pathan and a Muslim."[30] Here and elsewhere in this introduction, Gandhi's Hindu universalism (as championed by Bhalla) is presented as the only ethical, unbiased, and patriotic perspective to take on such matters as understanding Partition and evaluating Partition literature.[31] Bhalla's vision for this literature soon becomes a sentimental lament in which what is measured with regret is the gap between Gandhian idealism and literary writing.

Cowasjee and Duggal's *Orphans of the Storm* is one of the earliest anthologies of Partition fiction and has won praise for not having a heavy-handed editorial agenda guiding either the selection or the organization. Muhammad Umar Memon finds *Orphans of the Storm* the most readable and the "least shrill in its ideological pronouncements" of the anthologies that predate his own edited volume, *An Epic Unwritten*.[32] Cowasjee and Duggal begin their introduction by stating that, through the selected stories, their anthology examines not Nehru's much-quoted "tryst with destiny," but "the tryst of the common people caught between the greed of politicians for power and the unseemly haste [with which power was transferred]."[33] Yet, beyond the inclusion of a minimal copyrights page, a brief glossary, and short notes on the contributors, this anthology too is unconcerned with how exactly this alternative view to high nationalism's "tryst with destiny" was to become visible to the reader. There is no discussion of the implications of translating these stories from Urdu, Hindi, and Punjabi into English, nor is there any indication of the previous literary terrains in which such stories circulated. As with Bhalla's anthology and almost all such collections, the stories are presented as *finally* finding their best fit in the context of being translated and showcased as part of this retrospective collection.

Two additional collections, one edited by Mohammad Umar Memon and the other by Ravikant and Saint, do address some of the concerns raised in this chapter. In his introduction to *An Epic Unwritten: The Penguin Book of Partition Stories* Memon notes that fiction does not moralize or teach us life lessons; it writes the history of individuals and not that of a society. He wryly adds that if literature had lessons to teach us, then "none of what is occurring today in South Asia [a reference to contemporary communal violence] would have occurred as we would have been wiser for our perusal of the fictional works written in the immediate aftermath of Partition."[34] Memon suggests that the "ideological underpinnings articulated in the learned introductions" to earlier collections (that go unidentified) work as "a sort of distorting filter against the material presented."[35] Hence, his own decision to "steer clear in my own presentation of any such narrowly nationalistic aspirations on the one hand, and of a kind of mealy-mouthed, neo-Gandhian mumbo jumbo on the other."[36] Memon's own anthology is of course not without plan or focus – his collection includes Partition stories and those written in response to later communal violence but with the shadow of Partition falling across them.

In his introduction, Memon states his concerns with the problem of shabby translation in the published collections. Writing of the efforts he has made in his collection to preserve the integrity of the original Urdu material, he laments the fact that so often in the process of translation into English, cultural references that are integral to the content of the work were "flattened out or glossed over in silence."[37] Thus Memon protests that often "entire trajectories of feeling and thought are nullified by a single stroke of cultural hubris."[38] However, he goes on to comment on his decision to omit copious annotation. Arguing that such annotation would not be expected of contemporary French or Russian literature, he does not see why such annotation is necessary for a piece written in a South Asian language: "An obscure allusion in a foreign text calls for some minimal effort on the part of its reader."[39] For the absolutely necessary annotation Menon advises turning to the extensive and informative glossary and notes. Refreshingly, the notes on the contributors include some information on the original publication venue for each story included in this collection.[40]

The one contemporaneous anthology that stands out is *Translating Partition* edited by Ravikant and Tarun Saint. Like Mohammad Umar Memon, these editors also view the literature that emerged in the aftermath of Partition as "a repository of local truths" that "offer insights into the nature of individual experience, and break the silence in the collective sphere."[41] More than any other anthology, this one is attentive to how translation into English transforms the stories. Thus along with eight stories translated from Urdu into English, *Translating Partition* also includes essays by the translators and critics that "attempt at close reading of chosen stories to emphasize the difficulty of conveying certain culture specific references in the target language. The multiple layers of the texts become visible in terms of language, culture and historical context."[42] These essays by Asaduddin, Stuti Khanna, Anuradha Marwah Roy, and the two editors are exceptional in that they detail the many aspects of successfully translating these stories from Urdu into English. For example, in their essay on their translation of Manto's "The Dog of Tetwal," Ravikant and Saint discuss the difficulty of recreating in English translation the local language politics of the long-standing tensions between Hindi, Gurmukhi (the Punjabi script), and Urdu that are embedded in the Urdu original of this story. Part of the impact of this story in Urdu, which Ravikant and Saint strived to recreate in their translation, is Manto's brilliant "critique of the processes that led to language itself becoming a casualty, as nationalist jingoism prevailed."[43] Similarly, their extended discussion of the mystical and romantic weight of the "Heer Ranja" poem by the seventeenth-century poet Waris Shah helps the reader see how Manto uses this well-known narrative in this story about lonely and bored soldiers at the newly created border between Pakistan and India who recite snatches from Waris Shah's poem or shoot at a stray dog to pass the time. This discussion of the shared cultural traditions on both sides of this border, which is as everyday as the brewing of tea in the bitter cold mornings by both set of soldiers, restores a great depth of meaning to the story that is visible in the English version if read alongside this commentary by the translators. Ultimately what Ravikant and Saint demonstrate in this collection is that with painstaking effort – on the part of both editors and readers – it is possible to apprehend stories about Partition and its aftermath in English translation without the fading out of "localized truths." But such an enterprise requires extensive editorial commentary that recreates some of the resonance of the original story and it also requires careful and dedicated reading. Sadly, commercial value

Partition and the "birth" of national literature 183

lies in the presentation of an easily understood, smoothly translated set of stories unburdened by academic baggage such as annotations, editorial commentary, and the nuances of multiple languages. Consequently, of all the anthologies discussed in this chapter, *Translating Partition* is least likely to be found in airport bookstores.

Moving on to the collections of Indian and Pakistani "national literature" published around this fiftieth anniversary, the most widely discussed anthology (and the one most likely to be found in airport bookstores) is undoubtedly the one edited for Random House by Salman Rushdie and Elizabeth West.[44] In his introduction to this collection, Rushdie makes the provocative statement that in the postcolonial period, Indian writing in English "represents perhaps the most valuable contribution India has yet made to the world of books."[45] Acknowledging that this is a large claim, Rushdie nevertheless insists on the validity of his viewpoint. This assessment drew the ire of Indian critics, especially since Rushdie cannot read any other Indian language besides English. As will be discussed in the epilogue to this study, Rushdie has a vague sense that there is a literary and historical explanation to the preponderance of English language texts in his anthology, but he is unable to account for it except through the faulty logic of literary excellence. He suggests that the poor quality of translation may have something to do with his disappointment with Indian literature written in languages other than English, but to his "considerable astonishment" only one translated text – Sadat Hassan Manto's "Toba Tek Singh" – made his final cut.[46] As a result, *The Vintage Book of Indian Writing, 1947–1997* (1997) includes an English translation of Manto's story, the only entry of the total thirty-two that Rushdie and West present as not written originally in English.[47] This editorial decision displays the apparent necessity of a Partition story to even this otherwise non-representative (despite the title of the book) collection. "Toba Tek Singh" is one of Manto's most effective stories, in which a Sikh inmate of a lunatic asylum makes an incoherent yet very powerful protest of the Partition-driven exchange of populations of lunatic asylums: Hindu and Sikh inmates to institutions in India and Muslim inmates to Pakistan. Rushdie and West's collection is resolutely nation-centric as evident in the organization of the entries: The collection begins with Nehru's much-admired "Freedom at Midnight" speech followed by an excerpt from the memoir written by Nehru's niece, the writer Nayantara Sahgal, about her return in the late 1940s from Wellesley College to the Prime Minister's house where she played hostess for her uncle, and "Toba Tek Singh" by Manto. As with Rushdie's most lauded novel, *Midnight's Children* (1980), which was discussed in Chapter 1, this collection is also "handcuffed to history" and once again "history" for Rushdie is the history of the nation.[48]

Unlike with the Sahitya Akademi anthologies in English discussed in the previous chapter, which made heroic attempts to connect to and showcase literatures in other Indian languages, commercially produced anthologies like Rushdie's decisively cut through the multiple links between English and the other Indian languages. In Chapter 4, I critiqued the fact that the Akademi was so intent on its mandate to cultivate linguistic diversity that no other form of diversity was recognized or nurtured. So the question to ask is whether, despite its lack of linguistic diversity, Rushdie's anthology steps out of the caste and gender parameters of the previously discussed anthologies of Indian literature. While Rushdie and West include a significant number of female writers and more than the token number of minority writers, they do not breach the class or caste circle of elite India.

The fiftieth anniversary of national independence becomes a time to mark beginnings and to identify a common pattern to the events in different arenas (political, social, cultural, economic) as well as to braid together a national destiny from these developments. In Pakistan, too, several literary anthologies of national literature were published toward the end of the century to celebrate the fiftieth anniversary of the creation of this nation. No editor makes as close a link between the nation and its literature than Asif Farrukhi does in *Fires in an Autumn Garden: Short Stories from Urdu and the Regional Languages of Pakistan* (1997). Farrukhi, himself a fiction writer, states: "What follows is an attempt to read my country in its stories, to see how Pakistan is narrated in its stories."[49] He goes on to suggest that Pakistan's history is so extraordinary that it comes close to being fictional. And correspondingly, he insists that Pakistan's written "history" is so corrupted by political imperatives that fiction becomes the truer guide to the state of the nation, even as historical writing in Pakistan becomes fictional. In the preface to this collection, another prominent Pakistani scholar, Intizar Hussain, argues that an in-depth study of Pakistani fiction will reveal "the love for the nation" that is manifest below the surface in both patriotic and "seemingly anti-nationalist" writing.[50] Of the inception of Pakistani national literature, he writes:

> In the host of stories written in those days [around the creation of Pakistan] I am trying to locate that particular point which can be called the starting point of Pakistani fiction. I am fully conscious of the absurdity of such an attempt... However, at times a literary work turns into a milestone and

gives the impression of being the starting point of a new trend or movement or tradition. Manto's short story "Khol do" [Open It] appears to me a work of this kind. What a dramatic starting point provided to Pakistani fiction![51]

Hussain elaborates by arguing that this story by Manto (which is discussed later in this chapter) bursts the bubble of idealism and optimism with which the idea of Pakistan had been conceived, because as early as 1948, it forced Pakistanis to face harsh realities about their new nation.

Readers whose English knowledge is held within a bilingual or even multilingual context, and who have some understanding of the larger cultural terrain in which the stories were originally written, can access the registers in these stories that are beyond and below the nation-centric. However, for the reader who is completely reliant on the glossaries and on the interpretations proffered in the introductions to the anthologies, or on the generic "third world literature equals national text" logic, some of these other more local articulations are rendered mute and invisible. Hence, for the most part, as these stories circulate nationally and globally, the interpretive frame that is bought to bear on them becomes generic and broad. And translation into English becomes the first step toward a separation from location and language that seems necessary to transition the stories into the genre of "Partition fiction." And then this genre is positioned to lead the national literature of India, or Pakistan as the case may be, so that then these literatures can become recognizable as contenders on the field of world literature. Following a similar logic, Rushdie concludes his introduction to *The Vintage Book of Indian Writing: 1947–1997* with:

> The map of the world, in the standard Mercator projection, is not kind to India, making it look substantially smaller than say, Greenland. On the map of world literature, too, India has been undersized for too long. This anthology celebrates the writers who are ensuring that, fifty years after Indian's independence, that age of obscurity is coming to an end.[52]

These anthologies in English give "undersized" literary texts the heft they need to belong alongside the literature from other nations. However, the "obscurity" that comes to an end with translation into English and with inclusion in national anthologies in its turn obscures a whole range of local cultural and linguistic contexts.

III

As the fiction that takes Partition as its theme repeatedly demonstrates, for those who traveled across newly drawn borderlines, old attachments could not be submerged into or easily grafted on to the newly born independent nation. This fiction is diasporic in that it pays lingering attention to the pains of separation, to the sense of inappropriate attachment to the place left behind, and to the inability to fall in line with the new regime/land/object of patriotism. And yet, fifty years later, these stories of lament and looking back to the land left behind are rounded up in anthologies that canonize the national via the literary. Read in purely nationalist terms, Partition was a once-in-a-nation's-lifetime extraordinary event: it was the downside of achieving independence for India and the cost of establishing Pakistan. Thus, in terms of national history, this Partition is firmly in the past and will not be repeated. As Alok Bhalla writes in his introduction to his anthology, Partition and its communal violence constitute "*an exceptional moment of disorder* in a continuing history of a life lived together [by Hindus, Muslims, and Sikhs] in all its complex variety" (emphasis added).[53] Instead, if we read them through a diasporic lens, such partitions and dislocations are *routinely* replayed from the beginning of settled societies to the present day. As Vijay Mishra defines it, diasporas are ethnic groups that, for a variety of reasons, "live in displacement."[54] Framed in this context of trading diasporas, indentureship, evictions, forced/economic migrations, and dislocations, this Partition becomes less of a singular event in a national history and more liable to be repeated in varying form and degree.[55]

Every aspect of the violence associated with Partition demands our attention, not because it was extraordinary but because of what it reveals about the ordinary. The fiction is very clear on this point. I first examine what is possibly the most anthologized Partition story, "Khol Do" (Open It), written in Urdu in Pakistan in 1948 by the best-known, allegedly anti-nationalist writer on Partition in both India and Pakistan, Saadat Hasan Manto.[56] My reading of the fictional texts by Syed Mohammad Ashraf and Jamila Hashmi will demonstrate the ways in which Partition fiction partakes of, and in turn reproduces, the popular gendered vocabulary in circulation in folktales, iconic religious texts, and Indian cinema to simultaneously register, protest, absorb, and interpret the experiences of 1947 and its aftermath. There is, of course, much more to these three stories than I present here: my reading of them can only allow for a glimpse of those earlier literary worlds to which my access is limited primarily by my own limitations of language and cultural knowledge, and also by the paucity of record keeping on the early publication history.

In "Open It" Manto's plotting of gendered violence can be read as following the nationalist script in that it reproduces (even as it critiques) the patriarchal/nationalist prescription of woman standing in for the nation

Partition and the "birth" of national literature 187

as an object to be either violated or enshrined. In the exceptional moment of disorder that Partition violence is said to stem from, this story easily allows for a reduction of men and women to perfect binaries – rapists and raped, protectors and protected, villains and victims, buyers and bought, sellers and sold. And in making this violence the central event of the tale, some Partition fiction and the literary criticism it engenders further entrench these limited gender categories by allowing no space for either gender outside these binaries. An extreme example of such binary readings is provided by Bhalla, who notes that Manto's stories belong to the category of Partition fiction that is "marked by a sense of rage and hopelessness."[57] Such writers, Bhalla argues, "record with shock as people in an obscene world become either predators or victims, as they either decide to participate gleefully in murder and loot [*sic*] or find themselves unable to do anything but scream with pain as they are stabbed and burnt or raped again and again."[58]

"Open It" is very short and very dramatic in its violence. The story begins innocuously enough: "The special train left Amritsar at two in the afternoon and reached Mughalpura eight hours later."[59] But to the reader who knows that this distance is about thirty-five miles and can be covered in less than an hour, this is a chilling detail. We know that something awful must have happened en route from Amritsar in India to Mughalpura in Pakistan. In the beginning of this story a refugee family – aged parents and a teenage daughter – is on the run from a rampaging mob. The mother is attacked, and with her dying breath she urges the father to save the daughter. We know that this is a Muslim family trying to make it to Pakistan only because of the direction in which the train they are trying to catch runs (from Amritsar to Mughalpura) and because the daughter's name is Sakina and the father's name is Sirajuddin. Manto is always very insistent that the same violence is repeated on both sides – the names are only coincidentally Hindu or Muslim or Sikh. Manto forces the reader to participate, to infer from the few details that he does give us the details that he doesn't. For example, while father and daughter are on the run, her scarf falls off her shoulders and the father stops to pick it up – this scarf, worn over the shirt or kurta and around the chest and sometimes over the head, is a symbol of respectability and decorum for women in north India – whether they are Muslim, Sikh, or Hindu. She screams at him to leave it behind and to continue running. The father and daughter are soon separated, and while he ends up in a refugee camp, there is no sign of the daughter. The father is distraught because all he has is her *duppatta* or scarf that he had shoved into his pocket while on the run. When we next see the daughter Sakina, she is "rescued" by eight young men in a truck – who, because they are associated with the refugee camp the father is at, we can assume, are of the same community. They find Sakina, and we are told "the eight young men were very kind to Sakina."[60] We are also told that she is now very conscious of her missing *duppatta*. As readers we are forced to imagine what might have happened to her prior to this rescue to make her so conscious of her female body. A few lines down in the short story we read that when the father meets these men, they assure him that they have not found his daughter but that they will keep looking. We are now forced to go back and reread the few lines about the rescue and reinterpret the brief sentence about their having been "very kind" to Sakina.

A paragraph or so after the father questions these men, we are told that an unconscious Sakina is found abandoned by some railway tracks and is brought to the camp's makeshift hospital. When the male doctor requests that a window be opened to let in some reviving air, the semi-conscious girl who has been raped so often obeys the male command to "open it" by slowly and painfully unknotting the drawstring to her *salwar* (drawstring pants) and pulling them down. The old father sees her movement as a sign of life and shouts with joy. The story concludes with a single sentence that captures the doctor's mortification: "The doctor broke into a cold sweat."[61]

Most readings of this story have focused on the father's traumatized haplessness and ineffectuality in the face of terror and his inability to protect his daughter from the worst of the violence. In contrast, the refugee camp doctor is assertive and focused, the citizen rebuilding his community. The doctor's shame and mortification at the end of the story becomes a sign of his masculine virtue. Manto is masterful in inducing national/masculine shame. He lets the men of neither community off the hook: clearly both Sakina's Hindu or Sikh (it is not specified) abductors and her Muslim rescuers sexually assault her. As in the final scene in Deepa Mehta's Partition film *Earth* (1998), when the beautiful young Hindu heroine is carried aloft by a mob of rapacious Muslim men, it is a culmination of all the danger inherent in being female in these locations.[62] In most accounts, these sexual assaults become both symbolic of many other violations and at the same time the embodiment of that violence. Manto's text evokes protective, patriarchal sentiments and a certain helplessness in "decent" male readers, and simultaneously makes female readers aware of their gendered vulnerability and their need for protection. It performs a kind of gendering that pulls the reader into the limited gender positions that are available to women (and to men) in this scenario. Such a triangular cast is common in some Partition fiction – the rapacious crowd or individual villain, the helpless innocent male bystander, and the innocent passive female victim – with the shame and details of sexual violation wrapped together.[63]

The degree of the dramatic impact of these stories in English translation will depend on the readers' degree of familiarity with the ethos of the world evoked in these texts. Much of the impact of Manto's story in English translation depends on whether the reader knows the location of and distance between Amritsar and Mughalpura, knows the significance of the *duppatta*, and the meaning of the word *salwar*. Having to turn to the glossary to understand the horrible climax of the story makes for a different reading experience. The story "works" when the reader understands (either immediately or slowly) the full implications of the final scene between father, daughter, and doctor.

Given Manto's cryptic style, his general refusal to explicitly identify protagonists by the religious community they belong to, some English translations "help out" the reader by inserting explanatory phrases and sentences into the story.[64] In his translator's note to Manto's *Partition: Sketches and Stories*, Khalid Hasan writes: "While in the subcontinent the irony of the pieces would be quite clear in every case to the reader, it may not be so outside the region. I have, therefore, taken the liberty here and there, of identifying an occasional character by the religion he professes, in order to aid understanding. For this I apologize to Manto who, I am sure, would have understood."[65] Hence, for example, the various translations of this story add additional phrases (such as "she untied the knot at her waist" or "she spread her thighs") to spell out the significance of the very slight action and utterances in the chilling climax to this story. The translations also use different titles that make more explicit or shield the reader from the ugly denouement of the story. Some English translations use the Hindi/Urdu words "Khol Do" [Open It] as the title (as in the original Urdu version) and others such as Alok Bhalla's translation use "Open It." The anthology edited by Cowasjee and Duggal uses the title "The Reunion" for this story.[66] *Kingdom's End and Other Stories* by Manto translated by Khalid Hasan includes this story under the title "The Return."

Very few Partition stories actually produce the forward-looking, patriotic national subject who, one might imagine, is the proper subject of national literature. Hence when I argue that Manto's story performs gender within the nationalist model, I argue that his terms of critique are specified by notions of nation, of masculine decency (in contrast to masculine madness), and of civic responsibility (evoked in its very abdication).[67] Given the solidly patriarchal social arrangements in the communities affected by Partition, there are very few cultural modes of narrating shame, humiliation, dislocation, and displacement as experienced by men that do not undermine masculinity as popularly understood. Within the rhetoric of the nation and citizenry, the paucity of words with which normative masculine subjects can express these multiple traumas and still continue to occupy the position of the patriarchal masculine subject/citizen is especially stark. This is an argument that I will explore with the help of another short story, titled "Separated from the Flock," written in the 1970s in Urdu by the Indian writer and civil servant Mohammad Ashraf.[68]

IV

In "Separated from the Flock" Mohammad Ashraf presents a discomfiting masculine narrative of diminished authority in the face of a deep yet shameful affiliation to the country left behind, an attachment we easily recognize as diasporic. In this first-person narrative, a Pakistani superintendent of police is forced by a series of encounters into a wrenching acknowledgement of his longing for and inability to revisit the Indian state of Uttar Pradesh, or UP, in which he was born and grew up. As a senior Pakistani civil servant based in Lahore, he cannot travel to enemy territory, which is what India has become after the wars of 1965 and 1971. He views this inappropriate homesickness as a weakness that he hopes to keep hidden. In the short story, on his way to a recreational hunting trip, the civil servant is quizzed by his Pakistan-born driver about India and his hometown, which he left thirty years ago at the age of eighteen. At the lakeside where the hunters gather in the early dawn, the civil servant meets a childhood friend (who had also moved to Pakistan) and reluctantly allows himself to reminisce about the past in a way that he has not done for a while. The third and most discomfiting encounter is with his driver's wife who, against her husband's wishes, pleads with the civil servant to get her a travel pass so she can visit her native place in India, which happens to be in the civil servant's own home state. To be able to visit one's natal home, evocatively referred to as one's *maike* (place/home of a married woman's natal family), after marriage is culturally understood to be the most poignant wish of all young married women. Men/husbands are understood to be, are supposed to be, at home and not in a feminized and vulnerable position of pining for a home left behind. After the dislocation forced by Partition, this is no longer such a stable gendered difference and, as the story demonstrates, requires much effort to restabilize. The police superintendent decides to support his driver in this domestic battle and so, when confronted by the tearful wife, feigns his helplessness in expediting such official business.

By the end of the story, however, despite the elaborate arrangements that he and his subordinates made for this duck shoot, the civil servant finds himself unable to shoot the migrating birds. He is himself "separated from the flock." Unable to enjoy the masculine sport of hunting and compelled (most unwillingly) to compare himself both to a woman denied her husband's permission to go to her natal home and to ducks with broken wings, Ashraf's hero is caught in the emasculating and therefore humiliating discourse of homesickness and displacement. At the end of the story he lies to his friend and subordinates about old cartridges being responsible for his failure to shoot – and he is allowed the ruse. In his introduction to the collection, Bhalla writes that in refusing to shoot the birds, the hunters ensure that "suffering is not forgotten, for it can never be... Their own loss does not have to be repeated."[69] Interestingly, the understated yet explicit comparison that Ashraf makes between the driver's wife and the protagonist is eclipsed in Bhalla's critical reading. The radical blurring of gender boundaries that is so delicately recorded in this story is covered over by Bhalla's sentimentality.

Ashraf's "Separated from the Flock" does not have the harsh horrific clarity of Manto's "Open It" or of the final abduction scene of Mehta's film *Earth*. The police superintendent's discreet longing for his home state of UP now in India leaks the past into the present and disrupts his laboriously disciplined sense of Pakistani citizenship. Written from the perspective of an established male citizen, the diasporic features of the story threaten to unravel the patriarchal certainties of nationalism, but the police superintendent is able (just about) to rein in these disruptions: at the end of the story, self-discipline, proper masculinity, and proper national affiliations continue to hold sway.

I turn to a third and final story, "Banished" (1998), written by the female Pakistani writer Jamila Hashmi (1929–88), who was a well-known novelist and also a schoolteacher in Lahore.[70] "Banished" was written in Urdu in the 1960s and published under the title "Ban Vaas," which has been variously translated as "Banishment" and "Exile."[71] I follow the diasporic trope used in this particular story for the insight it provides into the agency of abducted women who were, as feminist critics have asserted, stripped of the basic rights of citizenship in these new nations. While national affiliations are presented in crisis in the very literature that ostensibly gets the post-independence national literary canon going, one needs to look *beyond and below* both national and diasporic features of this literature to get at the radical gender critique that some Partition fiction presents.

The original title, "Ban Vaas," is taken from the Hindu epic the *Ramayana*. Literally translated it would mean "forest dwelling" – a reference to the hero Prince Rama and his wife Sita's banishment from their kingdom and their fourteen years of joint exile in the forest. More poignantly and of specific importance in this story by Hashmi, "Ban Vaas" refers to Sita's second exile. When first exiled with her husband, Rama, Sita is abducted by Ravana, king of Lanka, and though she is eventually rescued by Rama, her virtue is suspect after the abduction. After the return to his kingdom, Sita is soon banished by her husband to a second round of exile because he is unable to reconcile himself to the shame of her abduction. It is not surprising that the *Ramayana* story became a popular metaphor and comforting parallel for the trials faced by Partition refugees (and by other South Asians who are part of the global diaspora). Similarly, some Muslim refugees sought religious solace by comparing their migration in 1947 and the trauma it entailed to the *hijrat* (the flight of Muhammad from Mecca to Medina). The very name given to refugees from India in Pakistan, *Muhajirs*, was a reference to the original *muhajirs* who accompanied the Prophet to Medina. And the Muslims already living in Pakistan were seen as Ansars, modern equivalents of the people of Medina who, legend has it, had so warmly welcomed the first set of Muslim migrants.[72]

Hashmi's story, "Banished," gives us the first-person narrative of a young upper-class Muslim woman who, at the time of the Partition riots, has been abducted from her home in an unnamed city in India by a Sikh farmer who installs her as his "wife" in his village of Sangraon in Punjab, India. This protagonist, identified only as "Bahu" – the term for daughter-in-law in Hindu and Sikh families – has borne three children to her "husband" and dutifully serves her dominating mother-in-law. From the story:

> Whenever anyone calls me Bahu I feel insulted. I have been hearing this word for years, ever since the evening when Gurpal dumped me in this courtyard and cried to Badi Ma . . . : "Look ma, I've brought you a bahu. A real beauty! The best of the lot."[73]

When Pakistani soldiers come to this village in Punjab, several years after Partition, to rescue abducted women like this protagonist, she hides herself in the fields.[74] She will go only if her two brothers come to rescue her. Meanwhile, she compares herself to Sita, and Gurpal, her abductor and now "husband," is her very own Ravana. In the present time of the narrative, about seven or eight years after the abduction, this woman is

Partition and the "birth" of national literature

walking "home" with her "husband" and children from a *Dussehra mela* (a religious country fair). This rare "family" outing is the occasion for her to contemplate her life along the pattern provided by the story of Rama, Sita, and Ravana.[75] Commenting on this story, Kaul sees this "mythic precedent" as "showing up" in Hashmi's story "in a rhetorical reversal," from which he concludes that "Partition stories point out, like no other, the vulnerability of women in times of social turmoil."[76] A close reading of the story, however, reveals that there are no reversals here – just stark parallels drawn between the experiences of everyday life for women both in patriarchal societies and in times of social turmoil.

In this story Hashmi follows the fine tradition of women and subaltern groups who use the *Ramayana* story to explain and protest their own predicaments.[77] By using the most iconic Hindu story to narrate her own predicament, this Muslim protagonist is shown to demonstrate her integration into the "family" she now belongs to (with all the ownership connotations of *belongs to* intact). The use of the *Ramayana* story is also an acknowledgement and incisive critique of the centrality of abduction, sexual dishonoring, and doubting of women's virtue (all essential ingredients of the Sita story) in this region. Over the course of this particular short story, the reader is made to appreciate that many of the trials that women suffered as the Partition and exchanges of population proceeded were not new inventions of fanatical menfolk. Against the oft-repeated lament that men went mad during these times, Hashmi makes clear that these *agni parikshas*, or trials by fire, such as the one Sita went through in the *Ramayana*, are scripted into the very texture of everyday life for women in this location. It is noteworthy to add here that in the songs sung by women at traditional Hindu weddings and other related rituals in northern India, Sita's marriage and the trials that follow serve as a comforting narrative for the young brides and as a means of expressing their grief at leaving home as well as their trepidation about the future.[78]

The protagonist in "Ban Vaas" does not draw on the rhetoric of nation in order to articulate her suffering, her compromises, or her process of adjusting to her new life.[79] Rather, she relies on the stories and wisdom that young girls in the subcontinent are well acquainted with – they marry and leave their natal home, and the rest of their life is spent missing home, waiting for their brothers to come and take them home to their *maike* for precious visits. It is in articulating the ways in which her own life as an abductee both fulfills and parodies this well-worn course of events that this nameless Bahu makes her most trenchant critique of everyday acts of patriarchal control and exchange of women:

> And besides, every girl must one day leave her parental home to join her in-laws. Well, maybe Bhaiya and Bhai [a reference to her two brothers] weren't present at my wedding – so what? Hadn't Gurpal rolled out a carpet of corpses for me? Painted the road red with blood? Provided an illumination by burning down city after city? Didn't people celebrate my wedding as they stampeded, screaming and crying? It was a wedding alright. Only the customs were new: celebration by fire, smoke, and blood.[80]

Commenting on this passage, Kaul identifies irony as a central trope in this and other Partition fiction. Irony in his reading is present when "everyday reality is represented via its own inversion."[81] However, one could argue that the irony lies not in inversions but in parallels – in the deftness with which the protagonist presents her own situation through the language of weddings and leave-taking of the natal home. Earlier in the narrative, she notes:

> Many such 'brides' were brought to the village of Sangraon, but without the customary fanfare: no festive music, no racy songs to the beat of drums, no comic antics or spins or hip-thrusts of nautch girls. No one oiled my dust-coated hair. No *na'in* was sent for to make me up. I became a bride without a single piece of jewellery, without any sindhur for the parting of my hair... Since that day I too felt like Sita, enduring her exile, incarcerated in Sangraon.[82]

For women, this transfer from natal to "marital" home through abduction as represented in fiction, while severe in its effects, was often presented as an intensification of the usual patriarchal discourse about women as property. A daughter is understood to be property that is only temporarily attached (on loan, as it were) to her natal home; property whose ultimate destination and destiny lies in the transfer to the marital home. This cultural understanding of women's inherent transferability, I will argue, is put to work in these accounts of Partition's particular forms of violent dislocation of women and the subsequent attempt to return them to their appropriate place in their "real" family and community. In such texts there is a reliance on cultural vocabulary of women as *paraya dhan* (a stranger's wealth in the temporary safekeeping of a woman's parents), or as guests in their own homes, that was in circulation both prior to and after the trauma of Partition. Such reminders serve as the cultural disciplining that will ease young women's transition from *maike* to *sasural* (the home of a woman's in-laws). Note that colloquially *sasural* is used by men only to refer to a stay in prison; serving a prison sentence, then, is the analogy for men to the transition that women make in marrying. Travel, displacement,

Partition and the "birth" of national literature

the trauma of the bride's leaving of her natal home, a ritual part of the wedding ceremony (*bedhai*, often pronounced and transliterated as *vidai*, and also called the *rukhsati* in Muslim weddings), and homesickness are all scripted into a commonplace understanding of a woman's normal lifecycle and ironically provide a means of narrating and adjusting to Partition's particular forms of violent separation.

The well-documented silence about Partition violence in official historiography is given voice albeit indirectly throughout popular culture. After reading the many accounts (fictional, testimonial) of Partition trauma, one finds the repeated use of available terms for voicing the grief of separation and homesickness that are present everywhere in the culture. Note, for instance, the consistent referencing of grief and longing that is done via parallels to some of the folkloric love stories of this region, especially the Romeo-and-Juliet-like tragic and doomed romances of Heer and Ranjha, Sassi and Punnun, and Soni and Mahiwal. The popularity of these folkloric romances between beautiful and faithful young women (Soni, Sassi, Heer) and lovelorn young men (Mahiwal, Punnun, Ranjha) is in no way diminished by the fact that each story ends with the separation of and tragic death of the young lovers.[83] Another cultural saying that is attributed to the first of the ten Sikh gurus, Guru Nanak (1469–1539), states that all humankind are like lost children in the world which is like a fair/carnival/mela. In 1928 when Mulk Raj Anand, newly transplanted to England, wrote his first short story, he titled it "The Lost Child" and deliberately evoked this saying of Guru Nanak even as he described an incident when he had become separated from his parents as a young child at a Baisakhi mela (spring fair) in a village on the banks of the River Beas in northern Punjab.[84] For millions in northern India, Partition resulted in traumatic exile and thus heightened the meaning of Guru Nanak's saying. In this short story by Jamila Hashmi, this trope of children lost in the "mela" is raised when the protagonist and her husband, Gurpal, have a brief altercation after he complains about careless mothers who are so distracted by the pleasures of the fair, that they "lose themselves" to the extend of forgetting "to hold on to their children."[85] The protagonist quietly reminds her husband that "Children become separated from their mothers even outside fairs."[86] Gurpal then urges his "wife" to forget the violent separation from kith and kin that he forced on her in the past.

The notion of life itself as a "mela" with pleasures, distractions, and dangers was commonly understood folk wisdom in the local idiom that continues to hold after Partition. I would like to speculate on the subterranean link between the dislocation caused by Partition trauma and the "lost-at-the-*mela*" trope in Hashmi's short story which is paralleled in the plots of so many Hindi films in the post-independence era. In their introduction to *Translating Partition*, Ravikant and Saint discuss the practical concerns about censorship that filmmakers faced if their work made explicit reference to Partition. They note that the "virtual ban" on explicit reference to Partition led cultural producers to resort to allusions and metaphorical references to Partition.[87] I propose that the very popular filmic plotline of a family that is separated at a country fair or by a traumatic event is obliquely patterned on the many unspoken and unspeakable stories of travel, separation, and sorrow that Partition generated. Note that in most Indian movies that use this formulaic plot, the separation scenes are placed before the opening credits as a kind of prelude to the story that will unfold, and the grand finale of the film includes a happy and tearful reunion of lost kin at the end. Literary narratives on Partition rarely offer such optimistic conclusions. A Hindi film called *Mela* released in 1948, starring the very popular duo of Dilip Kumar and Nargis, included a theme song "Yeh zindagi ke mele" [These Fairs that are Like Life] that is sung by a street singer at a village fair complete with hand-turned ferris wheel, crowds, peep shows, and a hero and heroine looking for each other through the crowds. The simple yet profound philosophy expressed in this opening song's lyrics and picturization frames the entire plot and time-frame of the film. This song's lyrics urge acceptance of life's ups and downs and the inevitability of death, and can be very easily glossed as referring to the losses induced by Partition: as the song notes, someday we all have to leave, regardless of the fitness of time or era; no one will lend support or walk alongside, everything will remain behind, we will have to go forth alone. The film both starts and ends with this song.

As with the excessive use of the life-is-a-*mela* trope in Hindi movies, one could note the excessive scripting in post-independence Indian cinema of pathos-laden renditions of *bedahil rukhsati* scenes in which the new bride leaves her parental home after her wedding for her *sasural*. Many such scenes, presented with and through songs about the sorrows of leaving home, being scattered, torn from the bosom of the family and friends, banished to a foreign land, looted of everything beloved and flung into an unknown future, and so on, can be viewed, I will insist, as Bombay cinema's discreet voicing of the lingering trauma that so many in north India were subjected to around Partition. Many of these *bedhai* songs are worked into scenes that have a romantic plot twist in that either the bride, the groom, or the lover who is an onlooker, loves inappropriately and therefore grieves secretly and silently, thus intensifying the sorrow woven into the song.

Partition and the "birth" of national literature

This commonly used plot detail heightens the understanding that there are secret sorrows that cannot be voiced but are palpable in these scenes.[88] An example of a *bedhai* song that becomes excessive in its grief can be found in the haunting lyrics of Majrooh Sultanpuri's "Chal re sajni, ab kya sochey?" [Come [keep walking] Dear Girl, Now What is There to Think About?] from the 1960 film *Bambai Ka Babu* [Gentleman from Bombay]. In this scene from the conclusion of the film, a tearful young bride, the heroine, leaves her *maike* while the song in the background laments that the young woman has set off on her journey with no one to call her own. In this example of the *bedhai* scene, the bride knows that the man masquerading as her brother is an imposter who is in love with her, but neither of them can stop the wedding or the *bedhai*. The song traces the father's regret at sending "this broken morsel of his heart" out to a foreign land. The singing voice is not attributed to any character, but functions as an omniscient narrator's commentary on the sorrow of leaving a beloved home: of having childhood friends scattered here, there, and who knows where? Home and the familiar alleys around it are lost for ever, but none of this bears thinking about, because it is time to leave and everything beloved is going out of one's grasp. Once again the lyrics and orchestration are excessively loaded with emotional charge, but the *bedhai* occasion is one where it is socially sanctioned to lament the loss of home, childhood, family, and of everything that was held dear. The lyricist for this song, Majrooh Sultanpuri (1919–2000), chose at Partition to remain in India like many other successful and well-entrenched Muslim poets, writers, actors, and others in the Bombay film industry, even as they saw so many of their friends and family leave for Pakistan. As the well-known female writer Ismat Chugtai, their fellow writer in the Bombay film industry and comrade from the Progressive Writers' Association, wrote in her memoir: "and in the end many souls remained behind in Hindustan [India] while their bodies started off for Pakistan."[89] Also noteworthy is the fact that the screenplay for *Bambai Ka Babu* was written by Rajinder Singh Bedi, author of "Lajwanti," the best-known Partition story about an abducted woman's changed relations with her husband after she is rescued and returned to him.[90] Not surprisingly, the plot twists in this film include a prior family history in which, twenty years in the past, the legitimate son apparently loses hold of his father's finger at a country fair and is lost forever.

Many of these filmic *bedhai* songs are of course based on traditional marriage songs from the region and have been sung for generations.[91] A bilingual collection of lyrics for songs that are sung at traditional marriage rituals and other ceremonies in the states of Uttar Pradesh and Bihar in north India has been recently compiled by Shakuntala Varma. The title for her book, *Kahe Ko Byahi Bidesh* (2005), is taken from a popular wedding song that is particularly able to convey the extra burden that the lyrics may have taken on after Partition. I have used Varma's translation of this "daughter's lament" as the epigraph for this chapter because the lyrics gain an additional layer of poignancy after Partition and establish that there is an entirely different register from that of nationalism to articulate the sorrow around this event. The title of the song corresponds to the first two lines of the lyrics with a much clearer sense of being married off to (someone in) an alien land than Varma's English translation can render.[92] The gendering of this banishment to a foreign land via marriage is very clear. Sons, the song wistfully complains, get to stay and inherit the patrimony; daughters are led into exile through marriage arrangements. And yet, after the dislocations of Partition, sons too found themselves banished to alien lands. As in "Separated from the Flock," this is an emasculating predicament for men.

Paralleling the upsurge of scholarly and editorial work on Partition at the close of the twentieth century, there was a sudden burgeoning of Partition-themed popular Hindi films in the 1990s and early twenty-first century and a corresponding body of scholarly work that analyzes these films. It could be argued that rather than track the faint and submerged echoes of Partition grief and trauma through scenes of separation from kith and kin as in the lost-at-the-mela plot or the *bedhai* scene as I have done above, one might instead consider the explicit thesis on Partition proffered by films such as *Gadar: Ek Prem Katha* [Rebellion: A Love Story] (dir. Anil Sharma, 2001), *Pinjar* [The Skeleton], the 2003 film (dir. Chandraprakash Dwivedi) of Amrita Pritam's acclaimed Punjabi novel *Pinjar* (1950), and *Earth: 1947* (dir. Deepa Mehta, 1998) which was based on *Cracking India*, the 1988 novel by Bapsi Sidhwa. In these and other recent commercial "Partition films" from the late 1990s and early twenty-first century, Partition is narrated via the trials and tribulations of a cross-community, heterosexual romance between Hindu and Muslim or Muslim and Sikh protagonists. Such plots paradoxically reinforce rather than undermine the national borders. This sentimentalized narrative of love across the two communities serves as a means of securing India and Indian as an exclusively Hindu/Sikh space and identity. To be Muslim in these films is to be always already Pakistani. While this is easily visible in its crudest form in a box office hit like *Gadar: Ek Prem Katha* or *Veer Zaara* (dir. Yash Chopra, 2004), the 2003 film *Pinjar* provides a much more nuanced and complex translation of religion into national identity. *Pinjar*, as written by Amrita Pritam in 1950 in the immediate aftermath of Partition, chronicles the trials and fortitude of

Pooro, a Hindu girl who is abducted by a Muslim youth, Rashid, from her own village in 1936 because of an old vendetta between their two families. In Pritam's novel, eleven years after this abduction, at the time of the 1947 Partition, Pooro sees her own story repeated in the many abductions of Hindu women that she witnesses. Her outrage is, however, not limited to Partition violence against women; rather the plotline for the novel is driven by Pooro's encounters with girls and women who are oppressed in their own family, by their in-laws, or by society at large. However, in keeping with the way gendered oppression and Partition are narrated in late twentieth century Partition films, in the film of *Pinjar* these themes are routed primarily via religion and patriarchal arrangements in both Hindu and Muslim communities. The film (unlike the novel) relies on extensive use of the Ram–Sita story as a love story and as a religious metaphor that ultimately serves as a means of assuaging the trauma of Partition. This very arresting film is a product of the "exceptional moment in which men went mad" logic that has become the standard explanation of Partition's gendered violence. Predictably, in the film *Pinjar*, the time-frame of the novel is compressed so that Pooro's abduction seems to take place just prior to Partition rather than eleven years earlier as in the novel, and several of the other plotlines of the novel that highlight everyday oppressions that women face are deleted or merely hinted at.

Ultimately then, these Partition films from the end of the twentieth century are no different in their investment in nationalism than the many contemporaneous Indian films that focus on recent border wars in the subcontinent. In its filmic interpretation, Pritam's "love story," which was about everyday oppressions faced by women under patriarchy, is revised into an exceptional story of abduction and rescue, villainy and victimage that is the gendered logic of Partition. As briefly discussed earlier in this chapter, when Bapsi Sidhwa's 1988 novel *The Ice-Candy Man* (also published under the title *Cracking India*) was made into a film by Deepa Mehta (*Earth: 1947*, 1998), it furthered the ruling gender logic of Partition as a time of exceptional violence in which men are rendered mad and/or bestial and women are subjected to unusual sexual violence. In the novel, the gang rape does take place and Shanta is traumatized and hardened by this and other violations. But this young Hindu woman refuses to "adjust" (as she is advised to by respectable social workers in the aftermath of her abduction) to her Muslim husband, the ice-candy man, who had both raped and pimped her before he married her. The ice-candy man, who is responsible for orchestrating the initial gang rape, is reduced at the end of the novel to a guilt-ridden, tormented, and broken shell of his former self. He is in his newly formed homeland and he has the girl whose attention so many men were vying for, but this is no victory. In Mehta's film, however, the shock value of the horrific scene of gang rape makes for a cinematically effective climax that unfortunately fixes the feisty, flirtatious Shanta in the final frames as the terrified victim of a horrifying sexual crime. We do not see her again on the screen. In the novel, by contrast, we do learn that Shanta survives, and she refuses her former employer's offer of safe passage to her community in India where she could perhaps find respectability again.

In Hashmi's story, the protagonist waits for her brothers to come rescue her. And they never do. Her abduction has led to her banishment – there is no return, and yet her thoughts are always on return. In Hashmi's story, all through the narrative, abduction is presented as causing a severe case of homesickness after a woman marries and leaves her natal home. For example, the protagonist is envious of other (Hindu, Sikh) village women whose brothers come to take them home: "Seasons change. Every year a father or a brother comes to take one or another woman back home. You should see how Asha, Rekha, Poroo, and Chandra seem to walk on air. They hug everyone before leaving. Their words sound like pure music."[93] Again, there are countless traditional folk songs from this region (and film songs) that joyfully and hopefully anticipate the next time, perhaps in the spring, that a married woman's natal family will send a brother to escort his sister home to her *maike* for a visit.[94]

In keeping with the metaphoric bent of this story, it is interesting to note that when Hashmi's protagonist in this short story does talk about her country or her homeland, the reference is not so much a geographical one but rather is to be understood in terms of time – past and present. As she states it:

> Still, I know well enough now that those dear to me live in a country I cannot possibly hope to reach. Like the pathways leading to Sangraon, all other paths criss-cross each other so often that they make one lose one's way. Besides what is to be gained from searching for a place which now exists only in stories?[95]

The term used in the Urdu original of the story for "country" or "homeland" is, surprisingly, the evocative Hindi term *janambhoomi*, which would most closely translate as "land of one's birth."[96] Like the use of the Sita story, the use of the Hindi term rather than Urdu alternatives such as *watan* (homeland) by this Pakistani writer deepens the ironic punch of this story. Of course, technically, this woman is still in her *janambhoomi*. She is still in India when she is in Sangraon, and yet this is not the "country" she longs to return to. There is a gap between the modern nation as country and the sense of the home country which is just as keenly felt as the distance between having citizenship and belonging to a place. Thus not only Muslims who leave for Pakistan but also Muslims and Hindus who remain in those Indian locations are rendered diasporic by time because this pre-1947 place of shared references has been left behind forever. Neither Pakistan nor independent India is adequate to the memory of the past. In a different context, Urdu scholar C. M. Naim has commented on the "syncretic *ganga-jamni* (Indo-Muslim) culture that was once the primary defining element for much of elite society in the towns and cities of the Gangetic plain."[97] Naim notes that while Partition destroyed this shared ethos, it often resurfaces in fiction written after 1947. Hashmi's use of Hindu legends and Hindi terms in this short story can be understood in this context. What is often dismissed in critical readings as romanticized sentimentalizing of the Other (such as the huge popularity of Hindi films categorized as "Muslim socials" in post-independence India) could be a nostalgic evocation of the loss of this shared *ganga-jamni* ethos.[98]

In Hashmi's story, then, the language of cartographic displacement – which is how the term *diaspora* is strictly interpreted – is itself simply a deferral of the profound out-of-placeness that this abductee experiences as the Bahu in a rural Sikh family. The Sita story, the diasporic tropes, are all simply metaphoric "paths that criss-cross," allowing her to express her dislocation but ultimately leading her back to the present life in Sangraon. The story ends with the line "How far do I still have to go?"[99] She is going nowhere, and yet the journey is not done. The narrative repeatedly emphasizes the ordinary drudgery of walking a long distance with a tired child to carry – an ordinary activity that is never sundered from the metaphoric journey: "All the same, I must keep on walking. Exile or not, one is compelled to move on in life's fair [*mela*]."[100] An abducted woman's suffering in this story is represented as keenly felt homesickness – and yet, while some Partition narratives elevate the horrific events of gendered violence into special stories full of heroism, villainy, and shame, this story consistently represents abduction and banishment as standard events in women's lives. Ashraf's and Hashmi's fiction makes diaspora a metaphoric category in itself, one that serves to wrench us from the familiarity of the customary national groves, derails us, and sometimes allows for a glimpse of a place that, as our protagonist sorrowfully tells us, "now exists only in stories."[101]

V

This chapter has attempted to extend the new scholarship on Partition by providing a glimpse into the long-standing literary and cultural ethos where nationalism is not the only reverberating axis of meaning, especially for voicing gendered dislocations. I read such texts as sites where vast non-national registers are voiced and made visible through formative cultural narratives such as the *Ramayana* and folk songs which equip women with a vocabulary for their exile, transferability, banishment, and homesickness. Butalia, Menon, Bhasin, and other feminists in their wake, work within the framework of the nation and, in their analysis of Partition's gendered violations, respectfully refrain from forcing into speech the many silences around the issue of rape and abduction. I see my contribution to this discussion as one that points to other routes toward an understanding of how gendered expectations and oppressions are voiced and protested in literary and other cultural narratives. These routes are made visible and audible within Partition literature, but they are routes that require reading (and listening) outside the official rhetoric of nation and, in the last instance, outside the customary language of diaspora.

Epilogue

In his note on the selections for *The Picador Book of Modern Indian Literature* that he edited in 2000, the novelist and cultural critic Amit Chaudhuri writes "this anthology happens to be in English."[1] Almost half of the selections in this hefty anthology are in English and the rest are English translations of texts originally written in six other Indian languages. Given this preponderance of English, Chaudhuri's description of the collection's contents as "a slight tipping of the scale toward the 'regional' or 'vernacular'" is inexplicable.[2] Despite being acutely aware of the politics of language and literature in the Indian context (which is in fact the central theme of the two essays by Chaudhuri that frame his anthology), the language in which the collection reaches the reader is presented as mere happenstance. And in a way it is. By the dawn of the twenty-first century, nothing needs to be said by way of explanation or justification when one writes in or translates into English. Indian intellectuals have mastered this art of making English an unobtrusive vehicle to convey modern Indian thought; it is apparently no less and no more than a convenient vehicle.

The motivation for writing this book came from my conviction that this banal presence of English in postcolonial Indian literary contexts had a multifaceted history and specific outcomes that remained under-examined. There are of course occasional outbursts against the continued hegemony of English, but these are not accompanied by any sustained consideration of the history of this language and of literature in this language in India.[3] In one of the two essays that together serve as an introduction to his anthology of modern Indian literature, Chaudhuri cleverly notes: "In fact, the word 'Indian' is almost only ever used, as a taxonomic term in contemporary literature, in connection with the word 'English'; no one speaks of the Indian novel in Bengali, or Urdu, or Kannada."[4] The reason for this easy linking of Indian with English is not self-evident. It is not just as simple as the fact that other nations besides India produce novels in English, thus requiring the clarification afforded by "Indian" when referencing the novel in this language. After all, one could, if one so desired, distinguish the Indian novel in Urdu or in Bengali from those produced in the neighboring postcolonial states of Pakistan and Bangladesh. Chaudhuri goes on to offer his explanation for the singularity of this linkage of "Indian" and "English":

> There is an implication here that only in the English language do Indian writers have the vantage-point, or at least feel the obligation, to articulate that post-colonial totality called "India" (on the other hand, it sometimes seems that the post-colonial totality called "India" only exists in the works of Indian English novelists, or in the commentaries they engender).[5]

The totality called "India" that Chaudhuri refers to had, as I have demonstrated in this book, a prior discursive existence to its appearance in postcolonial fictional and literary critical discourse. It is a construction that was born in the Indian English discourses of nation and national identity. English discursively constitutes this "India" which is the very locus of the national project. This totality called India became widely accepted as fact in the independence era and was subsequently adopted and adapted by postcolonial literary discourses which are also conducted in English. But Chaudhuri's pronouncements in this essay are more a dismissal of this entire genre than an explanation of why this genre has evolved the way it has and become representative of Indian literature.

As I have explored in this book, this extraordinary situation, whereby the literature in the one language that was considered not Indian became representative of "Indian Literature," has a dense history to it. Chaudhuri and other Indian commentators who are deeply invested in literatures in other Indian languages may find this situation annoying; but it is an undeniable consequence of the high status afforded to English both in India and globally in the colonial and the postcolonial era. Paradoxically, a language that had migrated into the subcontinent roughly two hundred years earlier had become, by the early twentieth century, *the* language in which all ideas, actions, and literary texts had to be expressed, or into which they had to be translated, in order to be recognized as non-parochial, not regionally biased, in short, as Indian. As I argued in Chapter 1 of this book, nationalist pride made Indians newly self-conscious about their reliance on English even as nationalists composed India as a nation in this language. After independence, English was the very Indian language of caste privilege and class authority in most public addresses pitched to the nation at large or to the world beyond. This is especially the case in Indian academia, where the only way to proceed with scholarly work seems to be to ignore

English, the elephant in the room, or to berate it as eternally foreign or everlastingly colonial.

English was and remains the global language of power and privilege. And as the chapters of this book have demonstrated, the need to compose and curate a particular India to the world in this language is not a recent imperative. The notion that the best of Indian thought could meet the world when expressed in English is an idea that is at least a hundred years old. As I have argued, from the efforts of Indian PEN and the first international All-Indian Writers' Conference in the 1940s to the anthologies edited under the auspices of the Sahitya Akademi and those published to celebrate the fiftieth anniversary of Indian independence, literary criticism in this language set out to establish that there was a representative Indian literature that could best be curated in English and that would thus reveal itself to be equal to the best in the world. Therefore, in 1997, when Salman Rushdie selected and wrote the introduction to *The Vintage Book of Indian Writing 1947–1997*, he was doing what many dedicated anthology editors before him had done, namely, showcasing Indian literature in a language that would earn it global respect.

From the early twentieth century onward, anthology editors have painstakingly gathered together their version of a representative Indian literature and have (usually with regret) noted the need to do so in the English language. Rushdie belongs to this long line of editors, except that unlike his predecessors, he is not apologetic for the reliance on English, nor does he see it as a necessary compromise undertaken in service to national unity. Rushdie instead declares that there is actually no better Indian literature than that which is written in English, hence his reliance on literary works in this language to represent the best work produced in the fifty years since independence. For Indian littérateurs, with this proclamation Rushdie's anthology embodies the most feared consequence of having retained English after independence: namely, that it would swamp the other languages and that it would force other, more "authentic" Indian literatures into the shadows. Rushdie's declaration forcefully insists that English, the language that was kept on for "convenience," that was supposed to efface itself, was instead the star of the past fifty years and the hope for the future.

In the early 1940s, Srinivasa Iyengar, the father of Indian literary criticism in English, had firmly declared that in a post-independence India, English would be "shown its place"[6] Rushdie deliberately and flagrantly violates this commonly accepted protocol attached to the Indian use of English. Of course, he had been doing precisely this in his brilliant manipulation of

English in his novels, but to extend this creative license to literary analysis was deemed beyond the pale. Chaudhuri, who very pointedly does not mention Rushdie's anthology but seems to have it in mind, begins his essay "Modernity and the Vernacular" with the question: "Can it be true that Indian writing, that endlessly rich, complex and problematic entity is to be represented by a handful of writers who write in English, live in England or America and whom one might have met at a party, most of whom have published no more than two novels, some of them only one?"[7] Chaudhuri could of course be one of this handful of writers — clearly he attends the same parties and writes his critically acclaimed novels in English. But, more seriously, what he protests is that all other languages and literary traditions are eclipsed by a post-Rushdie coterie of writers who have charmed the world and have occupied or, worse still, been *given* the entire Indian territory on the world literary map.

Fifty years after independence, when Rushdie looks forward to an era when Indian obscurity on the map of world literature ends, his cosmopolitanism actually echoes the ambitions of early Indian nationalists. Rushdie's essay, especially in his concluding lines quoted in the previous chapter, echoes the sentiments presented in the first entry to his collection — the iconic "tryst with destiny" speech made by Nehru at midnight on August 14, 1947 to the Indian Constituent Assembly, the new nation, and the world at large. That Rushdie for all his worldly sophistication, his elegant prose (the familiar archness of his writing), and his seeming distance from third world nationalism, echoes Nehru should come as no surprise to readers of *Indian English and the Fiction of National Literature*. We have seen repeatedly that the continuity between the elite nationalist and postcolonial discourses on the nation is steady and unshaken. Nehru ended his monumental speech made on the eve of Indian independence with:

> And so we have to labour and to work, and work hard, to give reality to our dreams. Those dreams are for India, but they are also for the world, for all nations and people are too closely knit together today for any one of them to imagine that it can live apart.[8]

As I have argued earlier in this study, from the start, aspirations for a national identity were also international aspirations at the very same time. In the decolonizing post-war era of the mid-twentieth century, it seemed more possible than ever before that "all nations and people" could live together in some more equal, more democratic union than under the colonial relationship. But as Nehru's speech notes, participation in this world community required a distinct national identity. Recognition on a global scale, as the editors at India PEN in the 1940s and as the Sahitya Akademi officials had well understood, would come only after a distinct national identity had been established. This need to render oneself or a cultural product as "Indian" was a crucial prerequisite to being heard or recognized in an international arena. And, as we have seen, everything that is lost in translation into this discourse of the nation and necessarily into English is soon forgotten. Most scholars like Chaudhuri who have noted that its global currency gives English an advantage over more local languages have lamented the resultant loss of recognition of vernacular literatures. What I have stressed in this book is that this lack of recognition applies not just to what is being written in other Indian languages, but also to Indian literary works in English that are not invested in the national. But venturing into the non-national requires the postcolonial critic to tread through unfamiliar grounds – to go past the familiar terrain of the nation and into everything that lies beyond.

Interestingly, both Rushdie's and Chaudhuri's introductory essays and the anthologies themselves are pitched at an international audience that includes an Indian readership within and outside India, as well as a western academic and mainstream audience. It is crucial to note that both these introductory essays were also published, albeit under different titles, in very influential western literary/cultural arenas: the *Times Literary Supplement* for Chaudhuri's two essays and *The New Yorker* for Rushdie's essay.[9] In these internationally circulating cultural venues, each author-turned-literary-commentator was deliberately penning the last word on Indian literature. The ease with which their essays were multi-purposed as introducing anthologies and as stand-alone assessments of a nation's literature as it enters the arena of world literature is worth noting. Is this path from the national to the international so easy because it is as smoothly aligned as the path from Miss India contests to Miss World contests? In other words, is it that, as with the beauty contests, one needs to emerge as the winner of the national title before one can enter and compete in the international arena? In such a situation, even the national selection is made with an eye to eventual success on the international circuit; hence, it is not just any small-town beauty or literary gem in a vernacular language that can hope to represent the nation. Both Rushdie and Chaudhuri are vying to bring a different contestant to the fore in the national and subsequently the international arena.

This study is also addressed to the same inter/national audience even as it hopes to circumvent the beauty contest. Its chapters trace the massive negotiations of language, of literary lineage, of theme and scale undertaken by individual writers and literary institutions in their very particular locations. Some of these negotiations are marked on national and world literary maps. Others are not. But the critical apparatus we bring to literature needs to be able to recognize all kinds of investments and not just those which reverberate on a national register. The genres that were appropriated for the literary projects studied in this book – whether novel, autobiography, or critical anthology – were transformed in usage. Each writer, each editor discussed in this book was a pioneer. Some were recognized as such, others were not. The heterogeneity of the literary scene even within one Indian language, English, was and is remarkable. Hence Narayan and Anand, both writing their first books in the same language and published in the same year, produce radically different texts that are enriched by radically different vernacular traditions, caste affiliations, and political motivations. English serves as a literary language to both Anand and Narayan; it is neither mother-tongue nor national language, but everything about these two authors and their books demonstrates the importance of not using the colonial or the national as the only stencil that will impart meaning to these novels.

In each chapter of this study, I have worked to record other riveting stories besides that of nation building that are narrated by literary texts. Each chapter has exposed the delicately etched effects of caste affiliation, gender dynamics, folklore, religious texts, regional and/or international literary movements, linguistic politics and other social changes that can be apprehended when we are not solely guided or blinded by the notion of the national. Each chapter offered detailed analyses of what is rendered invisible if authors and institutions are viewed strictly through the lens of the national. I considered whether a much favored writer like R. K. Narayan, who seems untainted by nationalist ideologies, is popular precisely because of the similar caste underpinnings of both stories set in Malgudi and the dominant narrative of the Indian nation. I show how Mulk Raj Anand's first novel *Untouchable* (1935) is rendered valuable when recuperated into a national narrative in the postcolonial era by both the author and the critics so that it moves from being a critique of Gandhi's approach to caste to being read as a Gandhian novel. In Chapter 4, on the Sahitya Akademi, I surveyed the successes and failures of this institution that was to establish a united Indian literature out of diverse sources on terra firma. In the final chapter on the anthologies produced in the late twentieth century to celebrate the fiftieth anniversary of Indian independence, I examined the collaborations (between publishers, critics, and writers) that produce a "national literature" in English for the Indian nation and the English reading world at large. I tracked the emergence of Partition as now inaugurating not just the nation but national literature well. Drawn from heterogeneous sources and translated into English, these stories are presented as reaching their full resonance in these new anthologies. But what is gained in this elevation to the national and thereby to a global audience? And what is lost?

Unlike other disciplines, literary criticism has no compulsion (except for convention and ease) to confine itself to the rubric of the nation. What, then, is national literature? Literary academics are currently quite comfortable with the category of national literature, especially when the focus is on literature that emerges from decolonizing contexts. However, the precise criterion for belonging to this category is hard to specify. Such literature cannot be equated with straightforward patriotic writing which simply follows the official narrative on the birth and fortunes of the nation. Clearly, there are very few literary examples that cleave to the kind of "no-fault nationalism" that Suvir Kaul suggests is the usual textbook account of national history that schoolchildren are subjected to.[10] National literature is usually that which critics assess as the best literary response to national crises, triumphs, or both. As a category it includes literary works that are expressly patterned by authors as a response to significant events in national history, works that even in their dissent from official narratives remain invested in the nation. Unlike diasporic fiction, it is understood to be committed to a single national space.

Does postcolonial literary criticism rely so heavily on the "transformation from colony to nation" narrative because it allows analysis to run repeatedly on a familiar track and through domesticated territory? In his essay "Modernity and the Vernacular," Amit Chaudhuri evaluates the postcolonial literary critical approach to Indian literature, and concludes from what he has read that:

> The only way India enters history is, evidently via colonialism: and as colonialism is seen basically as an encounter between Western colonizer and native colonized, it is perhaps fair to say that colonial India is interesting because at least in one crucial sense it is a part of Western history.[11]

This is a devastating assessment. But is it accurate? It would not be fair to say that colonialism is viewed in the scholarship simply as "an encounter between Western colonizer and native colonized," but certainly the colonial enterprise and the subsequent struggle for independence provide even the most sophisticated postcolonial scholarship with a historical logic and structure within which specific regions of the non-west are easily situated. In postcolonial analysis, does the motivation to hold on to the interpretive frame of nation and nationalism stem from an unwillingness to venture beyond this framework that leads so directly from the colonial state?

The caste and gender complexities of the turn to English as the language in which modern Indian literature, as much as a modern Indian identity, is gathered has been one of the central foci of this book. Despite my insistence on paying attention to the particular circumstance of English in India, my study is not motivated by a sense that the use of English in India is exceptional. Rather, I see my detailed study of the Indian context as a clear indication that the imbrications of English or other colonial languages in other once-colonized parts of the globe are absolutely worthy of study *on their own terms* and regardless of whether such scholarship confirms a comparative thesis about literature, language, and nationalism in all postcolonial locations. I hope this book helps postcolonial scholars resist the publishing and pedagogical pressures to "map" the non-west as tidy variations on the same difference. Several scholars have noted that because many of its leading theorists were of Indian origin, postcolonial criticism was tailor-made for the Indian context; and yet, as explored in this book, the fit is far from perfect. It would be flawed logic to assume that English or any other once colonial language – or literature for that matter – functions in identical fashion in all postcolonial literary contexts.

In the Indian context, I view this study as helping to create a more hospitable space for alternative voices and other themes in creative and critical writing in English. For example, from the late twentieth century onward, the most significant and yet studiously ignored claim to greater representation and access to literary circles and to the use of English has, in my estimation, been made by Dalit intellectuals. Substantial social, political, and economic changes need to be wrought in tandem with this recognition of Dalit cultural production; the overturning of popular paradigms is never easy. The transformed understanding of the role of the literary, which will come when Dalit literature and critical writing in English and in English translation are given their due, will no doubt confirm that what is currently considered "national literature" by Indian elite and western critics is necessarily partial. In interrogating the very creation and fabric of national literature through a close examination of institutions and individual authors who have fared differently under this rubric of consideration, this book has tried to illustrate the argument that so-called "national literature" is a fiction that serves and is maintained by nation-centric literary criticism produced in the early years of the nation, and then echoed and amplified by postcolonial literary discourses in the late twentieth century and beyond.

Notes

PROLOGUE

1. Casanova, *The World Republic of Letters*, p. xi.

CHAPTER 1 MANY A SLIP BETWEEN THE LITERARY AND THE NATIONAL

1. See U. R. Ananthamurthy, "The Flowering of the Backyard," in V. M. Narayanan and J. Sabarwal, eds., *India at 50*, pp. 235–246. Many of the essays in Vinay Dharwadkar, ed., *The Collected Essays of A. K. Ramanujan* explore aspects of language use in the Indian context.
2. There is of course a small Eurasian community of British or part-British descent in India, but clearly these are not the only Indians claiming English as their mother-tongue or as their first language. The 1991 census revealed that 0.55 percent of total households used English as a first or second language. In contrast the national language Hindi was spoken by 40–43.36 percent of households in India. See hhtp://censusindia.gov.in/. Confounding this issue of a minute sliver of the population being English users is the literacy level (according to the 2001 census) of 86.3 percent for urban males and 72.9 percent for urban females, where literacy is defined as the ability to read and write in any language. See www.censusindia.gov.in/Census_Data_2001/India_at_Glance/literates1.aspx. Also see http://censusindia.gov.in/Census_Data_2001/Census_Data_Online/Language/Statement1.htm. For a detailed analysis of the linguistic complexity of post-independence India, see Harihar Bhattacharyya's *Federalism and Regionalism in India*.
3. Different scholars read census data differently especially when it comes to gauging language use with an accounting for second and third language. See Sheth, "The Great Language Debate." Also see Viyaunni, "The Bilingual Scenario in India," for a nuanced consideration of bilingualism and trilingualism as gleaned from the 1991 Indian census results. Also see Trivedi, *Colonial Transactions*, which brilliantly examines the many aspects of English usage in multiple Indian and British literary contexts. Tabish Khair's *Babu Fictions* also discusses the caste and linguistic features of elite Indian literature which he refers to as "babu fiction."

4. In his "The Great Language Debate," p. 267, n. 1, D. L. Sheth remarks that "the term vernacular is used in two senses: linguistic and cultural. In the former sense vernacular refers to all non-English Indian languages as a diffused countervailing reality confronting the preeminence of English in India." Sheth notes that Hindi continues to be referred to as a vernacular, regional language despite its vast coverage (more than 40 percent of the population).
5. See Guha, *A Disciplinary Aspect of Indian Nationalism*, p. 38.
6. Sheth, "The Great Language Debate," pp. 288–289.
7. The Indian National Congress (INC) was the main political party in the pre- and post-independence years. The INC had Hindu, Muslim, and Dalit members but operated under the umbrella of a distinctly Hindu nationalism. The Muslim League was formed in British India in 1906 by non-Congress Muslims; by 1913 it, like the INC, began agitating for Indian self-rule, by the mid-1930s for separate political representation of Muslim interests, and eventually, by the 1940s, for the creation of Pakistan.
8. Ambedkar, *Pakistan or the Partition of India*, pp. 11–12 (emphasis in the original).
9. Note, however, that Ambedkar had repeatedly argued (from his Columbia University dissertation onward) that India had one culture. In claiming this he was arguing against those who had tried to depict Dalits as having different racial origins from upper-caste Hindus.
10. Ludden, *India and South Asia*, p. 181.
11. Ibid., pp. 161–163.
12. Interestingly the census questionnaire from 1901 to 1941 had one very specific question about the respondent's knowledge of English in addition to questions about the mother-tongue and knowledge of other Indian languages. However, from the very first census after independence (1951) this question about English knowledge was dropped from the total of twenty-odd questions respondents were expected to answer. For census questionnaires from the 1872 census to the 1971 census, see http://censusindia.gov.in/Data_Products/Library/Indian_perceptive_link/Census_Questionaires_link/questions.htm (accessed September 11, 2009).
13. Speech at Banaras Hindu University, February 6, 1916. See *Collected Works of Mahatma Gandhi*, vol. XV, p. 149.
14. Ibid., pp. 150–151.
15. Ibid., p. 150.
16. See Lelyveld, "The Fate of Hindustani," p. 191.
17. Elsewhere Gandhi advocated for both Hindi and Hindustani (an amalgam of Hindi and Persianized Urdu that was in use in the north and could be written in either Nagri or Urdu/Persian script). In 1945, Gandhi resigned from the Hindi Sahitya when it advocated that Hindi was to be written exclusively in the Devanagri script. Over time, as both Hindi and Urdu became increasingly linked with Hindu and Muslim identity respectively, Hindustani had few advocates in India with voices powerful enough to drown out the opposition to it, especially after the trauma of partition. Hindi was deliberately Sanskritized

to underline its Hindu roots and to create a purer etymology for the language. At the debates on the national language in the Constituent Assembly meetings, advocates of both Hindi and Hindustani tried to portray the late Gandhi as invested in their side of the debate. See the speech by Mohammad Hifzur Rahman to the assembly in which he proposed that Hindustani written in either the Hindi or Urdu script be chosen as the national language, even as he argued that Gandhi had shifted his advocacy from Hindi to Hindustani precisely to protest the Hinduization (via Sanskritization) of the language. Rahman insisted that three days prior to his death, Gandhi had told him that he was going to "propagate the cause of Hindustani" (see *Constituent Assembly Debates: Official Report*, Volume IX (July 30, 1949–September 19, 1949), pp. 1341–1342.

18. Note, for example, that when All-India Radio was set up in 1937, all news broadcasting was directly controlled by the British colonial offices in New Delhi. All news broadcasts were prepared in English and then translated into select Indian languages and transmitted from New Delhi. This practice was continued by AIR in the post-independence years and Lelyveld claims was in place when his research was conducted (early 1990s). See Lelyveld "Transmitters and Culture: The Colonial Roots of India broadcasting." Further investigation suggests that for the government-controlled news channels this translation from English to regional languages continues to the present day.

19. For example, see what is commonly referred to as the "CR Formula" – C. Rajagopalachari's offer to Mr. Jinnah made in 1944 in which he proposed (with Gandhi's assent) that instead of demanding Pakistan, the Muslim League endorse the Indian demand for independence and cooperate with the Congress, in return for which the Congress would promise that after a transitional period, a plebiscite would be held in places where Muslims formed an absolute majority, which would ultimately decide the issue of the establishment of a separate state for Muslims. Here, despite speaking across communities, there was no real equity being offered to the other side.

20. For example, see the "Address" presented to Lord Minto (then viceroy and governor-general of India) by "A Deputation of the Muslim Community of India on 1st October 1906 at Simla." This was an important document in that it has been viewed as the first instigator of the subsequent British policy of making separate provisions for Muslims in constitutional reform acts. This document is included as Appendix XII in Ambedkar's *Pakistan or the Partition of India*, pp. 428–443.

21. See especially Rai, *Hindi Nationalism*, which passionately tracks the creation of a Sanskritized "Hindi" from the nineteenth century, which he argues has been to the detriment of what was a dynamic, hybrid, "people's vernacular." See especially Rai's astute discussion of the language debates in the Constituent Assembly in chapter 7, "Roads to the Present," pp. 106–120.

22. This discussion is developed later in this chapter and then picked up in earnest in Chapter 4 on the uses of English in the Sahitya Akademi's efforts to develop

and coordinate a single national literature out of the multiple literary traditions in multiple languages.
23. See Asha Sarangi ("Introduction," in *Language and Politics*) and Selig Harrison (*India: The Most Dangerous Decades*, p. 282) who both quote Ambedkar's recollection of the negotiations that resulted in the writing of the new constitution for which he headed the drafting committee: "No article produced more opposition. No article, more heat."
24. Granville Austin has expressed doubts that this vote was so close. He suggests that Ambedkar and other participants, like Seth Govind Das, who recollect it were confusing the vote that established Hindi as the official language with another related (and close) vote about the use of international or Nagari numerals. Austin insists that, given that the Constituent Assembly operated on the principle of consensus, a one-vote victory would not have been enough to determine so important and so highly contested an issue as the official language for the nation. See "Language and the Constitution," pp. 83–84.
25. Sarangi, "Introduction," in *Language and Politics*, p. 23, n. 75.
26. See Constituent Assembly Debates: Official Report, Sept. 12, 1949, Vol. IX, pp. 1332–1333.
27. Ibid., p. 1330.
28. Ibid., pp. 1334, 1335. Also see the repeated attention that members draw to the language in which the debate on all matters is conducted and the attention drawn to any divergence from English use, as well as the occasional demand made from the floor that a particular speaker use English, Hindi, or even Sanskrit.
29. For more on the place of Sanskrit in these debates, see Ramaswamy, "Sanskrit for the Nation." There are interesting parallels between Sanskrit and English as language of the elites. See the comparison of English and Sanskrit by A. K. Ramanujan (English language poet and renowned translator of ancient literary works from classical Tamil to English) in his much-cited essay "Is There an Indian Way of Thinking?" Ramanujan argues that "Indian borrowings of Western cultural items have been converted and realigned to fit pre-existing context-sensitive needs. When English is borrowed into (or imposed on) Indian contexts, it fits into the Sanskrit slot; it acquires many of the characteristics of Sanskrit, the older native father-tongue, its pan-Indian elite character – as a medium of laws, science, administration, and its formulaic patterns; it becomes part of Indian multiple diglossia (a characteristic of context-sensitive societies)" (p. 437). In *The Discovery of India*, Nehru makes a similar comparison of the two languages. For further discussion of the parallels between English and Sanskrit, see Annamalai, "Nativization of English in India," pp. 152–153. Probal Dasgupta, in *The Otherness of English*, absolutely rejects this comparison: "Postmodern India's English, in contrast to classical India's Sanskrit has been a failure as far as independent creative expression is concerned" (p. 113; also see pp. 70–71 and 41). Also see Ananthamurthy, "The Flowering of the Backyard." See also Sheth, "The Great Language Debate," p. 289, for a detailed explication of how and in what ways English today is structurally in the position occupied

by Sanskrit and Persian, how both those languages allowed a similar hold on power by an elite minority, and how both lost out because they did not serve as the language of communication for large numbers. C. D. Narasimhaiah argues that if English was foreign at one time, then so was Sanskrit, both foreign and elite: "Were the authors of the Vedas, Upanishads, epics and dramas unpatriotic for not writing in the language of the masses?" he asks, implying that Indian English writers are in the same position in the present time (*The Swan and the Eagle*, p. 10). Narasimaiah insists that just as Sanskrit "in the past signified the first flowering of Indian sensibility and . . . represents the mainstream of Indian culture," so might English in the future (p. 8). And yet, by the twentieth century, despite all efforts at revival, Sanskrit was more or less a dead language. Sheth suggests that English will (or should) go the same way, that is, die out because of the small numbers who are comfortable in the language ("The Great Language Debate," pp. 283 and 291). Rita Kothari notes that Sanskrit has been an exalted scriptural language but never a spoken one. Persian too, she notes, was primarily an administrative language. English, on the other hand, is increasingly in use and hence she foresees a different trajectory for English from that of Sanskrit (Kothari, *Translating India*, p. 31). Other scholars insist that the global use of English will further motivate a larger part of the population to strive for competence in, if not mastery of, the language. Already the 2001 census shows that a larger percentage of young people are literate and more of them in English.

30. Iyengar, *Indo-Anglian Literature*, p. 62.
31. *The Constitution of Indian* (1950), Part XVII, Official Language, "Chapter I. Language of the Union."
32. Iyengar, "Introduction," in Iyengar, *Indian Writers in Council*, p. xviii.
33. The political and cultural ramifications of languages that appear and do not appear on the Eighth Schedule is discussed at greater length in Chapter 4.
34. See the Constitution of India. Part XVII Official Language, Chapter 1. Language of the Nation. Section 343. Official Language of the Union.
35. See Rai, *Hindi Nationalism*, pp. 114–115.
36. Pakistan, meanwhile, instated Urdu as the national language in its constitution. Even in West Pakistan, Urdu was the first language of no more than 10 percent of the population. The East Pakistan secession from Pakistan and the creation of Bangladesh in 1972 was directly linked to resistance to the imposition of Urdu against the claims of Bengali/Bangla which was the language of 99 percent of the population in what was East Pakistan.
37. For more analysis of language politics in the south, see Ramaswamy, *Passions of the Tongue*.
38. Narayan, "Fifteen Years," p. 14, in *A Writer's Nightmare*, pp. 14–16. Originally published in *The Hindu* (date unknown) and printed in *Next Sunday: Sketches and Essays* (1960).
39. Ibid., p. 16.
40. Kachru, *The Alchemy of English*, p. 1.
41. Iyengar, "Introduction," in Iyengar, *Indian Writers in Council*, p. xviii.

42. Ibid., p. 9.
43. See Annamalai, "The Anglicized Indian Languages," quoted by Kachru, *The Alchemy of English*, p. 9.
44. See E. Annamalai's comprehensive "Nativization of English in India." Annamalai's work is also instructive on the language rivalries that ultimately led to the decision against the original plan at independence to end the official use of English fifteen years after the Indian constitution was prepared in 1950. Also see Annamalai, "English in India."
45. See the brilliant analysis of the Dalit rejection of the BJP Sanskrit plan of 1999–2000 in Anand "Sanskrit, English, Dalits."
46. See Lahiri, "A Dalit Temple to 'Goddess English.'"
47. This has been changing in recent years with films like *Dhobi Ghat* (2010, dir. Kiran Rao) (literally "Washerman's Docks" but released in the west with the title *Mumbai Diaries*) that have a substantial proportion of the dialogue in English, which have been enthusiastically received by urban youth in India. Small films like *In Which Annie Gives Those Ones* (1989, dir. Pradip Krishen) and *Massy Sahib* (1985, also directed by Krishen) had sizeable amounts of dialogue in English but were not commercially distributed or successful.
48. See Lelyveld, "Talking the National Language."
49. Anderson, *Imagined Communities*, especially Chapters 2 and 3.
50. For example, Indian rock bands, like the highly regarded Indian Ocean, who write and perform their own music, turn to all of the "western" musical sources mentioned above but the lyrics are rarely in English. Despite having a primary following among English-speaking Indian college students, young first-generation Indian diaspora, and world music aficionados, the band turns to Indian folk and vernacular songs and musical genres for their inspiration. Rahul Ram, the guitarist and one of the vocal leads for Indian Ocean, notes that in their vast repertoire, there is only a single four-line section of a particular song that is in English. Conversation with author, March 2008. By the early twenty-first century numerous Indian rock bands had been formed, enough to sustain several annual festivals.
51. As C. D. Narasimhaiah explains in his "Preface to the Second Edition" of *The Swan and the Eagle*, the adoption of "Indian English" instead of earlier terms is a "demonstration of [the language's] mature self-confidence, for in colonial days 'Indian English' was a pejorative term to denote a sub-standard deviant of Standard English" (9).
52. Ahmed, *Literature and Politics in the Age of Nationalism*, p. 21.
53. The entire text of the PWA manifesto as published in *New Left Review* is reproduced in "Over Chinese Food: The Progressive Writers' Association," in Mir and Mir, *Anthems of Resistance*, pp. 4–6.
54. Ibid., p. 5. For more information on the Progressive Writers' Association, see Cappola, *Marxist Influences and South Asian Literature*; Mir and Mir, *Anthems of Resistance*; Talat Ahmed, *Literature and Politics in the Age of Nationalism*.
55. See Ahmed, *Literature and Politics in the Age of Nationalism*, p. 111.

56. See Mahmud, "*Angāre* and the Founding of the Progressive Writers' Association."
57. Ibid., p. 451.
58. See Chapter 3 in this book on Mulk Raj Anand, where the impact of the PWA on the writing of Anand's early fiction, especially on his first novel, *Untouchable* (1935), which was written in England in the same time period, is discussed.
59. Born in New York, Sophia Camacho (1901–1986) was a theosophist who was inspired to work in India by Bahman R. Wadia (1881–1958), a visiting fellow theosophist from India who was on a tour of theosophical centers in the USA in 1927. Camacho and Wadia wed in London in 1928. They returned to India in May 1929 and set up several branches of the United Lodge of Theosophists (ULT). Known for her oratory skills and fluent in several European languages, Sophia Wadia served as editor of ULT publications and in 1933 organized the first Indian branch of PEN in Bombay. In all her essays and editorials, Sophia Wadia presents herself as an anti-imperial nationalist devoted to spreading the word about theosophy and national independence for India via literature, the arts, and culture. Her position within the Indian literary context exemplifies the "network of public spheres" that Mrinalini Sinha describes, in the context of her study of the debates around Katherine Mayo's work, as a global configuration that "demands far more in the way of historical understanding than the supposedly seamless logic of imperialism and nationalism" (*Specters of Mother India*, pp. 23–24). Also see Leela Gandhi, *Affective Communities*, for a nuanced framework in which to place a figure like Sophia Wadia.
60. Interestingly the PWA leader Sajjad Zahir was very dismissive of Sophia Wadia's literary and political views which he gauged through the speech she made at the first International Congress of Writers for the Defense of Culture that was convened in Paris in June 1935 under the direction of André Gide. Wadia participated in a session on "For the Defense of Culture" in which she located the cradle of civilization in India but also insisted that "we consider the root of all Indian culture to be Aryan." Zahir thought such views to be the antithesis of the PWA stance against facism and imperialism, and Talat Ahmed quotes Zahir noting in his *Reminiscences* that "it would have been better to leave India unrepresented rather than send her to represent her" (Ahmed, *Literature and Politics in the Age of Nationalism*, p. 26).
61. Wadia, "Editorial Foreword," in Iyengar, *Indo-Anglian Literature*, pp. i–iii. This same foreword ran in all the volumes published in the pre-independence era, of which I have examined the following: Barua, *Assamese Literature*, Annadasankar and Lila Ray, *Bengali Literature*, and Raju, *Telegu Literature*. The twelfth volume in this series, Chandrasekharan and Sastri, *Sanskrit Literature*, was published after independence and after a gap of seven years, and carried a partly rewritten foreword. It is not clear whether all the books in the series were published.
62. Wadia, "Editorial Foreword," in Iyengar, *Indo-Anglian Literature*, p. i.

63. Ibid., p. i.
64. Ibid.
65. Ibid.
66. Ibid., p. ii.
67. Ibid.
68. Ibid.
69. Ibid.
70. Ibid., p. iii.
71. *The Twice Born Fiction* (1971), written by Meenakshi Mukherjee decades later, notes that it is with the publication of the assessment of "Indo-Anglian" literature by K. Srinivasa Iyengar in the early 1940s (specifically in *Indo-Anglian Literature* (1943) and *The Indian Contribution to English Literature* (1945)), that this writing was formally established as a field that could be studied.
72. As Chapter 4 on the Sahitya Akademi (SA) will show, when this academy of letters was established in 1954, many of these same political and cultural luminaries were at the helm there as well. The leaders of the all-India PEN, of the central government, and in 1954 of the governing body of the SA were all drawn from this same roster of English-educated literary elite. The governing principle of the Sahitya Akademi was this very same notion of Indian literature as a means of ensuring, as well as a manifestation of, Indian unity.
73. Iyengar, "Introduction," in Iyengar, *Indian Writers in Council*, p. xi.
74. Ibid., p. xvii.
75. Ibid.
76. Ibid.
77. Pannikar, "The Desirability of an All-India Encyclopaedia," in Iyengar, *Indian Writers in Council*, p. 148.
78. Ibid., p. 150.
79. Ibid., p. 151.
80. See the "Vote of Thanks" offered by Dr. Md. Shahidullah at the last session of the conference; Iyengar, *Indian Writers in Council*, pp. 227–229.
81. Also see "Popularization of the Indian Literatures outside India," a presentation at the conference made by Gertrude Sen.
82. Kabir, "Foreword," in *Contemporary Indian Short Stories*, p. xv.
83. Ibid.
84. This was the case with the princely state of Hyderabad where the Nizam was compelled by military force to join the union of independent India in 1947. It would be interesting to reconcile this violence with the Nizam's sponsoring of the first All-India Writers' Conference in Jaipur in 1945 discussed earlier in this chapter. A total of 565 royal states were integrated into the Indian union, acceding with varying degrees of enthusiasm.
85. I thank Nandita Dhume Majumdar for reminding me of these two "family planning" slogans from this era.
86. See Chapter 2 on R. K. Narayan for a detailed examination of the sentiments and sentimentalism evoked by his fictional world of Malgudi which serves as a compelling example of symbolic equity.

87. Iyengar, *Indo-Anglian Literature*, pp. 55–56.
88. For an excellent discussion on the curricula aspects of English in India, see Trivedi, *Colonial Transactions*, "Chapter 10: *Panchadhatu:* Teaching English Literature in the Indian Literary Context."
89. While more sophisticated critics might dismiss these books as "bazaar" or "pavement books," they are bought by university libraries in South Asia and beyond and, in the absence of other scholarship on Indian writing in English from the mid-twentieth century, these writings constitute the definitive "local" reading of such works.
90. A good example of this determined application of aesthetic theory from classical Sanskrit traditions to literary works in English is on view in the collection edited and introduced by C. D. Narasimhaiah for the Sahitya Akademi, *East West Poetics at Work* (1994), which includes essays ranging from applications of *rasa* theory as applied to T. S. Eliot, Blake, Nabakov, and Achebe, to arguments for the advantages of using these classical aesthetic theories (which remain central to performing and interpreting other Indian cultural forms like dance, music, and dramatic arts) over western poetics. See especially Narasimaiah's "Introduction" which is an impressive display of his erudition in Sanskrit aesthetic theories as well as in the literature of the west and of the decolonizing globe. Professor Narasimhaiah (1921–2005), who established the literary retreat Dhavanyaloka and the Center for English Studies and Indigenous Arts in Mysore, as well as publishing the English language journal *The Literary Criterion* from 1952 onward, is himself an institution worthy of study. His vision for Dhavanyaloka was to build a haven for the study and practice of Indian literary aesthetic theories which was both shaped by his own training under F. R. Leavis in Cambridge, but also sought to have at its core "a marked Indianness in . . . approach and values" ("Director's Announcement for McAlpin Resident fellowship"). "Indianness" here is clearly marked as that which is aesthetically legible only through Sanskrit poetics.
91. Mehrotra, "Further Reading," in *A History of Indian Literature in English*, p. 381.
92. Mehrotra's edited book provides leading scholars with the opportunity to jointly write a history of this literature which is unlike "the earlier attempts at a history [which] have been more like acts of enumeration" (*A History of Indian Literature in English*, p. xx). The general tone of this collection of essays (presented without the burden/benefit/constraint of citations and footnotes) is of a refreshing, often speculative, but thought-provoking reexamination of established figures and a championing of almost forgotten figures. And Mehrotra exemplifies the volume's openness to new readings and juxtapositions in his thoughtful introduction which acknowledges that: "[t]o write or even compile, a literary history is to build on shifting sands. And yet the task cannot be wholly futile" (p. xxi).
93. Mukherjee, "Preface," in *The Twice Born Fiction*, unnumbered first page.
94. Ibid.

95. Also see A. V. Krishna Rao, *The Indo-Anglian Novel and the Changing Tradition*. In his introductory chapter Rao makes the argument that "the Indo-Anglian novel, properly speaking, made its first uncertain, but significant start in the thirties."
96. Mukherjee, *The Twice Born Fiction*, p. 17.
97. See my earlier work on English language novels by female writers of this generation whose commonly used plot presents female protagonists who have every comfort of home (domestic comforts, social status, leisure, language) and yet find themselves unsatisfied with their privileges, unable to articulate this angst, and unable to significantly alter their lives. See "Elite Plotting, Domestic Postcoloniality," in George, *The Politics of Home*, pp. 131–170.
98. See the excerpt from Sujit Mukherjee's "Propositions" (1981), reprinted in *Cultural Diversity, Linguistic Plurality and Literary Traditions in India*, p. 8.
99. Devy, *After Amnesia*, p. 10.
100. Ibid.
101. Ibid., p. 7.
102. For more on this second stage of Kamala Das's career when she flourished as a regional cultural icon in Kerala, see *Kamala, Madhavikutty, Suraiya: Writing Self, Writing Kerala*, currently in preparation, edited by Muraleedharan Tharayil and myself, with essays by leading literary and cultural critics who trace Kamala Das's transition from the national to the regional literary arena and closely examine these two distinct linguistic and cultural spheres that coexist on a global terrain with some overlap in the late twentieth and early twenty-first century.
103. Naik, *A History of Indian English Literature*, p. 191. Published in 1982, M. K. Naik's literary history of Indian English provides a detailed assessment of important texts and themes from roughly 1906 to 1979.
104. Ibid., p. 284.
105. Sharma, "Introduction," in *Nationalism in Indo-Anglian Fiction*, pp. xii–xiii.
106. Neil Lazarus has argued in a similar vein in his essay titled "The Politics of Postcolonial Modernism" where he writes: "I am tempted to overstate the case, for purposes of illustrations, and declare that there is in a strict sense only one author in the postcolonial literary canon." Lazarus's reference is to Salman Rushdie whose novels, especially *Midnight's Children* and *The Satanic Verses*, are, he claims, "endlessly and fatuously cited" in postcolonial criticism (p. 772).
107. During Rushdie's book tour to India in 1982, when organizers expected small decorous gatherings, thousands turned up for each event. No venue was large enough, and in Delhi, Calcutta, and Bombay the author often had to jump up on the table and shout out his words to enthusiastic audiences that overflowed into the aisles, the foyers, and lawns of buildings and even into the streets.

108. By the 1980s it would be safe to say that the Indian English writers and readership were predominantly *not* bilingual as they had been in the late nineteenth and early twentieth century when many of the writers who chose to write in English were also fluent in a mother-tongue that they shared with their immediate audience (Tagore, for example). In earlier interviews (like those compiled in *Conversations with Salman Rushdie*, edited by Michael Reder) Rushdie is quite frank about his inability to write in Urdu, though the fault is placed with the language: Urdu is "beautiful" but "bound by rules" and therefore has "no elbow room" in it for a writer like himself. (See the interview with David Brooks from 1984, pp. 63–64.) In recent years Rushdie has variously assessed his competence in written Urdu in the many interviews that he has given.
109. Rushdie, *Shame*, p. 87.
110. Ibid., p. 29.
111. Beyond its impact in the literary field and in shaping postcolonial literary theory, thirty years later the very term "midnight's children" has entered the Indian lexicon so that, for example, in 1997, the fiftieth anniversary of independence, almost every assessment of India published in English carried this phrase in its title or text. Thus the English language press in India also echoed back Rushdie's evocation of the national.
112. Narasimhaiah, *The Swan and the Eagle*, p. 13. And yet, despite the seeming generosity of this statement, Narasimhaiah exhibits a high degree of vitriol, sexism, anger, and disdain for contemporary Indian English writing in his critique titled "Spurious Reputations" on Rushdie, Seth, and Roy. In an astonishingly harsh chapter he refuses to see any merit whatsoever in this writing (*The Swan and the Eagle*, pp. 244–255).
113. For example, Indianness and authenticity are crucial to the evaluations in M. K. Naik and Shyamala Narayan, *Indian English Literature: 1980–2000*, which they present as a sequel to the influential *A History of Indian English Literature* (1982) by Naik.
114. And yet, as my recently published work on Kamala Markandaya tries to demonstrate, this continued focus on the nation and the national has very severe consequences for a writer like Markandaya whose writing very quickly set off on a trajectory that took her away from the role of an Indian woman writer who would serve as an "Indian literary ambassador to the world," to that of a "European intellectual" in an era where an Indian expatriate could find very narrow footholds that would support such a self-fashioning. Hence, because her later work was not nation-centric, Markandaya became an outlier on the postcolonial literary map. See Rosemary George, "Where in the World did Kamala Markandaya Go?" pp. 400–409.
115. Jameson, "Third World Literature in the Era of Multinational Capitalism," p. 69. See my detailed discussion of this essay and of the critical response to it in "Nostalgic Theorizing: At Home in 'Third World' fictions," in *The Politics of Home*, pp. 101–130.
116. Bhabha, "DissemiNation," in Babha, ed., *Nation and Narration*, p. 297.

117. For a longer discussion of this essay by Homi Bhabha, see the chapter "Traveling Light: Home and the Immigrant Genre," in George, *The Politics of Home*, pp. 186–191.
118. Ramakrishnan, "Introduction," in *Narrating India*, p. 1.
119. Vijaysree *et al.*, *Nations in Imagination*, p. xvi.
120. See the introductions by Christopher Shackle and Vasudha Dalmia to *Nationalism in the Vernacular: Hindi, Urdu, and the Literature of Indian Freedom*, ed. Shobna Nijhawan, for a nuanced discussion of the varying degree and nature of nationalist sentiment in the many nineteenth- and twentieth-century texts translated from Hindi and Urdu which are excerpted in that book.
121. "Damne, This is the Oriental Scene for You!" This argument put forth by Rushdie is discussed further in Chapter 6 and in the Epilogue to this book.
122. Ramakrishnan, *Narrating India*, pp. 12–13.
123. Ibid., p. 12.
124. Menon, "No, Not the Nation."
125. Ibid., pp. 41–42.
126. Ibid., p. 42.
127. Ibid., p. 53.
128. Ibid., p. 47.
129. Ibid., p. 58.
130. Natwar Singh, "Keynote Address," in Mukherjee, *Early Novels in India*, p. 4.
131. Ibid., p. 5.
132. See Moretti, "Conjunctures on World Literature," and Moretti, *The Novel*. This discussion is picked up again in the Epilogue to this book.
133. See Sheth, "The Great Language Debate." For a larger discussion of these distinct worldviews, see Chapters 2 and 3 in this book which will address the different worldviews and worlds that upper and lowest castes inhabited, the intersections of these two worlds, and the intervention that an English language novel like Mulk Raj Anand's *Untouchable* makes in exposing the divergences between the national struggle for independence from the British and struggles for freedom from caste-based oppression. Chapter 3 will also consider the very important role of English in Dalit articulations of self-worth and self-empowerment.
134. Sheth, "The Great Language Debate," p. 272.
135. See Reddy, "Midnight's Orphans."
136. Deshpande, "English's Inter Alia."
137. See the Indian magazine *Outlook* (February 25, 2002).
138. See Sarkar, *Modern India 1885–1947*, p. 10.

CHAPTER 2 R. K. NARAYAN AND THE FICTION OF THE "ORDINARY INDIAN"

1. See David Ludden's analysis of the 1911 census which would support such an interpretation: "One group stands out for its literacy: Brahmans. All

Brahmans in British India combined to form about six per cent of the 1911 populations and as an official census category they had exceptionally high rates of literacy: forty per cent in Bengal and Madras presidencies and in some native states, like Baroda; thirty per cent in Bombay presidency and among Kashmiri Pundits. English literacy was also more common among literate Brahmans. More than twenty-five per cent of all literate Brahmans were literate in English in Madras and Bengal presidencies; and the figure hovers around twenty per cent in Bombay, Kashmir, Baroda, and Mysore territories. Brahman stature in imperial society is reflected in high Brahman English literacy" (Ludden, *India and South Asia*, p. 161).

2. See Ludden on the link between high-caste, male, urban culture, and writing in English and the vernacular languages: "Though English literates were the most prominent members of imperial society, they numbered less than one per cent of the total population in the early twentieth century. Most were men from high status groups, many were Brahmans, and they mostly lived in big cities. Most literate people who participated in public life read and wrote in other languages. Only fifteen per cent of all the books officially recorded as being published in British India in the 1920s were in English" (ibid., p. 163).

3. In 1938 when C. Rajagopalachari (Rajaji), the Congress Party premier of Madras, ordered the compulsory study of Hindi in secondary schools in the region, this anti-Hindi sentiment grew to a head and English, more than ever, was viewed as Tamil's ally. This law was repealed in 1940.

4. For the relationship between English and Tamil in the late nineteenth and early twentieth century, see Stuart Blackburn's afterword to his translation from Tamil of *The Fatal Rumour*, B. R. Rajam Aiyar's late nineteenth-century domestic novel. First serialized in the popular Tamil monthly journal *Vivekachintamani* from February 1893 to January 1895, *Fatal Rumour*, a story of how pride and gossip destroys the relationship between a husband and wife, was published in book form in 1896 and went through many editions. By 1932 this novel was placed on the government college syllabus in Madras Presidency and enjoyed wide circulation.

5. The burgeoning anti-Brahmin movement in this same period had also rallied support around an anti-Sanskrit, anti-Hindi, anti-north, pro-Tamil, pro-Dravidian politics. And, with the establishment by E. V. Ramaswamy Naicker (Periyar) of the self-respect movement in 1925, the issue of language was highly charged, with Tamil aligned against Hindi (the language of the north) and Sanskrit (the language associated with the Brahmin caste). For more on the complex, triangular relationship between Tamil, Hindi, and English in this period, see Ramaswamy, *Passions of the Tongue*.

6. For a reading of Narayan that places his work within a Tamil literary context, see Shanker, "Reading the Vernacular."

7. In *R. K. Narayan: The Early Years, 1906–1945*, his biographers Susan and N. Ram note: "In late 1933, his published output comprised a book review, a short story and a satirical essay... On this slender basis, he held firm to the ambition to be a full-time writer" (p. 119).

8. Ram and Ram, *R. K. Narayan*, pp. xxxii–xxxiii.
9. Ibid., pp. xxii–xxiii.
10. Iyengar, *Indo-Anglian Literature*, p. 36.
11. Krishnan, "Editor's Introduction," in *Malgudi Landscapes*, p. ix.
12. Narayan mentions this short essay in his autobiography *My Days*, p. 107. Also see the discussion of this essay in Ram and Ram, *R. K. Narayan*, p. 118.
13. "How to Write an Indian Novel," p. 341.
14. Ram and Ram, *R. K. Narayan*, p. 118.
15. Narayan, *My Days*, p. 107.
16. Narayan, "How to Write an Indian Novel," p. 341.
17. See Ram and Ram, *R. K. Narayan*, especially the chapter titled "Enter Greene," pp. 143–158.
18. In November 2009, an abridged version of *Swami and Friends* with an insertion of two of Narayan's stories featuring Swami was published (with approval from the author's estate) under the title *Malgudi Schooldays* by Penguin Indian books in collaboration with Ranga Shankara foundation in Bangalore India. This book is included (for "free") with a six DVD boxed set of the TV serial *Malgudi Days* distributed by Padamrag TV International. This TV serial is discussed at length at the conclusion to this chapter.
19. Iyengar, *Indo-Anglian Literature*, p. 44.
20. Tharoor, "Comedies of Suffering."
21. Walsh, *R. K. Narayan*, p. 6.
22. See Mukherjee's very effective contrasting of Narayan's style with that of other eminent Indian writers of his time in *The Twice Born Fiction*, pp. 199–200.
23. Ibid., p. 199.
24. Walsh, *R. K. Narayan*, p. 166.
25. Ibid., p. 1.
26. Ibid., p. 166.
27. Narasimhaiah, *The Swan and the Eagle*, p. 177.
28. Naik, *A History of Indian English Literature*, p. 160.
29. See Pandian, "One Step outside Modernity," pp. 240–241.
30. Ibid., p. 241.
31. Ibid.
32. In rare instances in his writing, Narayan deals directly and explicitly with caste tensions between Brahmin and other castes. See, for example, the short story "Fellow-Feeling," in *Malgudi Days*, which was first published in a collection of stories called *An Astrologer's Day*, pp. 52–60, and has since been reprinted in Rushdie and West, *The Vintage Book of Indian Writing*, pp. 102–108. In this short story Narayan presents a confrontation in a third-class train compartment between a rude and obnoxious low-caste passenger and a well-mannered, civic-minded Brahmin, Rajam Iyer, who takes on the role of the protector of his "meek" fellow passengers from low-caste "bullying." This is in itself a stereotypical depiction of the castes and, not surprisingly, Rajam Iyer is presented as possessing the intellectual superiority that allows him to slap the

physically stronger and unnamed low-caste passenger across the face without any retaliation. Despite being nine inches taller and despite his general belligerence, the low-caste man is shown to retreat in fear of Iyer's self-professed Brahmanical powers to permanently alter his face with the next set of slaps. This story records a fantastical insistence on Brahmanical superiority in the face of self-assertion by lower castes.
33. Ganguly, *Caste, Colonialism and Counter-Modernity*, p. x.
34. Ibid., p. 11.
35. Pandian, "One Step outside Modernity," p. 248.
36. Ganguly, *Caste, Colonialism and Counter-Modernity*, p. x.
37. Ibid., p. x.
38. Sankaran, "Narrating Race, Gender and Sexuality," p. 103.
39. Ibid., p. 95.
40. Ibid., p. 107.
41. See especially M. N. Srinivas's first book, *Religion and Society amongst the Coorgs of South India.*
42. For effective analyses of the caste politics of "Sanskritization" theory, see Pandian, "One Step outside Modernity," which insists that Srinivas's theory is unaware of its upper-caste positioning and can be summarized as "lower castes Sanskritize and upper castes Westernize" (p. 248). Using Johannes Fabian's notion of the "denial of coevalness," Pandian argues that Srinivas sets caste as the Other of the modern. It is in this context that Pandian makes the above quoted remark that "what looks like the unmarked modern is stealthily upper caste in orientation" (p. 248). Also see Dilip Menon's brilliant description of Sanskritization as "a category that has become corpulent over time consuming all articulations of social mobility" (*The Blindness of Insight*, p. xi). In his introduction to *The Blindness of Insight: Essays on Caste in Modern India*, Menon writes: "It [Sanskritization theory] is a model of a deferred ideal of perfect mimesis, wherein subordinate castes, given time, shall become behaviourally more and more like those above them in the hierarchy. Here too, the creativity of the subordinate castes lies in replication, not in innovation" (p. xi). Menon goes on to ponder if this mimesis carries with it any of the subversive potential that Homi Bhabha identified in the very act of mimesis – "at once resemblance and menace" (p. xii). However, the wide popularity of Narayan's fiction amongst all readers of variant caste, class, and gender belies any such subversive potential.
43. Ibid., p. 6.
44. Narayan's last collection of short stories, *Grandmother's Tales* (1993), is exceptional in that it is not set in Malgudi.
45. Narayan, *Malgudi Days*, p. 8.
46. See Chapter 3 on Anand's novel *Untouchable*, published in the same year as *Swami and Friends*, which is also set in a fictional small town, Bhulandsher. The very different caste location of the young hero of Anand's novel makes for an entirely different narrative on the nexus of urban and rural in the fictional small town.

47. For a detailed analysis of the "classroom scene" in Dalit writing, see Gajarwala, "Miseducation.".
48. See Omprakash Valmiki's *Joothan* (1997), for example, which begins with a devastating account of the caste discrimination in the village school experienced in the mid-1950s. Also see Arun Mukherjee's introduction to her English translation of *Joothan* where she notes that Valmiki's portrayal of village life is "very unlike the lyric mode of Hindi nature poetry where the sickle-wielding, singing farm worker is just an accessory of the picturesque landscape" (p. xxxv).
49. See Srinivas, *The Remembered Village*. Interestingly, Srinivas was one of R. K. Narayan's close and lifelong friends.
50. See the "Author's Introduction" (dated September 1981) to *Malgudi Days* in which Narayan writes of detecting Malgudi characters on West Twenty-Third Street in New York where he had "lived for months at a time, on and off since 1959" (8). He writes with affection for the Chelsea Hotel, for the five and ten, the deli on the corner, the synagogue with the drunk lolling on the steps, the barber shop – "all are there as they were, with an air of unshaken permanence and familiarity" (8).
51. I am grateful to Ashis Nandy who, while visiting San Diego in April 2005, read an early version of my work on Narayan's Malgudi (published in *Antipode*, 2003) and suggested that I read his examination of very similar issues in *An Ambiguous Journey to the City*, especially chapter 1, "The Journey to the Past as a Journey to the Self," pp. 1–41.
52. Ibid., p. vii.
53. Ibid., p. 13.
54. Ibid., pp. 16–17.
55. Ibid., p. 21.
56. Ibid., pp. 19–21.
57. This kind of romantic triangle is a recurring trope in vernacular satire written in this period. I thank Dilip Menon for discussing this with me in San Diego, January 2010. Also see chapter 4, "Marrying for Love: Emotion and Desire in Women's Print Culture" in Sreenivas, *Wives, Widows, Concubines*, pp. 94–120, in which Sreenivas suggests that "appropriate domesticity" for upper-caste Tamils was adapted freely from English culture, so that by the late nineteenth century there was a convergence of upper-caste or Brahminical and Victorian morality, which both valued chastity for women, the marriage ideal of conjugal companionship, privacy, and the emphasis on emotion, feelings, sentiment, etc., all articulated through literary depictions of family life (p. 98).
58. See, for comparison, the overt reformist message of Mulk Raj Anand's 1935 novel in English, *Untouchable*, which is discussed in the next chapter.
59. Mukherjee, *The Twice Born Fiction*, p. 213.
60. Ibid., p. 213.
61. It is in this context that Dalit writers have remarked that readers have challenged the veracity of their accounts of caste-based oppression. See, for example, Omprakash Valmiki, the Dalit writer and author of *Joothan*, who writes in his Author's Preface to his autobiography, that some readers have found his

account "unbelievable and exaggerated" and have claimed that "these things don't happen here" (viii).
62. Narasimhaiah, *The Swan and The Eagle*, p. 177.
63. See Larsons, "Review of Walsh's *R. K. Narayan*."
64. Krishnan, "Editor's Introduction," p. xii.
65. See Ganesan's *The Journey*, and her second novel *Inheritance*. For a detailed discussion of the relationship between Narayan's Malgudi and Ganesan's Madhupur, see my "Of Fictional Cities and Diasporic Aesthetics."
66. "Misguided 'Guide'" was first published in *Life* and then reprinted in *The Writer's Nightmare*, pp. 206–217, and also in Krishnan, *Malgudi Landscapes: The Best of R. K. Narayan*, pp. 323–334.
67. Narayan's objections seem to be to the "lost" English language film *Guide* (1964) directed by Ted Danielewski, with an English language script written by Pearl S. Buck, and produced by Vijay (Goldie) Anand, with Dev Anand and Waheeda Rehman in the lead roles. Danielewski's son, the author Mark Danielewski, has a copy of this film and is currently seeking funding for a rerelease (email correspondence, December 2010). Some of Narayan's criticism would apply to the Hindi version of *Guide* (1965), also produced and directed by Goldie Anand, starring Dev Anand as Raju and Waheeda Rehman as Rosie.
68. Narayan, "Misguided 'Guide,'" in Krishnan, *Malgudi Landscapes*, pp. 326–327.
69. Ibid., unnumbered last page.
70. Narayan, *Swami and Friends*, p. 20.
71. See Khaled Hosseini's *The Kite Runner*, Arundhati Roy's *The God of Small Things*, and Shyam Selvadurai's *Funny Boy*, where terrible and deeply traumatic events evict protagonists and readers out of their prelapsarian childhoods.
72. See Ram and Ram, p. 154, for the letter from Hamish Hamilton to Narayan that explains the logic behind the change of title.
73. Ibid., pp. 78–79.
74. See Sreenivas' *Wives, Widows Concubines* and Sivaramans, *Fragments of A Life*.
75. Cited by Sivaraman, *Fragments of a Life*, p. 128.
76. Note that Swami's fourth friend is Samuel (also called "Pea" because of his small size) who is a Christian convert. His unremarkable presence in the school and among the boys suggests that his family belonged to one of the higher castes prior to conversion.
77. Narayan, *Swami and Friends*, p. 75.
78. Ibid., p. 91.
79. Ibid., pp. 91–92.
80. See Dilip Menon's essay on the veteran communist leader E. M. S. Namboodiripad which asks how upper-caste intellectuals in this location write without the shadow of the anti-Brahmin movement falling across the pages. See, "Being a Brahmin the Marxist Way," also reprinted in Menon *The Blindness of Insight*.
81. Kaliappan and Srinivas, "On Castes and Comedians."
82. See James and Prout, *Constructing and Reconstructing Childhood*, p. 7.
83. The director Shankar Nag died in 1990 in a road accident. In 2004, T. S. Narasimhan, the producer of the series, approached Kavitha Lankesh to direct

Notes to pages 83–89

a second set of episodes which were aired on Doordarshan from April 2006. These twenty-six episodes were based on short stories written by Narayan over the course of his long career and were in Hindi.

84. I am extremely grateful to Girish Karnad, actor, playwright, and littérateur, who played Swami's father in this TV serial, for answering my numerous questions concerning decisions made about language use, the details of accents, and other aspects of this production. I am also very grateful to Padmavati Rao, the actress who played Jagan's wife in the *Vendor of Sweets* episodes under her screen name Akshata Rao, who also served as dubbing director for the serial, for answering additional questions on language choice, accents, and dubbing. This entire section of this chapter could not have been written without their help.

85. By the 1980s, the small-town milieu of a Malgudi in the 1930s could only be captured in a village, and by the next round of production in the early twenty-first century even Agumbe village was too overrun by cars and other modern developments to serve as an ideal location for the serial, according to the new director, Kavitha Lankesh: "The Return of Malgudi Days."

86. For example, a close-up of a newspaper from which Swami makes a paper boat that he sets sailing in a ditch carries the headline "Wellington succeeds Lord Irwin"; the reference sets the time-frame as 1931, the year in which the Earl of Wellington took over command of British India from Lord Irwin.

87. See the horizontal caste marks on Swami's forehead and the sacred thread around his torso which are visible in the first minutes of episode 19, the first episode based on the novel.

88. Narayan, *Swamiyum Snegithargalum*, trans. V. Krishnaswamy.

89. Email correspondence with the dubbing editor, Padmavati Rao, December 11, 2009.

90. However, the Hindi version was dubbed into a few south Indian languages like Telugu for distribution to local TV stations (email correspondence between Rao and the author, December 11, 2009).

91. Ibid.

92. Mishra, "R. K. Narayan," p. 199.

93. Ibid., p. 199.

94. Cited in Krishnan, "Editor's Introduction," in *Malgudi Landscapes*, p. xiv.

95. Ibid., p. xiv.

96. See Varadarajan, "In Madras Once." This essay by Varadarajan was also published in India in *The Indian Express*, Saturday, May 19, 2001 under the title "In Chennai Once, a Sweet Talk with Narayan."

97. Tharoor, "Comedies of Suffering."

98. Letter to the Editor, *Wall Street Journal*, June 1, 2001, p. 15.

99. The epigraph to L. P. Hartley's novel *The Go-Between* begins with the sentence: "The past is a foreign country. They do things differently there." I thank Dilip Menon for correcting my recollection of the exact source for this sentiment.

100. See Katz, "Vagabond Capitalism and the Necessity of Social Reproduction," p. 718.

CHAPTER 3 THE IN-BETWEEN LIFE OF MULK RAJ ANAND

1. See Anand, "Self-Obituary," pp. xvi–xxxi.
2. The life chronology that follows is based on the one provided by Saros Cowasjee in his authoritative study, *So Many Freedoms*; especially see chapter 1 "The Making of a Novelist," pp. 1–35.
3. Some sources give Anand's caste as falling within the third caste of traders and craftsman, broadly known as Vaisya. Anand's father was said to have belonged to the copper craftsmith community and to have joined the British army when the traditional means of earning a living from working with metals became untenable owing to the competition offered by cheap machine-made tin items for everyday use.
4. Recent scholarship like Ruvani Ranasinha's *South Asian Writers in 20th Century Britain* (2007) refers to Anand as an "early nationalist Indian writer" (p. 2). For Amir Mufti, Anand's *Untouchable* is centrally framed by nationalist struggles when read in comparison with the Urdu literature of the period. See *Enlightenment in the Colony*, p. 183.
5. M. K. Naik's respected *A History of Indian English Literature* discusses Anand's work at length along with the work of Narayan and Raja Rao in a chapter titled "The Gandhian Whirlwind: 1920–1947." Naik notes that it is a "mark of their stature that they revealed, each in his own characteristic way, the various possibilities of Indian English fiction" (p. 155).
6. I am very grateful to Saros Cowasjee for alerting me to the possibility that only one or two of these early novels were perhaps banned by the British, despite the repeated references to a total ban of all these books in the critical work on Anand (phone conversation with Cowasjee, September 2010).
7. See Gandhi, "Novelists of the 1930s and 1940s"; also see Narasimhaiah, *The Writer's Gandhi*, pp. 62–70.
8. Iyengar, *Indo-Anglian Literature*, pp. 43–44.
9. See the fifth edition revised in 1985 of which I consulted a 1993 reprint.
10. In *A History of Indian English Literature*, Naik characterizes and contrasts Anand's and Narayan's work as follows: "Narayan's delicate blend of gentle irony and sympathy, quiet realism and fantasy stands poles apart from Anand's militant humanism with its sledge-hammer blows and his robust earthiness" (p. 160).
11. Mukherjee, *The Twice Born Fiction*, p. 78.
12. See Rawat, *Reconsidering Untouchablity*; also see Ram, "Ravidass Deras and Social Protest."
13. For a detailed consideration of the impact of the PWA on the writing of *Untouchable*, see Baer, "Shit Writing."

14. The entire text of the PWA manifesto as published in *New Left Review* is reproduced in "Over Chinese Food: The Progressive Writers' Association," in Mir and Mir, *Anthems of Resistance*, pp. 4–6.
15. There were of course other PWA members who wrote in English, notably Ahmed Ali.
16. Anand, "Afterword," p. 177. This afterword was printed in the revised Indian edition by Arnold Publishers, New Delhi, first published in 1970. All references to this novel will be to the 1981 reprint of this Indian edition.
17. Berman, "Comparative Colonialisms," p. 467.
18. Ibid.
19. Ibid., p. 476.
20. Ibid.
21. Ibid., p. 482.
22. Anand, *An Apology for Heroism*, p. 84.
23. Anand, "Author's Preface," p. x.
24. Ibid.
25. Ibid.
26. Bluemel, *George Orwell and the Radical Eccentrics*, p. 3.
27. See ibid., pp. 189–190 n. 2, where Bluemel cites several sources to convincingly make the case that Anand's version of particular events is erroneous.
28. Also see Cowasjee's chapter "The Making of a Novelist" in *So Many Freedoms*, especially pp. 26–33, for more on the scant references to Anand in European accounts of the literary modernism of this period.
29. Bluemel, *George Orwell and the Radical Eccentrics*, p. 70.
30. Nasta, "Between Bloomsbury, Gandhi and Transcultural Modernities," p. 6 (emphasis in original).
31. Talat Ahmed, "Mulk Raj Anand: Novelist and Fighter."
32. See Anand, *An Apology for Heroism*, p. 59.
33. Ibid., p. 60.
34. Ibid.
35. Ibid., p. 62.
36. See Anand, "The Story of my Experiment with a White Lie," p. 8.
37. In a published interview with the Indian painter Amrita Shergill (at her studio at Summer Hill, Shimla, in May 1938), Anand describes his participation in the Spanish Civil War thus: "I have been to the Spanish war [*sic*] for three months. I joined the international brigade, but fainted on seeing blood. So I was advised to do reporting. On my return to Paris Tristan Tzara, art critic took me to see Picasso..." See Anand, *Splendours of Himachal Heritage*, p. 113.
38. Quoted by Ambedkar in *What Gandhi and Congress Have Done to the Untouchables*, p. 68.
39. Quoted in ibid.
40. Ludden, *India and South Asia*, p. 22.
41. Hubel, *Whose India?*, pp. 150–151.
42. Ibid., p. 166.

43. Mukherjee, "The Exclusions of Postcolonial Theory and Mulk Raj Anand's *Untouchable*," p. 37.
44. Ibid., p. 35.
45. Ibid., p. 38.
46. Ibid., p. 42.
47. Ibid., p. 40.
48. S. Anand, *Touchable Tales*, p. 38.
49. Ibid., p. 17. For more on the debate as to who can be called a Dalit writer, see Kumar, *Dalit Personal Narratives*, pp. 146–151.
50. See Appendix IV, "Statement by B. R. Ambedkar on Gandhi's Fast: Statement on Mr. Gandhi's attitude at the Round Table Conference to the Untouchables and their Demand for Constitutional Safeguards, 19th September 1932," in Ambedkar, *What Congress and Gandhi Have Done to the Untouchables*, p. 326.
51. Anand, "Self-Obituary," p. xxix.
52. "You Wrote from Los Angeles" (emphasis in original), in Daya Pawar, *Kondwada* [Cattle–pen] (1974), translated by Graham Smith, reprinted in Zelliot, *From Untouchable to Dalit*, p. 301.
53. See Anand, *Conversations in Bloomsbury*, p. 39, for the occasional reference to rude landladies and other travails of being Indian in London in this period. Also see "Author's Preface," where he writes briefly of being "shunned" on account of his skin color and therefore often "forlorn" in England (p. ix).
54. See chapter 8, "On the Way to Pretoria" and chapter 9, "More Hardship" in Gandhi, *An Autobiography or My Experiments with Truth*, pp. 103–109.
55. Anand, "The Story of my Experiment with a White Lie," p. 11.
56. Guru, *Humiliation*, p. 1.
57. Ibid., p. 4.
58. Ibid.
59. For a full discussion of titles and terms of reference, see Zelliot, *From Untouchable to Dalit*, p. 74, n. 1.
60. Rawat, "The Problem," p. 3.
61. Forster, "Preface." Also see Cowasjee, *So Many Freedoms* for a detailed discussion of the debt to E.M. Forster, as well as the influence of Bonamy Dobrée on Anand's work (pp. 17–19).
62. Anand, *Untouchable*, p. 157.
63. Ibid., pp. 157–158.
64. Baer, "Shit Writing," p. 581.
65. Indeed, Baer argues that the capital 'U' of *Untouchable* is "readable as an intertextual tribute to Ulysses" and to Gandhi's "Uka" (ibid., p. 581). Surely, the more direct reason to use this "U" word Untouchable is because it immediately conveys the condition that Bakha grapples with on a daily basis.
66. See S. Anand, "Sanskrit, English, Dalits," for further discussion of Ambedkar's decision to write in English, of the pan-Indian circulation of Dalit texts that are written in English, and of the significance of English language acquisition to Dalit efforts at achieving parity with upper-caste Indians.
67. Anand, *Untouchable*, p. 19.

68. In his autobiography, *Joothan*, the Dalit writer Omprakash Valmiki describes his difficulties as a young boy: "If we went to the school in neat and clean clothes, then our class fellows said, 'Abey, Chuhre ka, he has come dressed in new clothes.' If one went wearing old and shabby clothes, then they said, 'Abey, chuhre ke, get away from me, you stink'" (p. 3). The physical and emotional violence with which Dalit children are repeatedly assaulted is portrayed as escalating from such sartorial "provocation."
69. Even today, in many parts of India, to gift a sari without an accompanying "blouse piece" (material with which to stitch a sari blouse) is considered a caste insult because in these regions until recently low-caste women were expected to wrap the sari around their torso in lieu of wearing a blouse.
70. Thus, to wear what is marked as upper-caste clothing is a deliberate act of self-empowerment for Dalits: for example, Ravidass, the Chamar saint and central figure in the Adi Dharam movement of the early 1920s, adopted the prohibited dress of Brahmins: the full dhoti (cloth covering the lower half of the body for men), the sacred thread (usually an indication of Brahmin caste), and the red tilak (caste mark) on the forehead. Despite attiring as Brahmin, followers of this sect do not hide their caste, abandon their work as cobblers (Chamar), assimilate to upper castes, or Sanskritize themselves or their lifestyles. As Ronki Ram states in "Ravidass Devas and Social Protest," "In other words, [this movement] rendered Dalit social mobility without sacrificing the social ties and customs of the group of origin" (p. 1345).
71. See http://blogs.wsj.com/indiarealtime/2010/04/30/a-dalit-temple-to-goddess-english/ (accessed June 1, 2010).
72. Zelliot, *From Untouchable to Dalit*, p. 61.
73. See Rawat's *Reconsidering Untouchability* for a detailed discussion of the positive reception of the British and of English in Dalit communities.
74. Baer, "Shit Writing," p. 578.
75. Anand, *Untouchable*, p. 160.
76. Ibid., p. 159.
77. Ibid., p. 44.
78. Quoted in chapter 1, "A Strange Event: Congress Takes Cognizance of the Untouchables," in Ambedkar's *What Congress and Gandhi Have Done to the Untouchables*, p. 1.
79. From Mrs. Annie Besant, "The Uplift of the Depressed Classes," quoted in its entirety in Ambedkar, *What Congress and Gandhi Have Done to the Untouchables*, p. 5 (emphasis added).
80. In his autobiography, *Joothan*, Valmiki provides many examples of the harassment he faced as a Dalit child who was determined to get an education and of his father's absolute helplessness in preventing the violent cruelty and humiliation heaped on him by the upper-caste school principal, teachers, and children. Valmiki writes: "The children of the Tyagis would tease me by calling me 'Chukre ka' [low-caste name used as an epithet]. Sometimes they beat me without reason. This was an absurd tormented life that made me introverted and irritable. If I got thirsty in school, then I had to stand near the handpump.

The boys would beat me in any case, but the teachers also punished me. All sort of stratagems were tried so that I would run away from school and take up the kind of work for which I was born, According to these perpetrators, my attempts to get schooling were unwarranted" (p. 3).
81. See "Statement on Temple Entry Bill, 14th February, 1933," in *What Congress and Gandhi Have Done to the Untouchables*, pp. 108–113.
82. Ibid., p. 110.
83. Anand, *Untouchable*, p. 89.
84. Ibid., p. 57.
85. Ibid., p. 144.
86. Ibid., pp. 146–147.
87. Mukherjee, "The Exclusion of Postcolonial Theory and Mulk Raj Anand's Untouchable," p. 42.
88. Quoted in Zelliot, *From Untouchable to Dalit*, p. 206.
89. Ambedkar, *The Untouchables*.
90. Zelliot, *From Untouchable to Dalit*, p. 208.
91. Anand, *Untouchable*, pp. 164–165.
92. For more on the Jagjivan Ram protest see Zelliot, *From Untouchables to Dalit*, p. 170.
93. Anand, *Untouchable*, p. 168.
94. Ibid.
95. Anand, *Untouchable*, Penguin Classic Edition, 1940, p. 150.
96. To briefly follow up on the promise of the flush toilet as a possible liberator of Dalits: by the 1960s, only 15 percent of the Indian population had access to a sewage system and flush toilets. The other 85 percent of Indians relied on human scavengers who emptied the bucket latrines or slop pits or took to available open space to defecate in public. In 1970, Dr. Bindeswar Pathak founded the Sulabh International Trust that provided public flush toilets that now serve ten million Indians per day. Pathak's investigations began with his work for the *Bhangi-Mukti* (scavenger-liberation) branch of the government-run Bihar Gandhi Centenary Celebration Committee in 1968. Pathak's intention was to free scavengers from the stigma of manual collection of human excreta and his organization does much to educate and integrate former scavengers into caste Hindu society. Manual scavenging was banned by law in 1993 and the same law also banned the use of dry or unplumbed toilets (which necessitated manual scavenging of human excreta). See Pathak, "A History of Toilets," presented at the "International Symposium on Public Toilets" in Hong Kong, 1995, www.sulabhtoiletmuseum.org/pg02.htm (accessed on March 12, 2010) Dr. Pathak notes that, as in most parts of the developing world, sewage-based toilets remain out of the reach of the majority of the Indian population. In this website's online guest book, the last listed comment is by none other than "Dr. Mukh [*sic*] Raj Anand, Eminent Writer" who wrote: "What Abraham Lincoln did for Blacks in America, Dr. Pathak has done for scavengers in India. Both are great redeemers" (accessed on March 13, 2010 at www.sulabhtoiletmuseum.org/guest.htm).

97. Anand, "Preface to the Third Edition," in *Apology for Heroism*, unnumbered first pages. A second, much shorter "Preface to the Third Edition" is printed right after this seventeen-page essay.
98. Anand and Zelliot, *An Anthology of Dalit Poetry*.
99. See especially Dangle's introduction to the collection which is a manifesto that declares the difference, new foci, and power of Dalit literature (*Poisoned Bread*, pp. xi–xv).
100. S. Anand, *Touchable Tales*, p. 1.
101. See, for example, the dismal editing and proofreading on display in Anand, *Mulk Raj Anand: A Reader*.
102. For English language scholarship on Dalit literature, especially the life-writing or autobiography genre, see especially Beth, "Hindi Dalit Autobiography." See also Bannerji, "The Violence of the Everyday"; Bhongle, "Dalit Autobiographies"; Chauhan, "I am the Witness of my History and my Literature"; Ganguly, "Pain, Personhood and the Collective"; Nayar, "Bama's *Karukku*"; Pandian, "On a Dalit Woman's Testimonio" *Writing Rege, Writing Caste, Writing Gender*. See Kumar, *Dalit Personal Narratives*, chapters 4–6, pp. 115–256. Also see Kothari, "The Translation of Dalit Literature into English" for an assessment of the translation of Dalit works into English as a "translational intervention that interrogates and challenges traditionally held power relations" (p. 40). English, Kothari argues, "comes close to being the most ideal language in internationalizing the Dalit suffering and conferring upon the Dalits a sense of confidence" (ibid.).
103. Beth, "Hindi Dalit Autobiography," p. 567.
104. Ibid.
105. Nayyar, "Bama's *Karukku*," p. 85.
106. Ibid., p. 89.
107. Pandian, "On a Dalit Woman's Testimonio," p. 130.
108. Ibid., p. 131.
109. Ibid.
110. Ganguly, "Pain, Personhood and the Collective," p. 434.
111. Beth, "Hindi Dalit Autobiographies," pp. 567–568.
112. See Anand, "Author's Preface," p. xiii.
113. See especially Berman, *Comparative Colonialisms*; Nasta, "Between Bloomsbury, Gandhi and Transcultural Modernities"; Baer, "Shit Writing."
114. See Anand, "The Story of my Experiment with a White Lie." Ostensibly, the "white lie" in the title refers to what Anand claims Gandhi said to him at their first meeting – that fiction writing was about love, lies, and fine words. Anand concedes that "novels were made up and, therefore, full of lies, but perhaps they were full of 'white lies.'" We are told that Gandhi was amused at this response and so allowed the author to stay in his ashram (p. 13).
115. Anand, "Afterword," p. 179.
116. I wish to thank R. Sivapriya from Penguin India and Jessica Harrison from Penguin UK for their kind responses to my query about why the decision

was made not to reprint the Author's Afterword in the Penguin Twentieth-Century Classics edition of the novel. According to Harrison, since decisions on this edition of *Untouchable* were made more than twenty years ago there is no record at the press of why Anand's afterword was omitted (email correspondence, February 2010).
117. Anand, "Author's Preface," p. xi.
118. Naik, *Mulk Raj Anand*, p. ix.
119. I am very grateful to Saros Cowasjee for sharing this short unpublished interview with me and for graciously entertaining my questions about Anand. In our email correspondence, Prof. Cowasjee asserted that while Anand may have exaggerated aspects of the visit to Gandhi's ashram, there is no doubt in his mind that such a visit took place (email correspondence February 2010).
120. Gandhi's day-to-day correspondence and meetings have been closely chronicled in several different sources. I have consulted Desai, *Day-to-Day with Gandhi* and Gandhi, *Collected Works*. There are 98 volumes of the latter and volumes 36–41 cover the years 1926–1928, during which there is no mention of Mulk Raj Anand in any of the letters. Specifically there is no mention of Anand in the volumes of correspondence 37–41 which cover the period from July 1926 to May 1928. There is also no mention of Anand in correspondence from 1931–1933. Cowasjee, Naik, and Narayan date Anand's trip to the ashram in 1932; however, Gandhi and Mahadev Desai (as well as other leaders and associates) were in jail from January 4 through all of 1932 until May 1933 and then again jailed in August 1933 (see volumes 55–59). In fact, Gandhi's fast unto death to protest separate electorates for the Depressed Classes, which is mentioned in Anand's novel, was launched from Yeravda Jail in September 1932. There is no mention of Anand or Bakha or *Untouchable* the novel in Gandhi's correspondence from the early 1940; despite rumors of a ban on this novel, copies no doubt circulated in India. Anand could of course have met with Gandhi in England in late 1931 when the Round Table Conference meetings were held in November. Gandhi was also in Lucknow in April 1936, exactly at the same venue (Congress Nagar –the temporarily built township constructed to hold the annual session of the Indian National Congress) where the Progressive Writers' Association's first meeting was held on April 10, 1936. Desai's chronicle of Gandhi's travels and appointments places him there from April 8–16, 1936 where the annual meeting for the Congress Party was being held from April 12–15 of the same year. However, it seems clear that Anand did not attend this first meeting of the All-India PWA in Lucknow which was presided over by the Hindi/Urdu writer Munshi Premchand.
121. Cowasjee, *So Many Freedoms*, p. 34.
122. See Cowasjee, *So Many Freedoms* and Garimella, *Mulk Raj Anand*, for details on Anand's life in India after his return in 1945.
123. Ibid., p. 153.
124. In Cowasjee's opinion, after Nehru's death, Indira Gandhi was somewhat attentive to Anand out of deference for his relationship with her father, but

Notes to pages 130–131

by Rajiv Gandhi's time, Anand was certainly out of the circle of associates and friends around the Nehru/Gandhi family (phone conversation, September 2010).

125. Of the planned seven volumes, the following four were published: *Seven Summers* (1951), *Morning Face* (1968), *The Lover* (1976), *The Bubble* (1984). Anand's life in this fictionalized autobiography is presented through the story of Krishen Chand Azad, the primary protagonist and a fictionalized version of himself in all volumes. The fifth volume, *And So He Plays His Part*, was planned in seven parts, of which the first was published in 1991 as *The Little Plays of Mahatma Gandhi*. In this last book Anand sets these "little plays" in Sabarmati Ashram in an April in the 1920s. The first play is a dramaticized version of the meeting between Azad and Gandhi as described in the Afterward to the novel. The rest of the plays are also set in the ashram with Azad interacting with the Mahatma Gandhi as well as a cast of real people associated with the Mahatma such as Kasturba Gandhi, Mahadev Desai, Maluana Azad, Sarojini Naidu, and others.

126. See the especially devastating dismissal of Anand's later works in the chapter titled "Twilight of the Old Masters: The Novel-I" (pp. 18–34) in M. K. Naik and Shyamala Narayan's Influential and comprehensive *Indian English Literature, 1980–2000: A Critical Survey*.

127. Anand, *Conversations in Bloomsbury*, dedicated to Saros Cowasjee and Gulab Vazirani.

128. Ibid., p. 6.

129. Ibid., p. 22.

130. For example, see Ruth Vanita's translator's introduction to Ugra's *Chaaklat* for details on the controversy over Gandhi's opinion of these homoerotic stories: Sharma, *Chocolate and Other Homoerotic Writings*.

131. In late 2006 and 2007, I consulted several scholars in India, including those who had some acquaintance with Anand in the last decades of his life, and could not find corroboration of this visit and collaboration with Gandhi. In November 2006 I spent time at Lokayata with Kewal Anand who presents himself as the late Mulk Raj Anand's adopted son and assistant. Since Anand's death, Kewal has managed Lokayata (named after an ancient Indian atheist belief system which repudiated caste), the Mulk Raj Anand center and exhibition space that the author set up in Delhi in the last years of his life. Kewal claims that all Anand's papers from 1946 (the date of his return from Europe) and beyond are in the possession of his family and inaccessible to scholars. More recently, Saros Cowasjee, writer, critic, and long-time associate of Anand, has arranged for the National Archives of India to hold his papers when and if they are retrieved after various legal disputes on Anand's estate are settled (phone conversation with Cowasjee, September 2010).

132. Most scholars take their account of this visit verbatim from the Author's Afterword or many texts where Anand has referred to it. For example, Marlene Fisher, who in *The Wisdom of the Heart* frames her book with this visit to Sabarmati – relies entirely on Anand's own account. Even as recent and

researched a book at Priyamvada Gopal's *The Indian English Novel: Nation, History and Narration* assumes that the visit took place (p. 50).
133. See Berman, "Comparative Colonialisms," p. 469; Nasta, "Between Bloomsbury, Gandhi and Transcultural Modernities," p. 160; Gandhi, "Novelists of the 1930s and 1940s," p. 175.
134. See Mehrotra, *A History of Indian Literature in English*, pp. 1–26.
135. Ibid., p. 13.
136. Once Anand's papers are catalogued in the National Archives, a development that seems imminent, we may well find ample proof of this relationship between the writer and the Mahatma.
137. See all the contributions to Garimella, *Mulk Raj Anand*, but especially the introductory essay by Garimella, and Charles Correa's essay "Mulk Raj Anand at 100", pp. 66–73.
138. Garimella, *Mulk Raj Anand*, p. 18.
139. See the "Preface to the Third Edition" to Anand's *Apology for Heroism* (1942), unnumbered first pages.
140. Anand, *Apology for Heroism*, p. 163.
141. Ibid., p. 171.
142. See George, "Where in the World did Kamala Markandaya Go?" for a discussion of this author's work in the context of the global success of her first novel, *Nectar in a Sieve* (1954). Also see Antoinette Burton's outstanding study of Santha Rama Rau titled *The Postcolonial Careers of Santha Rama Rau* and see my review of the same in the *Journal of British Studies*.
143. From the "Preface to the Third Edition" to Anand's *Apology for Heroism* (1942), unnumbered page.

CHAPTER 4 THE SAHITYA AKADEMI'S SHOWCASING OF NATIONAL LITERATURE

1. *Sahitya Akademi Annual Report 1954–57*, Appendix II, p. 9. This Annual Report was published in both Hindi and English.
2. "Sahitya Akademi: Inauguration and Aims," in ibid., p. 9.
3. For a detailed analysis of the implications of the fact that this patriotic vision for a unified Indian identity was expressed in an English slogan "unity in diversity," see Chapter 1.
4. It would be worth noting that in the 1950s and early 1960s, several private and governmental cultural/educational institutions were either newly set up or refurbished and renamed to reflect their new role in the post-independence era. For example, construction of the National Museum in New Delhi began in 1955 and it opened to the public in 1960. The National Center for the Performing Arts was established in Bombay by the industrialist Jamshed Bhabha in the early 1960s and was registered as the National Institute of Performing Arts in 1966. The government-funded Film and Television Institute of India was set up in 1960 in Pune. The government-funded National School

Notes to pages 138–144

of Drama was established in New Delhi in 1959. Another government organization that is also very important in the context of academic and literary publishing is the National Book Trust of India, an autonomous body overseen by the Ministry of Education and established by Nehru in 1957.

5. The Sahitya Akademi was registered as a society on January 7, 1956 under the Societies Registration Act, 1860. A source of information on the Akademi that I have most relied on in writing this chapter is D. S. Rao's *Five Decades: A Short History of Sahitya Akademi (1954–2004)*.
6. See "Constitution," in *Sahitya Akademi Annual Report 1954–57*, Appendix I, p. i.
7. *Sahitya Akademi Progress Report (1956–57)*, p. 3.
8. Ramanujan, "Is There an Indian Way of Thinking?" p. 421.
9. S. Radhakrishnan, "Speech at Inaugural Ceremony," excerpted in *Sahitya Akademi Annual Report 1954–57*, p. 25.
10. Ibid., p. 4.
11. Ibid.
12. Ibid., p. 7.
13. For the full text Maulana Abul Kalam Azad, Minister of Education, "Inaugural Speech," in *The Sahitya Akademi Annual Report*, Appendix II, pp. 6–11, at p. 7.
14. Nehru, "Inaugural Speech," *Sahitya Akademi Annual Report 1954–1957*, p. 9.
15. In 1944 the Royal Asiatic Society of Bengal had submitted a proposal to the Government of India that a "National Cultural Trust" with three different academies be set up and this had been accepted in principle by the colonial government. As D. S. Rao notes in his history of the Sahitya Akademi, after independence, the Royal Asiatic Society's proposal was discussed, revised, and reworked in the many conferences and committee meetings that were convened in the late 1940s and early 1950s. See Rao, *Five Decades*, p. 7.
16. Azad, "Inaugural Speech," *Sahitya Akademi Annual Report 1954–57*, Appendix II, p. 10.
17. For details on these publications see the list of "Books Published" in *Sahitya Akademi Annual Report 1954–57*, pp. 4–8. A similar pattern of publications dominated by translation, and within that category by translations from and to Hindi, continues in the listing of "Books in Press," pp. 8–11 and "Manuscripts Ready for Press," pp. 11–14. Also see the comprehensive list by language of planned translations of Indian and foreign classics in "Books under Preparation," pp. 23–35.
18. For further details see ibid., Appendix VII, "Foreign Classics Selected for Translation into Indian Languages," pp. xxiii–xxiv. Most of these works were actually translated in the first five years of operation of the Sahitya Akademi.
19. See ibid., Appendix VIII, "List of Indian Classics Recommended to UNESCO for Translation into Foreign Languages," pp. xxvii–xxviii.
20. This sentiment was explicitly expressed in the Akademi's *Progress Report for 1956–57*. "There is, besides, the programme for translating important foreign classics into all the major Indian languages so that the great literary masterpieces

21. See the chapter titled "Coming Together" in Rao's *Five Decades* which lists the international and national seminars, workshops, lecture series, and symposiums organized by the Akademi on topics ranging from the work of Rabindranath Tagore, Premchand, Kabir, and Guru Nanak, to the work of international figures such as Shakespeare, Lenin, Gorky, Pablo Neruda, Pushkin, etc. (pp. 62–92).
22. See Rao, *Five Decades*, p. 143 for details.
23. See, for instance, the note dated March 16, 1962 from Leticia Baldrige, social secretary to Mrs. Kennedy, thanking the Akademi for the "beautiful books" presented to the First Lady of the United States, who was visiting India at the time. See "Important Letters, Notes and Literary Evaluations from the Sahitya Akademi Files" compiled by Z. A. Burney, Archivist, Sahitya Akademi, New Delhi, p. 321. Accessed November 2006 and July 2010.
24. In December 2003, the Sahitya Akademi passed a resolution condemning the destruction of the national library and museums in Iraq and presented this resolution to the Union Academique International. The Akademi's resolution stated that it wanted to "impress upon Governments their responsibility to protect the cultural heritage of a country" (quoted by Rao, *Five Decades*, p. 145).
25. In 1996, four more Honorary Fellows were chosen; all were Indologists of great repute: American scholars Edward C. Dimock and Daniel Ingalls, Czech scholar Kamil Zvelebil, and the Chinese scholar Ji Xianlin. In 2002, the Greek scholar Vasilis Vitsaxis and E. P. Chelyshev, a Russian scholar, and in 2007, the British linguist R. E. Asher were inducted into this select group.
26. For a list (compiled in 2003) of past and present Fellows and Honorary Fellows, see "Appendix V" in Rao's *Five Decades*, p. 294.
27. See George, "Where in the World did Kamala Markandaya Go?"
28. Casanova, *The World Republic of Letters*, p. xi.
29. Ibid., p. xii.
30. The earliest known Sanskrit texts were the four Vedas composed around 1500 BC, comprising hymns and chants in archaic Sanskrit for a pre-Hindu religion. Homer's *Iliad* and *Odyssey* were written in around 700 BC, that is 800 years later. The earliest written version of the epic poem *Ramayana*, written in Sanskrit and attributed to Valmiki, dates back to 550 BC, that is 250 years after Homer. The other important epic poem of this period is the *Mahabharata* and major portions of it were composed between 400 BC and 400 AD.
31. See Romesh C. Dutt, "Epilogue to the Maha-Bharata: By the Translator," in *The Ramayana and Mahabharat Condensed into English*, pp. 323–333.
32. Radhakrishnan, "Speech at Inaugural Ceremony," *Sahitya Akademi Annual Report 1954–57*, p. 7.
33. It is beyond the scope of this chapter to delve into the linguistic theories about a common origin for Sanskrit, Latin, and Greek which have been differently interpreted by Orientalist scholars from the eighteenth century onward and

in theories about the origin of civilization. For a recent reevaluation of the parallels, interactions, and collaborations between ancient Greece and ancient India, see McEvilley, *The Shape of Ancient Thought*.
34. Note that in Hindi, the alternative to the Persian word "zabaan" for tongue is "jeebh" which only connotes the body part.
35. Rai, *Hindi Nationalism*, p. 78.
36. And while this chapter is heavily indebted to D. S. Rao's official history of the Akademi, *Five Decades*, I find it remarkable that this study, published in 2004, has chapters titled "Men of Achievement" (chapter 3) followed by chapter 4: "Encouraging Men of Promise" which do, however, discuss women's work as well.
37. See Chapter 1.
38. The full citation and context for this statement is provided in Chapter 1.
39. This quotation serves as an epigraph to D. S. Rao's magisterial *Five Decades*.
40. It is beyond the scope of this chapter to catalog the many complaints that have been voiced by writers and public intellectuals on different aspects of the Akademi. There have been calls for increasing and for decreasing the autonomy of the Akademi, protests about censorship by the Akademi as well as calls to ban specific works. Almost every year there is some degree of disagreement with one or more of the award decisions. See the chapters titled "Autonomy and Accountability" and "Freedom of the Human Spirit" in Rao, *Five Decades*, pp. 172–200, for a glimpse at some of these battles.
41. See Rao, *Five Decades*, pp. 2–6 for a quick preview of the bouquets and brickbats the Akademi has received in the Indian popular press (mainly in the English language) since its inception. The Government of India has periodically assigned various committees to assess the workings of the three major Akademis and the committees have made recommendations that have been implemented where funding would allow.
42. For example, in 2006, when Arundhati Roy, the writer and activist, was announced as the winner of the 2005 Sahitya Akademi English language prize for *The Algebra of Infinite Justice*, a collection of political essays, she turned it down as a gesture of protest against the Indian government. Her statement said: "I have a great deal of respect for the Sahitya Akademi, for the members of this year's Jury and for many of the writers who have received these awards in the past. But to register my protest and reaffirm my disagreement – indeed my absolute disgust – with these policies of the Indian Government, I must refuse to accept the 2005 Sahitya Akademi Award." More specifically what she was protesting was the Indian government's aligning itself with the USA and "violently and ruthlessly pursuing policies of brutalisation of industrial workers, increasing militarisation and economic neo-liberalisation." The fact that *The Algebra of Infinite Justice* is very critical of both the Indian and the US governments, and yet a very distinguished academic jury selected this book for the Akademi's annual award, did not apparently ameliorate the charge Roy makes about the Akademi and its honors not being independent of the government. A case could be made based on the Akademi's overall record of

selecting prize winners that this is one arena where there is no attempt to shield the Indian government from its many lapses. For example, the 2008 prize for translation in Urdu was awarded to Kashmiri journalist Iftikar Gilani for *Tihar Kay Shab-o-Roz*, his horrific account of being falsely charged with treason and spying by the Indian government, publically vilified, sentenced to a fourteen-year prison sentence, and then tortured in Tihar Jail until he was able to prove his innocence. While controversies do erupt periodically over the announcement of these prestigious SA awards in the various languages, the complaint is usually about differing perceptions of the quality of the selected work.

43. Azad, "Inaugural Speech," *Sahitya Akademi Annual Report, 1954–1957*, Appendix II, p. 7.
44. Nehru, "Inaugural Speech,' *Sahitya Akademi Annual Report, 1954–1957*, p. 8.
45. See Chapter 1 for a detailed discussion of the arguments and counter-arguments made prior to the selection of Hindi as the official language of the nation. English was to remain in official use alongside Hindi in the business of running the nation.
46. In 1957, Sindhi was the next language that was included in the list of languages in which the Sahitya Akademi would conduct its programs. Like English, Sindhi was a language without a state – a factor that did not, however, stand in the way of its recognition. Ten years later, in 1967, Sindhi was added to the Eighth Schedule of languages in the Indian constitution. More recently, Mizoram, a territory in the north-eastern part of the country that attained the status of statehood in 1987, claimed both English and Mizo as its state languages, and yet English remains "unconstitutional."
47. See the official website of the Sahitya Akademi for full details on the awards: www.sahitya-akademi.gov.in/old_version/awa10309.htm. Also see Pollock, "The Death of Sanskrit." In *Five Decades*, pp. 44–45, Rao offers various logistical explanations why awards were not given in some languages in some years.
48. See Kothari, *Translating India*, p. 69.
49. See Rao, *Five Decades*, p. 29, which cites Bhattacharya's letter to the selection committee stating that "having considered this matter quite objectively," he is convinced that no better novel in English than his own (*So Many Hungers*) has been published since August 1947.
50. See "Important Letters, Notes and Literary Evaluations from the Sahitya Akademi Files," compiled by Z. A. Burney, Archivist, Sahitya Akademi, New Delhi, p. 327 (accessed November 2006 and July 2010).
51. Ibid.
52. See Rao, *Five Decades*, pp. 36–37.
53. The publication patterns for the Literary Histories produced by the Sahitya Akademi substantiate this claim. For details, see Rao, *Five Decades*, pp. 101–102.
54. See *Contemporary Indian Literature* (1957), with a foreword by S. Radhakrishnan. All page references are to the 1959 second edition of this collection.

55. Radhakrishnan, "Foreword," *Cantemporary Indian Literature*, unnumbered first page.
56. This was the case for the essay writers on Assamese, Gujarati, Marathi, and Sindhi literature in *Contemporary Indian Literature*. As with the essays, the book-length literary histories in each of these languages were also written in English.
57. See Kripalani, "Note on the Proposed Histories of Literature," in *Sahitya Akademi Annual Report 1954–57*, pp. 20–22.
58. Ibid., p. 20.
59. Rao's account of the writing of these histories notes that it took forty-eight years for the histories of literature in these twenty-one languages to be published and the volume on Sanskrit was still under preparation in 2004. Most of these histories were originally written in English and then translated into Indian languages. See Rao, *Five Decades*, p. 102 for details.
60. Kripalani, "Note," in *Sahitya Akademi Annual Report 1954–57*, p. 21.
61. Ibid.
62. Ibid., pp. 21–22.
63. Ibid.
64. See Chapter 1 for a discussion of these issues around the selection of the national language for India in the aftermath of Partition.
65. Raghavan, "Sanskrit Literature," in *Contemporary Indian Literature*, p. 52.
66. Singh, "Punjabi Literature," *Contemporary Indian Literature*, p. 199.
67. Ibid.
68. Gotak, "Kannada Literature," *Contemporary Indian Literature*, p. 100.
69. Vatsyayan, "Hindi Literature," *Contemporary Indian Literature*, p. 82.
70. Singh, "Punjabi Literature, *Contemporary Indian Literature*, p. 196.
71. For the full text of Ramdhari Sinha's letter to Kripalani protesting Ajneya's essay, see the facsimile collection in Rao's *Five Decades*, pp. 310–312.
72. See Vatsyayan, "Hindi Literature," in the first edition of *Contemporary Indian Literature*, especially passages on pp. 70 and 74, which appear unaltered on pp. 78 and 82 in the second edition of this book.
73. Kripalani, "Note on the Proposed Histories of Literature," in *Sahitya Akademi Annual Report 1954–57*, p. 20.
74. Gotak, "Kannada Literature," *Contemporary Indian Literature*, pp. 120–121.
75. See Rao, *Five Decades*, pp. 111–112.
76. See Chapter 1 for an in-depth discussion of the role that Wadia and others ascribed to the Indian PEN in the struggle for national independence and the concomitant efforts to win international recognition for "Indian culture."
77. See Wadia's letter of February 22, 1955 to Kripalani in which she refers to earlier correspondence and asks to know "in what specific directions the PEN all-Indian centre could effectively co-operate with the Sahitya Akademi in its program of activities." Her letter suggests that, based on Kripalani's response, Indian PEN would reframe its program to "avoid duplication of activities"

and aim to make its own work "more concentrated and compact." As an example she offers to stop production of their series on regional literature if the Akademi had plans for similar projects. "Important Letters, Notes and Literary Evaluations from the Sahitya Akademi Files," compiled by Z. A. Burney, Archivist, Sahitya Akademi, New Delhi, p. 235 (accessed November 2006 and July 2010).

78. Again, see Chapter 1 of this book for discussion of Iyengar, *Indian Writers in Council*.
79. See Iyengar, "Introduction," in *Indian Writers in Council*, p. xi.
80. Iyengar, "Introduction," in *Indian Literature since Independence*, p. vii.
81. Ibid., p. viii.
82. Ibid. p. xxiv.
83. Ibid., p. ix.
84. Ibid., p. xiv.
85. Ibid., pp. xvii–xviii.
86. Ibid., p. xi.
87. Ibid.
88. Barua, "Assamese Literature," in Iyengar, *Indian Literature since Independence*, p. 1.
89. Ibid., pp. 1–2.
90. Ibid., p. 2.
91. Ibid., pp. 8–9.
92. Dasgupta, "Bengali Literature," in Iyengar, *Indian Literature since Independence*, p. 11.
93. Ibid., p. 24.
94. Ibid., p. 25.
95. Ibid., p. 26.
96. Shivanath, "Dogri Literature," in Iyengar, *Indian Literature since Independence*, p. 27.
97. Ibid., p. 41.
98. See Rao, *Five Decades*, pp. 112–113, for details on the protests that ensued after the publication of *Indian Literature since Independence*.
99. Rao, *Five Decades*, p. 114.
100. As mentioned earlier in this book, in 1938 when C. Rajagopalachari (Rajaji) was the Congress Party premier of Madras, he had made the study of Hindi in secondary schools compulsory in the Madras Presidency, a sound patriotic plan which was nevertheless forcefully resisted until the law was repealed in 1940. But Rajaji, a south Indian leader who was an influential politician on the national stage, evidently had a change of heart about Hindi: his 1957 letter to Kripalani, which ridicules this plan for transliterations into Devanagari, was written a year after Rajaji joined the leading Tamil leaders Annadurai and Periyar (both staunchly anti-Hindi) in signing a resolution endorsing the continuation of English as the official language past the fifteen-year period from the signing of the Indian constitution. See Rao, *Five Decades*, p. 115, for a longer excerpt from this letter to Kripalani.

101. See "Sahitya Akademi: Inauguration and Aims," in *Sahitya Akademi Annual Report 1954–1957*, pp. 1–27.
102. Rao, *Five Decades*, p. 120.
103. See ibid., p. 118, for a longer excerpt from this speech.
104. Ibid., p. 118.
105. See Satchidanandan, "That Third Space," p. 19.
106. Ibid.
107. Quoted by Narayanan and Sabharwal in "Introduction: Anarchy!", p. xi.

CHAPTER 5 PARTITION FICTION AND THE "BIRTH" OF NATIONAL LITERATURE

1. See Varma, *Kahey Ko Byahi Bidesh: Songs of Marriage from the Gangetic Plains*, p. 104. This song is based on a poem attributed to the Sufi saint-poet, Amir Khusro (1253–1325).
2. For a political chronology of events and forces leading up to Partition, see Bhattacharjea, *Countdown to Partition*; Ravikant and Saint, *Translating Partition*; Sarkar, *Modern India*; Hasan, *India's Partition*. Once Partition was announced, driven by fear of escalating violence, hundreds of thousands of Muslims began to move to Pakistan, and Hindus and Sikhs from Pakistan began traveling to India. The scale of this population exchange was unanticipated by all governments and despite the severe restrictions on what refugees could take with them, and despite the unsafe journey, 10–15 million people (according to different estimates) crossed the borders in both directions. It was one of the largest and possibly the most violent of population shifts in history. Close to one million people were killed or died, and hundreds of thousands were assaulted, raped, and/or separated from their families in the violence that ensued on both sides of the newly demarcated border. Besides the 100,000 or more women estimated to have been sexually assaulted, official estimates state that about 75,000–80,000 women were "abducted" by men of communities other than their own.
3. I do not consider fiction from Bengal/East Pakistan/Bangladesh in this chapter because, while these texts share much of the gender and social dynamics of the north, the regional political, linguistic, and cultural particularities are significantly different.
4. This particular song with its roots in Sufism carries within it a long tradition of male devotees inhabiting a female persona to express love and longing for a male divinity, but more often as a love interest rather than, as in this song, a father figure (*babul*). In Sikh texts as well, God is sometimes referred to as *babul* – as in the Gurbani verse that states: "Babul mera wadd samartha karn kaaran prab hara" [My father is all powerful, he acts and is the cause for all action].
5. Note how most of the black and white photographic images that now immediately conjure up the Partition in the visual media show refugees on the move: especially in overcrowded trains, on foot in long caravans (*kafilas*),

in bullock carts, briefly resting or collapsed on the roadsides, in temporary refugee camps, etc. The cover illustrations chosen for books published as part of the new Partition studies are particularly illuminating of this aspect of Partition as it lives in the memory and imagination.

6. Much has been written within (and outside) of new Partition studies about the nexus of nation and gender: see Denise Kandiyoti, Partha Chatterjee, Dipesh Chakrabarty, Kumari Jayawardena, and Malati De Alwis. Butalia, Menon, and Bhasin, among others, have written eloquently of the patriarchal/nationalist prescription for appropriate femininity and masculinity.
7. Ravikant and Saint, "Introduction," in *Translating Partition*, p. xvi.
8. Ibid.
9. Ibid.
10. See Nandy, "The Invisible Holocaust: Silence and Testimony." Also see by Nandy, "The Days of the Hyena."
11. While communal violence continues to be a reality in all three nations, the Partition of 1947 has different resonance in the three locations: in independent India it was experienced as a vivisection, as the much-lamented loss of bodily parts of "Mother India," while in Pakistan it was read as the necessary birth pangs of a new nation. In Bangladeshi history, 1947–1971 is the occluded period in national history, a history that is recorded as really beginning in 1971, when East Pakistan became Bangladesh. The violence that ensued during that struggle for independence in 1971 overshadowed the violence associated with the 1947 Partition.
12. Specifically the anti-Sikh violence in New Delhi and elsewhere in 1984, after the assassination of Indira Gandhi by her Sikh bodyguards, and the national spates of violence after the December 1992 destruction of the Babri Masjid at Ayodhya (a sixteenth-century mosque built over what was considered by Hindu fundamentalists to have been the birthplace of the Hindu god Ram) led both intellectuals and ordinary folk to make comparisons with Partition violence. These violent anti-minority riots in the 1980s and 1990s resulted in a rethinking of the wisdom of having suppressed the memory of "those dark days" (the Partition months) in the national memory.
13. See Pandey, "In Defense of the Fragment," p. 559.
14. See especially Butalia, *The Other Side of Silence*; Menon and Bhasin, *Borders and Boundaries*.
15. Menon and Bhasin, *Borders and Boundaries*, p. 7.
16. Ibid., p. 20.
17. Ibid., pp. 20–21.
18. Ibid. p. 8.
19. Ibid., p. 17.
20. See Menon, *No Woman's Land*.
21. And yet, Menon repeatedly insists that one needs to acknowledge that unlike "master narratives," it is the "marginal voices" that need attending to because it is in the "interstices of history that real life is resumed" (p. 5).

22. See Bahri, "Telling Tales"; Hai, "Border Work, Border Trouble"; Priya Kumar, "Testimonies of Loss and Memory"; and Talbot, "Literature and the Human Drama of the 1947 Partition." For a review of some of the anthologies of Partition fiction, see also Francisco, "In the Heat of Fratricide."
23. See the following anthologies: Farrukhi, *Fires in an Autumn Garden*; Hameed and Farrukhi, *So That You Can Know Me*; Jack, *India! The Golden Jubilee*; Khwaja, *Pakistani Short Stories*; and Rushdie and West, *The Vintage Book of Indian Writing*.
24. For anthologies of Partition fiction, see Bhalla, *Stories about the Partition of India*; Cowasjee and Duggal, *Orphans of the Storm*; Memon, *An Epic Unwritten*. For critical evaluations of the genre, see Kumar, *Narrating Partition*; Pandey, *Remembering Partition*; Ravikant and Saint, *Translating Partition*. Also see Low, *North India: Partition and Independence*, special issue of *South Asia: Journal of South Asian Studies*; and Memon, *The Partition of the Indian Subcontinent*, special issue of *Interventions*; as well as innumerable essays in popular news magazines in South Asia.
25. See Hyder, *River of Fire*; Hyder, *A Season of Betrayals*; Manto, *Black Borders*; Nahal, *Azadi* [Freedom]; Nanda, *Witness to Partition*; and Pritam, *Pinjar* [The Skeleton]. See Rita Kothari's interview with Zamir Ansari, Marketing Manager of Penguin India (conducted on December 29, 1997) in which Ansari notes that successful translations in terms of sales include "anything related to the experience of Partition." Kothari, *Translating India*, Appendix 2, p. 107.
26. See Didur, *Unsettling Partition*.
27. Bhalla, "Editorial Note," in *Stories about the Partition of India*, p. xiii.
28. Ibid., pp. xix and xlix.
29. Ibid., pp. xxvi and xlix.
30. Ibid., p. xxix.
31. For more on Bhalla's Gandhianism, see the review essay by Francisco, "In the Heat of Fratricide," p. 377.
32. Memon, "Preface," in *An Epic Unwritten*, p. xi.
33. Cowasjee and Duggal, "Introduction," in *Orphans of the Storm*, p. xi.
34. Memon, "Preface," in *An Epic Unwritten*, p. xii.
35. Ibid., p. xiii.
36. Ibid.
37. Ibid., p. xiv.
38. Ibid.
39. Ibid., p. xv.
40. Also see Memon, *The Color of Nothingness*, which begins with a listing of the "sources" from which the translated stories were culled; Memon lists the venue and date of the original Urdu publication for each of the stories included in this anthology.
41. Ravikant and Saint, "Introduction," in Translating *Partition*, p. xi.
42. Ibid., p. xxv.
43. Ravikant and Saint, "'The Dog of Tetwal' in Context," in *Translating Partition*, p. 101.

44. Rushdie and West, *The Vintage Book of Indian Writing*; also published in the USA under the title *Mirrorworks: 50 Years of Indian Writing* (New York: Henry Holt, 1997).
45. Rushdie, "Introduction," in Rushdie and West, *The Vintage Book of Indian Writing*, p. x.
46. Ibid.
47. In an acerbic review of this anthology, Shyamala A. Narayan noted that the Satyajit Ray text included was translated from Bengali. See Nararyan, "Review of *The Vintage Book of Indian Writing: 1947–1997* by Salman Rushdie and Elizabeth West."
48. For further discussion of this anthology, please see the epilogue to this study.
49. Farrukhi, "Introduction: My Country's Stories," in *Fires in an Autumn Garden*, pp. xxi–xxii.
50. In Farrukhi, *Fires in an Autumn Garden*, p. xviii.
51. Ibid., pp. xv–xvi.
52. Rushdie, "Introduction," in Rushdie and West, *The Vintage Book of Indian Writing*, p. xxii.
53. Bhalla, "Editorial Note," in *Stories about the Partition of India*, p. xxv.
54. Mishra, "The Diasporic Imaginary," p. 423.
55. Today the horrors of dislocation that Partition literature testifies to are reenacted in the razing of urban slums, the dislocation of rural populations that are "resettled" in order to build dams and power plants, and the destruction of communities in the course of communal riots that swept over entire cities in the 1980s and 1990s and as recently as 2002 in Gujarat.
56. Manto (1912–1955) spent most of his adult life in Bombay, where he worked as a journalist and a screenwriter. It is documented that he moved very reluctantly to Pakistan in 1948. When he published his Partition fiction in the early 1950s, it was negatively received not just by right-wingers in Pakistan and India but also by progressive cultural critics who thought him voyeuristic, pornographic, and irreligious. In recent years, however, Manto's reputation has been resurrected by literary critics. See Mufti, "A Greater Story-Writer Than God" and Gopal, "Dangerous Bodies," for fuller discussions (in English) of the historical and Urdu literary milieu in which Manto's work was produced and received. For an English translation of some of Manto's critical commentary on his Partition-related writing, see Manto, *Kingdom's End and Other Stories* and *Partition: Sketches and Stories*, pp. x–xvi.
57. Bhalla, "Editorial Note," in *Stories about the Partition of India*, p. xxx.
58. Ibid., p. xxxi.
59. Manto, "Open It" (1948), in *Stories about the Partition of India*, pp. 358–362.
60. Ibid., p. 360.
61. Ibid., p. 362.
62. It is significant that the novel *Cracking India* by Pakistani writer Bapsi Sidhwa (1988) on which the screenplay for this film was based does not end with this horrific scene. In the film, we do not see Shanta the Hindu maid again on the screen. In the novel, by contrast, we meet Shanta after this ordeal, now

established as a well-patronized prostitute in the red light district of a Pakistani city. She firmly refuses the offer of respectability, of being rescued and sent back to India. *Cracking India* was also published under the title *The Ice-Candy Man* (1988). See further discussion of this novel and film later in this chapter.

63. For another story with this same triangular cast (young female victim, decent but helpless citizen, and a rapacious mob) written by one of Pakistan's most respected female writers, see Mastur, "They are Taking me Away Father, They are Taking me Away!" This story has also been translated by Moneeza Hashmi with a different title, "Farewell to the Bride," in Hameed and Farrukhi, *So That you Can Know me*, pp. 33–38.

64. I want to thank Prof. Memon for drawing my attention to the subtle differences in different English translations from Urdu which have resulted from each translator resorting to different strategies to make the English language best reflect the Urdu: lopping off sentences, forcing a logical or linear or chronological order on the material, abridgement, etc. (email exchange March 10, 2000). I am also grateful for Prof. Memon for another note of caution: in the interests of accuracy, "transliterations" between Hindi and Urdu should be classified as translations despite the overlap between the two languages because often significant liberties are taken with the original.

65. Hasan, "Translators Note," in Manto, *Partition: Sketches and Stories*, p. ix. First published in English in 1991, this book was originally published in Pakistan in the original Urdu in 1951, under the Urdu title *Siyah Hashye* [Black Margins]. In 1991 Hasan published an English translation of *Siyah Hashye*, taking the liberty of giving it a new title and of adding "five stories which relate to 1947 and two others" (p. xvi). The original title's complexity would be hard to translate given that "black margins" has such dense cultural signification. This title evokes a range of images of mourning and negativity: from the black borders of documents with tragic news, to dark commentary or marginalia attached to a document, to the dark hem of a skirt that signified a "soiled" woman. However, much is lost in the shift from *Siyah Hashye* to *Partition: Sketches and Stories* even as the thematic focus on Partition is made clear. I greatly appreciate Geeta Patel and C. M. Naim's help with the translation of the title. In 2003 Rupa & Co. published a new English translation of *Siyah Hashye* translated by Rakhshanda Jalil under the English title *Black Borders*. "Khol Do" by Manto was not included in this collection.

66. Saros Cowasjee notes that "The Reunion" was the title supplied to him, one of the editors of this anthology, by the translator of this story (email correspondence September 12, 2010).

67. For different equations of gender and the national in Manto's work, see Mufti, "A Greater Story-Writer than God" and Gopal, "Dangerous Bodies."

68. See Ashraf, "Separated from the Flock." The notes on contributors in Bhalla, *Stories of the Partition of India* in which this story appears state that Ashraf studied at Aligarh Muslim University in India and is a civil servant in the Government of India. This story, we are told, was first published in Urdu in the Aligarh University journal (date and citation not given) (p. 874). Also see

the notes on contributors in Memon, *An Epic Unwritten*, p. 361. For a brief literary biography of Syed Ashraf, see www.urdustudies.com/auinfo/ashrafSM.html (accessed July 18, 2006).
69. Bhalla, "Editorial Note," in *Stories about the Partition of India*, p. xxxix.
70. Three translations of the original story have been consulted. The first is "Banished," translated by Muhammad Umar Memon in *An Epic Unwritten*, pp. 87–105, and page numbers in the text correspond to this version. Also see "Exile" translated by Bhalla (in *Stories about the Partition of India*, pp. 50–67), and "Banishment" translated by Anwar Enayetullah in Hameed and Farrukhi, *So That you Can Know me*, pp. 61–80. For more information on Hashmi, see the notes on contributors in Memon, *An Epic Unwritten*, pp. 363–64. Despite my best efforts, I have been unable to locate the original publication venue and/or date for "Ban Vaas."
71. See Kaul, *The Partitions of Memory*, p. 27 for a brief discussion of this story. Also see Bodh Prakash's discussion of this story as framed by an extremely useful account of the literary representation of women in fiction from this region from the 1900s onward ("The Woman Protagonist in Partition Literature").
72. See Low, *North India*, the special issue of *South Asia: Journal of South Asian Studies* which includes several essays, especially by Sarah Ansari, Gyanesh Kudaisya, and Ian Talbot, on the comforts of religious parallels. Contrary to other critics, Alok Bhalla, in his introduction to *Stories about the Partition of India*, argues that these religious parallels did not offer much comfort to the migrants (p. xxxv). This stance is inexplicable unless Bhalla's insistence on muting all religiously inflected influences in the interest of a sentimental Gandhianism is brought to bear on the position that he takes in this instance.
73. Hashmi, "Banished," in Memon, *An Epic Unwritten*, p. 88. The original Urdu text is much more explicit here: "Aaj jitni larkiyan hamare hath lagin, un mey sab say achchi hai." Alok Bhalla's version is more faithful to the original, which he translates as "of all the girls who fell into our hands tonight, she was the prettiest' (in *Stories about the Partition of India*, p. 52). A more exact translation would be, "Of all the girls we got our hands on today, she was the best." The original also makes clear that this grabbing of women is a daily occurrence.
74. By December 1949, under the aegis of state-sponsored "rescue" missions, about 20,000 formerly abducted women were "restored" to their "proper" homes on either side of the border (12,000 to India and 8,000 to Pakistan). Ritu Menon estimates the number of rescued women between 1947 and 1952 at 30,000 – of whom 12,000 were Muslim and 18,000 non-Muslim. See Menon, *No Woman's Land*, p. 154. This rescue and recovery process was conducted under the guidelines set by a series of agreements signed by India and Pakistan from as early as September 3, 1947 to the Abducted Persons (Recovery and Restoration) Act of 1949.
75. Ironically, Dussehra is a Hindu festival in which the triumph of good over evil is celebrated by the reenactment of the rescue of Sita from the clutches of her abductor Ravana by her husband, Lord Rama.
76. Kaul, *The Partitions of Memory*, p. 28.

77. There is a long tradition of variant versions of the *Ramayana* that were produced in Asia over the centuries. See Richman, *Many Ramayanas*.
78. See Varma, *Kahey Ko Byahi Bidesh*, pp. 110, 116, 122, 134, 142, 144.
79. "Adjust" is a much-favored South Asian English term to describe the degrees of self-negation required and expected of women in difficult or new situations: consequently, this word has been imported into most other Indian languages. For a discussion on women's issues in popular magazines and the pressure to "adjust", see Singh and Oberoi, "Learning to 'Adjust'."
80. Hashmi, "Banished," in Memon, *An Epic Unwritten*, p. 102.
81. Kaul, *The Partitions of Memory*, p. 27.
82. Hashmi, "Banished," in Memon, *An Epic Unwritten*, p. 89.
83. The fact that this trope is not used in the three stories I focus on in this chapter should not detract from the importance of these frequently cited folktales of doomed love. For example, the title of Mastur's short story "They are Taking me Away Father, They are Taking me Away!" does not reference a father–daughter exchange from the story itself but is an easily recognized quotation from the Punjabi epic love poem *Heer Ranjha*, in which Heer protests being taken to a husband she does not love, while Ranjha, her lover, stands by helpless and heartbroken. See Mastur's short story and Tahira Naqvi's "Introduction" (p. xix) in Memon, *Cool, Sweet Water*.
84. For "The Lost Child," see Anand, *Mulk Raj Anand: A Reader*, pp. 3–6. See Anand, "Author's Preface," where Anand describes the genesis of this story written when he first arrived in London in 1925 (p. ix).
85. Hashmi, "Banished," in Memon, *An Epic Unwritten*, p. 98.
86. Ibid., p. 99.
87. Ravikant and Saint, "Introduction," in *Translating Partition*, p. xxi.
88. For example, consider the *bedhai* song ("Gayey ja geet milan ke" [Sing Songs of Meeting/mating/marriage as you Set out to your Husband's House]) from *Mela* (1948) with lyrics written by the respected Urdu poet Shakeel Badayuni and set to music by Naushad Ali.
89. Chugtai, *My Friend, My Enemy*, p. 3.
90. For "Lajwanti," see Memon, *An Epic Unwritten*, pp. 14–29.
91. It is important to note that despite the many similarities, Hindu and Muslim social arrangements were not identical. For example, Muslims in northern India in this time period often arranged marriages within extended family or kin and so brides may likely have known their husbands and their families from childhood; hence the rituals around the bride leaving her natal home are more pronounced in Hindu ceremonies.
92. Attributed to Amir Khusro, this poem has been performed by leading Sufi quawals like Nusrat Fateh Ali Khan and also by Ahmed Mohammed Warsi. Sung to the present day at Hindu, Sikh, and Muslim wedding ceremonies, this song was included in several Hindi films. See the film *Heer Ranjha* (dir. Walli Saheb, 1948), where this song was sung by Lata Mangeshkar, as well as *Suhag Raat* [Wedding Night] (dir. Kidar Sharma, 1948), with this song sung by Mukesh and in *Suhagan* [A Married Woman] (dir. Anant Mane, 1954),

where it was sung by Geeta Bali. More recently, a popular version of this traditional song was recorded by singer Jagjit Kaur for the film *Umrao Jaan* (dir. Muzafar Ali, 1981). A variation on this "daughter's lament," as Amrita Pritam calls it, is woven into Pritam's novel *Pinjar* [The Skeleton/Cage] (1950), p. 8. In the film *Pinjar* (2003), based on this novel, the traditional song "Charka Chalati ma" [The Mother Runs the Spinning Wheel] is sung by Preeti Uttam, and the lyrics are adapted from Pritam's novel. In Hashmi's short story, the same everyday scene is evoked in passages such as: "All these brides in the neighbourhood sit in the shade of the neem tree spinning their wheels and singing, but I remain quiet. What an aura of joy surrounds them! How sweet songs of their parental homes sound!" (p. 103).

93. Hashmi, "Banished," in Memon, *An Epic Unwritten*, p. 103.
94. See Bimal Roy's classic film *Bandini* [Female Prisoner] (1963) in which one of these traditional songs is performed by playback singer Asha Bhosle: "Ab ke baras bhej bhaiya ko babul" [In this Coming Year, Father, Send my Brother]. Picturised in a women's prison, where the heroine is incarcerated for killing her lover's wife, this song walks the knife edge of equating marriage with prison and presenting the pathos of the lack of domestic bliss in these female prisoners' lives.
95. Hashmi, "Banished," in Memon, *An Epic Unwritten*, p. 98.
96. I wish to thank Muhammad Umar Memon for this and other details about the original Urdu text of "Ban Vaas."
97. Naim, "Introduction," in *A Season of Betrayals*, p. xviii. In a literal sense the term *ganga-jamni* refers to two rivers (the Ganga and the Yamuna) that flow through this region and start out from the same source in the Himalayas. Colloquially, the term is used to describe two distinct and contrasting strands that are woven into one design; the beauty of the design is understood to stem from this interweaving of contrasting colors or patterns.
98. Muslim socials are films in which north Indian Muslim middle- and upper-class lives are depicted in a manner that stresses a fading but still gracious world of Persianized, Urdu-speaking lead characters stylized to evoke the gentility of the landed classes with their fabled exquisite appreciation of poetry and music.
99. Hashmi, "Banished," in Memon, *An Epic Unwritten*, p. 105.
100. Ibid., p. 104.
101. Ibid., p. 98.

EPILOGUE

1. Chaudhuri, "A Note on the Selection," in *The Picador Book of Modern Indian Literature*, p. xxxii. Three essays by Amit Chaudhuri frame this anthology and are gathered under the section titled "Introduction" (pp. xvii–xxxiv): "Modernity and the Vernacular" (pp. xvii–xxii); "The Construction of the Indian Novel in English" (pp. xxiii–xxxi); "A Note on the Selection" (pp. xxxii–xxxiv).

2. Chaudhuri, "A Note on the Selection," p. xxxii.
3. See Chapter 1, where I examine the heated exchange between Indian writers in English and writers in the vernaculars/regional languages in the aftermath of the first International Festival of Indian Literature that was held in New Delhi, February 2002.
4. Chaudhuri, "The Construction of the Indian Novel in English," in *The Picador Book of Modern Indian Literature*, p. xxiii.
5. Ibid., p. xxiii.
6. See Iyengar, "Introduction," in *Indian Writers is Council*, p. xviii.
7. Chaudhuri, "Modernity and the Vernacular," in *The Picador Book of Modern Indian Literature*, p. xvi.
8. Nehru, "Tryst with Destiny," in Rushdie and West, *The Vintage Book of Indian Writing 1947–1997*, p. 2.
9. Both the lead introductory essays in Chaudhuri's anthology were previously published in the *Times Literary Supplement* under different titles: "Beyond the Language of the Raj: How Indian Writers in Vernacular Tongues Scarcely Acknowledged their Colonial Masters," *TLS*, August 8, 1997, pp. 17–18 and "The Lure of the Hybrid: What the Post-Colonial Indian Novel Means to the West," *TLS*, September 3, 1999, pp. 5–6. Rushdie's introduction was also published with minor alterations under the title, "Damne, This is the Oriental Scene for You!" in *The New Yorker* (special issue on Indian fiction), June 23 and 30, 1997, pp. 50–61.
10. See Kaul, *The Partitions of Memory*, p. 9.
11. Chaudhuri, "Modernity and the Vernacular," in *The Picador Book of Modern Indian Literature*, p. xix.

Bibliography

Ahmed, Talat. *Literature and Politics in the Age of Nationalism: The Progressive Writers' Movement in South Asia, 1932–56*. New Delhi: Routledge, 2009.
"Mulk Raj Anand: Novelist and Fighter." *International Socialism: A Quarterly Journal of Socialist Theory*, no. 105. Posted January 9, 2005. www.isl.org.uk/index.php4?id=60&issue=105 (accessed October 28, 2010).

Ambedkar, B. R. *Pakistan or the Partition of India*. (1940). Bombay: Thackers, 1946.
The Untouchables: Who Were They and Why They Became Untouchables. New Delhi: Amrit Books, 1948.
What Congress and Gandhi Have Done to the Untouchables. Bombay: Thackers, 1945.

Anand, Mulk Raj. "Afterword. On the Genesis of Untouchable. A Note," in *Untouchable*. New Delhi: Arnold, 1970.
An Apology for Heroism (1946). New Delhi: Arnold Heinemann, 1975.
"Author's Preface," in *Mulk Raj Anand, a Reader: Selections from his Fictional and Non-fictional Writings*, ed. Atma Ram. New Delhi: Sahitya Akademi, 2005.
Conversations in Bloomsbury. New Delhi: Arnold Heinemann, 1981.
Guest Book Entry at Sulabh Public Toilet website. www.sulabhtoiletmuseum.org/guest.htm (accessed March 13, 2010).
"The Lost Child" (1925), in *Mulk Raj Anand, a Reader: Selections from his Fictional and Non-Fictional Writings*, ed. Atma Ram. New Delhi: Sahitya Akademi, 2005, 3–6.
"Self-Obituary," in *Mulk Raj Anand, a Reader: Selections from his Fictional and Non-Fictional Writings*, ed. Atma Ram. New Delhi: Sahitya Akademi, 2005, xvi–xxxi.
Splendours of Himachal Heritage. New Delhi: DK Fine Arts Press, 1997.
"The Story of my Experiment with a White Lie." *Indian Literature* 10.3 (1967). Reprinted in *Critical Essays on Indian Writing in English*, ed. M. K. Naik, S. K. Desai, and G. S. Amur. Dharwar, Karnataka State: Karnatak University, 1972, 6–20.
Untouchable (1935). New Delhi: Arnold, 1970.

Anand, Mulk Raj, and Eleanor Zelliot, eds. *An Anthology of Dalit Poetry*. New Delhi: Gyan Publishing House, 1992.

Anand, S. "Sanskrit, English, Dalits." *Economic and Political Weekly* 34.30 (July 24–30, 1999): 2053–2056.
  ed. *Touchable Tales: Publishing and Reading Dalit Literature*. Chennai: Navayana, 2003.
Ananthamurthy, U. R. "The Flowering of the Backyard," in *India at 50: Bliss of Hope and Burden of Reality*, ed. V. M. Narayanan and Jyoti Sabharwal. New Delhi: Sterling, 1997, 235–246.
Anderson, Benedict. *Imagined Communities: Reflections on the Origin and Spread of Nationalism*. London: Verso, 1983.
Annamalai, E. "The Anglicized Indian Languages: A Case of Code-Mixing." *International Journal of Dravidian Languages* 7.2 (1978): 239–247.
  "English in India: Unplanned Development," in *English and Language Planning: A Southeast Asian Contribution*, ed. Thiru Kandiah and John Kwan-Terry. Singapore: Centre for Advanced Studies, National University of Singapore, and Times Academic Press, 1994, 2612–2677.
  "Nativization of English in India and its Effect on Multilingualism." *Journal of Language and Politics* 3.1 (2004): 151–162.
Ashraf, Syed Mohammad. "Separated from the Flock," in *Stories about the Partition of India*, ed. Alok Bhalla. New Delhi: HarperCollins, 1999, 3–32.
Austin, Granville. "Language and the Constitution: The Half-Hearted Compromise," in *Language and Politics in India*, ed. Asha Sarangi, New Delhi: Oxford University Press, 2009, 41–92.
Baer, Ben Conisbee. "Shit Writing: Mulk Raj Anand's *Untouchable*, the Image of Gandhi, and the Progressive Writers' Association." *Modernism/Modernity* 16.3 (September 2009): 575–594.
Bahri, Deepika. "Telling Tales: Women and the Trauma of Partition in Sidhwa's *Cracking India*." *Interventions: International Journal of Postcolonial Studies* 1.2 (1999): 217–234.
Bama. *Karukku* (1992), trans. Lakshmi Holmström. Chennai: Macmillan, 2000.
Bambai ka Babu [Gentleman from Bombay], dir. Raj Khosla, 1960.
Bandini [Female Prisoner], dir. Bimal Roy, 1963.
Bannerji, Himani. "The Violence of the Everyday." *ARIEL: A Review of International English Literature* 34.4 (October 2003): 139–147.
Barua, Birinchi Kumar. *Assamese Literature* (The PEN Books: The Indian Literatures, Volume I). Bombay: The PEN All India Centre, 1941.
Bedi, Rajinder Singh. "Lajwanti," in *An Epic Unwritten: The Penguin Book of Partition Stories*, ed. and trans. Muhammad Umar Memon. New Delhi: Penguin, 1998, 14–29.
Berman, Jessica. "Comparative Colonialisms: Joyce, Anand, and the Question of Engagement." *Modernism/Modernity* 13.3 (2006): 465–485.
Beth, Sarah. "Hindi Dalit Autobiography: An Exploration of Identity." *Modern Asian Studies* 41.3 (May 2007): 545–574.
Bhabha, Homi K., ed. *Nation and Narration*. London: Routledge, 1990.
Bhalla, Alok, ed. *Stories about the Partition of India*. New Delhi: HarperCollins, 1999.

Bhattacharjea, Ajit. *Countdown to Partition: The Final Days.* New Delhi: Harper-Collins, 1997.

Bhattacharyya, Harihar. *Federalism and Regionalism in India: Institutional Strategies and Political Accommodation of Identity.* Heidelberg Papers in South Asian and Comparative Politics, Working Paper No. 27, May 2005. www.ub.uni-heidelberg.de/archiv/5500 (accessed April 29, 2013).

Bhongle, Rangrao. "Dalit Autobiographies: An Unknown Facet of Social Reality." *Indian Literature* 46.4.210 (July 2002): 158–160.

Bluemel, Kristin. *George Orwell and the Radical Eccentrics: Intermodernism in Literary London.* London: Palgrave MacMillan, 2004.

Burney, Z. A., ed. "Important Letters, Notes and Literary Evaluations from the Sahitya Akademi Files." New Delhi: Sahitya Akademi (unpublished collection).

Burton, Antoinette. *The Postcolonial Careers of Santha Rama Rau.* Durham, NC: Duke University Press, 2007.

Butalia, Urvashi. *The Other Side of Silence: Voices from the Partition of India.* New Delhi: Penguin, 1998.

Cappola, Carlo. *Marxist Influences and South Asian Literature.* East Lansing: Michigan Sate University, 1974.

Casanova, Pascal. *The World Republic of Letters*, trans. M. B. DeBevoise. Cambridge, MA: Harvard University Press, 2004.

Chandrasekharan, K. and Brahmasri, V. H. *Subrahmanya Sastri, Sanskrit Literature* (The PEN Books: The Indian Literatures, Volume XII). Bombay: The PEN All India Centre, 1951.

Chaudhuri, Amit, ed. *The Picador Book of Modern Indian Literature.* London: Picador, 2001.

Chauhan, Dalpat. "I am the Witness of my History and my Literature: The Making of a Dalit Gujarati Writer." *Journal of Postcolonial Writing* 43.2 (August 2007): 133–142.

Chugtai, Ismat. *My Friend, My Enemy: Essays, Reminiscences, Portraits*, trans. Tahira Naqvi. New Delhi: Kali for Women, 2001.

Constituent Assembly Debates: Official Report, Volume IX (July 30, 1949–September 19, 1949). New Delhi: Lok Sabha Secretariat, 1999.

The Constitution of India (1950). Part XVII Official Language, Chapter 1. Language of the Nation. Section 343. Official Language of the Union. http://indiacode.nic.in/coiweb/welcome.html (accessed March 6, 2012).

Contemporary Indian Literature, with a foreword by S. Radhakrishnan. New Delhi: Sahitya Akademi, 1957.

Cowasjee, Saros. *So Many Freedoms: A Study of the Major Fiction of Mulk Raj Anand.* New Delhi: Oxford University Press, 1977.

Cowasjee, Saros, with K. S. Duggal, eds. *Orphans of the Storm: Stories on the Partition of India.* New Delhi: UBS, 1995.

Dalmia, Vasudha. "Introduction: Hindi, Nation, and Community," in *Nationalism in the Vernacular: Hindi, Urdu, and the Literature of Indian Freedom*, ed. Shobna Nijhawan. New Delhi: Permanent Black, 2010.

Ganguly, Debjani. *Caste, Colonialism and Counter-Modernity: Notes on a Postcolonial Hermeneutics of Caste.* London: Routledge, 2005.
"Pain, Personhood and the Collective: Dalit Life Narratives." *Asian Studies Review* 33.4 (December 2009): 429–442.
Garimella, Annapurna, ed. *Mulk Raj Anand: Shaping the Indian Modern.* Mumbai: Marg, 2005.
George, Rosemary Marangoly. "Of Fictional Cities and Diasporic Aesthetics." *Antipode: A Journal of Radical Geography* 35.3 (2003): 559–579.
The Politics of Home: Postcolonial Relocations and Twentieth Century Fiction. Cambridge University Press, 1996.
"Review of Antoinette Burton's *The Postcolonial Careers of Santha Rama Rau.*" *Journal of British Studies* 47.4 (October 2008): 992–994.
"Where in the World did Kamala Markandaya Go?" *NOVEL: A Forum on Fiction* 42.3 (Winter 2009): 400–409.
Gilani, Iftikar. *My Days in Prison.* New Delhi: Penguin, 2002.
Tihar Kay Shab-o-Roz [My Days in Prison], trans. into Urdu by the author with Nusrat Zahir. New Delhi: Penguin, 2006.
Gopal, Priyamvada. "Dangerous Bodies: Masculinity, Morality and Social Transformation in Manto," in Gopal, *Literary Radicalism in India: Gender, Nation and the Transition to Independence.* London: Routledge, 2005, 89–122.
The Indian English Novel: Nation, History and Narration. Oxford University Press, 2009.
Guha, Ranajit. *A Disciplinary Aspect of Indian Nationalism.* Santa Cruz, CA: UC Santa Cruz and Merrill, 1991.
Guru, Gopal, ed. *Humiliation: Claims and Content.* New Delhi: Oxford University Press, 2009.
Hai, Ambreen. "Border Work, Border Trouble: Postcolonial Feminism and the Ayah in Bapsi Sidwa's *Cracking India.*" *Modern Fiction Studies* 46:2 (Summer 2000): 378–426.
Hameed, Jasmin and Asif Aslam Farrukhi, eds. *So That You Can Know Me: An Anthology of Pakistani Women Writers.* New Delhi: HarperCollins, 1998.
Harrison, Selig. *India: The Most Dangerous Decades.* Princeton University Press, 1960.
Hartley, L. P. *The Go-Between.* London: Hamish Hamilton, 1953.
Hasan, Mashirul, ed. *India's Partition: Process, Strategy and Mobilization.* New Delhi: Oxford University Press, 1994.
Heer Ranjha, dir. Walli Saheb, 1948.
Hubel, Theresa. *Whose India? The Independence Struggle in British and Indian Fiction and History.* Durham, NC: Duke University Press, 1996.
Hyder, Qurratulain. *River of Fire* [*Aag ke Dariya*] (1959), trans. by the author. New Delhi: Kali for Women, 1998.
A Season of Betrayals: A Short Story and Two Novellas (1960), trans. C. M. Naim. New Delhi: Kali for Women, 1999.

Dangle, Arjun, ed. *Poisoned Bread: Translations from Modern Marathi Dalit Literature*. Hyderabad: Orient Longman, 1992.
Dasgupta, Probal. *Otherness of English*. New Delhi: Sage, 1993.
Desai, Mahadev H. *Day-to-Day with Gandhi: Secretary's Diary*, ed. Narhari D. Parikh, trans. Hemantkumar G. Nilkanth. Varanasi: Sarva Seva Sangh Prakashan, 1972.
Desani, G. V. *All about H. Hatterr*. London: Aldor Press, 1948.
Deshpande, Shashi. "English's Inter Alia: An Open-Letter to Some Fellow Writers." *Outlook* (March 11, 2002), www.outlookindia.com/outlookarchive.
Devy, G. N., *After Amnesia: Tradition and Change in Indian Literary Criticism*. New Delhi: Oxford University Press, 1992.
Dharwadkar, Vinay, ed. *The Collected Essays of A. K. Ramanujan*. New Delhi: Oxford University Press, 1999.
Dhobi Ghat [Mumbai Dairies], dir. Kiran Rao, 2010.
Didur, Jill. *Unsettling Partition: Literature, Gender, Memory*. University of Toronto Press, 2006.
Dutt, Romesh C., ed. and trans. *The Ramayana and Mahabharat Condensed into English*. London: J. M. Dent and Sons, 1929.
Earth: 1947, Dir. Deepa Mehta, 1998.
Farrukhi, Asif, ed. *Fires in an Autumn Garden: Short Stories from Urdu and the Regional Languages of Pakistan*. Karachi: Oxford University Press, 1997.
Fisher, Marlene. *The Wisdom of the Heart: A Study of the Works of Mulk Raj Anand*. New Delhi: Sterling, 1985.
Forster, E. M. "Preface" (1935), to *Untouchable*, by Mulk Raj Anand. New Delhi: Arnold, 1970, 7–10.
Francisco, Jason. "In the Heat of Fratricide: The Literature of India's Partition Burning Freshly (A Review Article)," in *Inventing Boundaries: Gender, Politics, and the Partition of India*, ed. Mushirul Hasan. New Delhi: Oxford University Press, 2000, 371–393.
Gadar: Ek Prem Katha [Rebellion: A Love Story], dir. Anil Sharma, 2001.
Gajarwala, Toral Jatin. "Miseducation: Dalit and Beur Writers on the Antiromance of Pedagogy." *Comparative Literature Studies* 43:3 (2010): 346–368.
Gandhi, Leela. *Affective Communities: Anticolonial Thought, Fin de Siècle Radicalism, and the Politics of Friendship*. Durham, NC: Duke University Press, 2005.
——— "Novelists of the 1930s and 1940s," in *A History of Indian Literature in English*, ed. Arvind Mehrotra. New York: Columbia University Press, 2003, 168–192.
Gandhi, Mohandas. *An Autobiography or My Experiments with Truth* (1927), trans. M. Desai. Ahmadabad: Navajivan Trust, 2006.
——— *The Collected Works of Mahatma Gandhi* [electronic book]. 98 volumes. New Delhi: Publications Division, Ministry of Information and Broadcasting, Government of India, 1999.
Ganesan, Indira. *Inheritance*. New York: Knopf, 1998.
——— *The Journey*. New York: Knopf, 1990.

India at a Glance: Census Data 2001. http://censusindia.gov.in/Data_Products/Library/Indian_perceptive_link/Census_Questionaires_link/questions.htm (accessed September 11, 2009).
In Which Annie Gives Those Ones, dir. Pradip Krishen, 1989.
Iyengar, K. R. Srinivasa. *The Indian Contribution to English Literature*. Bombay: PEN All-India Centre, 1945.
— *Indian Writing in English*. New York: Asia Publishing House, 1973.
— *Indo-Anglian Literature* (The PEN Books: The Indian Literatures, Volume V). Bombay: PEN All-India Centre, 1943.
Iyengar, K. R. Srinivasa, ed. *Indian Literature since Independence*. New Delhi: Sahitya Akademi, 1973.
— ed. *Indian Writers in Council: Proceedings of the First All-India Writers' Conference (Jaipur 1945)*. Bombay: PEN All-India Centre, 1947.
Jack, Ian, ed. *India! The Golden Jubilee*, special issue of *Granta* 57 (1997).
James, Allison and Alan Prout, eds. *Constructing and Reconstructing Childhood: Contemporary Issues in the Sociological Study of Childhood*. London: Falmer Press, 1990.
Jameson, Fredric. "Third World Literature in the Era of Multinational Capitalism." *Social Text* 15 (Fall 1986): 65–88.
Kabir, Humayun, ed. *Contemporary Indian Short Stories*. New Delhi: Sahitya Akademi, 1959.
Kachru, Braj. *The Alchemy of English: The Spread, Functions and Models of Non-Native Englishes*. Oxford: Pergamon Institute of English, 1986.
Kaliappan, K. Sundar and Ravi Srinivas. "On Castes and Comedians: The Language of Power in Recent Tamil Cinema," in *The Secret Politics of our Desires: Innocence, Culpability and Indian Popular Cinema*, ed. Ashis Nandy. New Delhi: Oxford University Press, 2002, 213–233.
Katz, Cindy. "Vagabond Capitalism and the Necessity of Social Reproduction." *Antipode: A Radical Journal of Geography* 33.4 (2001): 709–728.
Kaul, Suvir, ed. *The Partitions of Memory: The Afterlife of the Division of India*. New Delhi: Permanent Black, 2001.
Khair, Tabish. *Babu Fictions: Alienation in Contemporary Indian English Novels*. New Delhi: Oxford University Press, 2001.
Khwaja, Waqas Ahmad, ed. *Pakistani Short Stories* (1992). New Delhi: UBS, 1995.
King, Robert. *Nehru and the Language Politics in India*. New Delhi: Oxford University Press, 1998.
Kothari, Rita. *Translating India: The Cultural Politics of English*. New Delhi: Foundation Books, 2006.
— "The Translation of Dalit Literature into English," in *Translation as Intervention*, ed. Jeremy Munday. London: Continuum, 2007.
Krishnan, S., ed. *Malgudi Landscapes: The Best of R. K. Narayan*. New Delhi: Penguin, 1992.
Kumar, Priya. "Testimonies of Loss and Memory: Partition and the Haunting of a Nation." *Interventions* 1.2 (1999): 201–215.

Kumar, Raj. *Dalit Personal Narratives: Reading Caste, Nation and Identity.* New Delhi: Orient Black Swan, 2010.

Kumar, Sukrita Paul. *Narrating Partition: Texts, Interpretations, Ideas.* New Delhi: Indialog, 2004.

Lahiri, Tripti. "A Dalit Temple to 'Goddess English'", April 30, 2010. http://blogs.wsj.com/indiarealtime/2010/04/30/a-dalit-temple-to-goddess-english/ (accessed June 1, 2010).

Lankesh, Kavitha. "The Return of Malgudi Days: A Rediff Interview with Kavitha Lankesh." http://ia.rediff.com/movies/2006/jul/21malgudi.htm (accessed February 6, 2010).

Larson, Charles. "Review of Walsh's *R. K. Narayan: A Critical Appreciation.*" *Modern Philology* 83.1 (August 1985): 89–90.

Lazarus, Neil. "The Politics of Postcolonial Modernism." *The European Legacy* 7:6 (2002): 771–782.

Lelyveld, David. "The Fate of Hindustani: Colonial Knowledge and the Project of a National Literature," in *Orientalism and the Postcolonial Predicament,* ed. Carol Breckenridge and Peter van der Veer. New York: Oxford University Press, 1993, 189–214.

"Talking the National Language: Hindi/Urdu/Hindusthani in Indian Broadcasting and Cinema," in Asha Sarangi, ed., *Language and Politics in India.* New Delhi: Oxford University Press, 2009, 351–367.

"Transmitters and Culture: The Colonial Roots of Indian Broadcasting." *South Asia Research* 10.1 (Spring 1990): 41–52.

Low, D. A., ed. *North India: Partition and Independence,* special issue of *South Asia: Journal of South Asian Studies* 18.S1 (1995): 1–212.

Ludden, David. *India and South Asia: A Short History.* Oxford: OneWorld, 2002.

McEvilley, Thomas. *The Shape of Ancient Thought: Comparative Studies in Greek and Indian Philosophies.* New York: Allworth Press, 2002.

Mahmud, Shabana. "*Angāre* and the Founding of the Progressive Writers' Association." *Modern Asian Studies* 30.2 (1996): 447–467.

Manto, Saadat Hasan. *Black Borders: A Collection of 32 Cameos* [*Siyah Hashye*] (1951), trans. Rakhshanda Jalil. New Delhi: Rupa, 2003.

Kingdom's End and Other Stories, ed. and trans. Khalid Hasan. New Delhi: Penguin, 1987.

Partition: Sketches and Stories, trans. Khalid Hasan. New Delhi: Viking, Penguin, 1991.

Markandaya, Kamala. *Nectar in a Sieve.* London: Putnam, 1954.

Massy Sahib, dir. Pradip Krishen, 1985.

Mastur, Khajida. "They are Taking me Away Father, They are Taking me Away!" in *Cool, Sweet Water: Selected Stories* (1984), ed. Muhammad Umar Memon, trans. Tahira Naqvi. New Delhi: Kali for Women, 1999, 1–6.

Mehrotra, Arvind, ed. *A History of Indian Literature in English.* New York: Columbia University Press, 2003.

Mela, dir. S. U. Sunny, 1948.

Memon, Muhammad Umar, ed. *The Color of Nothingness: Modern Urdu Short Stories*, trans. M. U. Memon. New Delhi: Penguin, 1991.

Memon, Muhammad Umar, ed. *An Epic Unwritten: The Penguin Book of Partition Stories*. New Delhi: Penguin, 1998.

Menon, Dilip. "Being a Brahmin the Marxist Way: E. M. S. Namboodiripad and the Pasts of Kerala," in *Invoking the Pasts: The Uses of History in South Asia*, ed. Daud Ali. Delhi: Oxford University Press, 2002, pp. 55–88.

 The Blindness of Insight: Essays on Caste in Modern India. Chennai: Navayana, 2006.

 "No, Not the Nation: Low Caste Malayalam Novels of the Nineteenth Century," in *Early Novels in India*, ed. Meenakshi Mukherjee. New Delhi: Sahitya Akademi, 2002, 41–72.

Menon, Ritu, ed. *No Woman's Land: Women from Pakistan, India and Bangladesh Write on the Partition of India*. New Delhi: Women Unlimited, 2004.

 ed. *The Partition of the Indian Sub-continent*, special issue of *Interventions* 1.2 (1999): 157–330.

Menon, Ritu and Kamala Bhasin. *Borders and Boundaries: Women in India's Partition*. New Delhi: Kali for Women, 1998.

Mir, Raza and Ali Husain Mir. *Anthems of Resistance: A Celebration of Progressive Urdu Poetry*. New Delhi: India Ink/Roli Books, 2006.

Mishra, Pankaj. "R. K. Narayan," in *A History of Indian Literature in English*, ed. Arvind Krishna Mehrotra. New York: Columbia University Press, 2003, 193–208.

Mishra, Vijay. "The Diasporic Imaginary: Theorizing the Indian Diaspora." *Textual Practice* 10.3 (1996): 421–447.

Mitchell, Lisa. *Language, Emotion and Politics in South Asia: The Making of a Mother-Tongue*. New Delhi: Permanent Black, 2010.

Moretti, Franco. "Conjunctures on World Literature," in *Debating World Literature*, ed. Christopher Prendergast. London: Verso, 2004, 149–162.

Moretti, Franco, ed. *The Novel*, Volumes I and II. Princeton University Press, 2006.

Mufti, Amir. *Enlightenment in the Colony: The Jewish Question and the Crisis of Postcolonial Culture*. Princeton University Press, 2007.

 "A Greater Story-Writer than God: Genre, Gender and Minority in Late Colonial India." *Subaltern Studies* 11 (2000): 1–36.

Mukherjee, Arun P. "The Exclusions of Postcolonial Theory and Mulk Raj Anand's *Untouchable*: A Case Study." *ARIEL: A Review of International English Literature* 22:3 (July 1991): 27–48.

Mukherjee, Meenakshi. *The Twice Born Fiction: Themes and Techniques of the Indian Novel in English*. New Delhi: Heinemann, 1971.

Mukherjee, Meenakshi, ed. *Early Novels in India*. New Delhi: Sahitya Akademi, 2002.

Mukherjee, Sujit. "Propositions" (1981), in *Cultural Diversity, Linguistic Plurality and Literary Traditions in India*, ed. Sukrita Paul Kumar, Vibha S. Chauhan

and Bodh Prakash. New Delhi: Macmillian India and Department of English, Delhi University, 2005, 7–18.
Nahal, Chaman. *Azadi* [Freedom] (1975). New Delhi: Penguin, 2001.
Naik, M. K., *A History of Indian English Literature*. New Delhi: Sahitya Akademi, 1982.
   Mulk Raj Anand. Delhi: Arnold-Heinemann India, 1973.
Naik, M. K. and Shyamala Narayan. *Indian English Literature, 1980–2000: A Critical Survey*. New Delhi: Pencraft, 2001.
Naim, C. M. "Introduction," in *A Season of Betrayals: A Short Story and Two Novellas*, by Qurrantulain Hyder, ed. C. M. Naim. New Delhi: Kali for Women, 1999, vii–xx.
Nanda, B. R. *Witness to Partition: A Memoir* (1948). New Delhi: Rupa, 2003.
Nandy, Ashis. *An Ambiguous Journey to the City: The Village and Other Odd Ruins of the Self in the Indian Imagination*. New Delhi: Oxford University Press, 2001.
   "The Days of the Hyena: A Foreword," in *Mapmaking: Partition Stories from Two Bengals*, ed. Debjani Sengupta. New Delhi: Shristi, 2003.
   "The Invisible Holocaust: Silence and Testimony." Keynote Address, Twenty-ninth Annual Conference on South Asia, October 13, 2000, Madison, WI.
Narasimhaiah, C. D. "Director's Announcement for McAlpin Resident Fellowships at Dhavanyaloka." *The Literary Criterion* 32.3 (1996): 101.
   The Swan and the Eagle: Essays on Indian English Literature. New Delhi: Motilal Banarsidass, 1987.
   The Writer's Gandhi. Patiala: Punjab University Press, 1967.
Narasimhaiah, C. D., ed. *East West Poetics at Work*. New Delhi: Sahitya Akademi, 1994.
Narayan, R. K. "How to Write an Indian Novel." *Punch* (1933).
   Malgudi Days. London: Penguin, 1982, 44–50.
   My Days (1974). Mysore: Indian Thought Publications, 2000.
   Swami and Friends. London: Hamish Hamilton, 1935.
   Swamiyum Snegithargalun, trans. V. Krishnaswamy. Madras: Ananda Vikatan, 1939.
   A Writer's Nightmare: Selected Essays 1958–1988. New Delhi: Penguin, 1988.
Nararyan, Shyamala A. "Review of *The Vintage Book of Indian Writing: 1947–1997* by Salman Rushdie and Elizabeth West." *Ariel: A Review of International English Literature* 29:1 (January 1998): 263–267.
Narayanan, V. N. and Jyoti Sabharwal, eds. "Introduction: Anarchy! Yes, but it Functions," in *India at 50: Bliss of Hope and Burden of Reality*. New Delhi: Sterling Press, 1997.
Nasta, Sushila. "Between Bloomsbury, Gandhi and Transcultural Modernities: The Publication and Reception of Mulk Raj Anand's *Untouchable*," in *Books without border; Volume II: Perspectives from South Asia*, ed. Robert Fraser and Mary Hammond. Basingstoke: Macmillian, 2008, 151–170.
Nayar, Pramod. "Bama's *Karukku*: Dalit Autobiography as Testimonio." *Journal of Commonwealth Literature* 41.2 (2003): 83–100.

Nehru, Jawaharlal. *The Discovery of India*. Calcutta: Signet Press, 1946.
Pandey, Gyanendra. "In Defense of the Fragment: Writing about Hindu–Muslim Riots in India Today." *Economic and Political Weekly* 26.11–12 (March 1991): 559–572.
  Remembering Partition: Violence, Nationalism and History in India. New Delhi: Cambridge University Press, 2001.
Pandian, M. S. S. "On a Dalit Woman's Testimonio," in *Gender and Caste*, ed. Anupama Rao. New Delhi: Kali for Women, 2003, 129–135.
  "One Step outside Modernity: Caste in the Middle-Class Imaginary," in *The Middle Class in Colonial India*, ed. Sanjay Joshi. New Delhi: Oxford University Press, 2010, 240–260.
Pathak, Bindeswar. "A History of Toilets," at *The International Symposium on Public Toilets, Hong Kong, 1995*. www.sulabhtoiletmuseum.org/pg02.htm (accessed March 12, 2010).
Pillai, Thakazi Sivasankara. *Thottiyude Makan* [Scavenger's Son] (1947), trans. R. E. Asher. New Delhi: Orient, 1993.
Pinjar [The Skeleton], dir. Chandraprakash Dwivedi, 2003.
Pollock, Sheldon. "The Death of Sanskrit." *Society for Comparative Study of Society and History* 43.2 (2001): 392–426.
Prakash, Bodh. "The Woman Protagonist in Partition Literature," in *Translating Partition*, ed. Ravikant Saint. and Tarun K. Saint. New Delhi: Katha, 2001, 194–210.
Pritam, Amrita. *Pinjar* [The Skeleton] (1950), in *The Skeleton and Other Writings*, trans. Khuswant Singh. New Delhi: Jaico, 2003, 1–84.
Rai, Alok. *Hindi Nationalism* (Tracks for the Times 13). New Delhi: Orient Longman, 2000.
Rajam Aiyar, B. R., *The Fatal Rumour: A 19th Century Indian Novel*, trans. and with an afterword by Stuart Blackburn. New Delhi: Oxford University Press, 1998.
Raju, P. T., *Telugu Literature* (The PEN Books: The Indian Literatures, Volume XI). Bombay: The PEN All India Centre, 1944.
Ram, Ronki. "Ravidass Deras and Social Protest: Making Sense of Dalit Consciousness in Punjab (India)." *Journal of Asian Studies* 67.4 (November 2008): 1341–1364.
Ram, Susan and N. Ram. *R. K. Narayan: The Early Years, 1906–1945*. New Delhi: Viking, Penguin, 1996.
Ramakrishnan, E. V., ed. *Narrating India: The Novel in Search of the Nation*. New Delhi: Sahitya Akademi, 2005.
Ramanujan, A. K. "Is There an Indian Way of Thinking?" (1989), in *The Picador Book of Modern Indian Literature*, ed. Amit Chaudhuri. London: Picador, 2001, 419–437.
Ramaswamy, Sumathi. *Passions of the Tongue: Language Devotion in Tamil India 1891–1970*. Berkeley: University of California Press, 1997.
  "Sanskrit for the Nation," in *Language and Politics in India*, ed. Asha Sarangi. New Delhi: Oxford University Press, 2009, 139–182.

Ranasinha, Ruvani. *South Asian Writers in 20th Century Britain: Culture in Translation*. Oxford: Clarendon Press, 2007.
Rao, A. V. Krishna. *The Indo-Anglian Novel and the Changing Tradition*. Mysore: Wesley Press, 1972.
Rao, D. S., *Five Decades: A Short History of Sahitya Akademi (1954–2004)*. New Delhi: Sahitya Akademi, 2004.
Rao, Raja. *Kanthapura*. Delhi: Orient, 1938.
Rawat, Ramnarayan S. *Reconsidering Untouchablity: Chamars and Dalit History in North India*. Bloomington: Indiana University Press, 2011.
  "The Problem." Special Issue on Dalit Perspectives, Seminar (February 2006): 1–8. www.india.seminar.com/2006/558/558%20the%20problem.htm (accessed May 2, 2010).
Ravikant and Tarun K. Saint, eds. *Translating Partition*. New Delhi: Katha, 2001.
Ray, Annandasankar and Lila Ray. *Bengali Literature* (The PEN Books: The Indian Literatures, Volume II). Bombay: The PEN All India Centre, 1942.
Reddy, Sheela. "Midnight's Orphans: How Indian is Indian Writing in English? Far Removed from Reality, Say Regional Writers." *Outlook*, February 25, 2002. www.outlookindia.com/article.aspx?214680.
Reder, Michael, ed. *Conversations with Salman Rushdie*. Jackson, MS: University of Mississippi Press, 2000.
Rege, Sharmila, ed. *Writing Caste, Writing Gender: Reading Dalit Women's Testimonios*. New Delhi: Zubaan, 2006.
Richman, Paula, ed. *Many Ramayanas: The Diversity of a Narrative Tradition in South Asia*. Berkeley: University of California Press, 1991.
Roy, Arundhati. *The Algebra of Infinite Justice*. London: Flamingo, 2002.
  The God of Small Things. New Delhi: Indiaink, 1997.
Rushdie, Salman. "Damne, This is the Oriental Scene for You!" *The New Yorker* (June 23 and 30, 1997): 50–61.
  Midnight's Children. London: Jonathan Cape, 1981.
  Shame. London: Jonathan Cape, 1983.
Rushdie, Salman and Elizabeth West, eds. *The Vintage Book of Indian Writing 1947–1997*. London: Vintage, 1997.
Sahitya Akademi: National Academy of Letters, Annual Report 1954–57. New Delhi: Sahitya Akademi, 1957.
Sahitya Akademi Progress Report (1956–57). New Delhi: Sahitya Akademi, 1957.
Said, Edward. *Orientalism*. New York: Vintage Books, Random House, 1979.
Sankaran, Chitra. "Narrating Race, Gender and Sexuality in R. K. Narayan's *The Painter of Signs*," in *Narrating Race: Asia, (Trans)Nationalism, Social Change*, ed. Robbie Goh. Amsterdam: Rodolpi, 2011, 89–107.
Sarangi, Asha, ed. *Language and Politics in India*. New Delhi: Oxford University Press, 2009.
Sarkar, Sumit. *Modern India 1885–1947*. Madras: Macmillan, 1983.
Satchidanandan, K. "That Third Space: Interrogating the Diasporic Paradigm," in *In Diaspora: Theories, Histories, Texts*, ed. Makarand Paranjape. New Delhi: Indialog, 2001, 15–23.

Sen, Gertrude. "Popularization of the Indian Literatures outside India," in *Indian Writers in Council: Proceedings of the First All-India Writers' Conference (Jaipur 1945)*, ed. K. R. Srinivasa Iyengar. Bombay: PEN All-India Centre, 1947, 63–77.

Shackle, Christopher. "Introduction: Urdu, Nation, and Community," in *Nationalism in the Vernacular: Hindi, Urdu, and the Literature of Indian Freedom*, ed. Shobna Nijhawan. New Delhi: Permanent Black, 2010.

Shahane, V. A. and M. Shivaramakrishna, eds. *Indian Poetry in English: A Critical Assessment*. New Delhi: Macmillan, 1980.

Shahidullah, Dr. M. D. "Vote of Thanks." *Indian Writers in Council: Proceedings of the First All-India Writers' Conference (Jaipur 1945)*, ed. K. R. Srinivasa Iyengar. Bombay: PEN All-India Centre, 1947, 227–229.

Shanker, Subramaniam. "Reading the Vernacular: R. K. Narayan's *The Guide* and its Adaptation into Film." 38th Annual Conference on South Asia, Madison, WI, October 23, 2009.

Sharma, G. P. *Nationalism in Indo-Anglian Fiction*. New Delhi: Sterling, 1978.

Sharma, Pandey Bechan ("Ugra"). *Chocolate and Other Homoerotic Writings*, trans. and ed. Ruth Vanita. Durham, NC: Duke University Press, 2009.

Sheth, D. L. "The Great Language Debate," in *Language and Politics in India*, ed. Asha Sarangi. New Delhi: Oxford University Press, 2009, 267–298.

Sidhwa, Bapsi. *The Ice-Candy Man*. London: Heinemann, 1988.

Singh, Amita Tyagi and Patricia Oberoi. "Learning to 'Adjust': Conjugal Relations in Indian Popular Fiction." *Indian Journal of Gender Studies* 1.1 (1994): 93–120.

Sinha, Mrinalini. *Specters of Mother India: The Global Restructuring of an Empire*. Durham, NC: Duke University Press, 2006.

Sivakumaran, Anil. "Letter to the Editor." *The Wall Street Journal*, June 1, 2001: 15.

Sivaraman, Mythily. *Fragments of a Life: A Family Memoir*. New Delhi: Zubaan, 2006.

Sreenivas, Mytheli. *Wives, Widows, Concubines: The Conjugal Family Ideal in Colonial India*. Bloomington: Indiana University Press, 2008.

Srinivas, M. N. *India's Villages*. Bombay: Asia Publishing House, 1961.

Religion and Society amongst the Coorgs of South India. Oxford: Clarendon Press, 1952.

The Remembered Village. Berkeley, CA: University of California Press, 1976.

Suhag Raat [Wedding Night], dir. Kidar Sharma, 1948.

Suhagan [A Married Woman], dir. Anant Mane, 1954.

Talbot, Ian. "Literature and the Human Drama of the 1947 Partition." *South Asia: Journal of South Asian Studies* 18.S1 (1995): 37–56.

Tharoor, Shashi. "Comedies of Suffering." *The Hindu*, online edition, July 8, 2001 (http://tharoor.in/articles/comedies-of-suffering/).

Trivedi, Harish. *Colonial Transactions: English Literature and India*. Manchester University Press, 1995.

Umrao Jaan, dir. Muzafar Ali, 1981.

Valmiki, Omprakash. *Joothan: A Dalit's Life* (1997), trans. Arun Mukherjee. Kolkata: Samya Press, 2003.
Varadarajan, Tunku. "In Madras Once, a Writer Pauses, Visitors Bear Gifts." *Wall Street Journal*, Taste page, Weekend Journal (May 18, 2001).
Varma, Shakuntala, trans. and ed. *Kahey Ko Byahi Bidesh: Songs of Marriage from the Gangetic Plains*. New Delhi: Roli Books, 2005.
Veer-Zaara, dir. Yash Chopra, 2004.
Vijaysree, C., Meenakshi Mukerjee, Harish Trivedi, and T. Vijay Kumar, eds. *Nation in Imagination: Essays on Nationalism, Sub-Nationalism and Narration*. Hyderabad: Orient Longman, 2007.
Viyaunni, M. "The Bilingual Scenario in India." *The Hindu*, July 16, 1999.
Walsh, William. *R. K. Narayan: A Critical Appreciation*. University of Chicago Press, 1982.
Wiser, William and Charlotte Wiser. *Behind Mud Walls 1930–1960*. Berkeley: University of California Press, 1963.
Zelliot, Eleanor. *From Untouchable to Dalit: Essays on the Ambedkar Movement*. New Delhi: Manohar Press, 2001.

Index

A. E.
   and Anand, 128
"Ab ke baras bhej bhaiya ko babul" (song), 252n94
academia, Indian
   use of English, 5, 205
Adi Dharam movement, 97
Adiga, Aravind, 48
Aga Khan
   and minority rights, 104
agni parikshas (trial by fire), 193
Ahmad, Naziruddin, 22–23, 215n28
Ahmed, Aijaz, 51
Ahmed, Talat, 218n60
   on Anand, 103
Aiyar, B. R. Rajam
   The Fatal Rumour, 224n4
All-India Progressive Writers' Conference (first, 1936), 32
All-India Radio
   languages used by, 214n18
All-India Writers' Conference (first, 1945), 35–36, 162, 205, 219n84
   attendees at, 35
Ambedkar, B. R., 56, 110, 120, 215n23, 215n24
   choice of dress, 114
   conversion to Buddhism, 121
   on Gandhi's fast, 107
   on Indian culture, 213n9
   Pakistan or the Partition of India, 17
   representation of Dalits, 105, 109, 118
Amma, Chinnamalu, 79
Ammal, Subhalakshmi, 79
Anand, Kewal, 237n131
Anand, Mulk Raj, 31, 48
   anti-imperialism of, 92, 102
   anti-nationalism of, 129
   An Apology for Heroism, 100, 102, 130, 134
   association with Gandhi, 92, 127–128, 130–132, 235n114, 236n120, 237n131, 238n136
   association with Nehru, 129, 130, 236n122
   autobiographical project of, 130–131, 237n125
   and Bloomsbury Group, 9, 101
   break with PWA, 129
   The Bubble, 100, 128
   caste of, 94, 230n3
   censorship of, 92, 230n6
   changes witnessed by, 133
   characters of, 96
   charges of exaggeration concerning, 94, 236n119
   as colonial subject, 108
   Conversations in Bloomsbury, 100–101, 130–131
   Coolie, 99, 100
   critical reception of, 92, 95–97
   Dalit affiliations of, 92, 93, 114, 124, 126
   Dalit anthology of, 124
   Dalit intellectuals on, 97
   death of, 95
   debt to Forster, 232n61
   Dobrée's influence on, 232n61
   early life of, 94
   early works of, 95
   education of, 93, 94
   elite status of, 107, 108, 111
   and English General Strike, 103
   English language works of, 112, 208
   on English working class, 103
   and European intellectuals, 100–103, 130–131, 231n28
   experience of racism, 108, 109, 232n53
   father of, 94, 230n3
   humanism of, 92, 133, 230n10
   in Indian arts establishment, 129, 132–133
   and Indian independence, 104, 223n133
   as intermodern, 102
   internationalist commitments of, 129
   involvement with *Marg*, 95, 129, 133
   Joyce's influence on, 98, 99, 100, 123, 232n65
   later life of, 93, 129, 237n131
   leftist views of, 91, 93
   Letters on India, 102, 129, 133

267

Anand, Mulk Raj (*cont.*)
  life chronology of, 95, 230n2
  limitations experienced by, 133
  in literary canon, 5, 92, 95
  literary output of, 95
  literary reputation of, 6, 94, 132
  literary style of, 95
  The Little Plays of Mahatma Gandhi, 128, 237n125
  "The Lost Child," 101
  marginality of, 93, 107, 109
  modernism of, 9, 92, 99–100, 112, 123, 231n28
  multifaceted character of, 93
  "My Experiment with a White Lie," 127, 235n114
  nationalism of, 5, 93, 95, 230n4
  national significance of works, 1
  "On the Genesis of Untouchable," 231n16
  in Orwell's circle, 101
  as outsider, 108
  papers of, 131, 237n131, 238n136
  participation in Spanish Civil War, 92, 95, 103, 231n37
  as public intellectual, 92, 96
  in PWA, 92, 93, 94, 129
  PWA influence on, 98, 218n58, 230n13
  radicalism of, 132
  reception post-independence, 130, 237n126
  relationship with Indira Gandhi, 236n122
  residence in England, 95, 101, 103
  return to India, 129
  role in cultural production, 133–134
  role in Indian modernity, 133
  Sabarmati Ashram visit, 127, 128, 132, 236n119, 236n120, 237n125, 237n132
  Sahitya Akademi fellowship, 144
  scholarship on, 94
  "Self-Obituary," 91, 93, 108, 129
  self-presentation of, 92
  semi-autobiographical works of, 93
  separation from nationalist discourse, 6
  social realism of, 96, 103
  socialism of, 9, 91, 92, 103
  on T. S. Eliot, 131
  Untouchable, 10, 28, 89–90, 105–108, 218n58, 223n121
    affiliations of, 92
    Afterword, 127, 235n116, 237n125
    aspiration in, 115, 116
    as *Bildungsroman*, 123
    caste discrimination in, 9, 92–94, 106–113, 118–121, 126
    censorship accounts concerning, 236n120
    childhood in, 66
    Christianity in, 120, 121
    composition of, 98
    content of, 94
    critical reception of, 92, 97
    English language in, 112, 115
    Forster's preface to, 127
    Gandhi in, 95, 108, 111, 115, 120–123
    Gandhi's contribution to, 127–128, 130–132, 235n114, 237n131
    Gandhian reform in, 9, 94, 105, 208
    independence in, 223n133
    influences in, 94
    Joyce's influence on, 98, 99, 123, 232n65
    as "Mahatma" novel, 95, 105
    modernism of, 94, 105, 123
    Muslim characters in, 120, 123
    nationalism of, 9, 92, 94
    publication of, 127
    PWA influence on, 98, 230n13
    reformist message of, 227n58
    setting of, 226n46
    socialism of, 9, 94
    western costume in, 113, 114, 115, 122
  and Virginia Woolf, 101
  at World Congress of Writers against Fascism, 103
Anand, S., 106
Ananthamurthy, U. R., 15
Anderson, Benedict, 29
  Imagined Communities, 47, 49
Angāre (short stories), 32
Anglo-Indians
  on Indian nation, 17
Annamalai, E., 27, 28
  on language rivalries, 217n43
Ansari, Sahah, 250n72
Ansari, Zamir, 247n25
anthologies, of Indian literature, i, 37, 38
  celebrating anniversary of independence, 7, 11, 179, 183–184, 205
  Dalit, 124
  English language, 1, 172, 184, 203, 205
  international audiences for, 7, 207, 209
  as national literature, 2, 7, 183–184, 209
  Pakistani, 184–185
  Partition fiction in, 179–186, 247n22, 247n24
  publication by Sahitya Akademi, 148, 205
  representation of linguistic diversity, 2
anti-Brahmin movement, 58, 224n4, 228n80
  language politics of, 26
Asaduddin, M.
  on Partition fiction, 182
Ashraf, Syed Mohammad
  education of, 249n68
  Partition fiction of, 173, 186, 190–191
  "Separated from the Flock," 190–191, 249n68

Index

Assam
  Bengali speakers of, 165
Assamese literature
  in CIL, 156
  effect of independence on, 165
  in *Indian Literature since Independence*, 165
Austen, Jane, 62, 64
Austin, Granville, 215n24
Ayodhya mosque
  destruction of, 246n12
Azad, Maulana Abul Kalam
  Sahitya Akademi inaugural address, 136, 142, 143, 150
Azmi, Kaifi
  Sahitya Akademi fellowship of, 148

Badayuni, Shakeel
  "Gayey ja geet milan ke" (song), 251n88
Baer, Ben Conisbee
  on Anand, 112, 115, 232n65
Bali, Geeta, 251n92
Bama
  Karukku, 125
Bambai ka Babu (film), 197
  screenplay for, 197
Bangladesh
  creation of, 216n36, 246n11
Barua, Navakanta
  on Assamese literature, 165
Basheer, Vaikom M., 148
bedahi songs, 197
Bengali language
  in Assam, 165
Bengali literature
  awards for, 151
  effect of historical events on, 166
  fiction, 61
  in *Indian Literature since Independence*, 166
Berman, Jessica
  on Anand, 99–100, 123, 131
Besant, Annie, 19
  on education, 115–116
Beth, Sara, 124, 125
Bhabha, Homi K.
  on mimesis, 226n42
  "Nation and Narration," 49, 223n117
Bhalla, Alok
  Gandhianism of, 180, 247n31, 250n72
  on Manto, 187, 189
  Stories about the Partition of India, 180, 186
Bharatiya Janata Party (BJP), 28, 152
Bharatiya Jnanpith Trust
  literary awards by, 151
bhāsā literature, 43

Bhasin, Kamla, 177–178, 202
  gender studies of, 177–178
Bhattacharya, Bhabani, 152, 242n49
Bhattacharyya, Harihar
  "Federalism and Regionalism in India," 212n2
Bhosle, Asha, 252n94
Bhutto, Zulfikar, 46
Bihar Gandhi Centenary Celebration Committee
  Bhangi-Mukti branch of, 234n96
Bildungsroman, European, 99
Blackburn, Stuart, 59
  translation of *The Fatal Rumour*, 224n4
Bloomsbury Group
  Anand and, 9, 101
  Indian intellectuals and, 101
Bluemel, Kristin, 231n27
  George Orwell and the Radical Eccentrics, 102
Brahminism
  girlhood in, 79
  morality of, 227n57
  Narayan's, 64, 65, 68, 69, 86
  see also anti-Brahmin movement
Brahmins
  literacy of, 223n1
Buck, Pearl, 228n67
Buddhism
  Ambedkar's conversion to, 121
Butalia, Urvashi, 177, 178, 202

Casanova, Pascal, 7
  La république mondiale des lettres, 145
caste, Indian
  comedic destabilization of, 82
  communalism of, 67
  in Dalit literature, 227n61
  in English academic discourse, 5
  and English usage, 18
  experience of modernity, 52
  expression in clothing, 112–114, 233n69, 233n70
  impact on literature, 4
  and independence movement, 9
  in Indian English literary criticism, 4, 67
  in Indian English literature, 11, 42, 52
  maintenance of, 68
  in *Malgudi Days*, 83
  modes of representing, 66
  Narayan's engagement with, 59, 66–68, 76–82, 208, 225n32
  in national literature, 2
  north Indian interests of, 26
  racism and, 123
  role in cultural production, 4
  role in nationalism, 117
  role in vernacular literature, 159

caste, Indian *(cont.)*
    and Sanskritization, 226n42
    in urban spaces, 70
    and vernacular languages, 224n2
    in village life, 70
    worldview differences in, 223n133
    and writing in English, 224n2
    see also Anand, Mulk Raj: *Untouchable*;
        Dalits; untouchables
censuses, Indian
    1911, 59, 223n1
    1951, 213n12
    1991, 212n2, 212n3
    2001, 15, 212n2, 216n29
    language use in, 212n3, 213n12
Central Advisory Board of Education
    three language formula of, 26
"Chal re sajni, ab kya sochey? (song)," 197
"Charka Chalati ma" (song), 252n92
Chatterjee, Bankim Chandra, 60
    Rajmohan's Wife (novel), 60
Chaudhari, Nirad, 18
Chaudhuri, Amit, 48
    "Beyond the Language of the Raj," 253n9
    on English, 206, 207
    interest in vernaculars, 204
    "The Lure of the Hybrid," 253n9
    "Modernity and the Vernacular," 206, 209
    The Picador Book of Modern Indian Literature,
        203, 204, 253n2, 253n9
childhood, Indian
    cultural construct of, 82
    in *Swami and Friends*, 9, 59, 76–82
    Tamil, 58
    see also girlhood, Indian
Child Marriage Act (1830), 79
Christianity
    Hindu converts to, 121
    in Indian public sphere, 52
    for untouchables, 120
Chugtai, Ismat, 197
cinema, Indian
    in English, 29, 217n47
    music of, 29–30
    "Muslim social," 201, 252n98
    Partition, 195–197, 198–200
        bedahil rukhsati scenes in, 197, 198
        cross-community romance in, 198
        gendered violence in, 200
        mela trope in, 196, 198
        nationalism of, 199
        separation in, 196–197
    vernacular
        cultural production in, 29
        Tamil, 82

clothing
    expression of caste, 114, 233n69, 233n70
    role in nationalism, 114, 122
colonialism
    impact on literary production, 3
    revised understandings of, 45
    see also India, colonial
community, imagined, 29, 47, 49
Conference on "Suppressed Classes"
    (Ahmedabad, 1921), 121
Constituent Assembly of India
    constitution of 1949, 23–24, 137
    national language debate in, 21–23, 151,
        215n24
    use of English, 22
constitution of 1949
    Eighth Schedule of, 25, 137, 151, 216n33,
        242n46
    language provisions of, 23–24, 215n23
    use of English, 23–24
Contemporary Indian Literature (CIL, 1957),
        161
    anti-Urdu statements in, 160
    Assamese literature in, 156
    bias in, 159–160
    choice of authors, 161
    Hindi in, 243n72
    Indian English in, 156
    instructions for authors, 154–156
    Iyengar's contribution to, 162
    Kannada literature in, 160
    Punjabi literature in, 158
    religious issues in, 159
    Sanskrit in, 157
    shaping of literary history, 157–159
    success of, 161
    translations of, 161
    Urdu in, 157
    vernacular literatures in, 157, 243n56
Cowasjee, Saros, 102, 249n66
    on Anand, 128, 129, 231n28, 236n119
    So Many Freedoms, 230n2
    work with Anand's papers, 237n131
Critical Essays on Indian Writing in English
    (Naik, Desai and Amur), 127
cultural institutions, Indian
    colonial, 239n15
    post-independence role of, 238n4
cultural production, Indian, 11
    Anand's role in, 133–134
    Dalit, 210
    English use in, 13, 30
    global remix of, 8
    international recognition for, 207
    national institutions for, 137

Partition in, 196
  role of caste in, 4
  in vernacular cinema, 29
  in vernacular languages, 8, 55
cultural unity, Indian, 164
  elites' interest in, 2
  under Sahitya Akademi, 137, 139, 140, 149, 153, 155, 161, 168, 172
  see also national unity, Indian
culture
  politics of, 45
culture, Indian
  city–village dynamic in, 73
  diasporic imaginary in, 75, 76
  role of English in, 10, 14
  swadeshi in, 30
  urban, 224n2
  village life in, 69–71
  western parallels of, 146–147
culture, Indo-Muslim
  ganga-jamni, 201, 252n97
culture, western
  Indian borrowings of, 215n29
  Tamil adaptation of, 227n57

Dalit literature, 232n49, 235n99
  autobiography, 125, 126
  caste oppression in, 227n61, 233n80
  classroom scenes in, 227n47
  community in, 106, 125
  in English, 232n66
  English language scholarship on, 235n102
  establishment of, 92
  by non-Dalits, 106, 126
  poetry, 124
  suffering in, 125
  translation into English, 235n102
Dalits
  activism of, 9, 97, 118, 121, 124
  Ambedkar's representation of, 105
  in Anand's fiction, 89, 107, 112
  animal imagery for, 122
  on BJP Sanskrit plan, 217n45
  conversion to Christianity, 121
  English education for, 28, 233n80
  narratives of village life, 70
  racial origins of, 213n9
  temple rights of, 121
  on untouchable terminology, 110
  upper-caste sentimentality toward, 106
  use of English, 112, 210, 223n133, 232n66, 233n73
  see also caste, Indian; untouchables
Dangle, Arjun
  Poisoned Bread, 124

Danielewski, Ted, 228n67
Das, Kamala, 221n102
  My Story, 44
  vernacular works of, 44
Das, Seth Govind, 22, 215n24
Dasgupta, Alokeranjan
  on Bengali literature, 166
Dasgupta, Probal
  The Otherness of English, 215n29
Depressed Classes, 110
  see also caste, Indian; untouchables
Desai, Mahadev H.
  on Gandhi, 236n120
Desani, G. V.
  All about H. Hatterr, 51
Deshpande, Shashe, 56
Devy, G. N.
  After Amnesia, 43
Dhobi Ghat (film), 217n47
diaspora
  aesthetics of, 89
  in Indian literature, 48, 75–76, 171, 175–176
  in nationalistic discourse, 176
  in Partition fiction, 11, 174, 175, 186, 192, 201
  temporal experience of, 201
  see also Partition (of India)
discrimination, caste/gender-based, 109
Dobrée, Bonamy
  influence on Anand, 232n61
Dogri literature
  in *Indian Literature since Independence*, 167
  local concerns in, 166
drama, Indian
  local traditions of, 29
Dravidian languages, 26
duppatta
  symbolism of, 187, 189
Dussehra (Hindu festival), 193, 250n75
Dutt, R. C.
  on Greek/Indian parallels, 146

Early Novels in India (essays), 52, 53
Earth: 1947 (film), 188, 198, 200
"Ek kay baad abhi nahi; dho kay baad kabhi nahi" (slogan), 39
Eliot, T. S.
  Anand on, 131
elites, Indian
  engagement with modernity, 52
  hegemonic ideologies of, 65, 87
  interest in cultural unity, 2
  regional versus national, 55
  role in Indian English literature, 30, 55, 56
  role in postcolonial studies, 54
  Sanskrit language use, 215n29

elites, Indian (*cont.*)
　use of English, 1, 3, 16, 26, 28, 39, 54
　view of national identity, 3
encyclopedia, Indian (proposed), 36
English language
　advantages of, 24, 207
　among Tamil population, 59
　Anand's use of, 112, 208
　anti-colonial sentiment concerning, 25
　championing of vernaculars through, 147
　in colonial India, 20
　communication across boundaries, 34, 112
　Dalit use of, 112, 210, 223n133, 232n66, 233n73
　elevation above vernaculars, 54
　global importance of, 44, 143, 204, 205
　hegemony in India, 16, 203–206
　high status of, 204
　in Indian academia, 5, 205
　Indian accent in, 85
　Indian elites' use of, 1, 3, 16, 26, 28, 39, 54
　in Indian independence movement, 8, 13
　Indian intellectuals' use of, 203
　as Indian mother-tongue, 15, 212n2
　loss of nuance in, 4, 170
　mediation with other languages, 18
　Narayan's use of, 59, 60, 208
　as national language, 23
　neutrality of, 27, 28
　non-elite use of, 28
　number of speakers, 18, 212n2, 216n29
　official imperial status of, 18
　as official Indian language, 8, 26, 242n45, 244n100
　parallels with Sanskrit, 146–147, 215n29
　postcolonial discourse in, 3
　in postcolonial India, 15, 37–39, 44, 203–204
　postcolonial literary context of, 210
　proficiency in, 16
　relationship to Tamil, 224n4
　representation of India, 1, 16, 205
　role in Indian national identity, 6, 14, 21
　role in Indian national literature, 2, 5, 10, 11, 14, 137, 172
　role in Indian national unity, 2, 17, 30, 56, 219n72
　role in Indian nationalism, 13–14, 21, 204
　role in social mobility, 18
　Sahitya Akademi's reliance on, 147, 148, 149, 150, 151, 153, 172
　Sanskrit phrases in, 146
　transmutation of subject, 28
　users of, 15–16
　vernacular writers' resentment of, 56
equity, symbolic, 39
European literature, communist-inspired, 32

Fabian, Johannes, 226n42
Farrukhi, Asif
　Fires in an Autumn Garden, 185
fiction
　Bengali, 60
　Malayalam, 52
　Tamil, 59
　Urdu, 173, 175, 182
　see also Partition fiction
fiction, Indian English
　babu, 212n3
　caste in, 52
　colonial modernity in, 52
　early works, 61
　freedom in, 53
　Gandhi's attitude toward, 132
　and Indian nationalism, 53, 61
　"Mahatma," 95, 105
　middle-class life in, 51
　nineteenth-century, 52, 61
　postcolonial, 204
　village life in, 70, 72–74
　women in, 53
　see also Indian English literature
Film and Television Institute of India (Pune), 239n4
film industry
　during Partition, 197
　see also cinema, Indian
Fisher, Marlene, 128
　The Wisdom of the Heart, 237n132
Forster, E. M.
　Anand's debt to, 232n61
　preface to *Untouchable*, 127
Francisco, Jason
　"In the Heat of Fratricide," 247n22
freedom
　in Indian English fiction, 53
French academy
　Sahitya Akademi's emulation of, 142

Gadar: Ek Prem Katha (film), 198
Gandhi, Indira, 38
　assassination of, 246n12
　on *The Guide*, 76
　relationship with Anand, 236n122
Gandhi, Leela, 131
Gandhi, Mohandas Karamchand
　advocacy of vernaculars, 213n17, 214n17
　Anand's association with, 92, 127–128, 130–132, 235n114, 236n120, 238n136
　attitude toward literature in English, 8, 132
　An Autobiography, 109
　clothing of, 114

contribution to *Untouchable*, 127–128,
   130–132, 235n114, 237n131
correspondence of, 128, 236n120
on English language, 20
experience of racism, 109
Hindu universalism of, 180
hunger strike (1932), 105, 107, 120,
   236n120
ideal of village life, 71, 72
in independence movement, 104
on Indian unity, 104
knowledge of vernaculars, 20
on Minorities pact, 104
on minority rights, 105
on Partition madness, 176
Suppressed Classes speech (1921), 122
"The Story of My Experiments with Truth,"
   127
in *Untouchable*, 95, 108, 115, 121–123
on untouchables, 105, 106, 110, 111, 120, 122,
   232n50
views on literature, 8, 131, 132, 237n130
Young India, 99
Gandhi, Rajiv, 236n122
Ganesan, Indira
   fictional cities of, 74, 228n65
Ganguly, Debjani
   Caste, Colonialism and Counter-Modernity, 66,
      67
   on Dalit literature, 125
"Garibi hatao!" (slogan), 38
Garimella, Annapurna, 133
gender
   in English language use, 210
   impact on literature, 4
   in Indian national literature, 2, 190
   in Manto's works, 249n67
   in Partition fiction, 175, 186, 189,
      192–193
   in Partition studies, 177, 246n6
   in use of vernacular languages, 15
gender bias, 109
   in Sahitya Akademi, 148, 149, 241n36
gender studies
   Bhasin's, 177–178
   Menon's, 177–178
gendered violence
   in "Banished," 192–193
   in "Khol do," 186–189
   in Partition, 175–178, 186, 195, 200, 202,
      245n2
   in Partition cinema, 200
General Strike (England, 1926)
   Anand and, 103
George, K. M., 170

George, Rosemary
   Kamala, Madhavikutty, Suraiya, 221n102
   on Kamala Markandaya, 222n114
Ghosh, Aurobindo
   writings in English, 143
Gilani, Iftikar
   Tihar Kay Shab-o-Roz, 242n42
girlhood, Indian
   Brahmin, 79
   in early twentieth century, 79
   marriage age in, 79
   see also childhood, Indian
Gokhale, Gopalkrishna, 72
Gopal, Priyamvada, 237n132
Gotak, V. K.
   on Kannada literature, 160
Government of India Act (1935), 9,
   104
Greene, Graham, 63
   on Narayan, 87
Guha, Ranajit, 16
The Guide (film, 1965), 76, 85, 228n67
Gujarat
   communal violence in, 248n55
Guru, Gopal, 109, 121

Hamilton, Hamish, 63, 78
Harijan Sevak Sangh, 105, 110
   see also untouchables
Harrison, Jessica, 235n116
Hartley, L. P.
   The Go-Between, 229n99
Hasan, Khalid
   translation of Manto, 189, 249n65
Hashmi, Jamila
   "Banished," 191–194, 201
      diaspora in, 192, 201
      gendered violence in, 192–193
      Hindu legends in, 201
      lost children trope in, 195
      mela trope in, 193, 195, 196
      Ramayana in, 192
      separation in, 200–201
      translations of, 250n70, 250n73
      wedding imagery of, 194, 252n92
      women characters of, 250n71
   Partition fiction of, 173, 186, 191–194
Hashmi, Moneeza, 249n63
Heer Ranjha (film), 251n92
hijrat
   parallel with Partition, 192
Hindi Consultative Committee
   on literary awards, 153
Hindi language
   compulsory use of, 224n3, 244n100

Hindi language (cont.)
  in Devanagari script, 24, 139, 147, 168, 213n17, 244n100
  as national language, 21, 23–24, 25–27, 148, 150, 157, 215n28
  number of speakers, 159, 212n2
  official status of, 17, 26, 83, 84, 168, 242n45
  Sanskritized, 25, 29, 146, 213n17, 214n21
  sentiment against, 17, 224n3, 224n5
  slogans in, 39
  untouchables in, 110
  as vernacular language, 213n4
Hindi literature
  awards for, 151
  in *Indian Literature since Independence*, 167
  nature poetry, 227n48
Hinduism
  in Narayan's works, 69
Hindustani
  advocates of, 98, 213n17
  in national language debates, 157
  PWA advocacy of, 32
Hubel, Theresa
  on Anand, 105–106
"Hum dho. Hamarey dho" (slogan), 39
Humiliation: Claims and Context (2009), 109
Hussain, Intizar
  on Pakistani fiction, 185
Hyderabad
  in union of independent India, 219n84
Hyderabad, Nizam of, 35, 219n84

independence, Indian
  anthologies celebrating, 7, 11, 179, 183–184, 205
  and artistic freedom, 166
  effect on Assamese literature, 165
  fiftieth anniversary of, 7, 176, 184
  literary effect of, 164, 166
  Narayan and, 73–76
independence movement, Indian, 104–106
  Anand and, 104, 223n133
  caste issues in, 9
  English language in, 8, 13
  Gandhi in, 104
  in Indian English literature, 8, 42
  Indian English literature following, 138
  minority rights in, 105
independence movements, global, 2
India
  communalism in, 67
  Eurasian community of, 212n1
  as goal, 17
  linguistic competence in, 15
  national language for, 21, 23–24, 25–27, 148, 150, 157, 215n28
  see also Partition (of India)
India, colonial
  cultural demoralization of, 43
  cultural institutions of, 239n15
  English language use in, 20, 217n51
  European fiction on, 61
  self-respect movement in, 224n4
  use of English in, 20
  in western history, 210
India, north
  caste interest of, 26
  Hindi belt of, 25
India, postcolonial
  English discourse of, 204
  English language in, 15, 37–39, 44, 203–204
  humanist aspirations for, 135
  in international literary community, 144–146
  language politics of, 156, 168, 203
  national cultural institutions of, 136
  role in global humanism, 135
India, south
  English users of, 26, 27
  language politics of, 216n37
Indian English literature, 30
  authenticity of, 6, 29, 31, 40, 45, 48, 56, 222n113
  authority of, 44
  awards for, 151–153
  British traditions of, 42
  canonical writers of, 5, 92, 95, 230n5
  caste in, 11, 42, 67
  childhood trauma in, 228n71
  CIL essay on, 156
  contribution to world literature, 183
  critical writing on, 47
  cultural production in, 13
  divergence from nationalism, 7, 10
  east and west in, 42
  effect on vernacular literatures, 2
  emergence of, 43
  expectations for, 1
  formative period of, 5
  heterogeneity of, 6
  independence in, 8, 42
  local concerns in, 51
  middle-class life in, 51
  of mid-twentieth century, 42, 134
  "minor" writers, 7
  nationalism of, 45
  of 1980s, 45–48
  nineteenth-century, 42
  non-national themes of, 207, 208
  nostalgia in, 48

postcolonial, 134, 138, 183
under PWA, 32
reception of, 42
relationship to nationalism, 51
representation of India, 1, 8, 31, 33, 36, 40, 56, 205
response to national situation, 55
role in Indian nationalism, 33–34, 154
role of elites in, 30, 55, 56
romance triangles in, 227n57
under Sahitya Akademi, 143, 151–153
standard issues in, 11
survival of, 44–45
themes of, 43
transnational literary discourse of, 31
"twice-born," 42
as uniting force, 35–36
see also fiction, Indian English; Indian writing in English; national literature, Indian
Indian literature
  caste in, 4
  children's, 156
  as construct of English language criticism, 56
  contribution to world, 142
  diasporic, 48, 75–76, 171, 175–176
  effect of historical events on, 164
  effect of independence on, 164, 166
  effect of world events on, 164
  expression of anti-imperialism through, 145
  folk, 156
  government policy on, 149–150, 162
  heterogeneity of, 208
  independence in, 156
  international readership of, 7, 11, 207, 209
  local concerns of, 5, 174–175, 182, 185
  modern, 156
  national, 137, 154
  poetry, 163, 227n48
  role in national unity, 139, 154
  Sahitya Akademi's position on, 154
  unity of, 156, 161, 164
  see also fiction; vernacular literatures, Indian
Indian Literature (journal), 153
Indian Literature since Independence (1973), 161
  Assamese literature in, 165
  authors of, 161
  Bengali literature in, 166
  bias in, 167
  Dogri literature in, 167
  Hindi literature in, 167
  Iyengar's editing of, 161–164
  Kannada literature in, 167
  sales of, 167
  single edition of, 167
  withdrawal from circulation, 167

Indian National Congress, 17, 104, 213n7
  Muslim League and, 105, 213n7, 214n9
Indian Ocean (rock band), 217n50
Indian writing in English, 30
  see also Indian English literature
Indianness
  in Narayan's works, 9, 48, 58, 77
  Sahitya Akademi's, 137, 141, 157
  in twenty-first century, 171
  of Urdu language, 157
Indo-Anglian literature, 23, 30
  see also Indian English literature; Indian writing in English
intellectuals, British
  view of colonial intellectuals, 103
intellectuals, Dalit
  access to literary circles, 210
  on Anand, 97
intellectuals, European
  Anand and, 100–103, 130–131
  relationship with former colonials, 133
intellectuals, Indian
  and Bloomsbury Group, 101
  and governmental cultural policy, 162
  use of English, 203
intermodernism, 102
International Festival of Indian Literature (first, 2002), 56, 253n3
Iyengar, Srinivasa, 23, 24, 27, 206
  and All-India Writers' Conference, 35–36, 162
  on Anand, 96
  contribution to *CIL*, 162
  on early Indian fiction, 61, 219n71
  editing of *Indian Literature since Independence*, 161–164
  on English literary criticism, 40
  on Indian poetry, 163
  Indo-Anglian Literature, 40, 162
  on Narayan, 63
  PEN work of, 162
  in Sahitya Akademi, 144, 167
  on vernacular languages, 163

Jadhav, Raj Narendra, 106
Jalianwala Bagh massacre (1919), 103
Jameson, Fredric
  on national allegory, 51
  "Third World Literature in the Era of Multinational Capitalism," 49, 222n115
Jnanpith Award for literature, 152
Joshi, Sharad, 84
Joyce, James
  influence on Anand, 98, 99, 100, 123, 232n65

Index

Kaali, Sunder, 82
Kabir, Humayun, 37
Kachru, Braj
  The Alchemy of English, 27, 28
"*Kahe ko Byahi Bidesh*" (wedding song), 173, 198
Kannada literature
  in *Contemporary Indian Literature*, 160
  in *Indian Literature since Independence*, 167
  post-independence security of, 158
Karanth, Kota Shivaram, 126
Karnad, Girish, 229n84
Kaul, Suvir, 209
Khair, Tabish
  Babu Fictions, 212n3
Khanna, Stuti
  on Partition fiction, 182
Khusro, Amir, 245n1, 251n92
Kothari, Rita, 152, 216n29, 235n102
Kripalani, Krishna, 162, 243n77
  instructions for Sahitya Akademi authors, 154–156, 159
  leadership of Sahitya Akademi, 139
Krishnan, S., 61
  Malgudi Landscapes, 74
  on Narayan, 87
Kudaisya, Gyanesh, 250n72
Kumar, Dilip, 196
Kumar, Ravi, 106

Lalit Kala Akademi
  establishment of, 136
language, national Indian
  in constitution of 1949, 23–25
  criteria for, 23
  debates over, 21–23, 44, 151, 213n17, 215n24, 215n29, 243n64
  English as, 23
  Gandhian ideal of, 28
  Hindi as, 21, 23–24, 25–27, 150, 157, 215n28
  rivalries for, 217n43
  versus official language, 25
languages
  choice of, 20
  code-mixing among, 27
Lankesh, Kavitha, 228n83
Larson, Charles, 74
Lazarus, Neil, 221n106
Leavis, F. R., 220n90
Lelyveld, David, 20
linguistic communities, Indian, 14, 212n2
  bilingual, 212n3
  worldviews of, 54
literacy, Indian
  of Brahmins, 223n1
  levels of, 29

literary criticism, Indian English, 47
  bhāsā, 43
  caste and, 4, 67
  changing norms of, 2
  encouragement of literary production, 40
  interest in Indian literature, 3
  Iyengar on, 40
  legitimacy of, 49
  nationalist, 6, 13, 54, 209, 211
  on Partition fiction, 178–179
  postcolonial, 14, 39–45, 48–54, 209
  postcolonial global discourse of, 14, 41
  professionalism of, 41
  Sanskrit aesthetics of, 41, 220n90
  subject matter of, 40, 41
  theories of, 41
  writers of, 41
literary criticism, postcolonial
  caste-free, 4
  championing of the subversive, 3
  comparative mode of, 3, 4
  nationalism in, 5
  themes of, 4
  see also postcolonial studies
literature, British
  in Narayan's fiction, 77
  postcolonial Indian view of, 46
literature, non-western
  global interest in, 48
  nationalism in, 53
literature, postcolonial
  nationalism of, 2
literature, world, 53
  Indian English contributions to, 183
  Partition fiction in, 185
  transcending of politics, 145
Lokayata (Mulk Raj Anand Centre), 237n131
Ludden, David
  India and South Asia, 18
lyrics
  of *bedahi* songs, 197
  in vernacular language, 30, 217n50

Mahmud, Shabana, 32
Malgudi Days (television serial), 82–85, 225n18
  cast of, 83
  caste in, 83, 229n87
  languages of, 84, 229n90
  Narayan on, 85
  nostalgia for, 86
  production values of, 83, 229n86
  screenplay for, 84
  second series of, 228n83
  shooting location for, 83, 229n85
Mane, Anant, 251n92

Mangeshkar, Lata, 251n92
Manto, Saadat Hasan
  career of, 248n56
  gender and nation in, 249n67
  "Khol do," 185–189
    English translations of, 189, 249n66
    gendered violence in, 186–189
    masculinity in, 188
    patriarchy in, 188
  Kingdom's End and Other Stories, 189
  literary reputation of, 248n56
  Partition fiction of, 173, 186–189, 248n56
  Siyah Hashye, 249n65
  "The Dog of Tetwal," 182
  "Toba Tek Singh," 183
  translations into English, 189, 249n65, 249n66
Marathi language
  Phule's use of, 112
  untouchables in, 110
Marg (arts journal)
  Anand's involvement with, 95, 129, 133
marginalized groups
  discourse of, 49
  see also Dalits; untouchables
Markandaya, Kamala, 222n114
  Nectar in a Sieve, 46, 238n142
marriage
  child, 79
  as leavetaking, 193, 195–198, 251n91
  varying customs of, 251n91
  see also wedding songs
Mastur, Khajida
  "They are Taking Me away Father," 249n63
Matr Bhasa (mother-tongue), 15
Mayo, Katherine, 218n69
Mehrotra, Arvind
  A History of Indian Literature in English, 41, 132, 220n92
Mehta, Deepa
  Earth, 188, 198, 200
Mela (film), 196, 251n88
mela trope
  in "Banished," 193, 195, 196
  in Partition cinema, 196, 198
Memon, Muhammad Umar
  The Color of Nothingness, 247n40
  An Epic Unwritten, 180
  The Penguin Book of Partition Stories, 182
  on translation, 181
Menon, Dilip, 53
  The Blindness of Insight, 67, 226n42
  on Namboodiripad, 228n80
  on Sanskritization, 67, 226n42

Menon, Krishna
  and Bloomsbury Group, 100
Menon, Ritu, 177, 202, 246n21
  gender studies of, 177–178
  No Woman's Land, 178
  on rescue missions, 251n77
minorities, Indian
  coalitions among, 120
  Gandhi on, 105, 120
  in independence movement, 105
  rights of, 104
Minto, Lord
  Muslim address to, 214n20
Mishra, Pankaj
  on Narayan, 87
Mishra, Vijay, 186
Mistry, Rohinton, 48
Mitchell, Lisa, 15, 25
  Language, Emotion and Politics in South India, 15
Mizoram
  state language of, 242n46
Modern English Literature (Sahitya Akademi publication), 170
modernism
  Anand's, 9, 92, 99–100, 112, 123, 231n28
  connection to politics, 100
modernity, Indian
  Anand's role in, 133
  castes in, 52
  elites' engagement with, 52
  in Indian English fiction, 52
Moretti, Franco, 53
Mufti, Amir, 230n4
Mukerjee, Hiren, 152
Mukherjee, Arun, 227n48
  on Christianity, 121
Mukherjee, Meenakshi, 52
  on Anand, 97, 98, 106
  on Narayan, 64
  The Twice Born Fiction, 42, 74, 96, 219n71
Mukherjee, Sujit, 43
music, Indian
  language of lyrics, 30, 217n50
Muslim League, 213n7
  C.R. formula and, 214n19
Muslims
  British policy concerning, 214n20
  compared with Dalits, 120
  refugees, 192
  in Round Table talks, 120

Nag, Shankar, 83, 84
  death of, 228n83
Naicker, Ramaswamy E. V., 224n4

Naik, M. K., 44
  on Anand, 128
  A History of Indian English Literature, 65, 221n103, 230n10, 230n5
  Indian English literature: 1980–2000, 222n113
  on Narayan, 65, 230n10
Naim, C. M., 201, 252n97
Namboodiripad, E. M. S., 228n80
Nandakumar, Prema, 162
Nandy, Ashis
  An Ambiguous Journey to the City, 73, 227n51
  on Partition violence, 176
Narasimhaiah, C. D., 220n90
  East West Poetics at Work, 220n90
  on Indian English, 217n51, 222n112
  on Narayan, 65
  on Sanskrit, 215n29
  The Swan and the Eagle, 48, 65, 74
Narasimhaiah, S., 84
Narayan, R. K., 1, 9, 27, 39
  admission to American Academy, 76
  apolitical vision of, 9, 57
  autobiography of, 66
  Brahminism of, 64, 65, 68, 69, 86
  caste of, 9, 59
  Chelsea Hotel residence of, 227n50
  cinematic adaptations of, 76, 228n67
  critical assessments of, 6, 65
  cultural success of, 67
  The Darkroom, 69
  death of, 86
  depiction of Utopia, 9, 58, 69
  early work of, 57, 59
  engagement with caste, 59, 66–68, 76–82, 208, 225n32
  "Fellow Feeling," 225n32
  "Fifteen Years," 27
  friendship with Srinivas, 67, 227n49
  Grandmother's Tales, 226n44
  The Guide, 75, 151
  Hinduism in works of, 64, 69
  "How to Write an Indian Novel," 57, 63
  Indian cityscape of, 9
  Indian critical accounts of, 65
  and Indian independence, 73–76
  Indianness in works of, 9, 48, 58, 77
  influences on, 62
  intelligentsia on, 88
  in literary canon, 5
  literary output of, 63, 224n7
  literary style of, 58, 64, 225n22
  Malgudi Days, 68
  "Misguided Guide," 75, 228n66
  modernity of, 86
  My Days, 71, 225n12
  ordinary Indian life in, 58, 61, 67, 68, 79, 89
  outsiders in works of, 69
  The Painter of Signs, 67, 69
  protagonists of, 68
  readers of, 58, 67
  readers' defense of, 89
  realism of, 87
  relationship to Ganesan's works, 228n65
  Sahitya Akademi fellowship, 144
  separation from nationalist discourse, 6
  Swami and Friends, 9, 56, 58, 59, 76
    abridged version of, 225n18
    caste in, 59, 76–82
    childhood in, 9, 59, 76–82
    outsiders in, 69, 78
    plot of, 62, 77
    publication of, 62, 63
    televised serial of, 82–85
    title of, 78, 228n72
  Tamil identity of, 59, 65, 68, 69
  in Tamil literary context, 224n6
  urban life of, 71
  use of English, 59, 60, 208
  vernacular languages of, 59
  village life (Malgudi) in, 8–9, 57–58, 68–72, 73–77, 208
  Waiting for the Mahatma, 95
Narayan, Shyamala
  Indian English literature: 1980–2000, 222n113
Nargis, 196
Narrating India: The Novel in Search of the Nation (2005), 50, 52
Nasta, Sushila
  on Anand, 131
  on non-white intellectuals, 103
nation building, Indian
  role of English in, 17
Nation in Imagination (essays), 50
National Book Trust of India, 239n4
National Center for the Performing Arts (Bombay), 239n4
national identity
  among colonial subjects, 31
national identity, Indian
  among feminists, 178
  elites' view of, 3
  international dimensions of, 207
  role of the arts in, 14
  role of English in, 6, 13–14, 21
  role of literature in, 139
  unity in, 238n3
national literature, Indian, 173–174
  alternative, 171
  anthologies of, 2, 7, 183–184, 209
  caste in, 2

consolidation of, 3
construction of, 1
Dalit role in, 210
formation of, 1
gendered, 2, 190
limiting aspects of, 2
maintenance by nation-centric criticism, 211
nation-centric discourse of, 12
responses to events, 209
role of English in, 2, 5, 10, 11, 14, 137, 172
role of marketplace in, 10
Sahitya Akademi's program for, 139, 140, 167, 171, 208
variations in, 3
see also Indian English literature; Partition fiction; vernacular literatures, Indian
national literature, Pakistani, 184–185
inception of, 185
National Museum (New Delhi), 239n4
National School of Drama (New Delhi), 239n4
national unity, Indian
in diversity, 38, 39, 54, 137, 138, 140, 147, 149, 172, 238n3
Gandhi's vision of, 104
Hinduization of, 36
under Nehru, 38, 138
role of English in, 2, 17, 30, 56, 219n72
role of literature in, 35–36, 154
see also cultural unity, Indian
nationalism
linguistic, 50
in non-western literature, 53
in postcolonial literary discourse, 5
nationalism, Indian
caste dynamics of, 117
continuity with postcolonial discourse, 206
diaspora and, 175–176
failures of, 50
and Indian English fiction, 53, 61
and Indian vernacular literature, 19–20, 223n120
invention through literary discourse, 11
in literary criticism, 6, 13, 54, 209, 211
in Partition fiction, 189, 202, 209
in Partition studies, 178
postcolonial discourse on, 117
relationship to literature, 51, 165
role of dress in, 114, 122
role of English in, 14, 21, 204
role of Indian literature in, 34, 154, 165
in Rushdie's works, 47
of Sahitya Akademi, 7, 10, 137
untouchable terminology of, 110
nationalists, Hindu
use of English, 21
Nayar, Pramod, 125

Nehru, Jawaharlal
at All-India Writers' Conference, 35
Anand and, 129, 130, 236n122
cosmopolitanism of, 172
death of, 39, 130
Discovery of India, 138
national unity under, 38, 138
role in Sahitya Akademi, 136, 139, 142, 149, 150, 151
on Sanskrit, 215n29
"Tryst with Destiny" speech, 183, 206
Nobel Prize
Indian nominees for, 144
nostalgia
in Indian English literature, 48
for *Malgudi Days*, 86
in Narayan's works, 87

Official Language Act (1963), 26
Orphans of the Storm (Cowasjee and Duggal), 180–181
alternatives to nationalism in, 180–181
Manto in, 189
Orwell, George
intellectual circle of, 101

Pakistan
national anthologies of, 184–185
partition fiction of, 174
in *Shame*, 47
Urdu use in, 216n36
Pandey, Gyanendra, 177
Pandian, M. S. S., 226n42
on caste, 66
on Dalit literature, 125
on Narayan, 66
Pannikar, K. M., 36
Partition (of India), 38, 138
Bangladeshi experience of, 246n11
censorship concerning, 196
in cinema, 195–197, 198–200
cultural narratives of, 202
discourse of romance in, 195
discourse of separation in, 195, 202
early histories of, 176
effect on patriarchal societies, 190
events preceding, 245n2
fiftieth anniversary of, 178
gendered analysis of, 177
gendered trauma of, 175, 177
gendered violence in, 175–178, 186, 195, 200, 202, 245n2
in literature, 156–157
madness in, 176, 193
"Mother India" imagery in, 246n11
Muslim refugees in, 192

Partition (of India) (*cont.*)
  Pakistani tropes of, 246n11
  parallel with *hijrat*, 192
  patriarchal discourse of, 194
  photographic images of, 245n5
  in popular culture, 195–196
  population exchange following, 245n2
  razing of slums during, 248n55
  religious comfort for, 192, 250n72
  rifts created by, 157
  rural dislocations during, 248n55
  silence concerning, 176
  suppression from memory, 246n12
  temporary insanity of, 176
  see also diaspora
Partition fiction, 11, 173–174
  in anthologies, 179–186, 247n22, 247n24
  Ashraf's, 173, 186, 190–191
  coherence of term, 178
  cultural tropes of, 174
  diasporic, 11, 174, 175, 186, 192, 201
  English translations of, 11, 173, 174, 179, 181, 182, 185, 189, 247n25, 247n40
  Gandhian assessment of, 180
  gendered themes of, 175, 186, 189, 192–193
  Hashmi's, 173, 186, 191–194
  historians' use of, 179
  hopelessness in, 187
  interpretive frame for, 185
  literary criticism on, 178–179
  local narratives of, 174–175, 182, 185
  male protagonists of, 175
  Manto's, 173, 186–189
  masculinity in, 190
  nationalism of, 189, 202, 209
  patriarchal society in, 174
  place in world literature, 185
  reprints of, 179
  separation in, 200–202
  South Asian, 174–175
  as transnational genre, 174
  Urdu, 173, 175, 182
  violence in, 174, 186–188
  see also fiction; national literature, Indian
Partition studies
  everyday life in, 177
  feminist, 177, 178
  gender in, 177, 246n6
  of late twentieth century, 176
  nationalism in, 178, 246n6
  new, 173, 176–177, 246n6
  social, 177
  sources for, 177
Patel, Sardar, 172

Pathak, Bindeswar, 234n96
Pawar, Daya
  Kondwada, 108
PEN
  International Conference (second, 1940), 35
PEN (Indian branch), 33, 218n69, 219n72, 243n76
  books on Indian literature, 33, 34, 162
  first All-India Writers' Conference, 35
  international aspirations of, 207
  Iyengar's work with, 161–162
  relationship with Sahitya Akademi, 162, 243n77
  reliance on English, 205
Persian language
  use in administration, 216n29
Phule, Jyotirao, 110
  use of Marathi, 112
Pillai, Thakazi Sivasankara
  Thottiyude Makan, 126
Pinjar (film), 198, 199, 248n62, 252n92
Poisoned Bread: Translations from Modern Marathi Dalit Literature, 124
politicians, Hindu
  on Indian nationhood, 17
Poona Pact, 105, 110, 120
postcolonial studies, 45
  colonialism in, 210
  English language use in, 210
  Indian origins of, 210
  Sahitya Akademi in, 170
  see also literary criticism, postcolonial
Prakash, Bodh, 250n71
Prasad, Chandra Bhan, 28, 114
Premchand, Munshi, 126, 158, 236n120
print commodities
  in imagined communities, 47, 49
Pritam, Amrita, 159
  Pinjar, 199, 252n92
Progressive Writers' Association (PWA), 33
  Anand in, 92, 93, 94
  Anand's break with, 129
  critique of status quo, 40
  first meeting (1936), 236n120
  on Hindustani, 98
  ideology of vernacular literature, 98
  Indian English writers of, 231n15
  influence on Anand, 98, 218n58, 230n13
  influence on *Untouchable*, 98, 230n13
  manifesto of, 31–32, 94, 97, 217n53, 231n14
public sphere, Indian
  emergence of, 52
  role of Christianity in, 52
Punjabi literature
  CIL essay on, 158

Index

post-independence survival of, 158
religious traditions of, 158, 159
Purna, Krishna Raghavendra ("Kittu"), 63

racism
   Anand's experience of, 108, 109, 232n53
   caste-based, 123
   against people of color, 109
Radhakrishnan, S.
   foreword to *Contemporary Indian Literature*, 154, 161, 163
   Sahitya Akademi fellowship, 144
   Sahitya Akademi inaugural address, 141–142
   on Sanskrit, 146
   use of Sanskrit, 146
Rahman, Mohammad Hifzur, 213n17
Rai, Alok, 25
   Hindu Nationalism, 214n21
   on Sanskritization, 146, 147
Rajagopalachari, C. (Rajaji), 214n19
   on Devanagari script, 169, 244n100
   on Hindi, 224n3, 244n100
Ram, Jagjivan, 122
Ram, Rahul, 217n50
Ram, Ronki
   "Ravidass Devas and Social Protest," 233n70
Ram, Susan and N.
   on Narayan, 60, 63, 71, 224n7
Rama Rau, Santha, 238n142
Ramakrishnan, E. V., 50, 52
Ramanujan, A. K., 15
   Collected Essays, 212n1
   "Is There an Indian Way of Thinking?," 140, 215n29
Ramayana
   trial by fire in, 193
   use in "Banished," 192, 193
   variant versions of, 251n77
Rao, A. V. Krishna
   on Indo-Anglian fiction, 221n95
Rao, D. S.
   on *Bharatiya Kavita* series, 168
   Five Decades: A Short History of Sahitya Akademi, 150, 240n21, 241n36, 243n59
   on *Indian Literature since Independence*, 167
Rao, P. V. Narasimha, 170
Rao, Padmavati, 84, 85, 229n84
Rao, Raja
   Kanthapura, 7, 95
   literary reputation of, 6
   village life in, 74
Rasa theory, 220n90
Ravidass (Bhakti saint), 97
   Brahmin dress of, 233n70
Rawat, Ramnarayan, 97

Ray, Satyajit
   experience of village life, 72
   on *The Guide*, 76
   Pather Panchali, 72
Reddy, Muthulakshmi, 79
rock bands, Indian, 217n50
romance, cross-community
   in Partition cinema, 198
romance, folkloric
   referencing during Partition, 195
Round Table Conferences (RTCs), 9, 104, 120, 236n120
   Minorities pact of, 104
Roy, Anuradha Marwah, 182
Roy, Arundhati
   The Algebra of Infinite Justice, 241n42
   on Dalit literature, 106
   The God of Small Things, 48
   refusal of Sahitya Akademi award, 241n42
Roy, Bimal
   Bandini, 252n94
Royal Asiatic Society of Bengal
   national culture proposal of, 239n15
Rushdie, Salman, 221n106
   "Damne, This is the Oriental Scene for You," 253n9
   diasporic writing of, 47
   early work of, 45
   on English use, 205, 206
   inauthenticity charges against, 47
   Indian book tour (1982), 221n107
   on Indian English fiction, 51, 223n121
   knowledge of Urdu, 222n108
   literary style of, 46, 206
   Midnight's Children, 45–48, 222n111
      colonialism in, 45
      historical events in, 47
      inauthenticity charges against, 47
      nationalism in, 7
      plot of, 46
      reception of, 46
      subject matter of, 46
   national narratives of, 47
   Shame, 45, 47
      Pakistan in, 47
   urban audience of, 46
   The Vintage Book of Indian Writing, 1947–1997, 184, 185, 205

Sabarmati Ashram
   Anand's visit to, 127, 128, 132, 236n119, 236n120, 237n125, 237n132
Sachidanandan, K., 171–172
Sackville West, Edward, 101
Saheb, Walli, 251n92

Sahgal, Nayantara, 183
Sahitya Akademi (SA)
  absence of British influence, 142
  advisory boards of, 168, 169
  anthologies of, 148, 170, 205
  anti-imperialism of, 146
  Asmita forum, 148
  autonomy of, 149, 161, 242n42
  awards decisions of, 151–153, 241n42
  Bharatiya Kavita series, 168–169
    Devanagari script in, 169
    failure of, 168, 171
    scope of, 168
    as vehicle for Hindi, 168
  caste bias of, 149
  colonial associations of, 137, 155
  complaints concerning, 241n40, 241n41
  constitution of, 139
  coordination of language traditions, 214n22
  creative productions under, 137, 139
  critical publications by, 143
  cultural unity under, 137, 139, 140, 149, 153, 155, 161, 168, 172
  development of scripts, 139
  diversity in, 149, 184
  early history of, 138
  emulation of French academy, 142
  encouragement of Hindi, 168–169
  English language prize of, 241n42
  establishment of, 1, 135, 136, 139, 219n72
  failed projects of, 168–171
  fulfillment of language mandate, 149, 151
  General Council of, 169
  global outreach of, 142–146, 172
  governing principles of, 139–140, 219n72
  governmental involvement with, 10, 149–150, 167, 241n42
  government leaders in, 149
  Hindi advisory board, 160, 167
  Honorary Fellows of, 144, 148, 240n25
  Indian English literature under, 143, 151–153
  Indianness of projects, 137, 141, 157
  inspirations for, 142
  international aspirations of, 207
  journals of, 153
  literary histories of, 154–156, 242n53, 243n59
  male gender bias of, 148, 149, 241n36
  name of, 141, 142, 146
  nationalist agenda of, 7, 10, 137
  national literature program, 139, 140, 167, 171, 208
  Nehru's role in, 136, 139, 142, 149, 150
  popular press on, 241n41
  position on Indian literature, 154
  in postcolonial literary studies, 170
  presentation copies from, 144, 240n23
  programs sponsored by, 240n21
  promotion of cultural exchanges, 139
  promotion of Devanagari script, 168–169
  promotion of education, 139
  publications of, 37, 143–144, 153–161, 171
  registration as society, 239n5
  relationship with PEN, 162
  reliance on English, 147, 148, 149, 150, 151, 153, 170, 172, 205
  resolution on Iraqi cultural heritage, 240n24
  Sanskritization under, 147
  self-assessment (2004), 150
  translation projects of, 169–170
  translations published by, 139, 143–144, 146–148, 155, 239n17, 239n18, 239n20
  Union Academique International membership, 144
  Urdu translation prize, 242n42
  use of Sindhi, 242n46
  vernacular languages under, 139, 151, 155
  women in, 148
Said, Edward
  Orientalism, 45
Saint, Ravikant and Tarun
  on Partition "madness," 176
  Translating Partition, 182–183, 196
    commercial value of, 183
    critical essays in, 182
Samakaleen Bharateeya Sahitya (Hindi journal), 153
Samskrita Pratibha (Sanskrit journal), 153
Sangeet Natak Akademi, 149
  establishment of, 136
Sangor, Leopold
  Sahitya Akademi fellowship, 144
Sanskrit
  advocates of, 26
  aesthetic concepts of, 41
  CIL essay on, 157
  expression of universalisms, 146
  as language of gods, 147
  in national language debates, 215n29
  parallels with English, 147, 215n29
  phrases in English, 145–146
  unity with ancient Greek, 141, 146, 240n30, 240n33
Sanskrit literature
  awards for, 151
  early, 240n30
Sanskritization, 67, 147
  among lower castes, 226n42
  caste politics of, 226n42
  of Hindi, 25, 29, 213n17, 214n21

mimesis in, 226n42
  of vernacular languages, 147
Sarabhai, Bharati, 36
Sarangi, Asha, 21
Sarkar, Sumit, 56
Scheduled Classes, 110
  see also caste, Indian; untouchables
scripts
  Devanagari
    Hindi in, 24, 139, 147, 168, 213n17, 244n100
    opponents of, 168–169
    Sahitya Akademi's promotion of, 139
    for southern languages, 169
  Gurmukhi, 158, 182
  Indi-Roman, 32, 98
  Sahitya Akademi's development of, 139
Seth, Vikram, 48
Shah, Rajendra
  literary awards of, 152
Sharma, G. P.
  Nationalism in Indo-Anglian Fiction, 45
Sharma, Kidar, 251n92
Sheth, D. L., 16
  "The Great Language Debate," 213n4
  on Sanskrit, 215n29
Shivanath
  on Dogri literature, 167
Sidhwa, Bapsi
  Cracking India, 198, 199, 248n62
Sikhs
  violence against, 246n12
Sindhi language
  post-independence vulnerabilities of, 158
  Sahitya Akademi's use of, 242n46
Singh, Khushwant, 152
  on Amrita Pritam, 159
  on Punjabi literature, 158
Singh, Namwar, 53
  on Hindi literature, 167
Singh, Rajinder, 158
Sinha, Mrinalini, 218n69
Sinha, Ramdhari (Dinkar)
  on Vatsyayan, 160
Sivakumaran, Anil
  defense of Narayan, 89
Sivaraman, Mythily, 79
small presses, Indian, 41, 220n89
Sobti, Krishna
  "Where is my Mother?," 180
social realism
  in Anand's writings, 103
social reproduction, 89
  Narayan's, 89
socialism
  Anand's, 9, 91, 92, 103

South Asia
  communal violence in, 181
Spanish Civil War
  Anand's participation in, 92, 95, 103, 231n37
Sreenivas, Mytheli, 79
  Wives, Widows, Concubines, 227n57
Srinivas, K. Ravi, 82
Srinivas, M. N.
  friendship with Narayan, 67, 227n49
  The Remembered Village, 71, 72
  Sanskritization theory of, 67
  sociological theories of, 67, 226n42
  Tamil identity of, 70
Strachey, Lytton
  Iyengar's study of, 40
subaltern studies, 45
Sufism
  female persona in, 245n4
Suhagan (film), 251n92
Suhag Raat (film), 251n92
Sultanpuri, Majrooh
  "Chal re sajni, ab kya sochey?," 197
  during Partition, 197

Tagore, Rabindranath, 5
  writings in English, 143
Talbot, Ian, 250n72
Tamil language, 83
  advocates of, 26
  anti-Hindi sentiment and, 224n3, 224n5
  fiction in, 59
  relationship to English, 224n4
Tamils
  adaptation of western culture, 227n57
  upper-caste domesticity of, 227n57
  use of English, 59
Tata, J. D. R., 129
television, Indian
  multilingual, 85
  of 1980s, 86
  see also *Malgudi Days* (television serial)
Tharayil, Muraleedharan
  Kamala, Madhavikutty, Suraiya, 221n102
Tharoor, Shashi
  on Narayan, 64, 87
toilets, flush
  Indians' access to, 108, 234n96

United Lodge of Theosophists, 218n69
unity in diversity (slogan), 38, 39, 54, 137, 138, 140, 147, 149, 172, 238n3
untouchables
  Christianity for, 120
  education for, 115–117
  Gandhi on, 105, 106, 110, 111, 120, 122, 232n50

untouchables (*cont.*)
   Harijan Sevak Sangh organization, 105
   national debate over, 105
   official designations for, 110
   terms for, 110
   see also caste, Indian; Dalits
Urdu language
   Indianness of, 157
   official use of, 216n36
   separation from Hindi, 139
   transliterations of, 249n64
Urdu literature
   CIL essay on, 157
   nationalist, 230n4
   Partition fiction in, 173, 175, 182
   pre-independence, 51
   translations into English, 173, 182–183, 249n64
Uttam, Preeti, 252n92

Vaikom Satyagraha (1924–1925), 121
Vajpayee, Atal Bihari, 153
Valmiki, Omprakash
   Joothan, 227n48, 227n61, 233n68, 233n80
Varadarajan, Tunku
   on Narayan, 87, 88
Varma, Shakuntala
   Kahe Ko Byahi Bidesh, 198
Vatsyayan, S. H. ("Ajneya")
   CIL essay of, 160
   on Progressive writers, 159
   self-praise by, 160
vernacular languages, Indian, 14
   advantages of, 34
   caste and, 224n2
   countervailing reality of, 213n4
   cultural production in, 8, 55
   emergence of, 43
   Gandhi on, 19, 213n17, 214n17
   gendered uses of, 15
   hybrid, 157
   and Indian nationalism, 19–20, 223n120
   Indians' knowledge of, 34
   in lyrics, 30, 217n50
   in national language debates, 21–23
   neutralization by English, 28
   as parochial, 16
   purity of, 15
   under Sahitya Akademi, 139
   Sanskritization of, 147
   translations among, 44
vernacular literatures, Indian, 203
   awards for, 153
   caste in, 159
   in *CIL*, 157
   effect of Indian English literature on, 2
   histories of, 33, 34
   in linguistic division of India, 158–159
   loss of recognition for, 207
   nationalism in, 19–20, 223n120
   nineteenth-century, 61
   Partition in, 156–157
   prior to western influences, 37
   PWA ideology of, 98
   see also Indian literature
vernaculars, cultural, 8, 213n4
village life, Indian
   caste in, 70
   Dalit narratives of, 70
   dynamic with city, 73
   Gandhian ideal of, 71, 72
   in Indian culture, 69–71
   in Indian English fiction, 70, 72–74
   in Narayan's works, 57–58, 68–72, 73–77
   post-independence investment in, 75
   in Raja Rao's works, 74
   Srinivas on, 71
   universality of, 74
The Vintage Book of Indian Writing, 1947–1997 (Rushdie and West), 183–185
   elite authors in, 184
   Indian English in, 183
   lack of linguistic diversity in, 184
   national history in, 184
   nation-centric aspects of, 183

Wadia, Bahman R., 218n69
Wadia, Sophia Camacho, 33–34, 161, 218n60, 218n59
   and Sahitya Akademi, 162, 243n77
Walsh, William, 64
Waris Shah
   "Heer Ranja," 182
wedding songs, 198
   see also marriage
West, Elizabeth, 183
women, Indian
   as allegory of oppression, 53
   Brahminical morality for, 227n57
   in early Indian fiction, 53
   in Partition fiction, 174, 195
   as property, 194
   relationship to nation, 174, 178
   "rescue" missions for, 250n74
   in Sahitya Akademi, 148
   self-negation of, 251n79
   trial by fire, 193
   violence against, 174–178, 186–189, 245n2
   writers, 6, 42, 148, 156, 221n97, 222n114

Woolf, Virginia, 98
  and Anand, 101
working class, English
  Anand on, 103
World Congress of Writers against Fascism (Madrid, 1935)
  Anand at, 103
writers
  bilingual, 222n108
  Indian women, 6, 42, 148, 156, 221n97, 222n114
  Pakistani women, 178
writers, Indian English
  PWA members, 231n15

writers, vernacular
  resentment of English, 56

Yadav, Rajendra, 125
Yeats, William Butler
  and Anand, 128
"Yeh zindagi ke mele" (song), 196
Yerawas (Dalit community), 121

Zahir, Sajjad, 31, 32, 97
  on Wadia, 218n60
Zelliot, Eleanor, 114, 124
  on Ambedkar, 121
Zia ul Haq, Mohammad, 47